The Principles of Biology

THE PRINCIPLES OF BIOLOGY

HAMAKER

THE PRINCIPLES OF BIOLOGY

BY

J. I. HAMAKER, Ph. D.
PROFESSOR OF BIOLOGY, RANDOLPH-MACON
WOMAN'S COLLEGE

WITH 267 ILLUSTRATIONS

PHILADELPHIA
P. BLAKISTON'S SON & CO.
1012 WALNUT STREET
1913

COPYRIGHT, 1913, BY P. BLAKISTON'S SON & CO.

THE·MAPLE·PRESS·YORK·PA

PREFACE

In an introductory course in biology a text-book is helpful because the notes taken by lower class students are usually unsatisfactory, if not useless, and require much time. This volume contains an outline of a course given by the author for more than ten years. It is designed to *supplement* the practical work in the laboratory and field, and to relieve the student of the greater part of the burden of taking lecture notes. Purely discriptive matter is reduced to a minimum and examples are largely omitted because the teacher is supposed to have sufficient command of the subject to supply these, and local and familiar examples are always better for illustration than those less well known. The figures in the book are regarded as an important part in the presentation of the subject and should be carefully studied. Many points omitted or only briefly alluded to in the text are explained by them.

Part I is designed to acquaint the student with the fundamentals of plant organization and life processes. Part II does the same for animals but in a different and more thorough method. Part III discusses the most important general biological phenomena. The difference in treatment of plants and animals rests on well-known pedagogical principles which need not be discussed here. There is little in the book for which originality can be claimed, but justification for publishing rests on the fact that there is at present no text which even approximately covers the field in subject-matter and method of treatment.

For the classification of plants and animals given in the appendices to Parts I and II, many authorities have been consulted but none followed consistently. In the interest of the beginner simplicity is desirable and to this end a number of unimportant, obscure or aberrant groups have been omitted and only three grades, or orders of groups, recognized, viz., Branch or Phylum, Class, and Order. The classification of animals given in the "Lehrbuch" of Claus-Grobben has been followed more closely than that of any other author.

Acknowledgment is due the publishers, Messrs. P. Blakiston's Son & Co., for the loan of many figures from the works of Galloway, Stevens, Folsom and others. The Macmillan Co. and Henry Holt and Co. have also kindly furnished several figures. More specific acknowledgment is made in connection with each borrowed figure.

J. I. HAMAKER.

COLLEGE PARK, VA.

TABLE OF CONTENTS

INTRODUCTION

	PAGE
Biology and the biological sciences	1
The living and the not-living	2
The living substance—protoplasm	4

PART I.—PLANTS

Laboratory and field exercises 7
Color. The light relation. The leaves. Phyllotaxy. The stem. The roots 15
Seeds. Germination. The seedling. The mature plant. Structure and function of the roots. Structure and function of the stem. Structure and function of the leaves. Photosynthesis. Respiration. Translocation of food substances. Other food substances. Differentiation of tissues 22
Modified roots. Modified stems and branches. Modified leaves . . 49
Homology of the flower. Inflorescence. Structure of the flower. Function of the flower. Pollination and fertilization. The seed. The fruit. Seed distribution 53
Classes of plants: Angiosperms, Gymnosperms, Cryptograms . . . 71
Ecology: Water, temperature, latitude and altitude, light, soil, relation of plants to each other, carnivorous plants, physiographic relations 75

APPENDIX TO PART I

CLASSES OF PLANTS

Branch I. Thallophyta 101
    Class 1. Myxomycetes 101
          2. Schizophyta 102
          3. Diatomeæ 105
          4. Conjugatæ 105

	PAGE
5. Chlorophyceæ	106
6. Characeæ	106
7. Phæophyceæ	107
8. Rhodophyceæ	107
9. Phycomycetes	108
10. Basidiomycetes	108
11. Ascomycetes	109
Lichenes	110
Branch II. Bryophyta	111
Class 1. Hepaticæ	111
2. Musci	112
Branch III. Pteridophyta	113
Class 1. Filicinæ	114
2. Equisetinæ	115
3. Lycopodinæ	115
Branch IV. Spermatophyta	116
Class 1. Gymnospermæ	117
2. Angiospermæ	117

PART II.—ANIMALS

Laboratory exercises 119
Introduction: Color and form. Locomotion. Axis of locomotion. Cephalization. Dorsal and ventral. Right and left. Bilateral symmetry. Radial symmetry. Universal symmetry. Asymmetry. Exceptional cases. Size and differentiation. Integument. Nerve-muscle Mechanism. Digestion. Circulation. Respiration. Excretion. Reproduction. Organization of the body. "Higher" and "lower" animals. Segmentation—metameres, antimeres 127
Integument: General integument of amœba, hydra, worms, arthropods, vertebrates. Specialized integumentary structures—cuticular, epidermal and dermal structures, glands. 141
Sense organs: General sense organs in amœba, hydra, worms, arthropods, vertebrates. Organs of special sense: The chemical senses—taste and smell. The organs of sight. The arthropod eye. The vertebrate eye. Types of vision. Mechanism for focusing and control of light intensity. Hearing and equilibration. Statocysts. The ear—of arthropods, of vertebrates. The senses of lower animals 151

TABLE OF CONTENTS

Organs of response: In amœba, hydra, annelids, arthropods, vertebrates. Skeleton and connective tissue. The endoskeleton of vertebrates. Muscular action........... 172
The nervous system: Cœlenterates. Annelids. The mechanism of response. Arthropods. Vertebrates. The brain and spinal cord. A spinal nerve. The cranial nerves 182
Energy relations of the animal: The food of animals a source of energy. Digestion in amœba. Fermentation and digestion. Digestion in cœlenterates, in worms, in arthropods. The digestive tract of vertebrates. Digestive ferments. Absorption... 191
Circulation: The gastro-vascular cavity of cœlenterates. Circulation in worms, in arthropods, in vertebrates. The lymphatic system. 204
Respiration: in minute animals, in aquatic animals, in insects, in vertebrates. The blood as respiratory vehicle 208
Metabolism: growth, secretion and excretion, muscular activity . . 213
Excretion: in minute animals, in worms, in crayfish, in vertebrates . 215
Reproduction: amœba, conjugation, hydra, annelids, crayfish, vertebrates 217

APPENDIX TO PART II

Classes of Animals

Phylum 1.—Protozoa: Classes of protozoa 224
Phylum 2.—Cœlenterata: Porifera. Structure of a sponge. Hydrozoa. Scyphozoa. Anthozoa. Ctenophora 230
Phylum 3.—Scolecida: Platyhelminthes. Aschelminthes. Nemertini 224
Phylum 4.—Annelida: Classes of annelids 247
Phylum 5.—Molluscoidea: Bryozoa. Brachiopoda. 248
Phylum 6.—Echinodermata: Pelmatozoa. Asteroidea. Structure of star fish. Ophiuroidea. Echinoidea. Holothuroidea . . . 250
Phylum 7.—Arthropoda: Branchiata. The orders of crustacea. Palæostraca. Arachnoidea. Protracheata. Myriapoda. Apterygogenea. Insecta. Structure of an insect. The orders of insects 259
Phylum 8.—Mollusca: Amphineura. Conchifera. Orders of Conchifera. Structure of a snail. Structure of a clam. Structure of of a squid.. 275
Phylum 9.—Adelochorda 284

x   TABLE OF CONTENTS

	PAGE
Phylum 10.—Urochorda. Classes of tunicates	285
Phylum 11.—Acrania	286
Phylum 12.—Vertebrata: Cyclostomata. Pisces. Orders of fishes. Amphibia. Orders of amphibia. Reptilia. Orders of reptiles. Aves. Orders of birds. Mammalia. Orders of mammals . .	287

PART III.—GENERAL PRINCIPLES

Spontaneous generation. Continuity of the living substance. Structure of protoplasm. The nucleus. Chemical structure of protoplasm. Function of cytoplasm and nucleus. Cell division. Number of chromosomes. Nucleoli. Centrosomes. Spindle fibres. Resting nucleus. Conjugation. Fertilization. Maturation. Conjugation in protozoa. Fertilization stimulus. Cleavage. The blastula. The gastrula. The medullary plate. The notochord. The mesoderm. Other types of cleavage. Origin of the tissues. Indirect development. Differentiation of germinal and somatic tissues. Division of labor and differentiation. Regeneration. Mechanics of growth. Progressive and regressive development. Sexual dimorphism. Polymorphism. Alternation of generations. Life habits depending on food. Parasitism. Protozoa as parasites. Bacteria as parasites. Immunity . . . 307

Species. Variation. Heredity. Mendel's law. Physical basis of heredity. Number of species. Origin of species. The Taxonomic Series. The Phylogenetic Series. The Ontogenetic Series. The struggle for existence. Natural Selection. Animals and plants under domestication. Geographical distribution. 382

Adaptations: Pollination. Care of young. Sexual dimorphism. Sexual selection. Welfare of the individual and of the species. Animal coloration. Protective resemblance. Feigning. Mimicry. Color changes. Luminescence. Electrical organs. Instinct. Intelligence 407

Index 439

THE PRINCIPLES OF BIOLOGY

INTRODUCTION

1. Biology is the science which treats of living things, or of objects having life. In the broad application of the term, as used here, Biology includes a number of more special sciences. Morphology, Anatomy and Histology treat of form and structure. On the other hand, Physiology deals primarily with the function of organs. In Embryology it is the development of the individual, especially during the earlier stages, that is kept chiefly in view. Paleontology treats only of fossils, that is, those types of living things which existed at some earlier period in the world's history but which have now become extinct.

2. Even with such a sub-division of the subject we have left special sciences which cover such a broad field that they become unwieldly. In Botany and Zoölogy the subject is divided on the basis of the kinds of living things considered, the former being the biology of plants, the latter the biology of animals. Still further sub-division leads to Cryptogamic Botany, Phanerogamic Botany, Invertebrate Zoölogy and Vertebrate Zoölogy. Bacteriology, Entomology (insect zoölogy), Ornithology (bird zoölogy), and still other more narrowly restricted branches of biology are recognized. The very extensive study of man has given rise to a number of biological sciences dealing only with this single genus; viz., Human Anatomy, Human Physiology, Human Embryology, Anthropology (dealing with the comparative anatomy of the various

1

races of men), and Ethnology (dealing with manners, customs, language and other activities of the races of men).

3. Biology deals with objects, that is, with the concrete, but its chief interest and value lies not in mere description or enumeration so much as in the generalizations, which may be made from accumulated facts. A single observation, or repeated observation of a single individual seldom justifies a general conclusion, but by the comparison of numerous examples one is enabled to distinguish the accidental and trivial from the general and significant. Therefore, the method of study by comparison is for the biologist of special importance.

(For the individual, and especially for the average college student who devotes a comparatively short time to the subject, the study of many individual examples is impossible and, therefore, in practice, an abridgement of the method of study by comparison is adopted. This is called the method of study by types, by which a series of examples are compared, each example being representative or typical of a considerable group. That the examples selected are typical, rests, of course, on the observation of previous students or investigators. By this method the student may in a comparatively brief time extend his studies over a large field.)

4. It is usually not difficult to distinguish a living thing from one not living, but to state formally what are the attributes of the living is not so simple a matter. On close analysis living things are found to be complex in structure, being composed of many parts, called organs, which differ in structure and in function. For this reason a living thing is called an organism, and is said to be organized.

5. Crystals are more like organisms than any other non-living thing, and a comparison of organisms and crystals will serve to indicate the most essential characteristics of living things.

6. One of the most prominent characteristics of objects that

have life is growth: crystals also grow, but not in the same way. The method of growth in crystals is by accretion, i. e., by addition of substance to the outside; but in the growth of living organisms the added substance is taken up into the interior of the body, i. e., by intussusception. Moreover, in crystals the chemical nature of the substance added is not altered, while in the case of organisms the substance added undergoes a series of chemical changes before it is finally really part of the growing body. This process of transforming food material is called assimilation and is wholly wanting in crystals.

7. Another prominent characteristic of organisms is the definiteness of the shapes which they assume. Each plant or animal is as much like every other individual of the same kind as if they were all made after the same pattern or cast in the same mold. Crystals are bounded by plane surfaces which meet at definite angles but within this limitation the shape may vary indefinitely.

8. The size of organisms is limited. The individual grows more or less rapidly until it reaches a certain size after which growth almost or wholly ceases. The size of crystals has no definite limitations.

9. Crystals may be formed under favorable circumstances wherever the substances of which they are composed are found. But we have no knowledge that a living thing is ever formed under any conditions except by development from what we may call a germ, which came from some pre-existing living thing, and which differs from the mature organism chiefly in being smaller and simpler in structure. The crystal may be reduced to its constituent elements which will again unite under the proper conditions to form a new crystal, whereas if the organism is similarly reduced, its elements will under no conditions recombine to produce a new organism.

10. Crystals may exist indefinitely, but the life of the in-

dividual organism is limited. It comes to an end by death and subsequent decay, by division, or by fusion of its body with another similar body. In either case the living individual, as such, ceases to exist.

11. Crystals are inert, while organisms possess to some degree the power of movement in response to an external stimulus.

12. Thus we have the material world made up of lifeless, or inorganic bodies, and living, or organic bodies. The following table exhibits in parallel columns the similarities and differences of the two classes of bodies:

CRYSTALS	ORGANISMS
1. Are unorganized.	1. Are organized.
2. Grow by accretion (so also hailstones, concretions, stalactites).	2. Grow by assimilation and intussusception.
3. Have indefinite shape and plane surfaces.	3. Have definite shape and curved surfaces.
4. Size not limited.	4. Size limited.
5. Generate spontaneously.	5. Develop from a germ.
6. May exist indefinitely.	6. Have a limited life period.
7. Are inert.	7. Have power of motion.

THE LIVING SUSBSTANCE

13. All the activities of an organism, by which it is distinguished from inorganic bodies, are the activities of the living substance, which is called protoplasm. But not all of the substance of an organism is protoplasm. Besides the protoplasm there is usually more or less inert substance which was formed by the protoplasm, but which does not of itself possess life. Of such substances are the hard parts of bones and the superficial layers of the skin, the corky layers of bark and the hard fibres of wood, etc. This inert substance may be wholly wanting, or it may constitute the larger part of the body of the organism.

14. Besides the protoplasm and the inert substances formed by it, there are in many cases foreign substances to be found within the various organs of an organism; such are, for example, the pebbles found in the gizzard of certain birds, the particles of sand found in the antennal organ of the crayfish, or the sand used by many minute animals in forming a skeletal shell or test.

15. Protoplasm is jelly-like in consistency, and transparent, but not perfectly homogeneous. Under the microscope it is seen to consist of an infinitely large number of minute particles of various sizes and of different optical and chemical characteristics. Chemical analysis shows that it is highly complex; consisting largely of carbon, oxygen, hydrogen and nitrogen, with small quantities of sulphur, and occasionally phosphorous, manganese, magnesium, calcium, sodium, and chlorine. It is regarded as a more or less definite aggregation of a large number of chemically complex bodies.

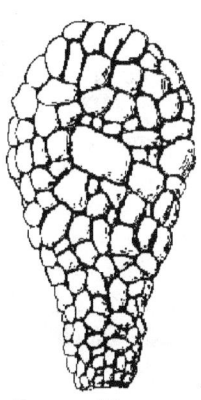

FIG. 1.—The test of a protozoan, Difflugia, composed of minute grains of sand cemented together.

16. In the smaller, microscopic organisms the protoplasm may usually be observed to consist of two parts, nucleoplasm and cytoplasm. The nucleoplasm, in the form of a round or oval body, the nucleus, occupies the centre of the mass and is surrounded by the cytoplasm. The nucleus and the surrounding cytoplasm together are called a cell. In larger organisms there are a large number of nuclei quite regularly distributed throughout the protoplasm. There are

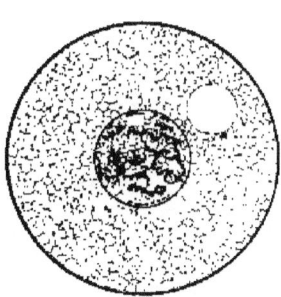

FIG. 2.—Diagram of the cell. For details see Fig. 179.

then as many cells as there are nuclei, and, frequently, each cell is marked off from its neighbors by a wall of inert substance secreted by the protoplasm. The character of this wall varies, not only with the kind of organism, but also with the organ in which it is found. In the central part of a tree trunk the thick cell walls form the firm substance of wood; similarly, near the surface they form the corky layers of the bark.

17. What has been said in the preceding paragraphs has a general application to all organisms, but the obvious grouping of living things into two kingdoms—the vegetable and the animal—is based on certain distinctive peculiarities which are of such far-reaching significance and which separate the more familiar forms of the two groups so precisely that it will be convenient to study each group separately. Plants are on the whole much simpler than animals and therefore better adapted for introductory study.

PART I.—PLANTS

LABORATORY AND FIELD EXERCISES

PRELIMINARY SURVEY

I. Light Relation of Leaves

1. An erect stem with opposite leaves (Coleus).
   a. Horizontal view showing stem (nodes and internodes) and leaves.
   b. Make a diagram showing arrangement of leaves as seen from above. How many vertical ranks are there?
2. An erect stem with whorled leaves (Galium). Horizontal view as in 1a.
3. An erect stem with alternate leaves (Quercus).
   a. Horizontal view as in 1a.
   b. Diagram as in 1b.
4. Leaf Rosette (Plantago) as in 1b.
5. Horizontal stem with alternate leaves (Castanea). Vertical view showing carefully how each leaf is connected with the stem.
6. Horizontal stem with alternate leaves (Tropaeolum). Horizontal view. Show relation of leaves with stem as in 5.
7. Leaf Mosaic (Ampelopsis Veitchii) seen from the direction of the midday sun.
8. Inverted stems.
   a. Wistaria. Relation of leaves to stem (note the pulvinus).
   b. Salix Babylonica. Relation of leaves to stem.

II. Form of the Plant as Related to Light

9. a. Form of a tree in an open space (Pinus).
   b. Form of same kind of tree growing in a thicket. Note difference in lower branches in *a* and *b* and explain.
10. An excurrent type of stem (Populus).
11. A deliquescent type of stem (Ulmus).

III. Phyllotaxy

12. Recall the opposite and whorled types of phyllotaxy.
13. a. Arrangement of leaves in grasses (Zea Mays).
    b. Arrangement of leaves in sedges (Carex).
    c. Arrangement of leaves in sour wood (Oxydendron), oak (Quercus), etc.
    d. Arrangement of leaves in mullein (Verbascum), goldenrod (Solidago), Easter lily (Lilium Harrisii).
    e. Arrangement of leaves (scales) in pine (Pinus).

IV. Morphology of the Leaf

14. Structure of a typical simple leaf (Pyrus). Identify: blade, petiole, stipules and (in the blade) midrib, veins, and veinlets.
15. Types of venation: Reticulate—a. Pinnate (Castanea), b. Palmate (Ampelopsis Veitchii). Parallel—c. Basal (Convallaria), d. Costal (Canna).
16. Form of the margin of simple leaves. Find examples among the leaves already studied of—a. Entire, b. Serrate, c. Lobed. In addition draw one that is d. Parted (Ricinus), and e. Divided (Bidens).
17. Compound leaves: a. Pinnately compound (Robinia)—note rachis and leaflets. b. Palmately compound (Parthenocissus).
18. Structure of the blade. a. With the edge of the scalpel strip off the thin membrane (epidermis) covering the upper and lower surfaces of the blade (Caladium). Study the epidermis with a hand lens and with a needle determine the texture. b. With the lens study both surfaces of the green part of the blade (mesophyll) where the epidermis has been removed. The denser portion is palisade mesophyll, the other, spongy mesophyll. Determine texture with the needle. c. Scrape out some of the mesophyll and soak it for a time in alcohol in a test-tube. Note the result. The green matter is chlorophyll. d. Can you find pores (stomata) in the epidermis?

V. Stems and Roots

19. Study a cross section of a stem (Paulownia) (Sambucus). Determine the texture of the wood, pith and bark.
20. Study a similar stem in longitudinal section in the region of the node, as in 19.
21. Compare the root of a similar plant with the stem, as in 19 and 20.

THE LIFE HISTORY OF A PLANT
VI. THE SEED

22. A dicotyledonous seed (Phaseolus).
    a. Draw two views of a bean seed to show the general form, the hilum, the micropyle and the chalaza.
    b. From a seed that has been soaked in water remove the seed coats (testa and tegmen). Study the coats.
    c. Draw the embryo, showing the cotyledon and caulicle.
    d. Separate the cotyledons and draw to show the cotyledons, the plumule and the caulicle.
23. Other dicotyledonous seeds:
    a. Study a seed of Pisum as in 22a, b, c, and d.
    b. Compare seeds of Trifolium and Raphanus (or Brassica) with those of Phaseolus and Pisum.
    c. Study a seed of Cucurbita as in 22a, b, c, and d.
24. A monocotyledonous seed (Zea Mays).
    a. Draw that side of a grain of corn which shows the embryo.
    b. Remove the seed coats from a specimen which has been softened in water and find the embryo embedded in the mealy endosperm. Study the seed coats, but do not try to homologize with those of the bean. They are more complex.
    c. With a sliding cut make a longitudinal section of a seed through the shorter diameter so as to exactly halve the embryo. Draw the section and identify cotyledon, plumule and caulicle.
    d. Cut another transversely at three points, so as to divide the embryo into quarters. Draw the three sections.
    e. Compare a seed of Triticum with that of Zea.
25. A seed of a Gymnosperm (Pinus). Study a pine nut noting the character of the seed coat, endosperm and embryo.

VII. Development of the Seedling

26. Where in a germinating bean does evidence of growth first appear? Where and how does the developing part first emerge from the seed coats? Compare plumule and caulicle with regard to rate of development during the first week of growth.
27. Compare pea, squash and corn with bean in regard to each point mentioned in 26.
28. How does each of the four kinds of seedlings emerge from the soil?

29. Compare the cotyledons of the seeds in regard to their behavior during the early stages of development.
30. Why does the primary root grow downward? To be determined by experiment 1.

Experiment 1.—Spread a piece of moist white filter paper in the bottom of a shallow plate or pan. On this set a bottle about three inches high with a cork projecting from the neck. Fasten several pea seeds to the cork with long pins in such a way that they will be suspended in mid-air at least an inch from the cork. The pins may be thrust through the seed coats or the cotyledons but the caulicle and plumule must not be injured. The seeds should be fastened so that the caulicle is directed downward in one case, upward in another and horizontally in another. Cover the whole with a bell jar and note the direction taken by the caulicle when it germinates. Interpret the result. See paragraph 49.

31. Why does the stem grow upward? To be determined by experiment 2.

Experiment 2.—Seal up the hole in the bottom of a four inch flower pot. Fill the pot with earth or sand and plant some pea seeds about an inch below the surface. Moisten the soil and then cover the pot with wire mosquito netting so that the earth will not fall out when the pot is inverted. Invert the pot and support it on an empty glass tumbler and cover the whole with a tall bell jar. The tumbler should be set in a shallow dish or pan on a piece of wet white filter paper. After a period of about ten days, carefully raise the pot, allowing the soil to fall away and expose the seedlings. Interpret the result. See paragraph 50.

32. What changes occur in the cotyledons and what is their ultimate fate? What is the function of the cotyledons?
33. The young plant—*a.* bean, *b.* pea, *c.* squash, *d.* corn.
34. Reviewing development as if in a moving picture, describe the development of the plumule.
35. As in 34 describe the development of the caulicle.
36. The hypocotyl is that part of the stem which develops from the caulicle. Compare the hypocotyl of bean, pea, squash and corn.
37. Root hairs (wheat). Study under glass cover.
38. Draw root system of well developed bean. Note, primary, or tap root, and, secondary, or lateral roots.
39. The cotyledons are the first leaves. Are the leaves that develop next like those of the mature plant? Are the third? Fourth? Compare bean, pea and squash.
40. Where do the branches appear? See also section viii.

VIII. The Mature Plant

41. The root (Quercus alba) in cross section. Draw x5. Study the details carefully with hand lens. Is there a central pith (medulla)? Medullary rays? Vessels or tracheæ in the wood. How arranged? Components of the bark?
42. With scalpel and needles determine the texture of the various parts of the root.
43. Are the vessels true tubes? Can you blow through them? (Exp. 3.)
44. Longitudinal section of root tips (microscope, prepared slide). Note the arrangement of the cells, and the root cap.
45. The stem (Quercus alba) (Aristolochia) in cross section. Draw x4. *a.* One year old stem. *b.* Two year old stem. *c.* Three year old stem. Note annual rings, medullary rays, epidermis, cork, chlorophyll. Compare in the three sections, the pith, the wood and the bark. What changes occur as the stem grows older?
46. A branch at least three years old. Can you determine from surface appearance the limits of the 1, 2 and 3 year old parts? How? Locate the limit of the last season's growth (the twig).
47. Draw the twig (white oak) showing the scale leaf scars, foliage leaf scars, terminal and lateral buds. What is the function of these buds? (see 48). Are there any branches? (see 48).
48. Study the growth of the preceding season. Are there any branches? How old are they? Where do they occur? What determines the position of a branch on a stem?
49. How old is the basal portion of your branch? Determine by surface inspection.
50. Dissect a bud (Hicoria or Æsculus). Note the character of the bud scales and their arrangement. What is their funtion? What do you find in the center of the bud?
51. Structure of the stem (white oak). Study: *a.* cross, *b.* longitudinal radial and *c.* longitudinal tangential sections of a block at least eight years old. Note epidermis, cork, chlorophyll, other tissues of the bark. What is the "grain" of wood? What are the flakes in quartered oak? Why must the wood be "quartered?"
52. Compare the vessels of the root and stem. Compare roots and stems of the same diameter with regard to rigidity.
53. Structure of the stem (corn). *a.* Study cross section of the corn stem noting carefully the arrangement of the pith and vascular bundles. *b.* Split the stem and draw. Are the vascular bundles continuous? *c.* Set a section of stem in red ink (Exp. 4). Does

the ink rise in the vascular bundles? *d.* A prepared slide under the hand lens showing the vascular bundles and the vessels. Draw one bundle x25.

54. The leaf: *a.* Surface view of the epidermis of a leaf showing the stomata (prepared slide, microscope). *b.* Cross section of the leaf (prepared slide, microscope). Identify the layers found in 18.

IX. MODIFIED STRUCTURES

Modified Roots

55. Fibrous roots (grasses).
56. Enlarged (storage) roots.
    (a) Enlarged tap-root (turnip).
    (b) Enlarged fascicled roots (Dahlia).
    (c) Enlarged lateral roots (sweet potato).
57. Prop roots (corn).
58. Aerial roots as holdfasts (ivy).

Modified Stems and Branches

(In each case note the nodes and internodes and the character of the leaves and buds.)

59. Procumbent stems (periwinkle).
60. Runner or stolon (strawberry).
61. Underground stems:
    (a) Rootstock (Smilax).
    (b) Rhizome (Solomon's seal).
    (c) Tuber (Irish potato).
    (d) Corm (Jack-in-the-pulpit).
62. Climbing stems:
    (a) Twining stems (morning glory).
    (b) Climbing by spiral tendrils (grape).
    (c) Climbing by adhesive tendrils (Virginia creeper).
    (d) Climbing by aerial roots (ivy).
63. "Stemless" plants:
    (a) Study a plant of salsify. Is there a stem? Where does the root begin? Note the leaf scars.
    (b) Make a longitudinal section of root and stem. Note distribution of pith and vascular bundles.
    (c) Make cross sections of the stem and the root. Note again as in b.
    (d) Compare a beet or turnip with the salsify as in a, b and c.

64. Storage stems (cactus). What is stored? Note the condition of the leaves. Where is the chlorophyll?
65. Cladophylls (Myrsiphyllum). What are the small scalelike structures borne by the stems? What are the leaf-like organs (cladophylls) borne in the axils of the scales?
66. Thorns:
    (a) What are the thorns on the black locust?
    (b) What are the thorns on the holly and barberry?
    (c) What are the thorns on the honey locust?
67. Tendrils: Compare the tendrils of the grape and Virginia creeper. Why are they branches? Note how the grape tendril is coiled.

Modified Leaves

68. Scale leaves. Recall various types already studied.
69. Tendrils. Compare leaves of the pea, vetch and vetchling. What are the tendrils in each?
70. Thorns. See paragraph 66, a and b.
71. Storage leaves:
    (a) Compare leaves of Portulaca and the houseleek.
    (b) Make a longitudinal section of an onion. What are the scales? (Where is the stem?)
72. Traps:
    (a) The sundew (Drosera). Note how the hairs on the leaves react to contact with a gnat or other small insect.
    (b) The pitcher plant (Sarracenia). What devices are employed for catching insects?
    (c) The Venus flytrap (Dionæa).

X. Flowers

73. A simple type of regular flower (Oxalis).
    (a) Make a diagram of the flower as it would appear in longitudinal section.
    (b) Make a "plan" diagram to show how the parts are arranged around the center.
    (c) Draw one member of each cycle. For terms see text.
    (d) Make a cross section of the ovary.
74. A simple type of irregular flower (Swainsona). Study as in 73.
75. Study other more modified types of flowers such as Primula, etc.

XI. Fruits

76. Simple fruits; dry, dehiscent.
    (a) A follicle (milkweed).
    (b) A legume (bean).
    (c) A pod (Yucca).
77. Simple fruits; dry, indehiscent.
    (a) A samara (maple).
    (b) An achene (sunflower).
    (c) A caryopsis (wheat).
    (d) A nut (oak).
78. Simple fruits, fleshy:
    (a) A drupe (plum).
    (b) A pome (apple).
    (c) A berry (cranberry, persimmon).
79. Aggregate fruits (Magnolia).
80. Multiple fruits (pineapple).

XII. Classes of Plants

For distinguishing characters see pages 71 ff. and 101 ff.

81. Dicotyledons.—Make a list of at least ten common dicotyledonous plants.
82. Monocotyledons.—Make a list of at least ten common monocotyledonous plants.
83. Gymnospermæ.—Make a list of all the kinds of Gymnosperms growing in your vicinity.
84. Pteridophytes.—Dig up a fern with all the roots and wash away the soil. Draw to show roots, rootstock and leaves. Study the under surface of a fruiting frond with the lens.
85. Bryophytes.—Musci—Collect a number of kinds of moss. Find plants with and without a spore capsule but otherwise alike. Draw both kinds.
86. Bryophytes.—Hepaticæ—Collect and study liverworts as in 85.
87. Lichenes.—Collect several kinds of lichens.
88. Algæ.—Collect several kinds of algæ.
89. Fungi.—Collect one or more kinds of each of the following fungi:
    (a) Mushrooms, toadstools, puffballs, rusts and smuts.
    (b) Mildews, blue and green molds and black fungi.
    (c) Water molds and black molds.

Color

18. Plants are usually green. This is so commonly true that perhaps the most general idea associated with the term plant is that of the green color. There are, however, many plants that are not green, as, for example, the "dodder" and "indian pipe." But these plants are also exceptional in other ways. The red and brown sea weeds and plants like the coleus are apparently exceptions, but in these cases the green is really present, though masked by other coloring matters. Besides, there is a large group of organisms like toadstools and molds, collectively called fungi, which are not green. These organisms are grouped by the biologist with the plants, but they are evidently very different from what is commonly meant by "plants," and for the present we may leave them out of consideration. So we may say that, with some exceptions, those organisms which are commonly called plants, are green. Such uniformity of color is not found among animals and, therefore, it is worth while to ask, why are plants so uniformly green?

19. Most plants which are normally green lose their color when grown in the dark. Thus grass growing beneath a stone is yellow; celery is blanched by covering it, and the shoots of potatoes sprouting in a dark bin have no trace of green.

20. Exposure to sunlight soon produces the familiar green in the leaves and certain parts of the stem of such etiolated plants. Frequently those parts of a plant which are not normally green become so on exposure to sunlight. This occurs when, for example, the tubers of an Irish potato, normally underground, are exposed by removal of the soil. The same is true of the roots of many plants.

21. Furthermore, it will be found that no green plants will continue to grow in places where they can get no light; while on the other hand fungous growths like toadstools flourish in

cellars, caves, hollow logs and similar dark situations where green plants are never found.

22. There seems, therefore, to be a direct relation between the green color of plants and the sunlight, and this becomes still more evident when we consider the distribution of the green on the individual plant. In the smaller herbaceous plants the green may be found in all parts above ground, in stem and leaves alike; but in the larger perennial growths, like the oak tree, the green is found only in the leaves and twigs; possibly also on the surface of the smaller branches and between the ridges of dead bark on the larger limbs and the trunk itself. But in the dark central parts of the branches and trunk, and beneath the thick ridges of dead bark there is no green. It may be wanting entirely in the stem, but, with the rarest exceptions, it is always present in the leaves.

The Leaves

23. In connection with its color it is also important to note the form of the leaf. This varies through an infinite variety of patterns from circular to linear, but in almost every case it is either very small, or else very thin or very slender in proportion to its other dimensions. From this it results that the surface of the leaf is large in proportion to its volume, and all of its substance lies near the surface, that is, exposed to the light. In other words, the form of the leaf is such as to give a maximum exposure of its substance to the light. As a general characteristic of leaves this one of form is second in importance only to that of the green color.

24. A typical leaf consists of three parts: (1) a broad, thin portion—the blade, (2) a narrow rounded or angular stem— the petiole, and (3) at the base of the petiole a pair of wing-like appendages—the stipules. Stipules vary greatly. They are usually more or less leaf-like, but may be reduced to mere

rudimentary structures or may even be entirely wanting. The leaf may also be without a petiole, in which case the blade is directly connected with the stem or branch of the plant and is then said to be sessile.

25. The petiole is stiff enough to support the blade and yet is flexible and elastic. It is composed largely of fibrous woody tissue, which extends on from the petiole into the blade, where it is so disposed as to constitute a framework upon which the more delicate tissues of the blade are supported. This framework is made up of one or a few large ribs which by branching give rise to numerous smaller veins and veinlets.

26. The veins may be arranged in one of two ways; they either lie parallel with one another and extend from the base of the blade to its tip or from the single large midrib to the edge of the blade, or else they unite with each other in such a way as to form a network. Leaves having the former arrangement of the veins are said to be parallel veined, while those presenting the latter condition are termed netted veined. Netted veined leaves may further be characterized as feather veined if there is only a single large midrib from which the principal veins branch on either side, or palmately veined when there are several ribs spreading in a fan shaped order from the base of the blade.

27. The upper and lower surfaces of the leaf blade are formed by thin, transparent, but rather tough, membranes, the epidermis, which may be stripped off. Between the two layers of epidermis lies the green mesophyll, which next the upper epidermis forms a rather firm tissue, but on the lower side is more spongy in texture.

28. In outline the leaf blade is extremely variable. All forms from circular to narrow ribbon-like or even thread-like are met with, and the margin varies from a continuous line or unbroken curve to conditions which may be described as toothed, lobed, cleft or divided, as the case may be. A divided leaf is one in

which the indentations of the margin extend completely to the midrib, thus producing a double series of leaflets ranged along a common midrib.

29. When the divisions of the blade are all distinct so that each resembles a miniature leaf, the leaf is said to be compound. The divisions are then called leaflets and the common leaf-stalk is the rachis.

Phyllotaxy

30. Leaves are usually arranged on the stem in a definite order. On a vertical shoot there are two or more vertical ranks of leaves. When there are two leaves at the same level they are opposite, and each pair crosses the pair above or below at right angles, making four vertical ranks of leaves. Sometimes there are three or more leaves at the same level, forming a whorl. If there is only one leaf at each level the leaves are said to alternate. In this case every 2nd, 3rd, 5th, 8th or 13th, etc., leaf, as the case may be, is in the same rank and there will be 2, 3, 5, 8, or 13, etc., ranks respectively. This order is in reality a spiral one, for if a line is drawn from one leaf to the next higher one in the nearest direction and continued in this way it will describe a spiral around the stem. This methodical arrangement of the leaves evidently gives each leaf a maximum of elbow room with respect to its fellows, and tends to equalize the conditions of light and shade.

31. The number of leaves which may receive sufficient light exposure on a stem of a given length depends on (1) the size of the leaf—a few large ones will shade each other as much as a large number of small ones, (2) the shape of the blade—long, narrow leaves or finely divided ones may be set more closely than broad and entire leaves, (3) the length of the petiole—other things being equal a long petiole will give the leaves more room than a short one and consequently long petioles

are usually associated with broad leaves. From this it follows that there is a correlation between the number of ranks of leaves on the stem and the distance between leaf levels on the one hand, and the form and size of the leaf on the other. Plants which normally grow in tussocks, i. e., many stems in a cluster, form a natural exception to the above rule, for in this case the crowding of the stems reduces the number of leaves possible on each stem.

32. On horizontal branches the leaves are attached to the stem in precisely the same order as on vertical stems, but the blades of the leaves are in many cases brought round into the horizontal plane by a twisting and bending of the petiole.

33. Still other devices are employed for securing equal and sufficient illumination of the leaves, but whatever the means employed all tend toward the same result, viz., a maximum exposure of green tissue to the light.

The Stem

34. From what has gone before, it is evident that one of the functions of the stem of the plant is to hold up the leaves to the light. This function may be performed in various ways, and much of the character of the stem and its branches depends upon how this function is performed. Among the low herbaceous forms the adaptation of the stem to this function is simple enough and nothing further need be said here, except to note that where the plants are crowded the stems are usually less branched, and more slender than where they grow singly. This is also true of trees, and the cause of it may be discovered by the comparison of a few examples.

35. A tree growing in an open space tends to have a relatively short and thick trunk, with large, spreading branches near the ground. One growing close by the side of another in an open field will have the large branches only on the side away from

20   PLANTS

the neighboring tree. If the tree is closely surrounded by others of approximately the same age, as in a forest, the trunk will be taller in proportion to its diameter and there will be no large limbs near the ground. These facts show clearly that the larger branches develop only where they can reach the light, whereas

Fig. 3.—Three oak trees in a group, showing the effect of one tree on another with regard to the development of the branches. In the middle tree the branches extend toward, and away from, the observer.

those twigs which appear from time to time in shaded situations fail to develop into large branches because of the lack of light, and, after a few seasons' struggle against adverse circumstances, ultimately die and fall away.

36. The stem of erect plants is usually a cylinder of woody

tissue. Woody tissue possesses in a large degree both rigidity and elasticity, while the cylindrical form is of all forms the one giving greatest rigidity. The stem cylinder is often hollow, but usually the axis is occupied by a core of spongy tissue—the pith. This by itself would be of little value as a supporting structure and yet in young shoots it probably adds greatly to the strength of the stem by preventing buckling of the cylinder. In far the greater number of the plants there is also a cylinder of bark which surrounds the woody part. This bark has a double function. It adds greatly to the elasticity of the stem through the layer of fibers—the bast—which lies directly over the wood and which possesses great tensile strength. The other function of the bark—that of protection—is subserved by its outer layers which consist either of a smooth and tough epidermis or thick layers of corky tissue, both of which are highly resistant to mechanical injury.

The Roots

37. The stem of the plant is firmly anchored in the soil by the roots. Continuing downward from the base of the stem there is often a short, rapidly tapering tap root, while other and longer roots pass out radially and usually at a small angle downward. These master roots branch repeatedly, giving rise ultimately to a vast number of minute rootlets which interlace and penetrate the soil in all directions and through a space of considerable radius. The tap root is often insignificant and the plant is held erect by the combined bracing and guying action of the lateral roots. Only the larger roots where they unite with the stem possess any great degree of rigidity. The more remote parts of the root system have little rigidity or elasticity in comparison with the stem and branches. They are, on the other hand, quite flexible and tough and capable of resisting a considerable pull longitudinally.

38. In many cases there are a large number of fibrous roots which spring directly from the base of the stem instead of a few larger roots. Such fibrous root systems occur principally on low herbaceous plants which do not require an especially strong supporting system.

39. The structure of the root, in the main, resembles that of the stem in that there is a central woody axis and an outer bark; but there is no pithy core. The woody portion is not as firm as that of the stem, but it is often very tough. The outer, dead, protective layer of the bark of roots is also relatively thin.

40. In the preceding paragraphs some of the most evident characteristics of ordinary plants have been noted for the purpose of showing that the form and structure of plants is in every case an adaptation to a certain end, and that even the peculiarities of each kind of plant are special adaptations to special ends. In continuing our studies we shall constantly keep in mind this idea of adaptation to functions, that is to say, at every point we shall seek to answer the question why?

41. In the following paragraphs we shall take up for consideration, in turn, the seed, the developing seedling and the mature plant, studying in each case the structure and functions of the principal sets of organs, so that at the end we may have a fairly comprehensive idea of the life-history of a plant.

Seeds

42. Seeds present a remarkable diversity of form and structure, but there are usually two distinct sets of organs to be recognized. The first of these are the seed coats, evidently organs of protection, often consisting of an outer firm layer, the testa, and an inner membraneous layer, the tegmen. However, the seed coats may be variously modified and cannot be generally characterized.

43. The other set of organs is the essential part of the seed and constitutes the germ or embryo. In the largest of the three grand divisions of seed-bearing plants, the Dicotyledons, the embryo consists usually of two symmetrical parts, the cotyledons, which are connected by a third part—the caulicle. At the end of the caulicle between the cotyledons there may also be a minute structure, the plumule, which when well developed shows clearly the outlines of one or more leaves in miniature.

44. In another division of the seed-bearing plants there is only one cotyledon, and hence the name applied to the group is Monocotyledons.

45. Besides the embryo there is frequently contained within the seed coat a mass of food material for the use of the developing embryo. This food material, called endosperm or perisperm, depending on the position it occupies in the seed, may consist either of starch, proteid, oil, or cellulose, or a combination of two or more of these food principles.

Germination

46. The conditions necessary for the germination of seeds are: First, a favorable temperature which might be designated as warmth. The range and limits of this favorable temperature are not sharply defined and may vary with the kind of seed. Cold, a temperature below the limit within which germination takes place, indefinitely retards development, though it does not necessarily destroy the vitality of the germ if the seeds are dry, while on the other hand, any considerable increase of temperature above that of germination destroys all power of further development.

47. A second condition of germination is moisture. This softens the seed coats, thus permitting the embryo to expand, and also supplies the water which is everywhere necessary to growth.

48. That oxygen is necessary to germination may be demonstrated by experiment either by placing the seeds of aquatic plants in water from which the air has previously been expelled by boiling, or by placing seeds in a vessel containing an atmosphere deprived of its oxygen.

49. Under the conditions just enumerated the embryo swells through the absorption of water, the seed coats burst and the caulicle grows out and down into the soil, the terminal part of it going to form the primary root. It will be noted here that the direction of growth, not only of the root, but also of the other growing parts of the plant, is very definite and that the determining cause of it must be sought in some external agency. By suitably conducted experiments we find that gravity acts upon the primary root as a stimulus, in response to which it grows downward. This response is known as positive geotropism. If the influence of gravity be eliminated the root will turn toward the source of moisture—this is positive hydrotropism.

50. The plumule also responds to external stimuli, but in a different way. It turns away from the earth, being negatively geotropic, and grows toward the light—positively heliotropic. (The student should note that unless light actually impinges on the seedling it can have no influence in determining the direction of growth. Hence, if the seed is growing in the dark the direction of growth must be determined by some stimulus other than light. In this connection analyze carefully the results of experiments 1 and 2 under paragraph 30, and 31, page 10.)

The Seedling

51. When the primary root has penetrated the soil some distance, lateral branches begin to appear on all sides of it at some distance above its tip. These branches are not positively geotropic, since they grow in an almost horizontal direction—diageotropism—with perhaps a slight tendency down-

ward. With the appearance of the lateral rootlets there can, of course, be no further elongation of that part of the radicle or tap root from which they spring, since this would result only in the destruction of the branch roots or a doubling of the tap root. Observation of a marked primary root shows, in fact, that elongation takes place only near the tip. The subsequent development of the root system is simple enough. The main branches increase in diameter, and, as they push out farther into the soil, give off numerous smaller branches. Successive branching in this way finally produces a system which ends in innumerable minute rootlets.

52. With the development of the lateral roots the seedling becomes firmly anchored in the soil. This is a necessary preliminary in many plants to the first steps in the development of the stem. In some cases the conical plumule pushes upward through the soil as the radicle grows downward, without moving the cotyledons. In other cases the cotyledons are forced up through the soil before the plumule has undergone any considerable development. This is accomplished by the elongation of that part of the seedling—called the hypocotyl—which lies between the cotyledons and the first lateral roots. With one end fixed by its root anchorage, the elongating hypocotyl carries the cotyledons upward in the direction of least soil resistance. During this process the seed coats are stripped off, and, as soon as the cotyledons appear above ground, the plumule is free to continue its development.

53. The several functions of the cotyledons now become evident. In those cases where they remain in the soil they are either greatly swollen by the reserve food contained in the cotyledons themselves, or else they are embedded in a large store of endosperm or perisperm. In either case they nourish the growing embryo from the stored food supply. The plumule of such seeds is a conical shaft, well adapted to bore its way through the ground.

54. In those cases in which the cotyledons appear above the ground they serve to protect the delicate plumule while the vigorous hypocotyl is pushing it up through the earth. If the cotyledons in this case are greatly thickened they are likely to become shriveled as they give up their food to the seedling, and finally they may fall off. Again they may become green and serve for a time the functions of leaves. Very often they are clearly leaflike at the beginning and remain for some time as the first pair of leaves. In every case the cotyledons nourish the seedling, either from endosperm or perisperm, or from the food contained within their own tissues, until green leaves are developed by transformation of the cotyledons themselves or by the development of the first leaves by the plumule.

55. The plumule is the last of the embryonic parts to begin its development. From it arise practically all the above-ground parts of the plant, i. e., stem and leaves. In the embryo it is essentially a bud, and, as it develops, one segment of the stem after another appears and leaf after leaf unfolds until we have the fully formed plant. The region of development, i. e., the formation of new parts, in the plumule is at the apex of its axis in the center of the bud, but after the parts have been formed and unfolded they continue to expand for some time. From this primary bud, which is first called the plumule, but later on is known as the terminal bud, is developed, directly, the main axis or stem of the plant with its leaves.

56. Secondary axes, or branches, are developed from buds (axillary buds) which appear in the angles (the axil) between the leaves and the stem. In the case of perennial plants the leaves which form last, but do not unfold in the fall, and which are the first to unfold in the following spring, are scale-like in form and serve to protect the tender parts which they enfold, from the winter weather.

57. In some cases accessory buds occur above or on either side of the axillary bud, and adventitious buds may occur on

any part of the stem. In case a terminal bud is destroyed, and also under certain other conditions, the development of the main axis may be continued by an axillary bud. Also, if an axillary bud is destroyed its functions may be taken up by accessory or adventitious buds.

58. Since branches normally develop from axillary buds, it follows that branches are arranged on the stem in conformity with the law which governs the arrangement of the leaves on the stem.

59. The terminal bud, because of its favorable position with respect to light exposure, and also possibly for other causes, is usually stronger than lateral buds, and therefore the main axis develops more rapidly than the branches. Many lateral buds, on the other hand, are in such unfavorable positions that even after having developed to some extent they are "choked" and the twig dies and falls away. Still others never develop at all. Thus it results that while the position of a branch on the stem is governed by the law of leaf arrangement, yet, because of the large number of buds that do not develop and of others that are choked out, the regularity of arrangement is seldom evident in the case of branches.

The Mature Plant

60. At the end of the growing season the foliage leaves of deciduous perennials fall off, leaving a scar on the twig. The bud scale-leaves fall away on the unfolding of the bud and also leave scars, which, however, are so crowded, because of the slight elongation of the axis, that they frequently form a continuous ring around the stem. The scale-leaf scar can also be distinguished from the foliage-leaf scar by its form. The position of the scale-leaf scars indicates the beginning of the year's growth, consequently the age of a twig may be determined by counting the successive rings of scale scars. Other

characters, such as the color and texture of the bark and the succession of branches, will also serve to determine the age of any particular section of the branch.

61. If we cut across a twig of one year's growth, we find that it consists of three parts, an outer bark which may be peeled off, a central core of soft tissue—the pith—and between them

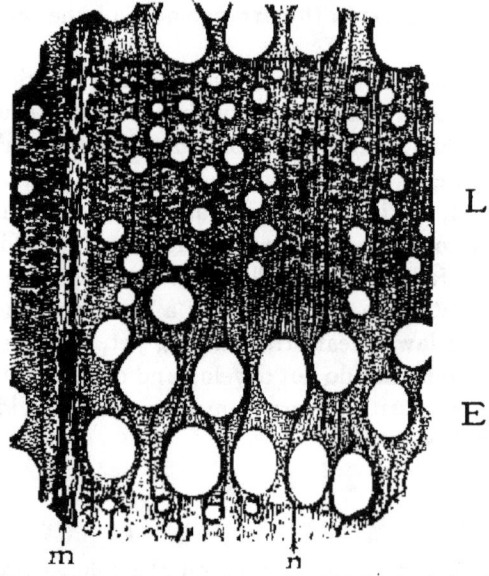

Fig. 4.—Photomicrograph of a cross section of oak wood showing one year's growth. *E*, Early growth; *L*, late growth; *m* and *n*, large and small medullary rays. (From Stevens.)

a firmer cylinder, the wood. The outer surface of the bark is smooth and rather tender, and covers a layer containing more or less green substance. The inner layers, those which are next the wood, are hard and consist largely of very tough fibers. The pith is soft and spongy in texture and contains no fibers. The wood is also fibrous, since it can be split lengthwise of the stem, but it is more compact than the fibrous tissue of the bark and cannot be as readily separated into strands.

62. If twigs two and three years old are cut across we find that there are differences besides merely that of thickness. In the older stems the surface of the bark has changed color, become firmer and also perhaps rougher. There is less, if any, evidence of chlorophyll, and the bark is thicker. The pith shows little change, but the woody cylinder is about twice or three times as thick as before and is divided by concentric circles into annual rings of growth. Crossing these circles of growth at right angles are narrow radial lines of pith which connect the central pith core with the bark. These are the medullary rays.

Composition of Plants

63. It is evident that water constitutes a very large per cent. of the substance of plants. If a portion of plant tissue be weighed and then subjected to a moderately high temperature until it is thoroughly dried and then weighed again, it will be found to have lost from 50 to 95 per cent. of its weight. In succulent herbs the percentage of water is very great, while in woody tissues it is much less. A moment's thought will show that the water contained in plants must be absorbed chiefly by the roots, for plants may grow and flourish even though water never falls upon the stem and leaves.

64. If after thoroughly drying vegetable tissue the temperature be increased to just short of the point of ignition the tissue becomes black and there finally remains only a mass of charcoal (carbon), equal in weight to about 25 per cent. of the dried mass. During the process of charring various vapors and gases are driven off; among others are the vapor of water (H_2O), carbon dioxide (CO_2), carbon monoxide (CO), marsh gas (CH_4) and other hydro-carbons. After complete ignition of the charcoal

30   PLANTS

there is left a small residue of ash, amounting to about 5 per cent. or less, of the dried substance.

65. The ash consists chiefly of the following mineral substances, viz.: Potash, soda, lime, magnesia, phosphorous,

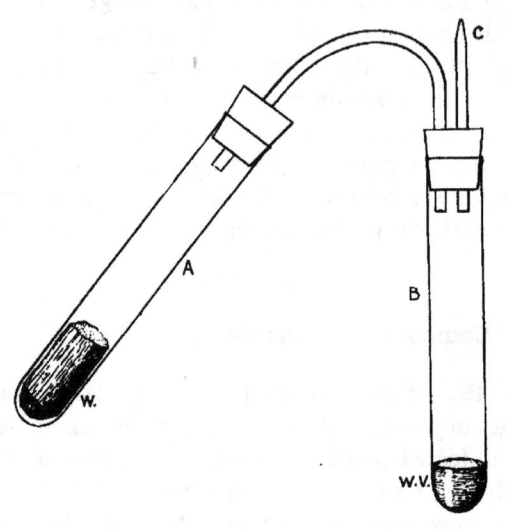

FIG. 5.—Experiment to determine the composition of vegetable tissue. A simple apparatus, consisting of test-tubes, glass tubing and cork stoppers, is fitted up as shown in the figure. The tube A should be of hard glass. A piece of dry wood (W) is then heated over a burner, at first gently, then more vigorously, until it is reduced to charcoal. At first water is driven off and condenses in the cold tube (B). Then other volatile substances pass over, some of which condense in B and others escape at C. The latter may be tested for H_2O and CO_2. The jet escaping at C may then be ignited and the flame tested for H_2O and CO_2. The liquid which has collected in the tube B, is wood vinegar and contains water, acetic acid, wood alcohol and tar. Test with litmus paper for acid. Then heat until it boils, when a blue flame may be obtained at C. This is due to the volatilized alcohol.

sulphur, silica, chlorine, and manganese, which are evidently derived from the soil and must therefore have been absorbed by the roots.

66. Plants will thrive if the water supplied to the roots contains only the above minerals and a trace of iron. But the

largest constituents of the plant are carbon, about 45 per cent. or more, and oxygen, about 45 per cent. or less. Since the carbon is not necessarily present in the water it must be derived from some other source. Carbon is present in the atmosphere in small quantities, combined with oxygen in the form of carbon-dioxide (CO_2), and in the absence of this gas the plant will not

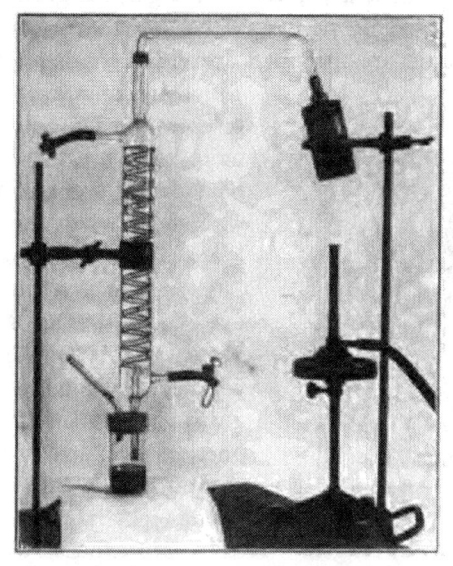

Fig. 6.—The preceding experiment may be performed more satisfactorily by substituting an iron capsule for the hard glass test-tube and connecting the delivery tube with a Leibig condenser. Such an arrangement is represented in Fig. 6.

thrive. Consequently we must assume that the carbon is absorbed from the atmosphere by the stem and leaves. This conclusion may be verified by experiment.

67. The oxygen taken up by the plant may be, and as a matter of fact is, taken up in part as free oxygen from the atmosphere, in part in combination with carbon as CO_2, and in part in combination with other elements absorbed by the roots.

Structure and Function of the Roots

68. The mechanism of water absorption by the roots may be discovered by the study of cross sections of the smaller rootlets. Such a section taken several centimeters from the tip, i. e., through the region covered by root hairs, presents three well marked kinds of tissues; viz., (1) a general ground tissue made up of rounded or polygonal cells with thin walls, (2) larger circular structures grouped around the axis of the root, which are longitudinal vessels in cross section, and (3) root hairs, which are tubular expansions of some of the thin walled cells of the surface layer. The vessels may usually be seen by the unaided eye, especially in the larger roots. The root hairs are very conspicuous and, when growing in a moist atmosphere, stand up rigidly from the surface of the root as slender cylindrical bodies several millimeters in length. If they are exposed for a few minutes to the dry air they soon become limp, topple over and shrivel. This fact shows that the watery content of the hair is rapidly extracted by evaporation from the surface, and that, therefore, the cell wall of the hair is highly pervious to water.

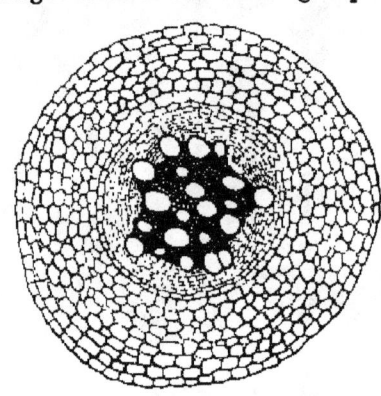

FIG. 7.—Cross section of a young root. ×40.

69. By cutting off the stem of a growing plant near the ground and connecting a glass tube with the stump it may be shown that the roots have the power, not only of absorbing moisture from the soil, but also of driving the sap up into the stem under considerable pressure. In all probability the force chiefly responsible for this root pressure is the osmotic

action which takes place between the contents of the root hairs and the soil water through the cell walls of the root hairs; these cell walls being admirably adapted to serve as osmotic membranes.

70. Soil water holds various mineral salts in solution in small quantities. These are absorbed with the water and furnish the mineral constituents of the ash. At the same time carbonic acid passes out from the root hairs into the soil and by its solvent action helps to break up the mineral constituents of the soil, thus serving at once to disintegrate the rocks and also increase the quantity of mineral salts contained in the soil water.

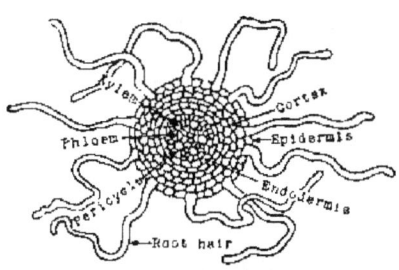

FIG. 8.—Cross section of rootlet in the region of the root hairs. (From Stevens.)

71. The fluids absorbed by the root hairs may then also be transferred from cell to cell by osmotic action and thus finally reach the tubular vessels which lie near the axis of the root. These vessels form a conducting tissue through which the fluids may travel freely, propelled by the osmotic force of the thousands of root hairs on the periphery of the root.

FIG. 9.—Diagram to show the arrangement of the tissues in the stem. The part between the dotted lines is shown on a larger scale in the next figure.

Structure and Function of the Stem

72. The structure of the stem differs somewhat in its significant features from that of the root. In a cross section of a young stem we find, as in the root, a ground tissue of thin

walled spherical or polygonal cells. Such tissue is generally termed parenchyma. In this case it occupies the axis of the stem and forms the pith. There are also radial extensions of the parenchyma from the pith toward the surface of the stem. The disposition of the parenchyma in a cross section might

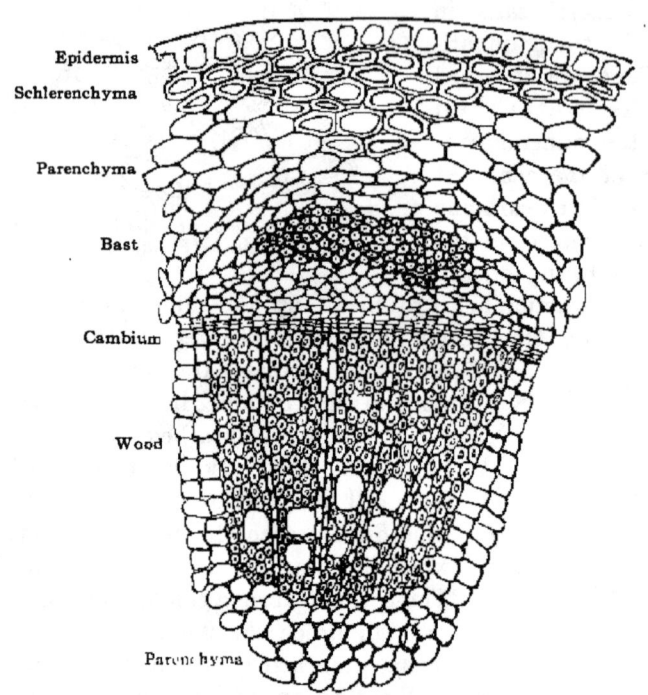

FIG. 10.—Cross section of a typical dicotyledon stem from the pith to the epidermis and comprising one vascular bundle. See preceding figure.

therefore be likened to the hub and spokes of a wheel. In the position corresponding to the felloes of the wheel there is also more or less parenchyma.

73. The tire of the wheel is represented by a single layer of brick-shaped cells whose outer walls are thickened and form

a continuous layer of smooth, tough and impervious cuticula. This layer of cells is the epidermis. It is sufficiently elastic to allow considerable expansion with the growth of the stem, but it may finally be ruptured and scale off, leaving the under parts exposed.

74. The spaces between the spokes of the parenchyma wheel are occupied by a system of fibers and vessels known as the vascular bundles. The fibers are usually of two distinct types, one, known as bast, is found nearer the surface of the stem, while the other is the chief element of the wood and lies

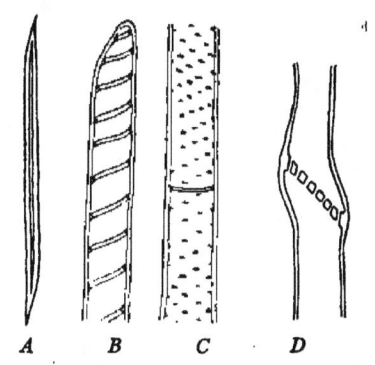

FIG. 11.—Diagrams representing the structural elements of the vascular bundles. *A*, A fibre of wood, or bast; *B*, one end of a tracheid, showing spiral markings; *C*, part of a trachea, or true vessel, with pitted markings and the remnant of the dividing wall which originally separated two of the cells which helped form the vessel; *D*, part of a sieve tube with the perforated cross wall (sieve).

nearer the pith. The bast fibers consist of greatly elongated cells with extremely thick walls. The fibers of the wood are similar but the walls are not so thick. The vessels are of several kinds; first, tracheides, consisting of single elongated cells whose walls are unbroken, but variously thickened in limited areas, forming rings, spirals, annular pits, etc.; second, the sieve vessels, formed by rows of elongated cells placed end to end with the dividing walls perforated by pores forming a sieve;

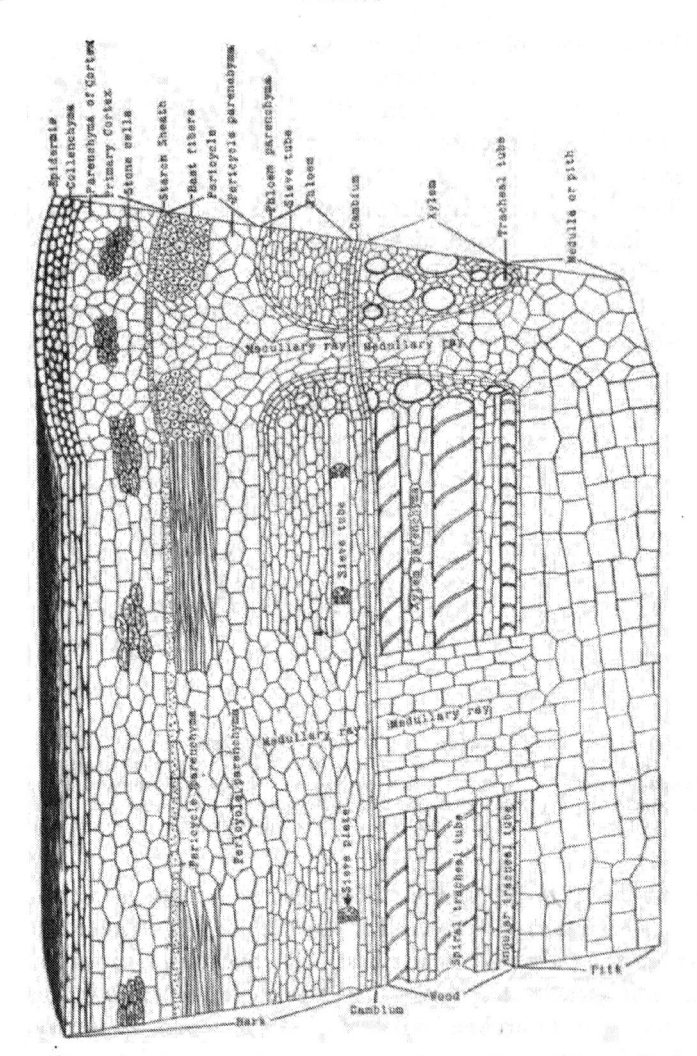

FIG. 12.—A diagram to show the character of the tissues and their disposition in a young stem of the typical dicotyledon type. (From Stevens.)

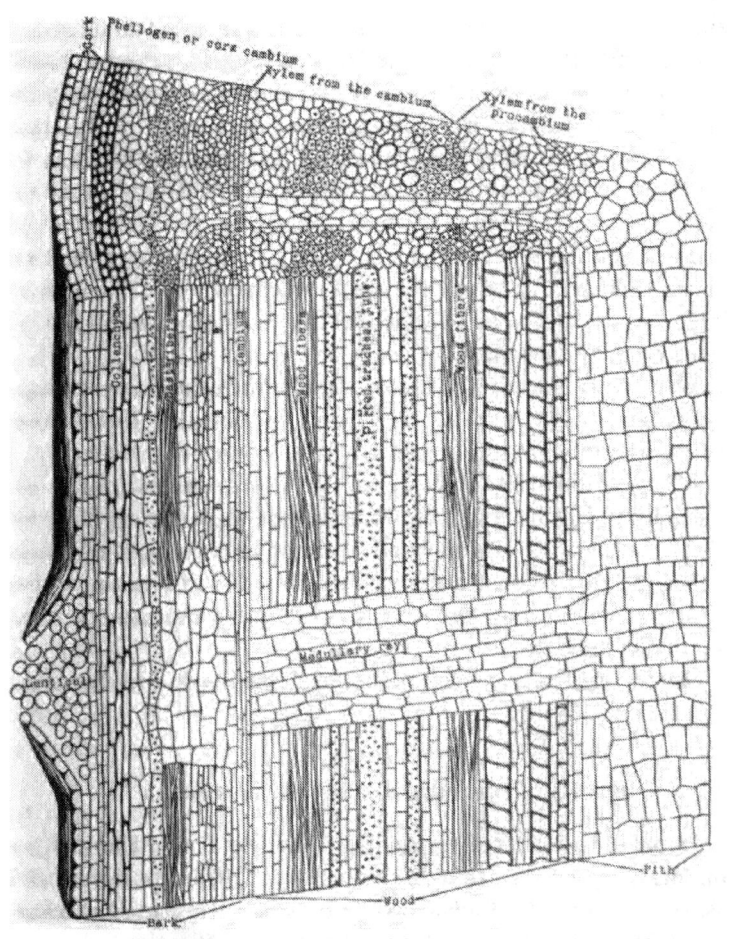

FIG. 13.—Diagram similar to the preceding but representing a later stage and showing the tissues formed by the cambium. (From Stevens.)

third, the true vessels, which originate from rows of cells whose dividing walls disappear, leaving a continuous passage from cell to cell. The walls of the true vessels are also thickened in spiral lines and otherwise as in the tracheides. The tracheides and vessels lie on the side of the vascular bundle next the pith, while the bast and sieve vessels lie next the surface of the stem.

75. The bast and wood portions of the vascular bundles are separated by a zone of very thin-walled cells. This is the cambium, the region in which the new cells are formed and added to the tissues on either side, increasing the thickness of the bark on one side and adding to the wood on the other. The delicate cambium is readily torn and forms the line along which the bark separates from the wood.

76. The woody portions of the vascular bundles are arranged side by side around the pithy axis, thus forming the cylinder alluded to above (paragraph 36).

77. By experiment it may readily be determined that the fluids absorbed by the roots rise through the stem through the vessels and cell walls of the wood and not through the bark. The same fact is demonstrated by the effect of girdling a tree, which operation does not prevent the rise of the sap nor cause wilting of the leaves.

78. Other functions of the wood and bark will be noted subsequently.

Structure and Function of the Leaves

79. In order to fully understand the function of the leaf and the important processes that take place within its tissues it is necessary to study the finer details of its structure by means of the microscope. Thus under moderate magnification a leaf seen in cross section presents the following essential elements of structure:

80. Both layers of epidermis consist of a single layer of brick-

shaped colorless cells, whose outer walls are thickened and cutinized, whereby they become tough and impervious. This modification of the cell wall is usually more marked in the case of the upper epidermis. The epidermis—usually the lower, sometimes the upper, frequently both—is pierced by numerous

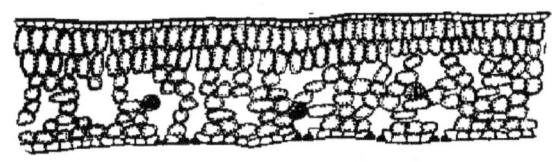

FIG. 14.—Cross section of a typical leaf. Five stomata are shown in the lower epidermis.

pores, the stomata, which open into a system of intercellular spaces filled with air. The outside atmosphere is thus given free access to all parts of the mesophyll through the stomata and this system of intercellular air spaces.

81. The more compact upper layer of the mesophyll consists of cells elongated perpendicularly to the epidermis and arranged in ranks, whence they have received the name "palisade cells." The lower, spongy layer of the mesophyll consists of cells less regular in form and arrangement and more completely surrounded by air spaces, but otherwise like the palisade cells.

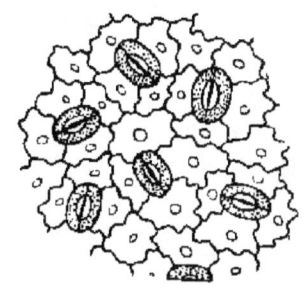

FIG. 15.—Surface view of the epidermis of a leaf showing several stomata. The guard cells are dotted.

82. The important characteristic of the cells of the mesophyll is the presence of numerous minute green granules embedded in the protoplasm. The granules are specialized parts of the protoplasm and are called chloroplasts. The substance which gives them color is called chlorophyll. It is

40   PLANTS

this chlorophyll which gives green plants their characteristic color. It may be extracted from green tissues by alcohol, in which it is soluble, the alcohol then becoming green and the chloroplasts colorless.

83. The function of the various parts of the leaf may be determined by suitably conducted, simple experiments.

84. The usual position of the stomata, on the underside of the leaf, indicates that the stomata are not organs for the absorption

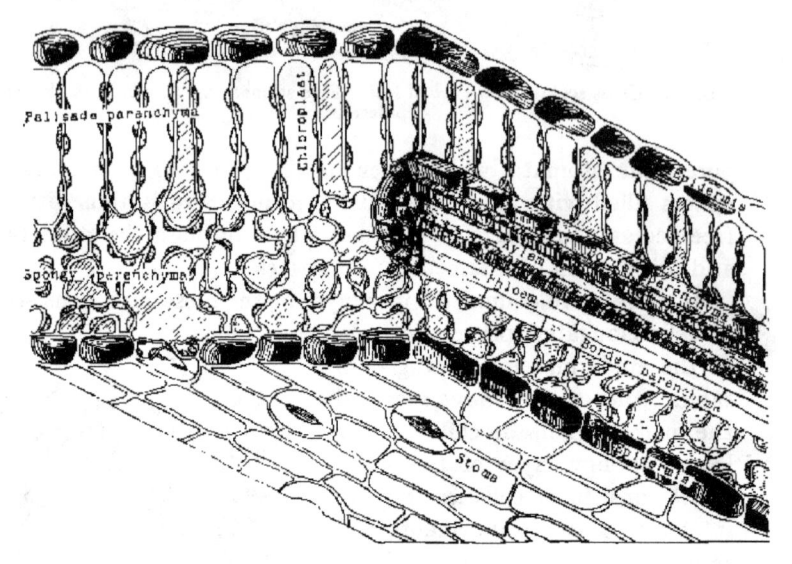

FIG. 16.—Stereogram of leaf structure. Part of a veinlet is shown on the right. Intercellular spaces are shaded. (From Stevens.)

of water. Besides, most leaves, due to the presence of a waxy secretion on the surface of the epidermis, do not wet and, consequently, water would not pass through the minute openings. The function of the stomata must be to permit an interchange of vapors and gases between the intercellular air spaces and the atmosphere; for by experiment it can be shown that water vapor is given off from leaves, but only from the surface provided with stomata, consequently the stomata must be regarded as the openings through which the vapor escapes. The term *transpiration* is applied to this process by which water in the form of vapor escapes from the leaves.

85. If the atmosphere surrounding a green plant growing in a closed chamber and exposed to the sunlight be tested from time to time for carbon dioxide and oxygen it will be found that the percentage of the former gas decreases, while that of the latter increases. Other tests will further show that the carbon dioxide is absorbed and assimilated by the leaf, in which process an excess of oxygen over that required by the plant is set free in the leaf, and, if the leaf is immersed in water, the oxygen may be seen to collect on the surface of the leaf in bubbles. These gases are not absorbed or eliminated through epidermal surfaces having no stomata, consequently we must conclude that the stomata give passage to carbon dioxide and oxygen, as well as to water vapor.

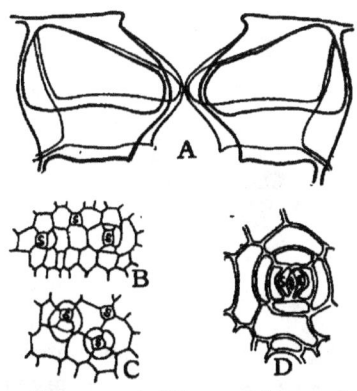

FIG. 17.—*A*, Diagram of stoma in open and closed condition (heavy lines represent stoma open). *B*, *C*, and *D*, successive stages in the development of the stoma. (From Stevens after Sachs.)

86. The rate of transpiration of water vapor is controlled by an automatic opening and closing of the stomata. Excessive transpiration results in the wilting of the leaf, which means that the cells having lost some water are less turgid. The cells which guard the stoma on either side are so constructed that with increased turgidity they open the stoma, while with loss of turgidity the stoma is closed. Of course the rate of absorption

of carbon dioxide and the accompanying elimination of oxygen is also dependent upon the opening and closing of the stomata.

Photosynthesis

87. The leaves of a green plant growing under normal conditions always contain starch when the plant has been exposed to sunlight for a time. The starch disappears at night or when the plant is placed in the dark. It also disappears if the plant is kept in an atmosphere which contains no carbon dioxide. Etiolated leaves contain no starch under any circumstances. It appears from these facts that starch is formed in the leaf only in the presence of chlorophyll, carbon dioxide and sunlight. The chemical formula for starch is $C_6H_{10}O_5$, a carbohydrate derivative formed by the combination of CO_2 and H_2O, thus, $6CO_2 + 5H_2O = C_6H_{10}O_5 + 6O_2$, the surplus oxygen being given off by the plant. It will be noted that the number of molecules of oxygen given off equals the number of molecules of CO_2 absorbed, which means that the volumes of the absorbed and eliminated gases are equal.

FIG. 18.—Starch grains, showing concentric lines of growth.

88. The power of forming starch from inorganic matter is a property peculiar to green plants, because of their chlorophyll, and gives them the distinction of being the source whence all organisms derive their food, since starch is the proximate organic form of almost all food substances. The starch is formed within, or in contact with, the chloroplasts and appears first as minute granules which grow by the addition of layers to the outside in such a way that the surface of the fully formed grain is marked by peculiar concentric lines.

89. We now see whence the plant derives its large amount of carbon. From the formula for starch it follows that 4/9 of

its weight is carbon, which is approximately the proportion of carbon in the total plant tissue. The CO_2 of the atmosphere finds its way, with the other constituents of the air, through the stomata of the epidermis, into the intercellular spaces of the leaf. From here it passes through the cell walls of the mesophyll by osmose and is then by photosynthesis converted into starch, the free oxygen passing out of the cell, also by osmose, to the air of the intercellular spaces and thus out of the leaf. This process must not be regarded as assimilation, since the substances absorbed have not been converted into living protoplasm nor built up into the structural elements of the plant. The starch is simply food material which has been manufactured by the plant from a substance which is not food. For CO_2 cannot be directly assimilated by protoplasm.

90. Starch is practically insoluble in water at ordinary temperature, yet it quickly disappears in an active cell when photosynthesis is not going on. There is an active principle called a ferment present in the protoplasm, which corrodes the starch grain, wearing away the surface until finally it goes to pieces and disappears. In place of the starch a form of sugar is found, dissolved in the cell sap. This is formed directly from the starch by the addition to the molecule of a molecule of water, thus starch $(C_6H_{10}O_5)+H_2O=$ sugar $(C_6H_{12}O_6)$, a substance readily soluble in water. This soluble food substance may be directly assimilated by the protoplasm of the cell in which it was formed, or it may be transferred to other cells by osmose.

Respiration

91. The fact that oxygen is liberated from the plant during photosynthesis must not be interpreted to mean that the plant does not need oxygen. As has been noted elsewhere, oxygen is necessary to the germination of seeds and it is as necessary to the growing plant. During photosynthesis more

oxygen is liberated than is needed by the plant and the excess escapes. But during the night, or when for any reason no oxygen is set free in the tissues by the synthesis of starch, the plant absorbs oxygen directly from the atmosphere. This is at all times true of plants which contain no chlorophyll. The process of absorbing oxygen of whatever source, by vegetable tissues, is called respiration and is identical with respiration in animals.

Translocation of Food Substances

92. The midribs and veins of the leaf are continuations of the vascular bundles of the stem. Besides giving support to the softer tissues they also bring the leaf into communication with the rest of the plant through the vascular system, permitting the passage of liquids and gases between the leaf and the stem.

93. Since starch and, consequently, sugar, are formed only in cells containing chlorophyll, all other cells must be dependent for their food upon those which contain chlorophyll. Consequently, in the larger number of plants, the leaves must elaborate all the food for the stem and root. Starch is frequently found in parts containing no chlorophyll. In such cases it has been formed from sugar by the action of colorless corpuscles, called amyloplasts, which differ from chloroplasts only in the absence of chlorophyll. The course of the sugar through the stem is chiefly along sieve vessels and the surrounding parenchyma. In passing from cell to cell it is frequently converted into starch and then reconverted into sugar preparatory to the next osmotic transfer.

Other Food Substances

94. Besides the carbohydrates, starch and sugar, there are several other kinds of food substances elaborated in the leaf.

Prominent among these are the various vegetable oils, which are also compounds of carbon, hydrogen and oxygen. Globules of oil may be found in the tissues of the leaf and in other parts of the plant, but it is especially in the seeds of certain plants that large quantities of oil are stored up, to serve the same purposes that is served by starch in other cases.

95. Aleurone is a substance which contains, besides carbon, hydrogen and oxygen, also a small per cent. of nitrogen. It is therefore called a nitrogenous substance and is very much like albumen. It is soluble in water and consequently disappears when immersed in a watery solution, but by mounting tissues of dry seeds containing it in a medium like glycerine, the aleurone may be seen under the microscope in the form of small granules.

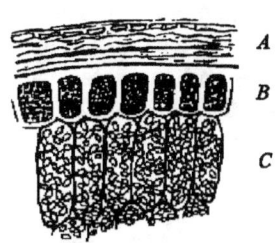

FIG. 19.—Section of a grain of wheat. A, Pericarps and seed coats; B, layer of cells in the endosperm containing aleurone grains; C, cells of the endosperm containing starch grains.

Differentiation of Tissues

96. All reserve food materials are ultimately converted into protoplasm and from protoplasm the various structural elements of the tissues are formed. Thus the undifferentiated cell walls of parenchyma consist of cellulose, $C_6H_{10}O_5$, a substance having the composition of starch. The cellulose is formed from layers of protoplasm by a process of chemical transformation.

97. By further alteration in the chemical nature of the cellulose walls by which the proportion of carbon is increased, the walls assume special characteristics; the surface wall of epidermal cells becomes cutinized (cutin), the walls of cork cells become suberized (suberin), and the walls of wood and bast fibres become lignified (lignin).

98. All parts of the plant are covered, at least during the early stages of their development, by a superficial layer of cells forming the epidermis. On parts exposed to the air the outer walls of the epidermal cells are cutinized, which renders them impervious and tough. These properties render the epidermis well fitted to prevent desiccation of the underlying tissues and to protect them from mechanical injury.

99. On the smaller rootlets, which are always surrounded by the moist soil and hence not subject to either desiccation

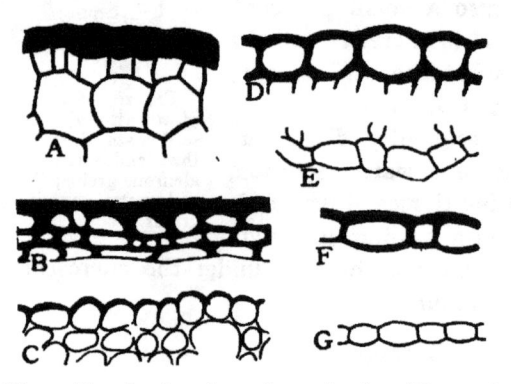

Fig. 20.—The epidermis of various plants showing different degrees of cutinization (in black). *A*, Leaf of Avicennia, a Xerophyte; *B*, the epidermis of an apple (fruit); *C*, petal of Japan quince; *D* and *E*, upper and lower epidermis of leaf of Hibiscus Moscheutos; *F*, epidermis of leaf of prickly lettuce, Lactuca scariola, in the sun; *G*, same, in the shade. (From Stevens.)

or mechanical injury, the epidermis is not cutinized, consequently it offers no obstacle to the transfusion of water and in fact is here specially modified for the function of absorption through the medium of the root hairs, which are only expansions of some of the epidermal cells.

100. Structures called hairs are also developed on aerial parts of the plant. These assume as endless variety of forms and serve various functions. Some are glandular, others are organs for water absorption, and still others serve a variety of

special functions. Most of those found on the leaf and stem, however, must be classed with protective structures, protecting the parts they cover from too intense sunlight, too rapid transpiration, attacks of animals, wetting and frosts, etc.

101. The epidermis is elastic and stretches to a remarkable degree as the parts covered by it expand with growth. But on the roots and stems of perennials the limit of elasticity is reached after a few years and then the epidermis gives way, breaking in various ways and exposing the tissues beneath. Its place as a protective structure is taken by the underlying layers of the bark which have then become modified into cork. This serves more efficiently the function of protection than did the epidermis, though at the expense of depriving the tissues beneath of the sunlight which had before been transmitted by the transparent epidermis. The corky layers are thick and opaque, though at the same time extremely impervious, extremely poor conductors of heat, not readily yielding to the claw or tooth of beast or the beak of bird, almost valueless as food for animals and offering an excellent protection against the attacks of fungous parasites. The outer layers of the cork are dead tissue, which usually splits into ridges as the stem expands, and later the outer layers even scale off and drop away, while new layers are constantly forming beneath from the cork cambium.

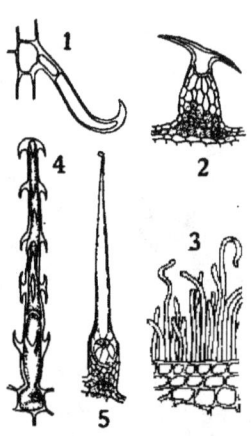

FIG. 21.—1, Hooked hair from the stem of Phaseolus multiflorus; 2, climbing hair on stem of Humulus Lupulus; 3, rod-like wax coating on stem of Saccharum officinarum; 4, climbing hair of Losa hispida; 5, stinging hair of Urtica ureus. (From Stevens, after deBary and Haberlandt.)

102. The most delicate tissues of the plant are those in which growth is taking place by the multiplication of cells. The three

48   PLANTS

chief regions in which this occurs are the centre of the bud, the cambium layer of the stem and roots and the root tip. The

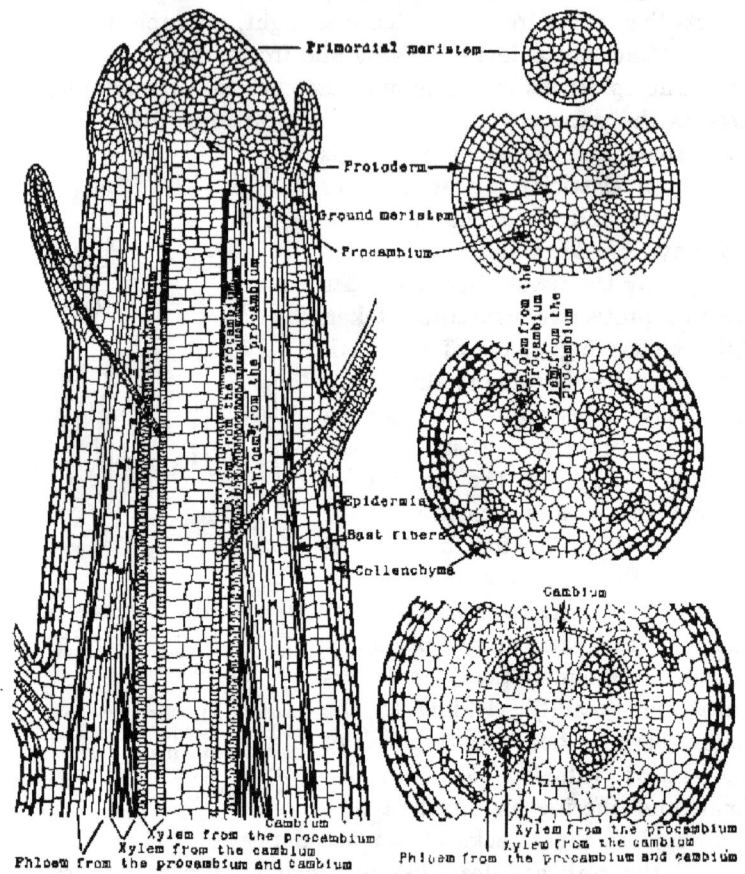

FIG. 22.—Diagram to show the development of the tissues (differentiation) near the tip of a growing stem. The four figures on the right represent cross sections at different distances from the tip of the stem. The figure should represent the tip of the stem covered by the young leaves. (From Stevens.)

growing tissue of the bud lies at the centre of a group of older structures and hence is not exposed except that the bud as a whole may suffer injury; and the cambium lies beneath the bark which gives it ample protection. But the tip of the root, as it grows, must push its way through the harsh soil and is therefore provided with a special protective structure, the root cap. This is a conical mass of cells fitting over the tip of the root. As the rootlet pushes forward through the soil some of the cells of the root cap are rubbed off or destroyed, while others from beneath take their places, new ones being continually formed for this purpose at the point of growth in the base of the cap.

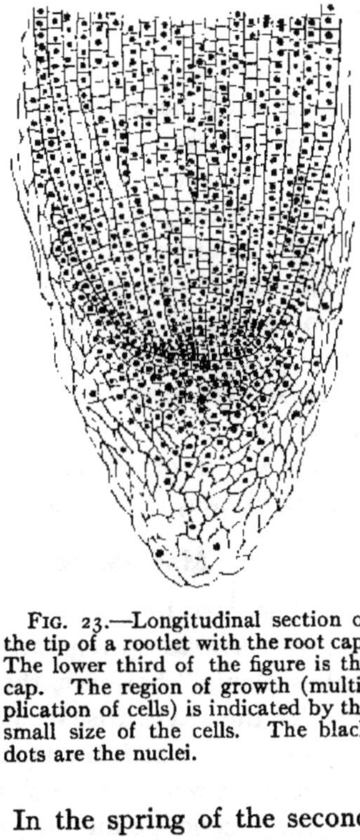

Modified Roots

103. In many plants, especially among biennials and perennials, the roots show peculiarities of form and structure which cannot be accounted for with reference to the usual functions of roots, viz., those of absorption and anchorage. These modifications are often in the nature of enlargements, as in the case of the turnip and sweet potato.

Fig. 23.—Longitudinal section of the tip of a rootlet with the root cap. The lower third of the figure is the cap. The region of growth (multiplication of cells) is indicated by the small size of the cells. The black dots are the nuclei.

In the spring of the second year such roots give rise to new shoots from undeveloped or adventitious buds. The root shrivels as the shoot grows because of the gradual absorption of the contained food store, the enlargement being due to the accumulation of starch or other elaborated food substances.

104. A less common type of root is the prop root, which

springs from the stem above ground, or even, in some cases, from the branches, and grows down to and into the soil. Such roots are found in special cases in which the plant would otherwise be top-heavy for its basal root system. The prop roots are primarily for anchorage though they may also serve for absorption.

105. Another form of modified root is found in certain climbing plants which have roots springing from the aerial parts of the plants. These aerial roots serve as hold-fasts, penetrating the superficial layers of the bark of the tree, or crevices of the rock, to which the plant clings for support.

106. The function of the aerial roots of epiphytes, so common in humid climates, is not only to attach the plant to its host but also to absorb moisture. In some cases the moisture is absorbed directly from the atmosphere; in others, it is drawn from the sponge of decaying leaves and other vegetable substance which collects among the tangled mass of roots. In the latter case the absorbed water is likely to contain more or less nourishing matter, extracted from the humus.

Modified Stems and Branches

107. Stems are frequently so much reduced in length that the leaves seem to spring directly from the roots. In such "stemless plants," however, the conical or disc-shaped surface from which the leaves arise must be regarded as the stem, at the apex or centre of which the terminal bud will always be found. Many biennials remain "stemless" during the first season, but during the second period of growth produce a normal stem and branch system by development from the terminal bud.

108. Another type of stem is that characteristic of the climbing and trailing plants. In these the stem is too slender to maintain itself in an erect position. The climbers depend on other objects for support, the stem serving merely as the conducting system connecting roots and leaves. In the

case of trailers the plant is enabled to secure a large light exposure by spreading over a large surface of ground. The stem, in this case also, serving only the function of conduction. Climbers from their habit are adapted to forested regions, while trailers flourish in open ground.

109. In many cases trailing stems take root at the nodes. Such stems are called runners, or stolons. The object of such a habit may be simply supplementary to the function of the basal root system or else, if the stem also produces a system of branches at the nodes, it may result in the production of new plants—an asexual method of reproduction. In this case, after the young plant has become firmly established the stolon connecting it with the parent may die, leaving the young plant independent. If the connecting stolons persist it is possible that the associated individuals may be of mutual physiological assistance at critical times in the way of furnishing each other nourishment, etc. It is certainly true that such plants growing on a shifting soil are of great mutual assistance in holding each other in place and thereby also holding the soil. Stolons may be either above or under the ground.

110. Underground stolons are sometimes greatly enlarged at the end, forming tubers. This is due to the accumulation of food substances for the purpose of storage, which is one of the normal functions of the stems of perennial plants. In the larger perennials the normal stem is large enough to provide sufficient storage and consequently no special enlargement is necessary. In the case of the smaller herbaceous perennials, however, there is insufficient storage room provided by the comparatively small normal stem and therefore the storage stems are enlarged. Moreover, since the normal herbaceous stems usually do not survive the winter, the stems which are modified for storage are developed underground, where they are protected, and whence they put forth shoots in the following spring from terminal and axillary buds.

111. Other types of underground storage stems are common. The root-stock differs from the tuber in that it has no slender connecting stem but is thickened throughout its length. It

FIG. 24.—Young shoots of the common cactus, Opuntia, showing the small, conical leaves. These soon disappear. Note that the spines develop in the axils of the leaves. ×2/3.

usually persists from year to year; a new segment consisting of one or more nodes, being added each season. When the root-stock is much shortened and vertical in position—in other words, merely an extremely short stem—it becomes a corm.

112. Many plants inhabiting semi-arid regions are adapted to the recurring long periods of drought following the brief periods of rainfall by the habit which they have assumed of storing up water. The stems form the reservoirs and are consequently of much greater bulk than the other functions of the stem would demand.

113. A less common type of modified stem is one in which the branch takes up the functions of the leaf. In this case the branch may become flattented and like the leaf in other respects. Thorns in certain cases are also modified branches.

Modified Leaves

114. Besides the endless diversity of form assumed by foliage leaves, there are also a number of leaf types in which the function of photosynthesis has been entirely lost. Such, for example, are the bud scale-leaves, which serve as protective organs, and the scale-leaves of underground stems, which are functionless rudiments. Certain kinds of thorns and tendrils, are modified leaves or parts of leaves. Even the function of food storage is sometimes assumed by leaves. The blade of the leaf in one group of plants is entirely wanting and its function is performed by the petiole, which is flattened laterally and has the appearance of a leaf blade turned into the vertical plane.

Homology of the Flower

115. While the modification of the type forms mentioned in the preceding paragraphs are all quiet common, still they are in every case limited to a small minority of plant species. There is, however, a most important and interesting kind of modification which is practically universal among seed-bearing plants.

This is the modification of a branch, involving both stem and leaves, which results in the structure we call the flower.

116. A leaf bud and a flower bud are in all essential points alike. There is a very short central axis around which are arranged the rudimentary leaves in regular whorled or spiral order. In the development of the leaf bud the axis elongates, separating the leaves, while the latter expand and assume the form and color of the typical leaf. In the case of the flower bud, however, the axis does not elongate regularly throughout its length. It may remain very short, in which case the flower remains sessile. If the axis elongates at all the elongation affects only a limited part, by which a stem (pedicel or peduncle) is formed. At the top of this stem the flower leaves still remain in closely set whorls or circles.

Inflorescence

117. The homology of flowers is also shown by their position on the stem and their groupings. When flowers occur singly they are either terminal or axillary and hence arise from terminal or axillary buds, or else they spring from accessory buds. In either case their origin is the same as that of branches. Whenever a flower terminates an axis the growth of that axis ceases with the growth of the flower, consequently further growth of the plant must proceed from another bud.

118. Flowers which occur in groups may be divided into two classes, depending upon whether the first flower to appear is terminal or lateral. In the former the grouping of the flowers is called a determinate or cymose inflorescence. In this case the first terminal flower is followed by two opposite, lateral ones which grow beyond the first, leaving it apparently in the angle of two equal lateral branches. This is a simple cyme. If the two lateral flower stalks also each put out, in a similar way, a pair of lateral flowers, the cyme becomes compound.

INFLORESCENCES

119. When the first flower of an inflorescence is lateral the terminal bud continues to grow for some time and new flowers

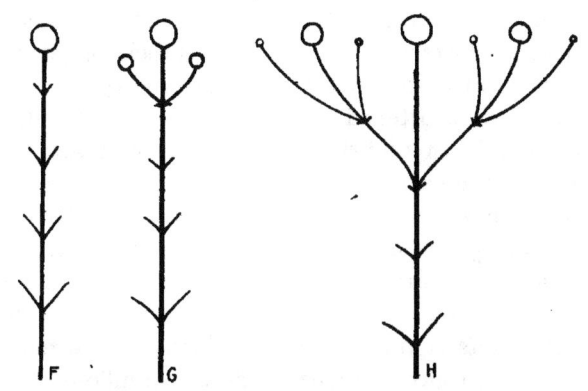

FIG. 25.—Cymose inflorescences. *F*, A terminal flower; *G*, a simple cyme; *H*, a compound cyme.

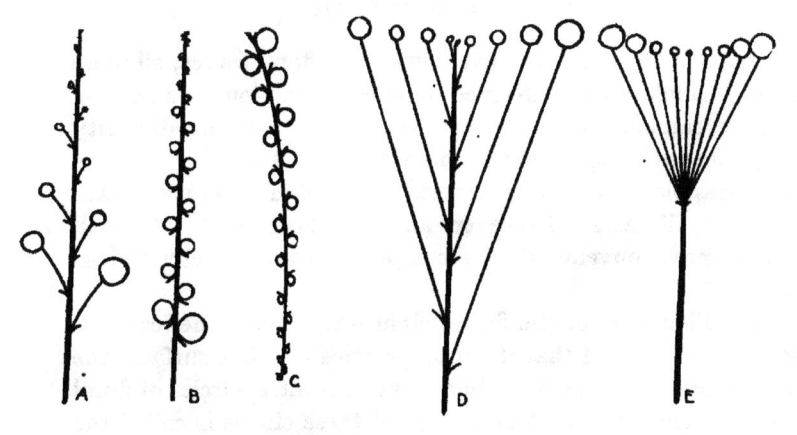

FIG. 26.—Types of racemose inflorescence. *A*, A raceme; *B*, a spike; *C*, a catkin; *D*, a corymb; *E*, an umbel. The flowers are represented by circles; the age of the flower is indicated by the size.

continue to develop above the first one along the main axis. Such an inflorescence is indeterminate and is called a raceme.

If the flowers of the raceme are sessile the inflorescence is a spike; if they are stalked it is a true raceme. A scaly, pendulous, deciduous spike is a catkin. If the older flowers of a raceme rise to the level of the terminal one because of their longer stalks, and thus form a flat topped cluster, we have a corymb. When the rachis is much shortened and the flowers equally stalked the inflorescence is an umbel and a similar condition of the rachis with sessile flowers is a capitulum.

120. That an inflorescence is made up of a system of branches is further shown by the fact that each flower springs from the axil of a bract, or rudimentary leaf. These are often green, but sometimes scale-like or chaffy. There is frequently a series of such bracts at the base of an inflorescence forming an involucre. This is especially true of capitulate inflorescences.

Structure of the Flower

121. A complete flower has four sets of floral leaves, all more or less completely transformed for special functions and bearing little resemblance to the foliage leaf. The extreme diversity of species with respect to the characteristics of the flower makes it impossible to give any general description of it which will apply to all cases. However, an ideal flower with which all others may conveniently be compared may be described as follows:

122. That part of the flower stem which bears the leaves is so much shortened that it forms practically a flat surface, the receptacle, upon which are borne the concentric circles of floral leaves. The outermost or lowest, of these circles is called the calyx. It is formed of from three to five leaves, which are green and enclose the other parts in the bud. The next circle within this is composed of a similar number of parts, characterized by some color other than green. This circle is called the corolla, and corolla and calyx together are sometimes called the peri-

THE FLOWER 57

anth. Neither calyx nor corolla are essential parts of the flower. One or both may be wanting without thereby impairing the function of the flower.

123. The third circle constitutes the andrœcium and is made up of parts called stamens, which ordinarily have little resemblance to leaves. There is usually a slender stalk (the filament)

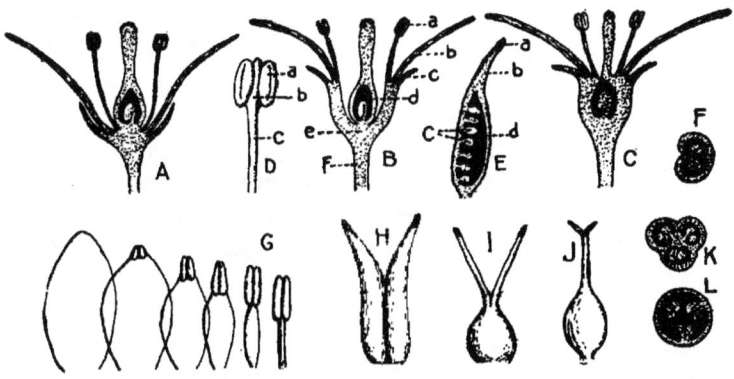

Fig. 27.—Diagrams of floral structures. *A* shows the relations of the floral parts in a hypogynous flower; *B*, the same in a perigynous flower; *C*, the same in an epigynous flower; *D*, a stamen; *E*, a simple pistil in longitudinal section; *F*, the same in cross section; *G*, transitional forms between true petals (left) and true stamens (right); *H*, slight union of two carpels to form a compound pistil; *I* and *J*, union of carpels more complete; *K* and *L*, cross sections of compound pistils, of three carpels. In *B*: *a*, stamen; *b*, petal; *c*, sepal; *d*, pistil; *e*, receptacle; *f*, pedicel. In *D*: *a*, anther cell; *b*, connective; *c*, filament. In *E*: *a*, stigma; *b*, style; *c*, ovules; *d*, ovary.

at the summit of which is attached a double sack-like organ (the anther) containing a powdery or granular substance (the pollen).

124. In certain flowers the stamens bear a close resemblance to a leaf. In such cases the filament is leaf-like in form and the cells of the anther are borne on its edge. The number of stamens is frequently the same as, or a multiple of, the number of parts of the calyx or of the corolla, but it may vary from one to many.

125. The gynœcium is the organ or set of organs formed by the fourth or inner circle of floral leaves. The individual leaves (carpels) composing it may be more or less united to form a single structure or, not infrequently, the number of carpels may be reduced to one, which then occupies the centre of the flower. In case there is only one carpel, or if the carpels are separate, each one constitutes a simple pistil, which must be regarded as having been formed by the rolling of the blade of the carpellate leaf, so that its opposite edges meet and unite and thus enclose a flask-shaped cavity. The pistil thus formed may be described as consisting of the ovary—the cavity of the flask with its enclosing walls, the style—the neck of the flask—and the stigma, a slight glandular enlargement at the top of the style. (See Fig. 27.)

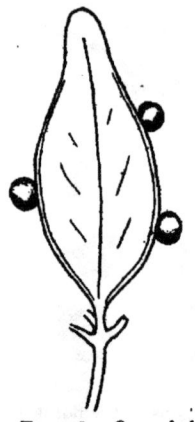

FIG. 28.—One of the four leaf-like carpels of the Chinese parasol tree (Sterculia) with several seeds attached to its margins. The carpels separate early and assume a leaf-like form.

126. Within the cavity of the ovary and attached to its walls are one or more minute bodies, the ovules, which are destined to develop into the seed. The specialized part of the ovary wall to which the ovules are attached is the placenta. (See Fig. 27.)

127. Pistils are frequently compound, i. e., made up of more than one carpel. In such cases there may be various degrees of fusion of the component leaves, ranging on the one hand from a slight external union of the ovary walls to such complete fusion on the other, that the only evidence of its compound nature is to be found in the number of placentæ. The number of pistils in one flower varies from one to many.

128. Both andrœcium and gynœcium are essential and without either one the flower is incapable of performing its function.

There are many plants, however, in which stamens and pistils are not found in the same flower. In such cases there are two kinds of flowers, one staminate, the other pistillate, both found on the same plant (monœcious) or separate plants of the same species (diœcious).

129. The number of deviations from the ideal flower just described are too many to be enumerated, but it will be necessary to indicate the most important ones in order that homologies may be recognized.

130. The receptacle may be either convex, flat, or concave. In the latter case the edges of the receptacle may rise so high around the gynœcium as to entirely enclose it within the concavity. (See Fig. 27.)

131. The calyx is very rarely wanting since its function is that of protection. Its parts may all be separate sepals, but frequently there is a more or less complete union of the edges of the sepals with each other so as to form a cup or tube (calyx gamosepalous).

132. The corolla is often entirely wanting. In other cases it is present, but inconspicuous. Usually, however, when the corolla is present it is very conspicuous because of the size and color of its parts. Like the calyx it may be made up of distinct parts, or the parts may be more or less united into a single structure (corolla gamopetalous).

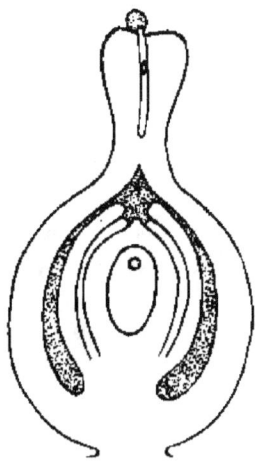

FIG. 29.—Diagram of a pistil with one ovule in the ovary. The cavity of the ovary is shaded. The ovule is attached by a stalk, the funiculus, and is provided with two protective layers, the inner and outer integuments, which develop into the seed coats. The embryo is developed from the egg nucleus (small circle) which lies in the embryo sac (large oval). The embryo sac is embedded in a mass of tissue called the nucellus. The growing embryo is nourished by the contents of the embryo sac and the nucellus. Reserve food contained in the embryo sac is called endosperm while that found in the nucellus is perisperm.

133. The stamens may also be distinct or united into one (monodelphous), two (diadelphous) or more groups, the union being due to the cohesion of either filaments or anthers.

134. A union of floral organs occurs, not only between members of the same series, but also between adjacent series. Thus, the petals may be united with the calyx cup in such a way that they seem to spring from the edge of the cup instead of from the receptacle. The stamens, likewise, may be adnate to the petals or fused with the calyx tube and thus, like the petals, apparently inserted upon it (perigynous). Still greater fusion may occur and calyx, corolla, and stamens all be more or less united with the ovary and thus apparently inserted on its side (perigynous) or top (epigynous) instead of on the receptacle. In the latter case the ovary is said to be inferior.

Function of the Flower

135. The function of the flower is to produce the seed, but this is accomplished only by the conjoint action of pollen and ovule. Under normal conditions, the ovule at a certain time begins a series of developmental changes by which it finally becomes a seed. This latter phase of its development is begun, however, only after pollination and fertilization. Pollination is the transfer of pollen from the anther to the stigma by the wind, by insects, or through some other agency. After reaching the stigma the pollen grain develops a tubular outgrowth which penetrates the tissues of the stigma and style growing down to and into the ovule. A certain nucleus of the pollen tube then fuses with a similar nucleus of the ovule. This fusion of elements from the pollen grain and ovule is known as fertilization, because, as a result of it, the ovule is stimulated to further development which finally results in the seed, whereas, if the fusion does not occur, there is no further development of the ovule and no seed is produced.

Pollination

136. A necessary preliminary to fertilization, however, is pollination, which is brought about in many different and often remarkable ways, all of which illustrate most clearly the nice adaptations, or correlations, of plants with other organisms and, in general, with their environment.

137. It may first be noted that most flowers are so organized as to effectually protect their pollen from wetting. This means in many cases merely that the flowers do not open except in fair weather and then require only a few minutes or hours for the accomplishment of pollination. Other flowers close at night or during threatening weather, i. e., the petals assume a position such as to protect the stamens from rain or dew. In other cases the petals, some or all, are so disposed as to give shelter to the stamens; and frequently the flowers are pendant, so that the stamens are sheltered even when the petals are widely spread.

138. It is a well recognized biological principle that cross-fertilization, i. e., fertilization by pollen from another plant of the same species, results in more vigorous offspring than does self-fertilization—fertilization resulting from the union of elements of the same plant. Accordingly we find that plants are so organized as to favor cross-fertilization.

139. One of the most important agencies of pollination is the wind. The plants for which the wind performs this service all have small and inconspicuous flowers, i. e., the petals are either wanting or, if present, are small and not brilliantly colored. The pollen in such plants is light and powdery and is, therefore, easily carried by the wind, sometimes to long distances. It is produced in great quantities and, as it is wafted along on the wind in clouds, some grains are likely to fall upon other flowers of the same species and be held there by the adhesive stigma.

62   PLANTS

140. To the fact that anemophilous flowers are inconspicuous must be added the evidently related facts that such flowers are

Fig. 30.—The inflorescence of Polygala. The flowers are clustered in the axils of the whorls of leaf-like bracts. These bracts are violet colored and render the inflorescence very conspicuous.

also devoid of odor and secrete no honey. These facts become significant when we learn further that all flowers which are conspicuous because of the color of the corolla or other parts,

POLLINATION BY INSECTS 63

or are scented, or secrete honey, have the office of pollination performed for them by insects which visit them for the pollen or honey; the pollen as well as the honey being used by insects as food. The colors and scents of flowers are evidently related to the senses of sight and smell of insects and serve to attract the insects to them.

141. Insects on visiting the flowers necessarily come in contact with the anthers and some of the pollen clings to the

FIG. 31.—The dichogamous flowers of Polygala. The flower A shows the anthers protruding from the hood. In B the stigma has advanced and is ready for pollination.

insect's body; for the character of the pollen grains in such plants differs from the powdery pollen of anemophilous plants in that it is sticky by virtue of a viscid or oily coating, or because of the prickles, grooves, ridges or other structural peculiarities of the wall of the pollen grain which cause it to cling more readily to the hairs of the insect's body. Now as the insect moves on to another flower it will in all probability

64 PLANTS

FIG. 32.—Bumblebees and wasps which carry pollen for Polygala. The hairs on the thorax of all these insects were covered with pollen.

brush off some of this pollen upon the parts of the flower with which it comes in contact. Because of its position and because of the character of the stigmatic surface, the stigma will be most likely to receive and retain some of this pollen, and thus pollination will be accomplished.

142. The question now arises, is not pollination by wind or by insects as likely to result in self-fertilization as in cross-fertilization? The study of further facts will lead us to answer this question emphatically in the negative. The facts are these: In the case of anemophilous plants the flowers are either diœcious, monœcious, or dichogamous. In the first case, of course, self-fertilization cannot occur. In the case of monœcious plants the staminate and pistillate flowers are not on the same level, consequently the pollen floating horizontally on the wind is not likely to fall upon any of the pistillate flowers of the same twig. If the flowers are hermaphrodite they are also usually dichogamous, which means that either the andrœcium or the gynœcium matures first and hence the pollen cannot fertilize an ovule of the same flower.

143. Entomophilous hermaphrodite flowers are usually either dichogamous, dimorphic or else by movements of stamen and pistil a result is brought about which is practically equivalent to that attained by dichogamy. In the case of dimorphic flowers there are two kinds of flowers which differ with respect to the length of the style and stamens, and the position of the stigma in one form of flower corresponds to the position of the anther in the other. The result of this is that when an insect visits the flower it receives pollen on that part of its body with which the stigma comes in contact when the insect visits a flower of the other type.

144. Self-fertilization is also known to occur in many hermaphrodite flowers. However, it takes place, usually, only after the methods for securing cross-fertilization have been employed by the flower; the result being to insure fertilization in case

66   PLANTS

cross-fertilization fails. Autogamy is secured in a great variety of ways. Some of these are; by movements of the anthers, by movements of the stamens or style, or both, by changes in length of stamens or style, by changes in the corolla, etc.

FIG. 33.—The inflorescence of the dog-wood. The flowers are small and greenish and occur in clusters. Beneath each group of flowers are four large white bracts which take the place of the petals in making the inflorescence conspicuous.

145. Some plants develop seed from flowers which never open. Such plants also produce blossoms under favorable conditions and the cleistogamic flowers are to be regarded merely as a special form of autogamy. The corolla is reduced and other parts of the cleistogamic flower may differ from the corresponding parts of the blossoming flower.

146. It undoubtedly often occurs that various kinds of pollen fall on the same stigma. This is quite likely to be the case with anemophilous pollen, but occurs less frequently in entomophilous flowers because many species of insects confine their attention to one or a few species of flowers; and also many species of flowers are visited by only one or a few species of insects.

147. When pollen from a distantly related plant falls on the stigma of a flower no fertilization occurs. If the pollen comes from a nearly allied plant, however, fertilization may take place and the resulting offspring will be a hybrid. But normally only pollen coming from a flower of the same species is efficacious in producing fertilization. If several kinds of pollen fall on the same stigma at about the same time there may, therefore, be a selection of the kind proper to the plant. As between pollen from the same flower and pollen from another flower of the same species it is quite probable that there may, also, be a selection in favor of that yielding cross-fertilization. This is known to be the case in certain plants and, by analogy, it may occur in others.

The Seed

148. Fertilization accomplished, the development of the seed begins. The embryo itself is developed from the germ nucleus which results from the fusion of the fertilizing pollen nucleus and the egg nucleus of the ovule. But the germ nucleus is only a small part of the ovule. The other parts also grow as the embryo develops, and form the masses of reserve food and the seed coats.

The Fruit

149. While the ovules in the ovary are developing into seeds, changes are also taking place in adjacent parts of the flower —changes which would not occur if the ovules failed of

fertilization. Sometimes all the tissues of a flower cluster are involved, more frequently the receptacle or calyx, but always the ovary. The structures become enlarged and fleshy or indurated and modified in various other ways. The resulting structure or organ is called a fruit and its function always has relation to the function of the seed.

150. With the ripening of the seed the plant seems to have fulfilled the object of its existence and soon dies, or if it is not an annual it becomes dormant until the following season, when another period of growth is closed by the ripening of the fruit. Occasionally the fruit is not matured until the following season, in which case the activity of the plant during the first season is devoted to the storing up of reserve food, which is then used in the development of the fruit during the second season.

151. The distinction between seed and fruit, then, lies in this, that the seed is only that part which develops from the ovule, while the fruit includes the seed and consists besides of the modified ovary and frequently other adjacent parts of the flower, which finally together constitute the seed-containing organ of the plant.

152. Simple fruits are either fleshy or dry, and the latter are either indehiscent or dehiscent, hence the following classes of fruits are recognized:

153. A berry is a fleshy fruit composed wholly of the pericarp, or of the pericarp and the adherent calyx-tube.

154. The drupe, or stone fruit, is also a fleshy pericarp, the inner layer of which is stony.

155. The pome is a fleshy fruit derived from the concave receptacle which encloses the dry papery pericarp.

156. An achene is a dry indehiscent fruit derived from a simple pistil and containing only a single seed.

157. A caryopsis resembles an achene, but has the seed coats intimately united with the walls of the ovary.

158. The nut also resembles an achene, but is derived from a pericarp consisting of more than one carpel.

159. A samara is an indehiscent fruit with winged appendages.

160. A schizocarp is a compound fruit which splits when ripe into two or more parts, each resembling an achene.

161. A follicle is a dry fruit derived from a simple pistil and opens when ripe by splitting down one side.

162. A legume, or pod, is like the follicle, except that it splits down both sides of the carpel.

163. A capsule is a dry, dehiscent fruit derived from a compound pistil and opens by splitting down the side, by separating a lid from the top, by opening of small pores or otherwise.

164. Aggregate fruits are those which are made up of the numerous distinct carpels of a single flower adhering together to form a single mass, or sometimes held together by the receptacle.

165. Multiple fruits are composed of the combined carpels and coherent parts of a number of flowers held together by the common receptacle. The common receptacle may be either convex or concave, in the latter case enclosing the carpels.

Seed Distribution

166. All the elaborate adaptations of the plant contribute directly to the one end—that seed may be produced from which a new generation of the species may proceed. However, to produce mature seed is not of itself a guarantee that from that seed a new plant will spring. The seed must be brought to a spot where the conditions are favorable for its germination and development. But because of constantly changing conditions this is frequently not the case at the place where the seed was brought to maturity. The seeds must be scattered abroad in order that some may by chance fall upon good ground.

167. Some seeds are so small and light that they are readily

carried by the wind to great distances. Larger seeds in many cases have special contrivances in the form of sails, parachutes, or feathery or hair-like appendages which offer such a large surface to the wind that they may also be carried by it in spite of their larger size. Seeds swallowed by animals are frequently not digested and may be carried abroad by this agency.

168. But aside from the protection which the fruit tissues may give the seed in some instances, it is often the function of the

FIG. 34.—A leaf of Bryophyllum developing new plantlets by budding at the edge of the leaf.

fruit to provide for the dissemination of the seed. This object may be accomplished in an endless variety of ways; sometimes by mechanically scattering the seed when the fruit opens; sometimes by the development of hold-fast organs which cause the fruit to cling to passing animals; or again by means of parachutes and sails by which the fruit is carried on the wind; or by floats on which the fruit drifts with the current of water. Edible fruits of all sorts are carried by animals from place to place and the seeds scattered in this way. In some cases the larger part of the plant is concerned in the process of scattering seed.

169. It is not in all cases necessary that a seed should be formed in order that a new plant may be developed. Many perennials also multiply by a process called budding, which consists essentially of the development from some part of the parent stock of a shoot which ultimately becomes an independent plant. The shoot may spring from the roots, from underground stems, from runners or branches where they touch the substratum or even from leaves. Some species belonging to the group of seed-bearing plants have adopted this method of reproduction almost to the exclusion of the formation of seeds.

Classes of Plants

170. All the so-called flowering plants have one characteristic in common, which is the formation of a reproductive body, the seed, developed from the ovule after fertilization, and consisting essentially of an embryo enclosed in a protective seed coat. This group of plants is called Spermatophytes and consists of two divisions, the Angiosperms and the Gymnosperms.

171. The Angiosperms are those seed-bearing plants in which the ovules are enclosed in the cavity of an ovary. Of these there are two classes, the Monocotyledons and the Dicotyledons. The difference between these two classes is shown in the following table:

Angiosperms

DICOTYLEDONS	MONOCOTYLEDONS
1. Two seed leaves.	1. One seed leaf.
2. Leaves netted veined and with broken margin.	2. Leaves parallel veined with margin entire.
3. Parts of flowers in 4s or 5s.	3. Parts of flowers in 3s.
4. Vascular bundles of the stem in a single circle forming two concentric cylinders of wood and bark.	4. Vascular bundles of the stem scattered and no distinction of wood and bark.

Either of the characters, 2, 3, or 4, may in some cases fail to apply.

72   PLANTS

172. The grasses, sedges, lilies, palms and orchids are the most important groups of the Monocotyledons. The Dicotyledons include most of the remaining seed-bearing plants except the "evergreens."

FIG. 35.—Inflorescences of the pine. 1, Terminal twig; 2, ovulate cone; 3, staminate cone; 4, two-year-old cone.

Gymnosperms

173. The Gymnosperms are distinguished from the Angiosperms by the fact that the ovules are not enclosed by the walls of an ovary, but are simply covered by a scale. To this group belong the cone-bearing "evergreens;" as e. g., the pine, cedar, yew, larch, and spruce.

Cryptogams

174. Not all plants produce seed. There is a great variety of organisms which are not included in the groups so far consid-

ered; e. g., ferns, mosses, sea-weeds, toadstools, molds, etc. These are all grouped together under the name of Cryptogams, but it is not thereby meant to indicate that there is a close relationship between the various members of the group. It signifies only that the members of which it is composed do not bear seed. As a whole the Spermatophytes are much more complex and for certain reasons are regarded as of a higher order than the Cryptogams.

175. Of the Cryptogams, the highest class—those most nearly resembling the Spermatophytes—are the Pteridophytes, including the ferns and their allies. Most of these have an underground stem (rootstock or rhizome) with a system of true roots and a series of leaves held aloft on long petioles or stipes. The microscopic structure of the organs, too, resembles in a general way that of similar organs in the higher plants. The common ferns, the scouring-rushes and the club-mosses are familiar examples of this group.

176. Next in order below the Pteridophytes come the Bryophytes, to which group belong the mosses and liverworts. These plants are all small. The moss plant consists of a slender stem, with scale-like leaves, but no true roots, and there are no well-developed vascular bundles in the stem. In liverworts there is usually no distinction of stem and leaf. The body of the plant consists simply of a flat expanse of green tissue. In place of roots the mosses and liverworts have organs which resemble root hairs and are called rhizoids.

177. All plants not included in the foregoing groups are classed together as Thallophytes—a large and heterogeneous group which comprises all the lower or simpler plants. The body of a Thallophyte is never differentiated into root, stem and leaves, as is usually the case in the higher groups, and there are more exact distinctions to be observed in the methods of reproduction. The Thallophytes are divisible into two very distinct groups, algæ and fungi, which are distinguished by the

presence of chlorophyll in the former group and its total absence in the latter. Most of them are small, many are microscopic in size, but there are a few marine algæ which are extremely large.

178. The algæ are found either in the water or else in moist places, for they have no elaborate protective structures which would prevent desiccation. There are many kinds which consist of only a single cell, others of similar cells arranged in rows or filaments. In others, again, the cells are arranged in sheets or masses having more or less definite forms. One group of marine algæ in which the structure is rather complex is characterized by a reddish color, due to the presence of a red pigment in the protoplasm, which to some extent obscures the green of the chlorophyll. Another group of marine algæ, simpler in structure, is similarly characterized by a yellow pigment which gives the plant a brownish color. A small group of extremely simple filamentous or unicellular algæ is characterized by a blue-green color due to the presence of a blue pigment. There are many algæ, however, which are neither red, brown nor blue-green, but have the yellowish-green color characteristic of chlorophyll. These vary in complexity of structure from the simplest to the most complex. The blue-green and the green algæ comprise both marine and fresh water forms.

179. The fungi vary as greatly in regard to complexity of structure as do the algæ and may be regarded as a parallel series, differing chiefly from the algæ in those points which are dependent on the presence of chlorophyll. Since they are destitute of chlorophyll, the fungi (excepting perhaps some of the lowest forms) cannot assimilate carbon dioxide and consequently are either saprophytic, i. e., nourished upon waste organic matter, or parasite, i. e., nourished upon the tissues of other living organisms. Some of the most familiar of the higher fungi are the toadstools, mushrooms, shelf-fungi, puff-balls, smuts and rusts of grasses, "cedar-apple," ergot, black-knot of plum trees, mildews, molds, yeast, etc.

180. The lowest fungi are the bacteria, a large and important group, though made up of the simplest and minutest of all organisms. The bacteria are minute unicellular or filamentous organisms, so simple in structure that the cell constituting an individual seems to be devoid of even the nucleus. To this group belong the germs of many diseases, and the active agents in various processes, such as putrefaction and decay, souring of milk, acid and vinous fermentations, etc.

181. Cryptogams reproduce by means of spores instead of by seeds. Spores are single cells specially set apart by the plant for the purpose of reproduction. In some cases they are formed by the union of two elements, as in the process of fertilization in Spermatophytes. Another kind of spore is formed merely by the separation from some part of the parent plant of a single cell, which has the power of developing a new plant without fertilization. Some of the lowest, simplest Cryptogams, consisting of a single cell, multiply merely by the division of the cell into equal halves (fission).

Ecology

182. In our study of the development, form, structure and life processes of a plant we have confined our attention almost entirely to the kinds of plants with which we have been most familiar, i. e., such as grow in soils that are at least moderately productive to the agriculturist and in climates which are the most habitable to man, neither extremely cold nor hot, nor extremely wet or dry. And besides, we have limited our study to the independent, chlorophyll-bearing plants. In these we have seen with regard to every feature of the plant's organization a remarkable adjustment to its external conditions of existence, or, in other words, adaptation to environment. This has been so apparent at every turn that one might well regard it as a law of nature. However, if there be such a law, it must

apply to all plants in all circumstances under which they are found to thrive, although the environment may be very different from that which is normal to the plants we have been considering. In order, then, to test the validity of this law, let us examine the flora of localities which present conditions different from those we have already considered.

FIG. 36.—A tree deformed by the action of the wind and salt spray. The buds are continually killed on the windward side. Coast of North Carolina. A similar effect is produced by the combined action of wind and cold, as on high mountain summits.

Water

183. With regard to conditions of moisture, plants have been grouped into three classes, mesophytes, hydrophytes and xerophytes. Mesophytes are the plants which grow normally under conditions of moderate supply of moisture, and hence include all those which we have heretofore been studying. Hydrophytes are plants which grow in the water, or, at least, in very wet soils. Xerophytes are the plants peculiar to arid regions.

184. Among hydrophytes we may have, first, those plants

which grow entirely submersed either in the sea, in fresh water streams or in quiet ponds. The most striking peculiarities common to plants living under such conditions is the almost complete absence of mechanical supporting tissue. Almost without exception, submersed aquatics are not rigid enough to support their own weight when taken from the water. Obviously the buoyancy of the water makes such a highly developed supporting system superfluous.

185. Some aquatics utilize the buoyancy of the water for support by specialized bladder-like floats which represent modified leaf blades, petioles, or other organs. Very generally, also, the tissues of such plants contain extensive systems of passages filled with air. These serve not only to aerate the tissues, but at the same time act as floats.

186. Other characters common to plants of this class are the undeveloped condition of the root system, which usually serves only as a hold-fast, and the absence of root hairs. The absorption of water is carried on chiefly by the epidermis of the stem and leaves. For the epidermis, not being exposed to the dry air, is not cutinized and, consequently, is in condition to serve the function of water absorption.

187. The leaves of submersed aquatics are commonly very narrow or finely divided. This offers several advantages under the conditions; the ratio of absorbing surface is increased, mutual shading lessened and there is less resistance to currents of water which would tend to dismember the plant. Besides, in a submersed plant, there would be no apparent advantage offered by a broad leaf over an equal expanse of narrow leaves.

188. Plant surfaces continually in contact with water have no stomata, hence the gases absorbed in the case of submersed aquatics are taken from the water by osmose.

189. In marked contrast with the finely divided leaves of submersed plants are the broad leaves of the floating aquatics. The under surface of leaves of this type is destitute of stomata,

but the upper, exposed surface, has the stomata and an epidermis like that of the mesophytes. These plants grow only in quiet, shallow water. They are firmly rooted in the mud,

FIG. 37.—Salicornia ambigua, a xerophytic plant found in salt marshes and sandy beaches of the Atlantic sea-board. The leaves are rudimentary. ×1/2.

from which the long stout petioles rise at an angle to the surface, where the broad leaf blades spread out in a single plane. These conditions allow the leaf to rise and fall with every change in the level of the surface. There can be no question of mutual shading and none of the considerations which gave advantage to the form of the submersed leaf can here apply.

Fig. 38.—A xerophytic habit of the prickly lettuce, Lactuca scariola. View as seen from the east.

190. A few plants are capable of growing either entirely under water or with at least some of the leaves entirely above

water. In these the effect of the water on the form of the leaf is clearly shown. Both kinds of leaf, the narrow ones below the surface and the broad ones above, may be found on the same plant.

FIG. 39.—Lactuca as seen from the south. This and the preceding figure show the leaves twisted into the vertical plane and bent toward the plane of the meridian.

191. Along the border of quiet waters another type of hydrophyte is to be found. The plants of this type stand in shallow

water, firmly rooted in the mud, but are erect, self-supporting and rise tall and slender, high above the surface of the water. The special adaptation here is in the height of the plant, which permits considerable change in level of the water surface without drowning the plant.

192. Marsh and swamp plants do not differ much from the mesophytes in structure, but nevertheless the continually saturated soil and other conditions which obtain in such localities, are sufficiently different from mesophyte conditions, on the one hand, and true hydrophyte conditions on the other, to give the floras of swamps and marshes a character of their own.

193. Comparing xerophytic plants with hydrophytes we find that in a number of particulars they present the opposite extremes of structures. Thus the epidermis of xerophytes is extremely well developed, often consisting of several layers of cells and provided with a very thick cuticular wall on the surface. Stomata are less numerous. The plant as a whole is more compact, thus reducing the ratio of surface to volume. All these peculiarities result in decreased loss of water by transpiration and evaporation and are clearly an adaptation to scanty water supply. The massive form of these plants also affords space for the storage of water obtained from occasional showers.

194. Under semi-arid conditions there is sometimes another device employed for preventing the excessive loss of water, namely, the vertical or meridional position assumed by the leaves or leaf-like organs (phyllodes) and the consequent tempering of the force of the sun's rays.

195. In those regions of the earth's surface which have alternately wet and dry seasons the vegetation also presents alternately mesophytic and xerophytic characters. This does not mean merely that at one season mesophytes are prominent and at another the xerophytes, but even the same plant alters in character with the seasons.

82   PLANTS

Temperature

196. There are certain parts of the earth's surface which are always destitute of vegetation because of the fact that the

FIG. 40.—A small fern, Polypodium, which grows as an epiphyte on the bark of trees. See next figure. ×1.

surface waters are always frozen, a condition which renders vegetable life impossible. On the other hand, in the hottest parts of the earth vegetation flourishes, provided there is a sufficient supply of moisture. In fact, it is in equatorial regions that vegetation grows most luxuriantly.

197. Between the two extremes of latitude, with the corresponding extremes of cold and heat and absence and profusion of vegetation, there are regions which present an alternation of conditions with respect to temperature, from winter to summer.

FIG. 41.—Same as the preceding figure but photographed on the preceding day. The plant has the xerophytic habit of curling up during dry weather as in this figure. In wet weather the leaves expand.

The change of seasons permits only of intermittent periods of growth, and this has affected most of the species indigenous to such regions to such an extent that the life processes succeed each other in a rhythmical manner, even though the conditions are temporarily altered. The lower orders of plants respond more directly to actual changes of the conditions, and they vary in character directly as the conditions vary, but the higher forms show a decided tendency to undergo their usual series of life processes and accompanying change of character, even though the seasonal changes of conditions fail to occur at the appropriate time. For example, the tropical plants present an expanse of leaf surface throughout the year, although the older leaves are continually falling, because new ones are as constantly developing. The deciduous perennials are characteristic of temperate latitudes, where there is alternately winter and summer. In the latter case there is evidently a relation between the fall of the leaf and the seasons. But the leaves do not fall only after they have been killed by a frost. Rather, they die, and physiological connection with the plant body is cut off before the time for serious frosts arrives. Otherwise not only would the leaves be killed, but the plant itself might suffer serious injury.

198. For the plant to retain its leaves during the snows of winter would also expose it to the danger of being overloaded and crushed by sheer weight of the snow.

199. Another example of this principle of the independence of the plant of the direct conditions of its environment is found in the period of rest required by seeds and other reproductive bodies, such as bulbs, which normally remain quiescent during the winter and resume their growth with the recurrence of the warmth of spring. But the rest is taken whether or not the winter conditions supervene.

200. Such adaptations of the plant are not responses to changing external conditions. The plant undergoes changes which anticipate the corresponding changes in the conditions. Such adaptations must be regarded as habitual responses.

201. Some other adaptations of the plants to rigorous climates are, for example, such modifications of the leafy shoot as the rosette and the creeper. By hugging the earth plants of this type avoid the great exposure to cold which a freer method of growth would entail.

202. Subterranean stems and reserve food stores generally are devices for tiding over unfavorable seasons and permitting the plant to make the best of a short growing season. The

FIG. 42.—Cassia, the wild sensitive pea.

annual and biennial plant habits are also evidently adaptations to seasonal changes, whether of temperature or moisture.

203. The usual fall of temperature at night, which is often very considerable, is a condition to which some plants apparently

show a very special response. The usual day-time disposition of the leaves is such as would at night result in the greatest loss of heat by radiation. The leaves of many plants droop at night and thereby come into a position which greatly reduces the loss of heat by radiation.

Latitude and Altitude

204. The traveler in passing from the equator to the latitudes of perpetual snow in polar regions observes a gradual change in the character of the vegetation from the most luxuriant evergreen tropical forests to the scanty herbage of those high latitudes where during the few weeks of the brief summer, while the ground is bared of snow, a few specially hardy mosses, a few rapidly maturing annual and biennial herbs and still fewer shrubby perennials succeed in bringing their fruit to maturity. So also in ascending mountain slopes from the sea-level at the equator to the snow line on the higher peaks a similar series of changes in the character of the vegetation occurs with the degrees of altitude. In middle altitudes, as in middle latitudes, there is an intermediate condition of vegetation characterized by the grasses of the prairies and the deciduous perennials and coniferous evergreens of the forests.

Light

205. The adaptations of green plants to light conditions has been discussed at considerable length with reference to the disposition of the leaves. It remains to show that the adaptation extends also to the formation of palisade tissue and the arrangement of the chloroplasts within the cells of the mesophyll. In order to determine whether the palisade tissue is the result of a response to light stimulus, the following experiment was performed. A developing leaf was artificially inverted so that

ECOLOGY 87

what should have been the underside was brought uppermost and facing the sun. The result was that the palisade tissue was developed on the side toward the light, that is, on the morphological underside.

FIG. 43.—Leaves of the sensitive pea closed. In this case the leaves close when touched. No explanation for this habit is known.

206. The position taken by the chloroplast in the cells is also determined by the intensity of the light. In bright light

they are found to be crowded on the vertical walls of the cells, while in subdued light they are ranged on the horizontal walls, thus exposing themselves broadside to the light. In this way the chloroplasts to a considerable degree control the light relation of the plant.

207. Plants might be classified with reference to the light conditions of their habitat. Many species grow only in shaded situations, while others seek the brightest light. Under the vertical rays of a tropical sun the light is much more intense than it is in higher latitudes. Consequently it penetrates the foliage of the taller forest vegetation with sufficient intensity to permit also of a vigorous undergrowth. The result is that other things being equal the intensity of the light in the tropics permits a denser growth of vegetation than could exist in higher latitudes.

208. The deep sea is known to be practically destitute of vegetation, although the conditions, except for darkness, are probably favorable. Along shore and on the surface of the sea there is an abundance of green and brown sea-weed vegetation, and farther down, on comparatively shallow bottom, the red sea-weeds are found. It has been suggested that the red and brown pigments of the red and brown sea-weeds have some significance with reference to the light relation.

Soil

209. Every farmer is familiar with the fact that the distribution of plants is largely determined by the nature of the mineral constituents of the soil. Thus limestone regions are better adapted for the cultivation of certain crops than are soils derived from sandstones or shales. So also other plants do well only on sands or clays. Analysis of the soils, however, shows that all the mineral substances necessary to any plant are present in sufficient quantities in any soil. It is also known that

plants differ greatly in regard to their ability to thrive on soil containing little organic matter, and it is probable that this is really the determining cause of this apparent soil relation. Soils of unlike mineral constitution do not retain the organic matter to the same degree and it is therefore probably the amount of humus present in the soil that determines its adaptability to any given plant.

210. Occasionally soils are too unstable to permit vegetation to secure a foothold. This is notably true of the shifting sand dunes of many windward coasts and in sandy deserts. There are a few plants, however, which are enabled to maintain their position in such soil by virtue of rapid and deep rooting or, better still, by means of stolons or runners which enable the individual stocks to cling to each other and finally, forming a felted carpet, protect the sand from the wind and hold it in place.

Relation of Plants to Each Other

211. We have heretofore spoken of the green plants as being independent in the sense of deriving their sustenance directly from inorganic matter. This might be regarded as quite generally true wherever the plant is provided with soluble nitrogen compounds. However, these salts are by no means everywhere present in the soil, and under such circumstances green plants become dependent upon certain fungi, as we shall presently see.

212. Plants may be dependent upon other plants in a great variety of ways, and in varying degrees. The climbers, for example, get only mechanical support from their stouter neighbors. Some cling to their support by means of aerial rootlets, which penetrate the outer layers of the bark of the host. Others spread their long slender tendrils, which, on contact with a solid object, coil around it and then draw the stem of the plant close

to the support by the contracting spirals. Tendrils in some instances end in adhesive discs by which the plant is enabled to cling to a smooth plane surface. Lastly, the twining climbers, swaying their growing tips in a spiral around the axis of support, coil themselves bodily about their host. In neither of these cases does the climber obtain any nourishment from the host,

FIG. 44.—The trumpet vine, a climber.

although the latter may be seriously handicapped or even finally destroyed through shading by its vigorous yet dependent hanger-on.

213. Epiphytes constitute another class of plants which depend upon others for mechanical support. They have no

connection with the soil and obtain their necessary supply of moisture from the humid atmosphere, from the moist bark of the host, or from the sponge of vegetable detritus which accumulates about the base of the plant. The epiphyte by its habit merely obtains advantageous exposure to light.

FIG. 45.—An epiphyte, Tillandsia, hanging from the branches of trees. Tillandsia is a flowering plant but is erroneously called "gray moss."

214. Saprophytes are plants found growing only on humus or other decaying organic matter. They are of great importance in the economy of nature because of their share in the process of decomposition and decay. They contain no chloro-

92   PLANTS

FIG. 46.—Puff-balls, Lycoperdon, a saprophyte. ×1.

FIG. 47.—The truffle, Tuber brumale; a saprophyte which grows underground.
×3/4.

phyll, have no power of photosynthesis and consequently bear no necessary light relation. The group includes chiefly fungi, but there are not a few flowering plants which have degenerated to the condition of saprophytes.

215. What has been said of saprophytes might be repeated for the group called parasites; excepting this, that they live in

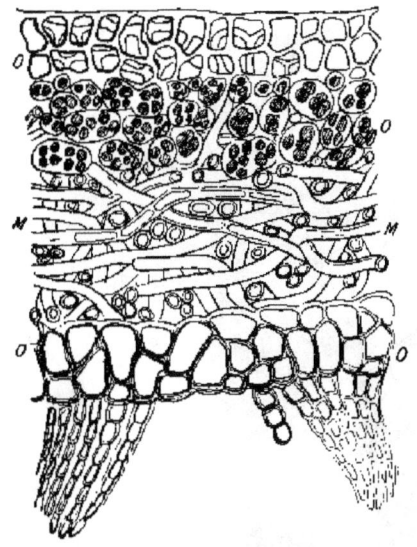

FIG. 48.—Section of a lichen. Near the upper surface are groups of rounded cells (shaded). These are algal cells, arranged in groups by fission. The remaining parts are formed by the filaments of the fungus. (From Sayre after Sachs.)

or upon the tissues of living organisms and the result of their activity is called disease. Most infectious diseases of both animals and plants are to be ascribed to this class of organisms. A few chlorophyll-bearing plants have a parasitic habit and hence are called partial parasites. Facultative parasites may live either as true parasites or as saprophytes, while obligate parasites can exist only as parasites.

94   PLANTS

216. Symbionts are organisms which are associated with other plants or animals for the advantage of one or both, but without serious detriment to either. Some forms are found normally only under such relationship. Lichens are a symbiotic combination of a fungus and an alga. A relation of this kind also exists between certain Spermatophytes and some of the

FIG. 49.—The sun-dew, Drosera. One leaf is shown, with the glandular hairs by which small insects are caught. ×5/3.

lower fungi. The mycorhiza, for example, consist of a filamentous fungus attached to the roots of seed plants, for which they seem to serve to some extent the office of absorption, and probably receive some compensation in return.

217. The most important of this class of plant relationship

ECOLOGY 95

is that which exists between bacteria and seed plants. Certain bacteria live in the soil and have the power of assimilating the free nitrogen of the air, of breaking up ammonia compounds, or of oxidizing nitrites into nitrates and thus bringing the nitrogen compounds into a form available for green plants. Such nitrogen bacteria accumulate in masses on the roots of leguminous

FIG. 50.—The trap of the Venus fly-trap, half closed. ×2.

plants, presumably finding there conditions favorable to their own development and certainly enabling the associated seed plant to thrive in soil which would otherwise be too poor in available nitrogenous compounds to support the plant.

Carnivorous Plants

218. A considerable variety of unrelated plants have acquired the power in one form or other of capturing small animals and

96   PLANTS

by a process analogous to digestion and absorption securing in this way the requisite nitrogenous matter. Such carnivorous plants are found in soils or situations which are in an unusual degree devoid of nitrogenous compounds of all kinds.

Physiographic Relations

219. Finally we may note briefly the physiographic relations of plants. From geological evidence we know that vegetation

FIG. 51.—The Venus fly-trap closed, showing interlocking teeth.

has existed upon the earth for vast ages and has undergone continual changes with the lapse of time. Long before the advent of man, vegetation flourished as it has not done since, and in certain regions of the earth's surface the remains of those early forests accumulated to such an extent as to form

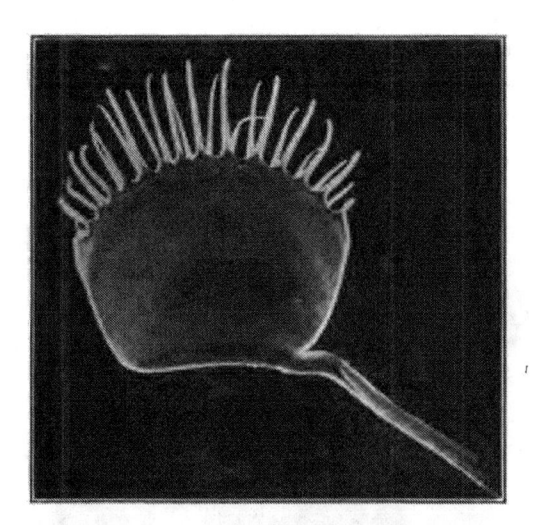

FIG. 52.—Venus fly-trap. Teeth unlocked but trap still closed. The dark shadow is cast by the bodies of two house flies caught by the trap.

FIG. 53.—Trumpets, one of the pitcher plants (Sarracenia flava).

98 PLANTS

the many deposits of coal, covering in the aggregate thousands of square miles of the earth's surface and varying in thickness from a few inches to hundreds of feet.

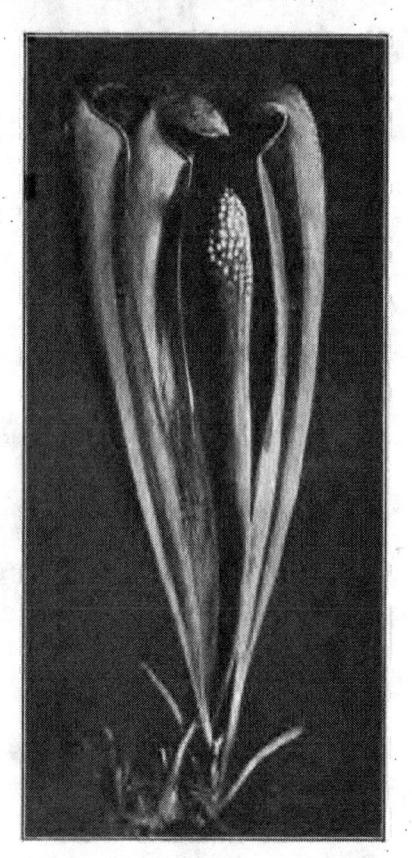

FIG. 54.—Sarracenia minor. ×1/2.

220. Practically all the coal-forming plants have long since become extinct. They belonged chiefly to the Cryptogams, and very few of the higher plants existed at the time. The

species of Spermatophytes living to-day have all appeared on the earth in comparatively recent times.

221. Plant remains, therefore, in the form of coal, constitute a very considerable part of the earth's crust and have largely determined the modern conditions of human activity. But

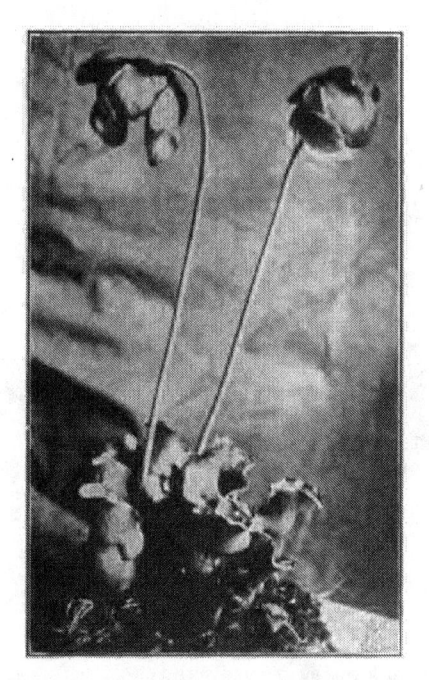

FIG. 55.—Sarracenia purpurea, in bloom. In this species the leaves are shaped like a pitcher. ×1/3.

vegetation is at the present time an important agency in both constructively and destructively modifying the physiographic features of the earth.

222. All forms of vegetation assist in breaking up rocks and dissolving minerals and thus contributing greatly to the general process of weathering or decay of rocks. Vegetation is also

a conservative force in protecting the surface of the land from erosion by holding the soil in position and breaking the force of the rush of surface waters, which rapidly wears away naked or unprotected soils. It is even a constructive agency in many cases, as, for example, in the formation of deposits of coal, peat, iron ore and other minerals, and in filling up swamps, ponds,

FIG. 56.—A solid-rock surface covered with lichens, mosses and ferns.

lakes and sluggish streams with the wash from the land, and even in places building out the land into the shallow open sea.

223. The general climatic conditions of a region may also be modified by changes in the vegetation so as to determine very materially the social and economic conditions of man. The deforestation of a region has in more than one instance resulted in the practical destruction of a highly developed civilization.

APPENDIX TO PART I

CLASSIFICATION OF PLANTS

224. **Branch I.** *Thallophytes.*—To this division of plants belong all of the lowest eleven classes. No single positive character is common to all. The plant body is never differentiated into true roots, stems and leaves. Classes 3–8 contain chlorophyll and are called algæ. Classes 9–11 are devoid of chlorophyll and are called fungi.

Fig. 57.—A slime mold creeping over dead grass. ×1.

225. **Class 1. Myxomycetes.**—This group is sometimes classed with animals under the name mycetozoa. The organism is saprophytic and is found creeping about on moist organic matter, as on the vegetable mold under trees. In the active condition a slime-mold plasmodium might be likened to a gigantic amœba, often several inches in diameter, with numer-

ous nuclei. It creeps about by an amœboid motion for a time but then comes to rest. The central part of the mass becomes transformed into spores while the superficial parts form a peridium or spore case which opens when the spores are ripe and permits them to scatter as a dry brown powder. When the spore germinates an active swarmspore with a flagellum emerges. This greatly resembles a flagellate. After a time the flagellum is lost and the organism assumes an amœboid (Myxamœba) condition. By the fusion of a number of these myxamœbæ the plasmodium is formed but in this fusion the nuclei are not concerned. There is nothing resembling a sexual method of reproduction. The vast number of spores produced results from the division of the nuclei of the plasmodium. A few slime-molds are parasitic in plants. There is no chlorophyll and the reason for placing these organisms under the plants rests on the very unanimal-like condition of the organism in the "fruiting" stage.

226. **Class 2. Schizophyta.**—The organisms belonging to this class are very simple in structure. There is no well-defined nucleus and the cells are usually very small. There is no sexual reproduction and multiplication takes place by fission. The cells are either free or adhere in chains, plates or masses held together by the gelatinous cell wall.

227. *Order* 1. *Bacteria.*—The bacteria are the smallest organisms. Many forms are so minute that even with the highest power of the microscope they appear as little more than a point. There is a cell membrane but no nucleus. Certain granules scattered in the cytoplasm stain like chromatin and are therefore supposed to represent the nucleus. The bacteria contain no cholorophyll, consequently most are saprophytic or parasitic. But some forms are holophytic. Some forms have one or more cilia and are motile, others are motionless and may be embedded in a jelly formed by the swelling of the cell membrane. There is comparatively little variety in form because of the simplicity of structure. Nevertheless there are many species and these can be distinguished by their physiological characters. The half dozen type forms which commonly

occur have been given special names as follows: A coccus is spherical in form, a bacterium or bacillus is short rod shaped, a bacillus slightly bent is a vibrio, while one more strongly curved is a spirillum; straight thread-like forms are called leptothrix and corkscrew forms are spirochæte.

FIG. 58.—Bacilli of various forms. (From Williams.)

228. After division the cells may adhere in chains or become free. When the cell walls become gelatinous the cells adhere in a large mass which is known as a zoöglea. Spores are formed by the contraction of a part of the protoplasm into a dense mass which then surrounds itself with a cell

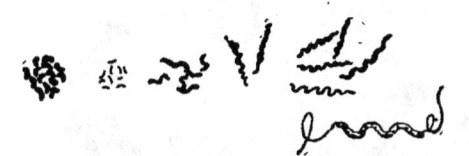

FIG. 59.—Spirilla of various forms. (From Williams.)

membrane. Because of their mode of formation these are called endospores. They are highly resistant.

229. The physiological differences between bacteria are very great. This is evident in the substances which they excrete and the effect produced by these excretions on the surrounding medium. A number of

FIG. 60.—Staphylococci. Streptococci. Diplococci. Tetrads. Sarcinæ. (From Williams.)

examples will be mentioned. Closteridium butyricum and many other bacteria thrive where there is no free oxygen. This is possible because they have the power of decomposing substances containing oxygen. On the other hand, Bacillus aceti, and others, cause the combination of alcohol and oxygen to form acetic acid (vinegar). The nitrite bacteria in the soil oxidize ammonia into nitrites and the nitrate bacteria continue the oxidation into nitrates. These bacteria and others are holophytic, assimilating carbon dioxide like green plants. Beggiatoa alba grows in water where there is sulphuretted hydrogen, H_2S, formed by the decomposition of organic matter. The bacterium causes the oxidation of the H_2S whereby the sulphur is set free and deposited in the cell in small granules. Leptothrix ochræa oxidizes iron carbonate into iron oxide (iron ore) which is likewise deposited in the cell.

230. Through the ferments formed by many bacteria sugar is formed from starch and the sugar is then split into alcohol and carbon dioxide, $C_6H_{12}O_6 = 2C_2H_6O + 2CO_2$. This is the common type of fermentation which takes place in the making of bread, wine, beer and other alcoholic

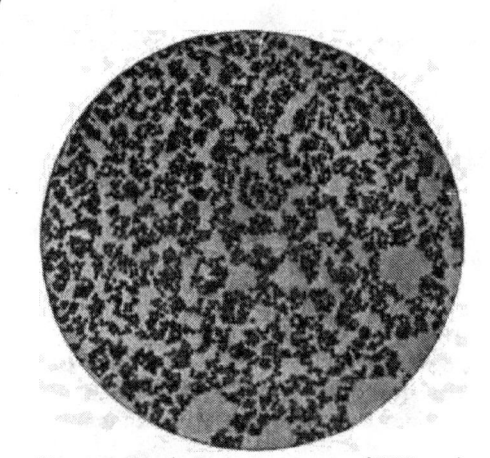

Fig. 61.—Staphylococcus aureus. (Williams.)

fluids. Another common type of fermentation is produced by the Bacillus vulgaris and other bacteria. The process here is ordinarily spoken of as decay. Nitrogenous substances, like flesh, are decomposed and, among other products, sulphuretted hydrogen is set free. It is this gas which produces the evil odor so characteristic of this type of bacterial activity.

231. Among the parasitic bacteria are some which cause little or no harm to the host. Some may even be useful, as when those inhabiting the digestive tract assist in the process of digestion (Bacillus coli communis). But again others may be the cause of the most malignant and contagious diseases. Species of Streptococcus and Staphylococcus are generally

the causes of local eruptions, such as boils, ulcers, gangrene, etc. Bacillus typhi in the digestive tract causes acute inflammation—typhoid fever. Bacillus pneumoniæ and the B. diphtheriæ on the mucous epithelium of the pharynx and adjacent cavities, and B. tuberculosis in the lungs and on other serous membranes of the body are well known. B. tetani in the blood is the cause of lock-jaw. B. anthracis causes a disease fatal to cattle and occasionally to man. Asiatic cholera, leprosy and many diseases of domestic animals, such as chicken cholera, foot rot, black leg, etc., are bacterial.

232. *Order 2. Cyanophyceæ (Schizophyceæ).*—The Cyanophyceæ are also called blue-green algæ because of the presence of a blue pigment (Phycocyanin) in addition to chlorophyll. These plants are found only in water or on moist surfaces. They multiply by fission like the bacteria and the cells adhere in threads or are enclosed in masses of jelly formed by the swollen cell membranes. The nucleus usually consists of scattered chromatin granules.

233. **Class 3. Diatomeæ.**—The Diatoms are a large group. They are also unicellular and the cells separate completely though they may adhere in chains or be attached by a common stalk. The cells are usually bilaterally symmetrical and the cell wall consists of a silicious capsule of two parts which fit into each other. The surface of the capsule is often very elaborately ornamented. There is a single central nucleus and one or more large lobed chromatophores containing a brownish-yellow pigment in addition to a substance similar to chlorophyll. Multiplication takes place asexually by fission and also by conjugation.

234. **Class 4. Conjugatæ.**—The Conjugatæ are unicellular, though the cells may be connected in filaments. The cell has a single nucleus, one or more chlorophyll green chromatophores of a complicated form and one or more pyrenoids. Sexual reproduction through the union of two non-motile gametes (conjugation) to form a zygospore, is characteristic of the group.

235. *Order 1.*—The *Desmidiaceæ* are single cells which consist of two symmetrical halves often joined by a narrower portion like a dumb-bell, the cells are frequently very bizarre in form. The nucleus lies in the

narrower middle part of the cell and the chromatophore is symmetrically doubled.

236. *Order 2.*—The *Zygnemaceæ* are always filamentous and the cells are cylindrical. In conjugation the entire contents of the cells is involved.

237. *Order 3.*—The *Mesocarpaceæ* are similar to the foregoing but only a part of the cell contents is concerned in conjugation.

238. **Class 5. Chlorophyceæ.**—The Chlorophyceæ are a large group of fresh water and marine chlorophyll green algæ. They reproduce asexually by the formation of pear-shaped zoöspores which have two or four flagellæ. Sexual reproduction usually consists in the conjugation of similar zoöspores but there is often a differentiation of gametes into eggs and sperms.

239. *Order 1.*—The *Volvocales* are motile throughout life. They are usually single and resemble the green flagellates, but some forms adhere by their gelatinous walls and form swimming colonies. The cell has a single nucleus and a chromatophore.

240. *Order 2.*—The *Protoccocales* are similar to the Volvocales but are only motile in the zoöspore stage.

241. *Order 3.*—The *Ulotrichales* are usually simple or branched filamentous forms but some marine species form flat ribbons of two layers of cells. The cells are uninuclear and have usually one chloroplast.

242. *Order 4.*—The *Siphonocladiales* are also filamentous forms, usually much branched. The filaments are composed of large multinuclear cells with one or more chloroplasts.

243. *Order 5.*—The *Siphonales* consist of a branching tubular thallus with few or no cross walls in the vegetative condition. The protoplasmic substance is therefore continuous, with numerous nuclei and chloroplasts.

244. **Class 6. Characeæ.**—The Characeæ are fresh-water algæ of rather complicated structure and with highly differentiated gametes and gametangia. The principal axis of the thallus consists of alternately long and short tubular cells forming nodes and internodes. A whorl of branches occurs at each node and the branches resemble the main axis in structure. Short branches of a second order may also occur and in the axils of these are found the oogonia and antheridia. The first

consist of an egg cell surrounded by a wall composed of five spirally wound branches. The antheridium is a complicated spherical structure with a wall of eight cells and containing a large number of spermatozoids each provided with two flagellæ. No swarm spores are produced.

245. **Class 7. Phæophyceæ.**—The Phæophyceæ are the brown sea weeds. Only a few small forms are found in fresh water. Among the marine forms, however, are the largest of all Cryptogams. Macrocystis pyrifera is said to attain a length of over 200 feet. The plants are usually attached to rocks by means of a hold-fast organ. No general statement can be made concerning the form but in the larger species the thallus is usually flattened and often forms broad sheets. The cells are uninuclear and contain a number of chromatophores which contain a brown pigment, phycophæin.

246. *Order 1.*—The *Phæosporeæ* reproduce asexually by means of swarm spores produced in large numbers in "unilocular" sporangia. Sexual reproduction occurs also through the conjugation of motile gametes developed in multilocular sporangia (gametangia) one gamete being developed from each cell of the sporangium.

247. *Order 2.*—The *Cyclosporeæ* are farther advanced sexually. There is a marked differentiation of egg and sperm. In one family, Dictyotaceæ, asexual aplanospores are also produced but in the Fucaceæ there is no asexual reproduction.

248. **Class 8. Rhodophyceæ.**—The Rhodophyceæ or Florideæ are the red sea weeds. A few forms occur in fresh water. The red sea weeds are small as compared with the brown. The form of the thallus is most often a bushy mass of branching delicate filaments or of thin sheets. Some species are encrusted with calcium carbonate. The color is due to a red pigment, phycoerythrin, found in the chromatophores in addition to the green. Asexual reproduction takes place through non-motile tetraspores, which are produced in groups of four on the surface of the thallus. The sexual reproduction is peculiar. The male

cells are minute non-motile "spermatia," cut off from the tips of certain branches. The female branch, carpogonium, is terminated by a slender filament, the trichogyne. When a spermatium comes in contact with this trichogyne a fusion takes place which effects a fertilization. The result is that by a more or less indirect process spores, carpospores, are developed farther down on the branch.

249. **Class 9. Phycomycetes.**—The Phycomycetes are fungi, that is, they contain no chlorophyll and are therefore saprophytic or parasitic in habit. But in many other respects they resemble algæ, especially the Siphonales. The thallus is tubular with few or no cross walls dividing it into cells, and the protoplast contains numerous nuclei. Spores are formed asexually by the division of the protoplasmic contents of a sporangium. These spores are motile in aquatic forms but those of terrestrial forms are simple rounded cells which are scattered like dust. In some genera a kind of spore, conidium, is formed by the cutting off of a cell from the tip of a filament (hypha).

250. *Order 1.*—The *Oomycetes* reproduce sexually by means of sperm and egg cells. In some cases the sperm cells are motile spermatozoids which are set free from an antheridium, make their way to the oögonium and fuse with the egg cell producing an oöspore. In most cases, however, the antheridium forms a tube which grows toward and into the oögonium. In this case the sperm cells are not provided with flagellæ. They pass through the tube of the antheridium directly into the oögonium and there reach the egg cell. The asexual spores are swarm spores. The oömycetes grow as saprophytes in fresh water or as parasites in plants and, occasionally, animals.

251. *Order 2.*—The *Zygomycetes* reproduce sexually by the fusion of the contents of two similar gametangia. The resulting body is called a zygospore. The asexual spores are produced either in sporangia or as conidia. The Zygomycetes are terrestrial and grow as saprophytes on vegetable or animal matter or as parasites in insects. The black mold on bread, etc., is a familiar example.

252. **Class 10. Basidiomycetes.**—The Basidiomycetes are distinguished by the club-shaped basidium upon which four

spores are produced by budding. The basidium is a terminal hypha and is either unicellular and bears the four spores at its free end or else it is divided into four cells each one of which bears one spore.

Rudimentary sexual organs are found but there is usually no sexual process connected with the formation of spores. The basidia are usually grouped and borne on the surface, or within special fruiting bodies. Besides the basidiospores there may be also one or more other kinds of spores formed by the same fungus.

253. *Order 1.—Hemibasidiales* are parasitic on plants. The black corn-smut is a familiar example. A short hypha which is supposed to represent the basidium is developed directly from the thick-walled brand spores. The mycelium developed from the basidiospores ramifies through the tissues of the host and ultimately produces large masses of brand spores.

254. *Order 2.—Protobasidiomycetes* have a basidium divided into four cells each of which bears a spore. The "rusts" are the most important members of this group. See p. 364 for the life history of the wheat rust. There are also some saprophytic forms which have a gelatinous thallus.

255. *Order 3.*—The *Autobasidiomycetes* have the basidium undivided but bearing four sterigmata with one basidiospore on each. The group is a very large one. In most cases the basidia are arranged in a well-defined layer called the hymenium and this is borne on a fruiting body of very definite form. The hymenium may form a single flat surface, or it may be variously folded into numerous tooth-like or finger-like projections or parallel plates. In other groups again it lines the walls of slender tubes or of numerous closed chambers. To this order belong the mushrooms and puffballs.

256. **Class 11. Ascomycetes.**—The Ascomycetes are characterized by the sack-like sporangium, the ascus. This is formed from the terminal cell of a hypha, the two nuclei of which fuse and then divide, usually three times so that eight spores are formed. Not all of the protoplasm of the ascus is used in the formation of the spores. The asci are usually clustered in characteristic fruiting bodies. Sexual reproduction by oögonia has been observed in a few cases.

257. *Order 1.*—The *Perisporeaceæ* comprise the mildews and the blue molds. In this group the asci are completely enclosed in a minute spherical fruiting body, the perithecium. The mildews are parasitic on the leaves of higher plants as exemplified by the common grape and lilac mildews. The blue molds are saprophytic on decaying fruits, preserves, bread, leather, etc., and are usually readily distinguished from the black molds (Phycomycetes) by the color and by the conidia.

258. *Order 2.*—In the *Discomycetes* the asci are borne in concave disk-shaped fruiting surfaces (apothecia). The species of this order are very common and are usually saprophytic. They are most frequently found on decaying wood. The edible morel (Morchella) belongs to this order.

259. *Order 3.*—In the *Pyrenomycetes* the perithecium is flask shaped with a pore through which the spores escape. In the mature condition the fruiting bodies are usually black. The Pyrenomycetes are in part parasitic; some on other plants as the black knot of plumb trees or the ergot of rye and some in the bodies of insect larvæ. Many forms are saprophytic on bark, decaying wood, etc.

260. *Order 4.*—The *Tuberaceæ* are saprophytic underground in forest humus. The perithecia are large spherical bodies without opening. Some forms are edible.

261. *Order 5.*—The *Exoasci* are parasitic on trees and stimulate the tissues of the host to abnormal growth thus forming in certain cases "witches' brooms."

262. *Order 6.*—The *Saccharomycetes* (yeasts) are microscopic unicellular, saprophytic fungi. They are important as the chief agents in the various fermentation processes connected with the making of bread, wine, beer and other alcoholic liquors. Reproduction takes place by budding (conidia) and under favorable conditions spores are formed endogenously within a cell (ascus).

263. *Lichens.*—The lichens are one of the most common and most widely distributed types of vegetation. They may be found on almost any kind of stable surface, on rocks, tree trunks, or on the surface of the earth. They are often confused with mosses but are readily distinguishable. The color is usually gray or brown but never chlorophyl green. The fruiting surfaces are frequently brilliantly colored. The form of the plant is thalloid, never differentiated into true stem and leaf. Serious objection may be made to ranking them as a class because a lichen is in reality only a symbiotic combination of an alga and a fungus, either of which may be grown independently of the other. The algæ concerned would by themselves be classed as Cyanophyceæ or as Chlorophyceæ of the simpler forms.

The fungi are usually Ascomycetes but a few Basidiomycetes also occur as lichens. The fungous filaments wind about the algal cells and usually form a firm superficial protective tissue. The specific characteristics of a lichen depend upon both the alga and the fungus components but the fruiting surface of the lichen is purely fungal. (See page 362.)

264. BRANCH II. *Bryophyta.*—The Bryophyta include the liverworts and mosses. They are distinguished from the Thallophytes by the structure of the gametangia. The sperm cells are provided with two long flagellæ and they are formed in large numbers within an oval capsule, the antheridium, whose walls are composed of a single layer of cells. The single egg cell is contained in the lower part of a flask-shaped gametangium, called archegonium. This is also formed by a single layer of cells. The upper portion, or neck, of the archegonium contains an axial row of cells (canal cells) which distintegrate and form a slime through which the spermatozoids make their way to the egg. A "ventral canal cell" cut off from the egg cell at the lower end of the canal cells also distintegrates with the canal cells.

265. The fertilized egg immediately begins development. There is ultimately formed an organism (sporophyte) which produces spores asexually. From these spores there then develops an organism (gametophyte) which bears the gametangia. In this way a regular alternation of sexual and asexual generations occurs.

266. The Bryophyta are called Archegoniates from the very characteristic female gametangium. They are always holophytic and are chlorophyll green.

267. **Class 1. Hepaticæ.**—The liverworts are usually thalloid or if there is a differentiation into stem and leaves the latter are arranged dorso-ventrally. The thallus branches dichotomously and is attached to the substratum by rhizoids, i. e., tubular, hair-like cells which serve as organs for the absorption of moisture. The spore capsules usually contain sterile elongated

cells (elaters) which serve to scatter the spores by hygroscopic movements.

268. *Order* 1.—The *Ricciaceæ* are aquatic or semi-aquatic thalloid forms. The sporophyte remains completely enclosed within the archegonium wall and embedded in the gametophyte thallus. It consists merely of a spherical capsule filled with spores.

269. *Order* 2.—The *Marchantiaceæ* are larger and more complex in structure. The thallus is perforated by pores on the upper side, which open into air chambers. Surrounding and projecting into these chambers are the green assimilatory cells. The deeper lying cells are larger, contain little or no chlorophyll and serve for water storage and conduction. The antheridia and archegonia are borne on stalked receptacles. The sporophyte is a stalked capsule which remains attached to the receptacle but projects beyond the old archegonium wall.

270. *Order* 3.—The Anthocerotaceæ are a smaller group. The gametophyte is irregular thalloid. Its cells contain each a single chloroplast. The archegonia are embedded in the thallus. The sporophyte projects beyond the thallus because of its greatly elongated form, but is not stalked. The capsule splits longitudinally and there is a slender axial "columella" of sterile tissue.

271. *Order* 4.—The *Jungermanniaceæ* are usually differentiated into a stem and dorso-ventrally arranged leaves one cell layer thick. The capsule is long stalked and usually opens longitudinally by four valves. There is no columella.

272. *Order* 5.—The *Calobryaceæ* are represented only by two exotic genera.

273. **Class 2. Musci.**—The moss plant is differentiated into stem and leaves. There are no true roots but at the base of the stem are found branching rhizoids by which water is absorbed. The stem sometimes contains an axial strand of elongated cells which serve for the conduction of fluids, but there are no true fibro-vascular bundles. The leaves are usually one cell layer thick and are arranged spirally on the stem.

274. The archegonia and antheridia are borne at the apex of the stem or on lateral branches. The sporophyte is stalked and remains attached to the gametophyte by a prolongation

of the stalk known as the foot. The capsule contains a central axis of sterile tissue, the columella.

275. When the spores germinate a branching green thread (protonema) like an alga is developed. From this the moss plants are formed by budding. By this protonema the mosses may be distinguished from the liverworts. The mosses are always holophytic and chlorophyll green.

276. *Order* 1.—The *Sphagnaceæ* are the swamp mosses. They grow continually upward while dying away at the base. The capsule is short stalked and the foot is broad. A pseudopodium is formed by the elongation of the branch below the foot. The archegonium wall breaks and its fragments remain at the base of the capsule. The capsule opens by a lid. The columella is hemispherical. There is only one genus, Sphagnum, with many species.

277. *Order* 2.—The *Andreaceæ* are usually found in small clusters on rocks. The capsule is short stalked with a broad foot and is elevated by a pseudopodium. The archegonium wall breaks around the base and remains on the capsule like a cap (calyptra). The capsule opens by four longitudinal slits. There is only one genus, Andrea.

278. *Order* 3.—The *Phascaceæ* are small, simple mosses with persistent protonema, and a short stalked capsule which does not open. The spores are set free only by the disintegration of the capsule.

279. *Order* 4.—The *Bryinæ* comprise most of the common mosses. In these the capsule is long stalked (seta) with a foot. The archegonium forms a calyptra. The capsule opens by a lid (operculum). On removal of the operculum the edge of the opening of the capsule is seen to be provided with a fringe, the peristome, which by hygroscopic movements assists in the scattering of the spores.

280. BRANCH III. *Pteridophyta.*—The ferns are differentiated into true root, stem and leaf. Conducting and supporting tissues in the form of fibro-vascular bundles occur, as in the higher plants. The ferns are like the mosses in regard to the structure of the gametangia and are hence archegoniata. Like the mosses they also have a distinct alternation of generations. The gametophyte, however, is reduced to an inconspicuous thalloid structure (prothallium) or still farther to a minute

cluster of colorless cells. The sporophyte, on the other hand is much better developed and constitutes the leafy plant.

281. **Class 1. Filicinæ.**—The Filicinæ are the true ferns, a large group of plants of moderate size. A few tropical "tree ferns" attain the size of a small tree but the more familiar forms have only an underground stem (root-stock) from which the leaves (fronds) rise on long petioles (stipes) to a height of from 1 to 5 feet. All ferns are holophytic. Many species, especially tropical ones, are epiphytic.

282. The gametophyte of the fern is a small green thalloid structure (prothallium) which lies flat on the ground. (Or colorless, saprophytic and underground, Order 1.) Embedded in its tissues are the antheridia and archegonia. The antherozoids are spiral bodies with a tuft of cilia at one end. The fertilized egg cell divides into four segments from which are developed root, stem, leaf and foot respectively. The foot is an organ by which the developing plant retains connection with the prothallus for some time. The prothallus finally disintegrates and the plantlet becomes independent. The plant with the root, stem and leaves is the sporophyte. The spores are developed in sporangia on the under surface of the leaves. Sometimes the spore-bearing portion of a leaf is especially modified, or again the spores are only borne on certain leaves which then are completely modified (sporophylls).

283. *Order 1.*—The *Ophioglossaceæ* or adder-tongue ferns, are a small group of slow growing and rather inconspicuous plants. The gametophyte is a small, saprophytic, underground thallus. The leaf is partly differentiated into sporophyll.

284. *Order 2.*—The *Marattiaceæ* are tropical ferns of large size. The prothallus is a green thallus resembling a liverwort. The sporangia are grouped in sori on the under surface of the foliage leaves.

285. *Order 3.*—The *Filices* are the order to which most of our common ferns belong. Most of the tropical tree ferns also belong to this order. The order comprises many genera and species. Many are epiphytic. The gametophyte is usually a small, green, liverwort-like prothallus which

bears antheridia and archegonia on its under surface embedded in its tissue. The sporophyte usually bears the spores on the under surface of undifferentiated leaves. The sporangia are stalked and grouped in clusters (sori). The sori are often covered by a scale (indusium).

286. *Order 4.*—The *Hydropterideæ* or water-ferns, are a small group of plants which bear little resemblance to common ferns. Some grow in the mud, partly submerged, others float on the surface of the water. They are of special biological interest because the sporophyte bears two kinds of spores, small "microspores" and large "megaspores." The microspores develop a very simple prothallus consisting of only a few colorless cells, and a few antheridia. The megaspores develop a slightly larger prothallus which, however, only projects slightly beyond the broken sporangium wall. (A megasporangium produces only one megaspore.) A few archegonia are formed in the prothallus but only one egg cell develops. The microspores therefore develop male gametophytes and the megaspores female.

287. **Class 2. Equisetinæ.**—This class contains only one genus, Equisetum, the common scouring rush or "horse-tail." These plants have an underground stem from which the erect fruiting and vegetative stems rise each season. The stem is fluted and jointed and green since there are no foliage leaves. The scale leaves sheathe the stem at the nodes. The fruiting stems are usually simple while the vegetative stems bear whorls of branches at the nodes. The epidermis is encrusted with silica which gives the stem a harsh feel and lends the name scouring rush. The fruiting stems bear a conical spike of umbrella-shaped sporophylls. The spores are all of one kind and are each provided with four ribbon-like hygroscopic appendages (elaters) by which the spores are scattered. The spores give rise to a branching prothallus which is usually unisexual.

288. **Class 3. Lycopodinæ.**—The Lycopodinæ are small plants with some affinities to the ferns but of very different appearance. The sporophylls each bear a single sporangium.

289. *Order 1.*—The *Lycopodiaceæ* are the lycopodiums, "trailing cedar" or "ground pine." The stem is usually trailing, with short ascending branches. Branching of stem and roots is dichotomous. The leaves are

broad awl shaped and thickly set. The sporophylls are usually borne in a spike with the sporangia on the upper side of the scale-like leaves. The spores are all of one kind. The gametophyte is bisexual. It is a club-shaped saprophytic organism in some cases, in others it forms a flat green thallus. The spermatozoids are provided with two flagellæ. The embyro develops a suspensor as in Selaginella.

290. *Order 2.*—*Selaginellaceæ* also all belong to one genus, Selaginella. Most of the species are tropical but a few delicate moss-like forms are found in our forests. The plant resembles lycopodium somewhat but the arrangement of the leaves is usually dorso-ventral. There are frequently two dorsal rows of very small leaves and two ventral rows of larger ones. The sporangia are borne in the axils of leaves near the tip of a branch. There are two kinds of spores found in the same spike. Some sporangia contain four megaspores, others numerous microspores. The microspores develop into a prothallium of one cell and an antheridium of eight cells within which a number of spermatozoids, each with two flagellæ, are formed. The megaspore develops a small colorless prothallium in which a few archegonia are formed. Only one or two of the archegonia are fertilized. The embryo develops an appendage, the suspensor, which consists of a row of cells, by which the embryo is pushed down into the nourishing prothallium.

291. *Order 3.*—The *Isoetaceæ* consist of the single genus, Isoetes. The plants are small, with long needle-shaped leaves arranged in a rosette around a short erect stem. The plants are found submerged in water or in wet soil. The sporangia are borne on the inner surface of the leaves, at the base. The outer leaves bear megasporangia, the inner ones microsporangia. The spermatozoids are spiral and have a tuft of cilia like those of the ferns. The embryo has no suspensor.

292. BRANCH IV. *Spermatophytes.*—The three branches of the vegetable kingdom already described are together called Cryptogams and in distinction to them all the higher forms are called Phanerogams. The latter are in general more highly developed, but the distinguishing character is the seed, like which nothing is found among the Cryptogams. In the Phanerogams the female gamete is developed within the megaspore wall and the egg cell is fertilized and develops an embryo while the megaspore is still within the sporangium and attached to the parent sporophyte. After the embryo is well formed

development comes to a standstill and the sporangium with the enclosed embryo is set free. This structure is the seed. The seed-bearing plants are called Spermatophytes and form a branch coördinate with Thallophytes, Bryophytes and Pteridophytes. In the Spermatophytes alternation of generation occurs as in the Archegoniates but the gametophyte is reduced even further than in the higher Pteridophytes.

293. **Class 1. Gymnospermæ.**—In the Gymnosperms the sporangia are borne on the surface of modified leaves (sporophylls). The microsporophylls are arranged spirally on a short branch. The megasporophylls are usually similarly arranged. The microspore (pollen grain) develops a rudimentary prothallus of from one to three cells and the sperm cells reach the megaspore through a tube developed by the gametophyte. The megaspore (embryo sac) develops a prothallus of many cells and several archegonia. The latter consists of a large egg cell and a few small neck cells.

294. *Order 1.*—The *Cycadinæ* are tropical palm-like plants, with an unbranched trunk and a rosette of pinnate leaves. The sperm cells bear a spiral band of cilia. The embryo consists of a suspensor, two cotyledons, a plumule and a hypocotyl.

295. *Order 2.*—The *Ginkgoinæ* contain only the Japanese genus Ginkgo, a deciduous tree with small fan-shaped palmately veined leaves. The sperm cells are ciliated. The embryo forms no suspensor.

296. *Order 3.*—The *Coniferæ* comprise the "evergreens" and a few deciduous trees. The pines, cedars, spruces, hemlocks, cypresses and junipers are familiar examples. In the structure of the stem they differ from most Spermatophytes in the absence of tracheæ. The tracheids are highly developed and take the place of tracheæ. The sperm cells are not ciliated. The embryo forms a suspensor.

297. *Order 4.*—The *Gnetinæ* contain only three genera of exotic plants. They constitute in many respects a connecting link between the Gymnosperms and Angiosperms.

298. **Class 2. Angiospermæ.**—The Angiosperms include all the true flowering plants. The most distinctive character

of the group is the pistil, a megasporophyll so formed as to entirely enclose the megasporangia. The flower consists of several circles of sporophylls surrounded by several circles of specially modified floral leaves. All these leaves are set close together on an extremely short axis. The typical flower bears at its apex or centre a circle of megasporophylls, around this two circles of microsporophylls and around these again two circles of floral leaves. Both circles of floral leaves may be colored or only the inner one.

299. The male gametophyte is represented only by a single pollen tube nucleus and a sperm mother nucleus which divides into two sperm nuclei. No division into cells occurs. The female gametophyte is represented by the endosperm and the archegonium by the egg apparatus (two synergids and the egg cell).

300. The first seven orders of Angiosperms are Monocotyledonous (see page 71). The Dicotyledons contain thirty-three orders.

301. For a detailed description of flowering plants the student should consult a manual of botany.

PART II.—ANIMALS

LABORATORY EXERCISES

I. Organization of Animals

90. Protozoa:
    (a) Observe an actively moving amœba for some time and sketch its outline five times to show the change of form. Trace in these outlines the changes through which each pseudopodium passes. Note the ingested food particles and, if possible, observe the process of ingestion. Note the contractile vacuole.
    (b) In a stained preparation note the structure of the protoplasm, the nucleus, the contractile vacuole and the food vacuoles.
91. (a) Study the movement of a ciliate protozoan (Paramecium). How many kinds of movement does it perform.
    (b) Study a living individual under higher magnification. Note the cilia, the buccal groove leading to the mouth, the food vacuoles and the contractile vacuoles.
    (c) In a stained preparation note the macronucleus and the micronucleus.
92. Cœlenterata:
    (a) Observe a living hydra in the aquarium, first with the unaided eye then with the lens.
    (b) A hydra (living or a fixed preparation) which shows reproduction by budding.
    (c) Preparations of hydra to show the gonads.
    (d) A cross section of the body to show ectoderm and endoderm. Note the muscle fibrils which show as dots between ectoderm and entoderm. Also the central gastro-vascular cavity.
93. (a) A hydroid colony (Obelia) (Pennaria). Sketch the colony. Compare a polyp with hydra. Is there evidence of budding?
    (b) A hydrozoan medusa (Obelia). In a stained preparation note the manubrium and mouth, the radial canals, the gonads, the tentacles and the velum.
    (b') The medusa of Gonionemus is larger than that of Obelia and may be studied with the lens.

94. Annelida:
    (a) If living Nereis is at hand study its movements.
    (b) In a dorsal view of Nereis note general form of body; head; sensory, locomotor, and respiratory appendages; segmentation; symmetry.
    (c) In a small living specimen the dorsal blood vessel may be seen. Note its rhythmical contractions. Note the direction of the flow.
    (d) Study the head with a lens. Note the proboscis, tentacles, palps, cirri and eyes.
    (e) Study a segment cut from the middle of the body. Note the four large muscle masses, the intestine, the body cavity, the dorsal and ventral blood vessels, the ventral nerve cord and the parapodia.
    (f) On a parapodium note its two divisions—dorsal and ventral rami—each bearing a cirrus, a ligula, setigerous lobes, setæ and an aciculum.
    (g) In a portion of the body from which the dorsal wall has been removed, note the intestine, the body cavity and the mesenteries.
    (h) In a microscopic preparation study the ova.
95. Compare the earthworm (Lumbricus) with Nereis.
96. Some of the smaller fresh-water annelids may be studied living, as transparent objects, under the microscope.
97. Arthropoda:
    (a) If living crawfish (Cambarus) or lobsters (Homarus) are available study the movements. Note how the tail fin is used in locomotion, also the legs. By adding a little carmine to the water can you detect any respiratory currents? What causes them? Feed with an earthworm and note activity of sense organs and the method of ingestion of food.
    (b) In a dorsal view note type of symmetry and character of segmentation of the body.
    (c) In a lateral view note in the cephalothorax: rostrum, head, nuchal groove, thorax. In the abdomen: segments (No. ?), telson. The appendages of the cephalothorax are: 1 antennules, 2 antennæ, (eyes), 3 mandibles, 4 first maxillæ, 5 second maxillæ, 6 first maxillipeds, 7 second maxillipeds, 8 third maxillipeds. (For appendages 3 to 8 see d). 9 Chelæ, 10–13 ambulatory appendages. Are these all alike? The appendages of the abdomen are: 14–18 pleopods, 19 uropods. Are the pleopods all alike?

Compare pleopods of male and female. Study with a lens a pleopod of segment 16 or 17; there is a basal protopod, a lateral exopod and a medial endopod.
(d) Study the region of the mouth in a ventral view, to show especially the appendages 3–8 (see c above). Begin with appendage 8 and work forward.
(e) In a ventral view of the entire animal note the openings of the green glands on the basal segments of the antennæ, the openings of the gonoducts at the base of the eleventh (female) or thirteenth (male) appendages, and the anal opening. Draw the appendages 9–13 in detail, showing all the joints.
(f) Note the sensory hairs. Where are they found? In the eyes note the eye stalk and the retina. Study a preparation of the retina with the microscope. With the point of a needle search the dorsal surface of the basal segment of the antennule for the opening into the statocyst.
(g) In a specimen in which the gill chamber has been laid open note character of the gills, their number, position and mode of attachment to the body. With a lens study a single gill under water in a watch glass.
(h) In a specimen that has been sectioned longitudinally near the median plane note: (1) the digestive tract with œsophagus, cardiac and pyloric portions of the stomach, the liver and the intestine; (2) the heart in the pericardial chamber under the posterior edge of the thoracic shield and the arteries (ophthalmic, sternal and abdominal), (3) the gonads lying below the heart, (4) the green gland above the basal joint of the antenna, (5) the large complicated muscles of the abdomen, (6) the ventral nerve cord communicating with the brain.
(i) In a side view of a grasshopper (Schistocerca) show in the body: head, prothorax, mesothorax, metathorax, abdomen. The appendages are; antennæ, labrum, maxillæ, with maxillary palps, labium with labial palps, legs. The parts of a leg are; coxa, femur, tibia and tarsus.
(j) Remove the wings and draw the thorax and abdomen on a larger scale. Note especially the tympanum and the ten spiracles—eight on the abdomen and two on the thorax. Note the number of segments in the abdomen and compare male and female.
(k) Draw both wings of one side expanded.

(l) In an anterior view of the head show the compound eyes, ocelli, antennæ. Raise the labrum to expose the mandibles.
(m) Compare Schistocerca with Cambarus.
(n) Study a wasp as above i—l.
98. Vertebrata:
(a) Draw a dorsal view of a fish (Perca) to show type of symmetry. Label as in b.
(b) In a lateral view note:
1. Head with mouth, nostrils, eyes (eyelids?), ears (?), operculum.
2. Body with dorsal and anal fins (count the number of spines and soft rays) and paired pectoral and pelvic fins. The lateral line.
3. Tail and tail fin.
(c) Note the arrangement of the scales. Remove some and study with the lens.
(d) Study the texture of the skin.
(e) In a specimen from which the operculum has been removed study the gills. Note the gill arches and the gill rakers and the gills. Compare this respiratory system with that of the crawfish.
(f) In a median longitudinal section of the lamprey (Petromyzon) note especially the notochord, also the brain and spinal cord, the mouth, pharynx and gill slits, œsophagus, stomach (?), intestine, liver, heart, kidney, gonad and gonoduct.
(g) In a lateral view of the entire skeleton of any mammal show:
1. Skull and mandible.
2. Spinal column divided into cervical, dorsal, lumbar, sacral and caudal regions. Count the number of vertebræ in each region.
3. Ribs (number?) and sternum.
4. Girdles.
A. The pectoral girdle consisting of a scapula and a clavicle on each side.
P. The pelvic girdle consisting of ilium, pubis and ischium on each side.
5. The appendages:
A. Humerus, radius and ulna, carpals, metacarpals, phalanges (how many?) digits (how many?).
P. Femur, tibia and fibula, tarsals, metatarsals, phalanges (how many?) digits (how many?).

(h) Draw both ventral and lateral views of a skull. Show the sutures and identify the bones.
(i) Draw lateral, dorsal and anterior views of a dorsal or lumbar vertebra to show centrum, neural arch, dorsal spine, transverse processes and articulating processes.
(j) Draw a cross section of bone from a prepared slide. Note the Haversian canals, the lamellæ, the lacunæ and canaliculi.
(k) In the leg of a frog from which the skin has been removed note how the fleshy mass is composed of distinct muscles. Note also the tendons and the relation of muscle to bone. Between the muscles may be found nerves and blood vessels.
(l) Study cross striped muscle fibres in a prepared slide.
(m) In a median longitudinal section of a dog fish (Galeus or Mustelus) study carefully the brain and spinal cord. Note also the vertebral column and compare the other organs of the body with those of lamprey as in f.
(n) In another specimen which has been dissected to show the cranial nerves and brain identify the following:
   1. Brain: Olfactory lobes, cerebrum, optic lobes, cerebellum, medulla oblongata.
   2. Cranial nerves: I Olfactory, II Optic, III Oculomotor, IV Trochlearis (slender), V Trigeminal, VI Abducens (slender), VII Facial, VIII Auditory, IX Glossopharyngeal, X Vagus.
   3. Spinal cord and spinal nerves.
(o) Draw dorsal and lateral views of the brain of a mammal showing cerebral hemispheres, cerebellum, and medulla.
(p) Slit the skin of a frog along the mid-dorsal line, lift the skin of one side and note the median dorsal cutaneous nerves passing out to the skin.
(q) With a lens search the inner surface of a piece of skin of a frog and observe the white nerves, the veins and the arteries, the three often running parallel.
(r) Study the digestive system of a frog or turtle. Note: œsophagus, stomach, small intestine, liver, gall bladder, pancreas, large intestine. Note also the mesentery and the spleen.
(s) Study as in r the digestive system of some mammal.
(t) On the surface of a tongue (mammal) find the circumvallate and fungiform papillæ. If present note also the character of the glottis and epiglottis.

(u) Study the internal surfaces of a mammalian stomach and intestine.
(v) The heart of a mammal. Sketch the organ as a whole showing auricles, ventricles and the aortic arch.
(w) In a freshly killed turtle observe the beat of the heart noting the order of the beat in auricles and ventricle.
(x) Observe the circulation of the blood in the tail of a tadpole, the web of a frog's foot or the gills of a larval amphibian.
(y) In an injected frog trace the principal arteries, viz: The truncus arteriosus which divides into three arches:
   1. The Carotid Arch with its branches.
      (a) The external carotid.
      (b) The internal carotid.
   2. The Systemic Arch with its branches.
      (a) The subclavian.
      (b) The dorsal aorta from which arise:
         1. The cœliaco-mesenteric.
         2. The urinogenital.
         3. The iliac.
   3. The Pulmo-cutaneous with its branches.
      (a) The pulmonary.
      (b) The cutaneous.
(z) An injected mammal may be studied as in y.
(a') Study the lungs of a frog or turtle from which the liver and stomach have been removed. Trace the trachea and bronchi from the glottis to the lungs. Study the internal structure of a lung which has been laid open.
(b') In preparations of a mammalian lung note the structure of the trachea, the division of the lung into lobes and the internal structure of a lung.
(c') In a male frog from which all other organs have been removed observe the testes, the kidneys and the ureters.
(d') In a female frog observe the ovaries and the oviducts.
(e') Compare a mammal (rat) with the frog with regard to the excretory and reproductive organs.

CLASSES OF ANIMALS

99. The following outlines may be used to extend the laboratory studies to some of the other more important phyla and classes.

LABORATORY EXERCISES

100. Porifera (Sponges):
    (a) Study a simple sponge like Grantia. Note the general form, the point of attachment, the large excurrent opening or osculum and the spicules.
    (b) In a dry specimen of Grantia cut longitudinally, note the central cavity or cloaca and the radial canals. Note also the form and arrangement of all spicules.
    (c) A longitudinal section treated with acid to remove the spicules and then stained and mounted will show the relation of the radial canals and the incurrent canals or interradial spaces.
    (d) A dry specimen in cross section should be studied in connection with b.
    (e) A cross section with the spicules, stained and mounted, will show further details especially with regard to the arrangement of spicules and may also show ova or embryos.
    (f) The spicules may be set free by dissolving the fleshy parts in boiling potash. How many kinds of spicules are there?

101. Cnidaria:
    (a) A sea anemone (Metridium). In a lateral view note: the column, the base, the crown of tentacles.
    (b) In an oral view note the mouth with the grooved lips and siphonoglyph (one or two).
    (c) In a cross section through the middle of the column note:
        1. The gullet with grooves and siphonoglyphes.
        2. The gastro-vascular cavity incompletely divided into chambers by the mesenteries.
        3. The mesenteries are of two kinds, complete and incomplete and on their edges may be found the mesenterial filaments and acontia and the gonads.
    (d) Study a fragment of a coral (Astrangia). The cups (theca) each contain a central columella and a number (?) of radial septa.

102. Platyhelminthes:
    (a) In a living planarian note the method of locomotion, the eye spots, the proboscis.
    (b) In an adult liver fluke note the terminal mouth and the ventral sucker.
    (c) In a tape worm note:
        1. The scolex with a circlet of hooks and suckers.
        2. The body of proglottides. Note the form of a proglottis in different regions of the body.

(d) A proglottis cleared and mounted may show the reproductive organs, viz: ovary, shell gland, vitelline glands, uterus, testes and genital pore.
103. Aschelminthes:
(a) Note the form and movements of a living "vinegar eel" or a thread worm from an aquarium.
(b) In Ascaris note the form of the body, the terminal mouth with its lips, and the anus. If the body is slit open the intestine and reproductive organs may be identified.
104. Annelida: Study a living leech in water. Note its method of swimming, and locomotion by means of its suckers.
105. Echinodermata:
(a) In an aboral view of a starfish (Asterias) note the type of symmetry, the central disc and the arms or rays. On the general surface will be found the hard spines and soft papulæ; on the disc the madreporic plate.
(b) If a living specimen can be had study it in sea water for the method of progression.
(c) On the oral surface are the mouth, the ambulacral grooves with the ambulacral feet, the radial nerve ridge in the middle of each ray and, at the tip of each arm, a tentacle and eye spot.
(d) If the aboral wall is removed the stomach and hepatic cæca come into view and beneath these the gonads and the ampullæ of the ambulacral system. Note also the structure of the skeletal system.
(e) Compare a sea-urchin with a starfish.
(f) Compare a sea-cucumber with a starfish.
106. Arthropoda:
(a) Compare a crab with the crawfish.
(b) Observe some living fresh water Entomostraca with the microscope.
(c) Study a "thousand-leg" or centipede.
(d) Study a spider.
(e) For further studies on insects consult a work on entomology.
107. Mollusca:
(a) Study the method of locomotion of a common snail. Note symmetry of body and shell.
(b) In a right lateral view note the head, the foot, the collar and shell. Note also the mouth, the tentacles, the eyes, the respiratory opening.

(c) In a small living snail the movement of the heart may be seen through the shell.
(d) When the shell is removed the lung chamber may be laid open. Note also the heart, kidney, liver, coils of the intestine and, at the top of the spiral mass, the gonad.
(e) If the dorsal body wall is removed from the tentacle to the heart the following organs come to view: The buccal mass, the œsphagus surrounded by the nerve collar, the crop with the salivary glands at either side, the complicated reproductive organs lying on the right side of the body.
(f) Draw a dorsal view of a clam. Note the symmetry. (The hinge is dorsal and the siphon posterior.)
(g) The clam may be studied with one valve of the shell removed. Note: The mantle, the two adductor muscles and the siphon with its two openings. At the dorsal edge of the mantle is the pericardial cavity in which lies the heart.
(h) Raise the mantle and observe the large chamber in which lie the visceral mass and the fleshy foot. Upon the visceral mass lie the two gills and at the anterior edge the palps which hide the mouth.
(i) Draw a lateral view of a squid. Note the head with the arms and eyes. Behind the head are the collar and funnel. The body is covered with a very thick mantle which is expanded at the end into a fin.
(j) Study the suckers on the arms. Find the mouth and jaws.
(k) The visceral mass and the gills are exposed by slitting open the mantle on the ventral side.
(l) The rudimentary shell is embedded in the dorsal surface of the mantle.

INTRODUCTION

302. **Animals and Plants.**—Animals present a much greater variety of types of organization than plants. This is largely because the higher animals are vastly more complex than the higher plants. The apparent complexity of a tree, for example, is in reality due chiefly to a repetition of similar parts; but in animals there is a progressive differentiation of parts from the lowest to the highest forms, so that even a single cell may have

a structure and function not duplicated by any other cell in the body. The gap between the simplest and most complex animals is occupied by many types of intermediate degrees of complexity and we shall therefore keep in mind several of the most significant of these types while seeking to obtain a conception of what constitutes an animal.

303. **Animal Types.**—As an example of the very simplest kinds of animals we shall frequently refer to the amœba, a minute speck of living jelly, quite common in the bottom slime of ponds.

304. As a slightly more complex form we will take hydra, which is also found in fresh-water ponds, attached to plants or other objects in the water. It is vase-like in form and has a circle of long slender arms or tentacles near the oral end.

305. As a still more complex form the common earthworm may serve very well, or a segmented marine worm, like nereis.

306. The crayfish will form another step forward. This animal is also common in most parts of the world and should be familiar to everyone. In this connection reference will occasionally be made to insects, which belong to the same phylum.

307. As an example of the most complicated type of animal organization any mammal may be kept in mind, such as the cat, dog or rabbit, or, better still, man. The student will be supposed to have some knowledge of human anatomy and physiology. Reference will also be made to other members of the vertebrate phylum, such as fishes, frogs, reptiles and birds.

308. **Color and Form.**—If we compare plants and animals with regard to color and form we find nothing in common. Animals contain no chlorophyl and they are therefore physiologically dependent upon plants. Nor do they have any other general color characteristic. The form of plants we found was determined by the necessity of exposing chlorophyll tissue to

the light, and for maximum efficiency this demands a branching, or what may be called a diffuse form of body. Since animals do not demand such light exposure the branching form of body is also not necessary. As a matter of fact the animal body is not only not diffuse, it is constructed in the most compact manner possible. The reason for this is, of course, not far to seek. It is demanded by the most distinctively animal characteristic—locomotion. For the purposes of respiration animals also require a large exposure of surface to the surrounding medium, but this is secured in the gills and lungs by folding surfaces in such a way as to make the respiratory organs occupy very little space in proportion to the surface which they expose. This of course secures protection to the organs but at the same time it also allows greater freedom of motion. That the latter is an important consideration is evidenced by the fact that many fixed animals are also diffuse in form.

309. **Locomotion.**—The ability to move from place to place is the most conspicuous animal character, but coördinate with it and inseparably connected with it is sensibility to external influences. This latter character is not wanting in plants but it is so much more greatly developed in animals as to amount practically to a different thing. Locomotion and sensibility go hand in hand because locomotion without sensibility would be aimless and sensibility without the power of motion would be without value. In this connection "motion" or "locomotion" must be understood in a broad sense as a muscular response which may involve only a part of the body. The power of locomotion carries with it a large train of interesting consequences which determine the form and structure of the animal even to the minutest detail. These will be considered at various points as the subject develops, but here we will examine only into the matter of the external form as resulting from locomotion.

310. **Axis of Locomotion.**—In the more primitive condition,

differentiation results in a repetition of similar parts and these parts must either be arranged radially or serially. But the serial arrangement results in an elongated body and this is better adapted for free locomotion. Consequently the body of the typical animal is elongated in the axis of locomotion.

311. **Cephalization.**—Since locomotion is generally in a horizontal direction the elongation of the body is horizontal. But the two poles of this body are not alike, because the principle of division of labor and efficiency would make locomotion in one of the two directions become the principal direction of locomotion. The animal usually moves with the same end forward and this end, which is called anterior, is very different from the opposite or posterior end. The difference is chiefly due to the development of special sense organs at the anterior end, because this end comes more positively into relation with the forces which affect the senses. The development of the special sense organs further carries with it the special development of the central nervous system of that region; that is, the development of a brain. The locomotion of the animal has to do largely with obtaining food and this probably determines that the anterior end is located near the mouth. Then the development of organs for ingestion and comminuting food, and the sense organs connected with this function still further differentiate the anterior end from the posterior. The development of all these organs at the anterior end of the animal forming a complex of organs called the head is called cephalization. The posterior end of the body is sometimes developed into an organ of propulsion or otherwise specialized, but never to the degree to which the more positive conditions bring the development of the anterior end. In this way are determined the elongation of the animal with its principal axis horizontal, and the differentiation of the two poles into anterior and posterior.

312. **Dorsal and Ventral.**—For animals which pass from one medium to another, as from water to dry land or from the latter

FORM OF THE BODY 131

into the air, two sets of locomotor organs might be necessary, but in general the principle of economy determines that only one set of appendages is developed. For those forms which move on the bottom of the sea or on land the locomotor ap-

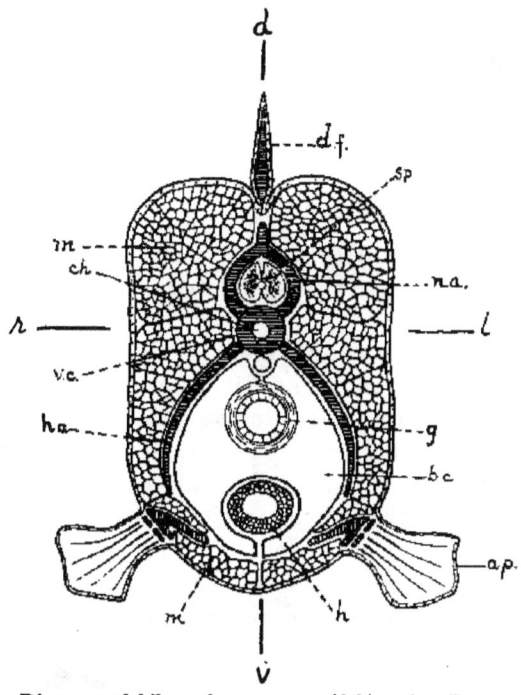

Fig. 62.—Diagram of bilateral symmetry (fish). *d–v*, Dorso-ventral axis; *r–l*, right-left axis; *ap*, appendages; *b.c.*, body cavity; *ch.*, notochord; *d.f.*, dorsal fin; *g*, intestine; *h*, heart; *h.a.*, hæmal arch; *m*, muscles; *n.a.*, neural arch; *sp*, spinal cord; *v.c.*, vertebral column. (From Galloway.)

pendages will necessarily be constructed with reference to the force of gravity. Since this force operates in one direction only, the appendages have a one-sided relation to the body. There are therefore an upper and a lower side of the body, and these two sides are not alike. Moreover, since light, which also affects the organism, impinges more strongly from above, it will also operate to differentiate the upper and lower sides. These two sides are distinguished as dorsal and ventral, respectively.

313. Fishes which do not rest on the bottom but always float suspended in the water do not present the same degree of dorso-ventral differentiation. In this case the action of gravity is practically eliminated by the buoyancy of the water.

314. **Right and Left.**—With the differentiation of anterior and posterior and of dorsal and ventral the animal comes to have a right side and a left side. These two sides are so related to the external world that every force which acts on one side affects the other side also in a symmetrical way. In consequence, the two sides are also symmetrical in form in every way.

315. **Bilateral Symmetry.**—An organism like the one just described is divided into right and left symmetrical halves by the vertical plane in which the principal axis lies. No other symmetrical division of such a form is possible. A body having such a form is said to be bilaterally symmetrical, and this is the type of symmetry found in most animals and generally in those having marked freedom of locomotion.

316. **Radial Symmetry.**—Those animals which are very sluggish in movement or actually fixed, show little or no evidence of bilateral symmetry. The principal axis is perpendicular to the substratum, and its two poles are differentiated; the mouth and associated organs for ingestion are at the free, oral, pole, while the opposite, aboral, pole is modified for attachment. If the animal is not actually fixed, the oral pole may be toward the substratum. In either case, the organization of the animal is more or less perfectly radial with respect to the principal axis, the number of rays being 2, 4, 6 or 5 or a multiple of one of these numbers. The oral-aboral differentiation in part corresponds to the dorso-ventral differentiation of bilateral forms.

FORM OF THE BODY

The radial symmetry is to be referred to the radial action of the environment, which is the same in all directions at right angles to the principal axis. This type of symmetry is characteristic of plants, and inasmuch as these radial animals approach plants in their life habit, they are affected by their environment like plants and consequently approach plants in their structure.

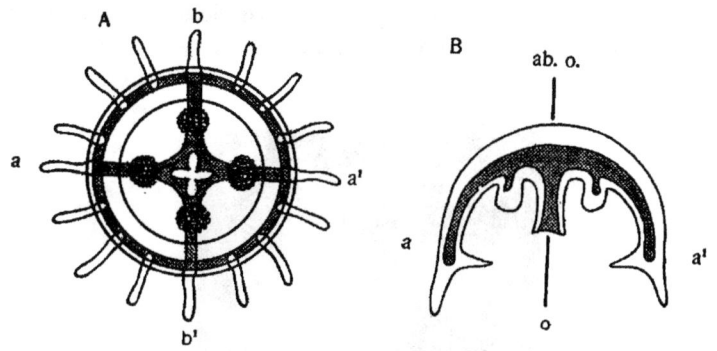

Fig. 63.—Diagram of radial symmetry as represented by a medusa. A, Oral view; B, lateral view; o-$ab.o.$, principal axis.

317. Universal Symmetry.—In case external forces are the same in all directions the corresponding response form would be a sphere. This might be called universal symmetry. Such a condition is actually approached only by a few protozoa which float in the water, unattached, and are continually turning over and over.

318. Asymmetry.—Varying degrees of asymmetry are found among fixed or sluggish types. This is more often true of colonial forms which grow by a process of budding and become asymmetrical by unequal growth. In these cases, however, the individual may be perfectly radial.

319. A study of some exceptional cases will serve to "prove the rule." The shell of gasteropod molluscs is asymmetrical. However, when the animal is completely withdrawn into the shell and is then completely asymmetrical, it is also to all in-

tents, so far as external forces are concerned, an inert body and has lost its animal character completely. When expanded and moving, on the other hand, the animal character reappears and at the same time the form of the animal becomes largely or completely bilaterally symmetrical.

320. The free swimming larvæ of the Echinoderms are perfectly bilateral, but when they assume the less active or fixed life habit of the adult, they become radial in symmetry. This change involves a radical metamorphosis. In the case of some

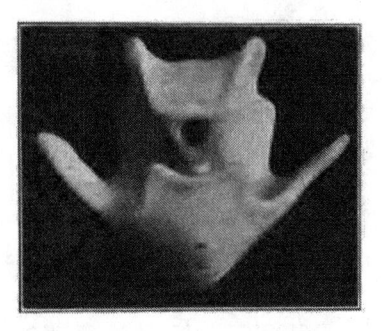

Fig. 64.—The bilaterally symmetrical free swimming larva of an Echinoderm. (From Ziegler's models.)

of the Holothuria a second change occurs, in which the radial symmetry is largely superseded by a secondary bilateral symmetry. This is brought about by the habit of the animal of assuming a horizontal instead of a vertical position of the principal axis.

321. The adult ascidians and barnacles also show a strong tendency toward radial symmetry, although the active larvæ are bilateral.

322. A striking example of a different type is offered by the "flat fishes," such as the flounder and sole. The young of these fishes have the ordinary type of bilateral symmetry, and in swimming they also assume the erect position characteristic

FORM OF THE BODY 135

of fishes. But they soon turn on one side and in the adult continue in this attitude, with one side toward the earth. In this case the principal axis is maintained in the same relative position, but the dorso-ventral and right-left axes are transposed in space. In response, the form of the animal also under-

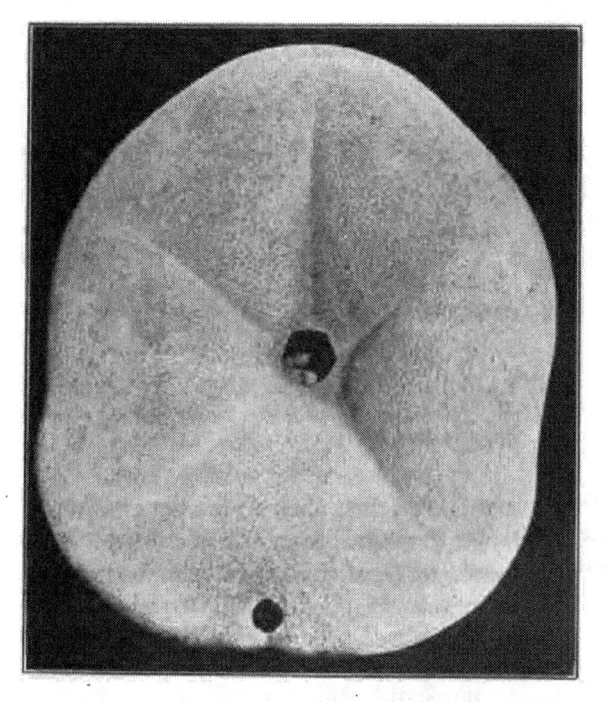

FIG. 65.—A sea-urchin (Clypeaster) in which a secondary bilateral symmetry is impressed on a radial organism. Oral view, slightly reduced.

goes a change, so that the dorsal and ventral surfaces become symmetrical and the right and left sides unsymmetrical. The plane of symmetry is thus revolved 90° on the principal axis. It would be more correct, however, to say that while the animal revolves 90° on its principal axis, its plane of symmetry remains fixed. That is, of course, what one should expect following the general principles already laid down; for since there is no change in the external forces which cause symmetry in the organism there should be no change in the plane of symmetry following the revolution of the animal on its axis.

Fig. 66.—The flounder, Pseudopleuronectes Americanus, showing approximate dorso-ventral symmetry. Note that both eyes are on the right side of the head. (From Hegner, after Goode.)

323. Size and Differentiation.—Animals vary greatly in size and complexity of structure, from the microscopic protozoa to the gigantic mammals, and it is of interest to note that, in a general way, size and complexity vary together. Superiority in size is of itself an advantage, especially where there is a contest between individuals. But more important is the advantage derived from complexity, which permits of differentiation, division of labor and consequent efficiency. Considerable differentiation may be found between the parts of the same cell, as in the protozoa, but when the body is composed of many cells the differentiation may be vastly greater, both in regard to the number of kinds of differentiation and the degree to which it is carried. Thus the functions of contraction, irritability, digestion, etc., may be taken up by the different cells or groups of cells and performed more efficiently.

The various kinds of differentiation may be grouped under the following heads:

324. Integument.—An extremely important set of organs are the various protective structures which cover the entire surface of the body of all but the very lowest animals. The most important of these structures are the hair, feathers, scales, bony plates, cuticular secretions, shells, glands and the unmodified skin itself. These together comprise the integument.

325. The Nerve-Muscle Mechanism.—The nervous and the muscular tissues are the most highly differentiated tissues of the body. For efficiency the **sense organs** must be very numerous, so that on the surface of the body there is scarcely a point large enough to be visible which is not occupied. The **muscles** for strength must be massive. The **central nervous system**, through which all the various organs of the body are brought into harmonious relations, especially the sense organs and the organs of response, is the most complicated organ of the body and is also of considerable size. The weight of a large body requires special supporting structures, and for the most efficient application of muscular energy for locomotion, a system of levers is necessary. These structures comprise the **skeleton** and the **connective tissues,** which together constitute the largest set of organs in the body.

326. Digestion.—The highly differentiated tissues just described have surrendered the function of digestion to other cells of the body, and these are connected with the central cavity, in which digestion takes place. The various phases of the digestive process are separated and distributed to distinct groups of cells, composing as many organs. These together constitute the digestive system.

327. Circulation.—The digested food is absorbed by the digestive tract in much larger quantities than is necessary to nourish the tissues of the digestive tract itself. It is in a fluid state as blood plasma and is available for assimilation by the other tissues of the body. But a large part of these tissues is too far removed from the digestive tract to be nourished by transfusion. A system of vessels becomes necessary for the conduction of the blood plasma and, in addition, a heart to force the blood along.

328. **Respiration.**—The smaller organisms absorb enough oxygen through the general surface of the body to supply the needs of all the tissues. But increase in size also brings some of the tissues too far from the surface to be supplied in this way. Moreover, the development of impervious integumentary tissues prevents the absorption of much oxygen through the general surface. There then becomes necessary a special respiratory organ—gills or lungs. From the organs of respiration the oxygen can reach the tissues through the channels followed by the blood plasma, either dissolved in the blood plasma or carried by special vehicles, the red blood corpuscles.

329. **Excretion.**—The waste products of metabolism are voided by the smallest animals through the general body surface. But this also becomes impossible in the higher animals, where they are taken up by the blood and are then in part eliminated through special excretory organs, the nephridia, kidneys, etc.

330. **Reproduction.**—Most of the protozoa reproduce by division of the body, or by budding. These methods also occur largely among the lower metazoa, but highly differentiated tissues lose the power of division and the more complex animals have not the power of reproducing in this way. In them there is a special organ, in which undifferentiated tissue is reserved for reproduction.

331. **Organization of the Body.**—We thus see that the development of the animal, i. e., the nerve-muscle mechanism,

to the highest degree involves the development of an organism made up of nine systems of organs:

1. The Integumentary System.
2. The Sensory-Nervous System.
3. The Muscular System.
4. The Skeletal System.
5. The Digestive System.
6. The Circulatory System.
7. The Respiratory System.
8. The Excretory System.
9. The Reproductive System.

332. **"Higher" and "Lower" Animals.**—The functions performed by these nine systems of organs are all performed by the undifferentiated protoplasm of the amœba and must likewise be provided for by every other animal. The higher forms are, therefore, not distinguished by the development of new functions, but by the effectiveness with which these functions are performed. Under favorable conditions the functions of the amœba are equal to the demands made upon them, but with a serious change in these conditions they fail and the amœba comes to naught. Against drouth, heat, cold, the lack of food in the immediate vicinity and the attacks of larger animals the amœba has no defense. On the other hand, a higher animal, say, e. g., a wolf, is effectually protected against dessication by his skin. Ordinary climatic changes of temperature are automatically compensated for and the body maintains an equable internal temperature. When food fails he travels far in search of more, and when attacked he knows how to defend himself. Indeed, he is a living demonstration of his superiority, for his life is maintained by the destruction of other living things which are not able to defend themselves against him. He demonstrates his superiority, and we habitually distinguish such capable forms from the less capable by the terms higher and lower. But there is still another way in which the wolf

140   ANIMALS

demonstrates his superiority. The life of the amœba is brief in time as well as circumscribed in space; the range of its experiences are as limited as its sensibilities are vague and the memory of them instantly vanishes. The wolf, however, lives on for days, months and years. His highly specialized nerve cells not only feel infinitely more acutely but they are able to retain impressions, and through his comparatively long life these accumulated experiences are made to serve to his advantage. **The intelligence of the wolf goes far to make him independent of his environment** and he thereby demonstrates his superiority. The highest animals are those most completely independent of the conditions under which they live.

333. **Segmentation.**—Comparing the larger and smaller animals again from another point of view: The greater size of the body may be due to larger organs, or it may also result from a repetition of similar organs, as in plants. The former condition is well exemplified by the phylum Mollusca, in which the repetition of similar organs (in this sense) does not occur, and yet one class of this phylum (Cephalopods) has attained a high degree of development, and counts, in some of its species, animals of the greatest size.

FIG. 67.—The anterior end of an annelid, Nereis. The body consists of upward of 130 similar segments or metameres. Hence the animal is said to be homonomously segmented.

334. When repetition of organs occurs it may affect some

systems of organs more than others, but usually there is a tendency for the various systems to be repeated in the same degree. In this way the body is divided into segments, each one of which contains a segment of each system of organs. In elongated animals the body segments are arranged in a linear series, and are called **metameres.** Within the metamere each system of organs is represented by a single segment if the system is median in position, or by a symmetrical pair if they are lateral.

335. The segments of radial animals are called **antimeres** and they are arranged radially about the principal axis of symmetry. The antimeres are also bilaterally symmetrical. (Why?)

336. Metameric segmentation introduces a new type of differentiation, the differentiation of segments. In the phylum Vermes there is little differentiation of segments and hence the segments are said to be homonymous. When the segments are differentiated they are heteronymous. This occurs in progressive stages through the phyla Arthropoda and Vertebrata, so that in the higher forms the segmentation is considerably obscured. Of course, differentiation of segments greatly increases the complexity of organization.

337. Segmentation of the body is a means by which its flexibility may be provided for. This is of special importance in animals having a skeleton.

INTEGUMENT

338. The amœba is said to be a naked cell, i. e., it has no cell wall, and therefore can scarcely be said to have an integument. The surface layer of the protoplasm, the pellicle, is slightly denser than that lying deeper, and its consistency is such as to maintain a well-defined boundary between the organism and the surrounding water. The protoplasm is so nearly the density of water and the animal so minute that little force is required

142   ANIMALS

to maintain the integrity of the body. The delicate pellicle is therefore sufficient for the amœba, although for larger forms it would be entirely inadequate.

339. The body wall of hydra consists of two layers of cells, an outer ectoderm and an inner entoderm. The cells of the

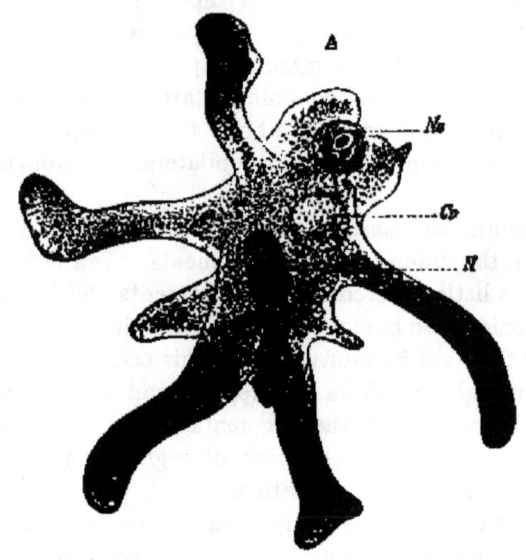

FIG. 68.—Amœba Proteus. *Na*, A cluster of algal cells which is being engulfed by the protoplasm of the amœba; *Cr*, contractile vacuole; *N*, nucleus. (From Marshall, after Doflein).

ectoderm are practically naked protoplasm on the exposed surfaces, but this protoplasm is so dense that it serves as an integument. In the closely related hydroids the ectoderm secretes a thin membrane known as the perisarc or cuticula. It is extremely tough and well adapted for protection and support.

340. The epidermis of worms corresponds to the ectoderm of hydra, but is much thicker because of the columnar form of

the cells composing it. It secretes a very thick and firm cuticula. Both epidermis and cuticula vary greatly in thickness in different species of worms, but this variation corresponds approximately with the size of the worm.

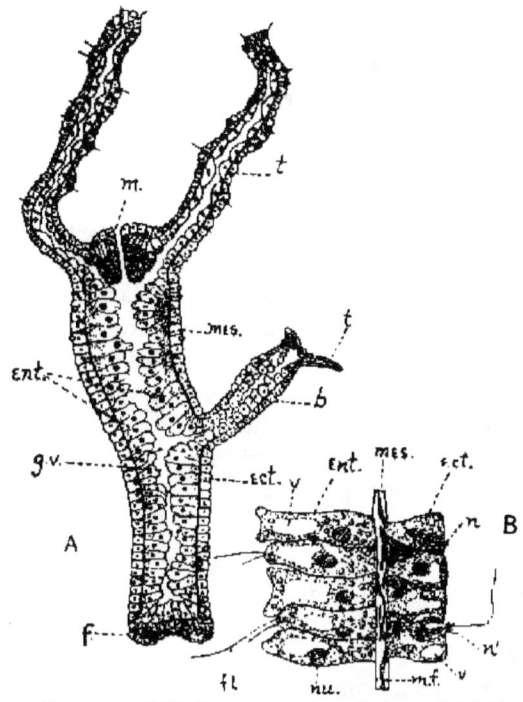

Fig. 69.—*A*, Diagram of Hydra; *B*, portion of the wall highly magnified; *b*, bud; *ect.*, ectoderm; *ent*, entoderm; *f*, foot; *fl*, flagellum; *g.v.*, gastro-vascular cavity; *m*, mouth; *mes*, supporting lamella; *m.f.*, muscle fibre of the ectoderm cells; *n*, nettling cells; *n'*, same, exploded; *nu.*, nucleus; *t*, tentacle; *v*, vacuole. (From Galloway.)

341. The integument of the crayfish is similar to that of the worm. The chief difference lies in the much greater thickness of the cuticula, which here consists of a peculiar substance called chitin. Chitin is an extremely firm and elastic substance,

344. This type of integument is extremely flexible and therefore does not impede locomotion or other movements. At the same time it is very tough, fairly resistent to mechanical injury, and the lifeless superficial layers of the epidermis are impervious to water and thus protect the living parts from the dry air.

345. In addition to these undifferentiated portions of the various types of integument there are also certain important specialized structures developed which serve as supplementary protective organs, as organs of defense and offense, as prehensile organs and as accessory organs of locomotion.

346. The most common type of differentiation consists simply of a local thickening of the cuticula or epidermis. Thus in many worms minute tubercles or larger jaw-like structures are found on the walls of the mouth and pharynx. The setæ and aciculæ on the parapodia and sometimes scales on the back, are of similar origin. In insects and crustacea the sensory hairs found especially on the antennæ and mouth parts, and around the joints of the appendages and body are also produced by the unusually active secretion of chitin by one or a few cells of the underlying epidermis.

347. In Vertebrates the epidermis becomes modified in a great variety of ways by the aggregation of the minute horny scales into exceedingly firm structures, which serve a great variety of purposes. Among the most important of these structures are nails, claws, hoofs, spurs, horns, beaks, "tortoise shell," "whale-bone," scales of certain kinds, hairs and feathers. The scales found on reptiles, birds and some fishes are merely thick and compact areas of the corneous layer of the epidermis. The hair differs from the scale only in its form. The feather may be likened to a hair greatly enlarged in diameter and hollow, with certain parts of its shaft splitting in a complicated fashion and thereby producing the vane.

348. The scales of most fishes are not horn but thin plates

of bone which are formed, not in the epidermis, but in the dermis. In some fishes there is deposited on the upper surface of the bony scale a layer of enamel which is due to the activity of the cells of the overlying epidermis. Teeth are also formed in this way, the dentine being merely a kind of bone. Antlers are bone and are formed by the dermis.

349. **Glands.**—Glands form another type of differentiated integumentary structures. They are of the simplest form in hydra and worms where they consist of single cells of the epidermis. These cells do not secrete a cuticula on their free

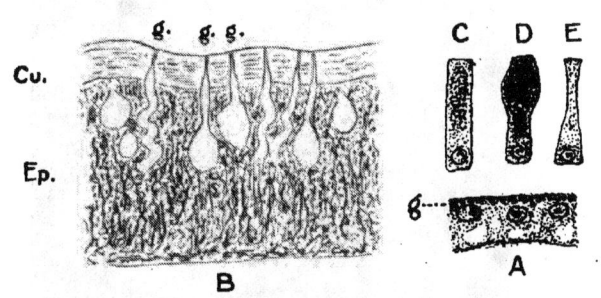

FIG. 71.—Glands. *A*, The ectoderm of hydra showing granules of cement (*g*) secreted by the cells at the surface; *B*, a section through the epidermis of nereis, showing a number of unicellular glands. Only the outlines of the outer ends of the gland cells are shown. The nuclear portions are below but not distinguishable in the figure. *Cu*, Cuticula; *Ep*, epidermis; *g*, pores of the glands; *C*, diagram of a unicellular gland at the beginning of secretion; *D*, the same when swollen with secretion; *E*, the same cell after its contents are ejected.

surfaces, but do secrete other substances which at first accumulate within the bodies of the cells but are later forced out through the pores in the cuticula which were formed by the non-secretion of cuticula by the gland cells. The secretions accumulate until the excess gradually oozes out through the pores or is suddenly forced out in larger quantities by the contraction of the surrounding tissues. In the case of worms and many other aquatic animals the substance secreted takes up water and forms slime. The function of the slime is probably in most cases

148   ANIMALS

protective, but in special cases it may serve a variety of other functions. Sometimes it serves to cement together the particles of earth to form a tube in which the animal lives. Some-

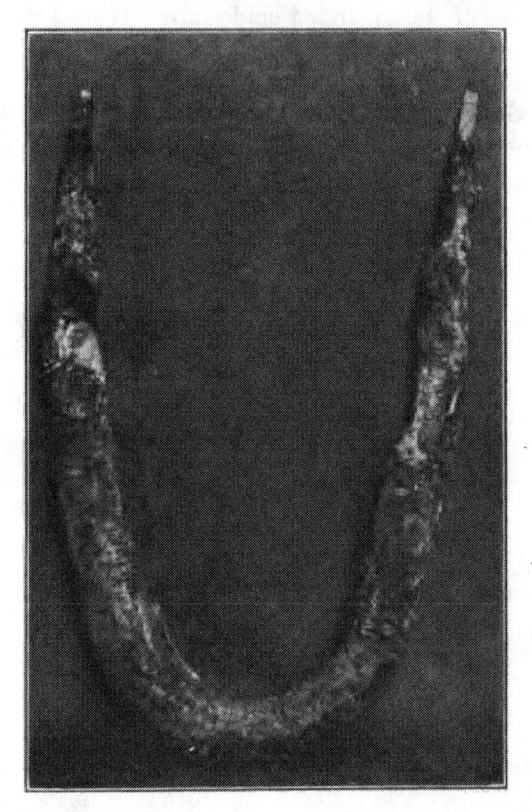

FIG. 72.—A parchment-like tube constructed by a marine annelid, Chætopteris. The tube is buried in the mud, except an inch or two of each end which project above the surface. Both ends are open to permit a current of water to pass through. × 2/3.

times it is used in locomotion, as in case of snails. The skin of fishes is richly supplied with slime glands. Hydra and many other animals attach themselves temporarily or permanently by a secretion which acts like a cement. Leathery tubes are formed by many worms by a secretion which hardens

FIG. 73.—Oven-shaped shelters of the caddice-worm, composed of pebbles fastened together with silk fibres spun from the mouth.

FIG. 74.—Another type of shelter tubes of caddice-worms, composed of sticks and pebbles. The caddice-worm is the aquatic larva of the caddice-fly (Trichoptera).

in the water into an exceedingly tough fibre. There is often considerable lime mingled with these secretions and sometimes

150   ANIMALS

the lime is deposited in great quantities. This is notably true of the corals, which are closely related to hydra. Many

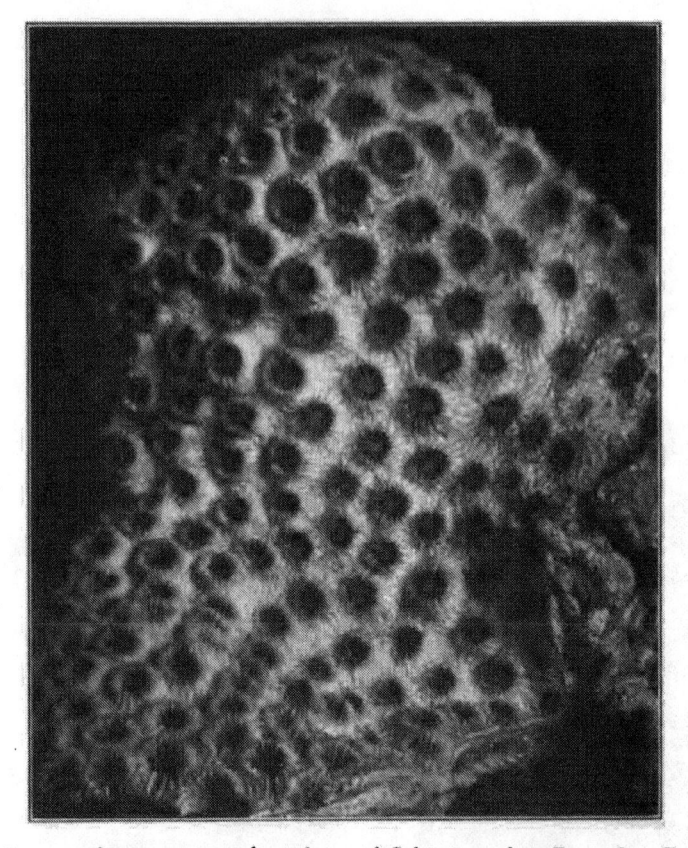

Fig. 75.—A common type of massive coral, Solenastrea, from Bermuda. Each cup is formed by a polyp and radial septa in the cups indicate the pairs of mesenteries of the polyp. Slightly reduced.

worms live in hard, limey tubes which they secrete. The shell of the mollusc originates in the same way, but here it forms part of the body of the animal.

350. The epidermis of Crustacea and Insects is generally devoid of glands. Fishes and Amphibia are well supplied with slime glands. Reptiles have practically no glands in the skin. In Birds there is one important gland or group of glands. This is the uropygal gland, located on the tail. It secretes an oil which is transferred by the bird by means of its beak to the surface of the feathers when preening. The oil keeps the feathers flexible and prevents wetting. For this reason "water rolls off a duck's back," as it also does from other birds.

351. The skin of Mammals is provided with two kinds of glands, sebaceous and sweat glands. The former are grouped around the hair follicles and their oily secretion escapes at the base of the hair. It not only serves to keep the hair flexible but also the corneous layer of the epidermis. This is a very important function, since the dead tissue would otherwise break and expose the living tissue beneath, which is what happens in the chapping of an abnormally "dry" skin. The oil also renders the skin impervious to water.

352. The sweat glands are the thermostatic organs of the body. They will be discussed elsewhere. (Page 411.)

SENSE ORGANS

353. Animals which live in the water may sense their food in one or more of three ways, viz.: Sight, smell, and taste. For amœba the first is excluded, since amœba cannot be said to have a sense of sight. The sensations of taste and smell are both due to chemical stimuli; that is to say, the substances which stimulate the sense organs must be in solution, and the stimulation itself is a chemical process. The distinction between the two sets of senses is largely a matter of position of the sense organs. The organs of taste are located in the mouth, while those of smell are elsewhere on the surface of the body, usually

in the vicinity of the mouth. For amœba no such distinction is possible, and we can, therefore, only speak of a chemical sense. Amœba has been observed to engulf particles of sand and other inorganic substances which could not serve as food, but in spite of this fact there is much evidence to show that there is a chemical sense. Ordinarily the animal distinguishes food particles from others and has even been observed to follow a moving protozoan, which it also captured and devoured. Many observations lead to the general conclusion that the protozoa generally are sensitive to the chemical condition of the surrounding medium. They are attracted to or repelled from the source whence such substances are diffusing through the water. Strong stimuli produce decided responses, such as a contraction of the amœba into a spherical mass.

354. Amœba is also sensitive to mechanical stimuli, such as a touch or a jar. By this means it "feels" the presence of a foreign object to which it may adhere. If the stimulus is irritating the response may take the form of a secretion of slime, the withdrawal of the pseudopodium or the complete contraction of the amœba into a spherical mass.

355. Amœba is also sensitive to strong light though not as much so as some other colorless protozoa. Usually, when other things are equal, protozoa may be observed to seek a point where the light is neither excessively strong nor weak.

356. To changes in temperature amœba is also sensitive. With increase in temperature it becomes more active, until at about 35° C. it contracts and remains motionless. With a falling temperature activity is also lowered until at a little above 0° C. it ceases entirely, often without contraction. When possible amœba will move out of a region of extremely high or low temperature to one more nearly normal.

357. Though amœba is sensitive to these various stimuli, yet it has no sense organs. There is no differentiation of organs for the reception of the different stimuli, nor yet for the re-

ception of stimuli in general. Sensibility is one of the primary functions of undifferentiated protoplasm.

358. Almost the same may be said of hydra. The organism is sensitive to the same stimuli and to no others. So far as is known there is no localization of sensory function. All the cells of the body consist largely of undifferentiated protoplasm, which is probably the organ of general sense as in amœba. It is true that some of the cells of the ectoderm project beyond the surface by slender protoplasmic processes which are probably organs for the reception of stimuli. Since these processes are more exposed they are more readily affected by stimuli and hence may be regarded as incipient sense organs.

359. In some other Cœlenterates as, e. g., the medusæ, the sensory cells and the nervous elements generally, are better developed. Many cells of the ectoderm are provided at their free surfaces with sensory hairs while the opposite ends of the cells are prolonged into long fibres which extend for some distance under the ectoderm.

360. In nereis the sense cells are clearly differentiated from the other cells of the epidermis. Each sense cell projects through the cuticula by a single protoplasmic process, while the remainder of the cell is elongated into a fibre which extends deep into the body to the central nervous system. The nucleus of the cell often lies in the epidermis, but it may also lie immediately beneath the epidermis or even at a considerable distance beneath the surface. In the latter case a number of such nuclei may be collected into a group which constitutes a ganglion, and if the fibres run parallel in a bundle they form a nerve.

361. The sensory cells of Arthropods are very much like those of nereis, but they do not always have the exposed protoplasmic terminations. Instead, the fibre may end at the base, or in the axis of one of the cuticular sensory hairs mentioned above. (Page 146.) The hairs serve mechanically to trans-

154   ANIMALS

mit the stimulus to the sensory element but are not themselves sensitive.

362. The sensory elements found in the skin of Vertebrates are of various types which may be divided into two classes. In one class the fibre ends in a bushy system of branches which penetrate among the other normal elements of the surrounding tissues. In the other class the fibre may end with or without

FIG. 76.—The blue crab. View of the region around the mouth to show the groups of cuticular hairs, which are in large part sensory. × 1 1/2.

terminal branching, but in either case there are always some of the cells of the surrounding tissues modified to form a special stimulating organ. The first class, the free nerve terminations, are found chiefly in the deeper layers of the epidermis, though they may also be found in the dermis. The second class, which for want of a better name may be called sensory corpuscles, are found chiefly in the superficial and deeper layers of the dermis, though some are also found in the epidermis (in man only in the dermis).

363. The nuclei of all sensory elements of the skin of vertebrates lie in the spinal ganglia and homologous ganglia of the cranial nerves.

364. The sense organs just described are those which are generally distributed over the whole surface of the body. The senses to which they correspond are, in man, touch, cold, warmth and pain. Each of these senses, with the possible exception of pain, has its own set of sensory elements, although the correspondence between sense organs and senses has not yet been completely determined. How far these senses are differentiated in the lower animals is also not known.

365. In the higher animals there are also deeper lying sense organs, which are located in the sub-cutaneous connective tissue, in the muscles and tendons and even in the mesentery. To these organs are ascribed a sense of weight and a sense of position, or attitude, of the member of the body with regard to the other members of the body.

ORGANS OF SPECIAL SENSE

366. Besides the general sense organs described above, we find in all the higher animals special sense organs, which are developed in very limited regions of the body and which are often very complex in structure. These are the organs of taste and smell, which are stimulated chemically; the organs of hearing and equilibration, which are stimulated mechanically, and the organ of sight, which is stimulated by ether vibrations.

367. From direct evidence we know little about the chemical senses of hydra, though as in the case of amœba we may infer that the choice of food indicates a sense of this kind, but this evidence is by no means conclusive. In the sea anemone, however, it is found by experiment that the tentacles distin-

156   ANIMALS

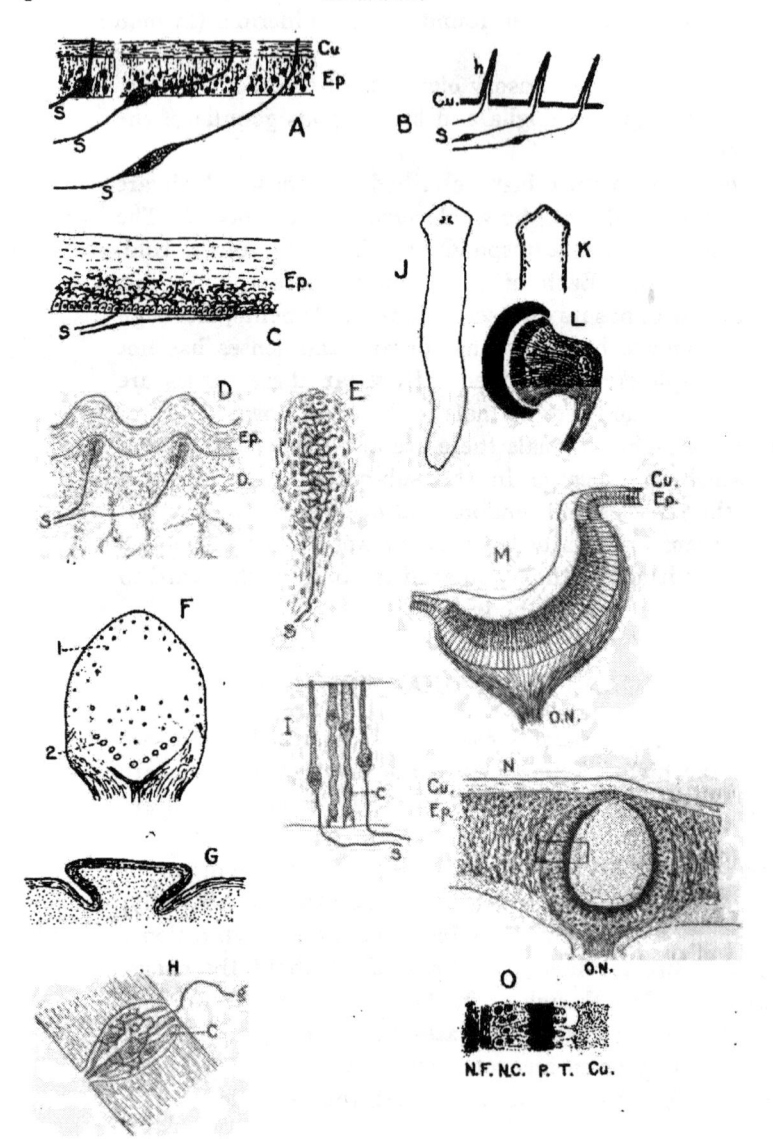

guish food from other objects in such a way as to indicate a chemical sense. No specialized chemical sense organs have been distinguished.

368. The earthworm is chemically sensitive over the entire surface of the body, but at the anterior end this sense is best developed. The function seems to be located in sensory cells, which occur in clusters, the clusters being distributed over the surface of the body in numbers which correspond approximately to the sensitiveness of the region.

369. The antennules of the crayfish are the seat of chemical sense. The sensory cells concerned are not specially modified, but their accessory terminal end-organs are peculiar club-shaped hairs, which are covered by an extremely thin cuticula. In insects, there is a differentiation of the chemical sense into an olfactory and a gustatory sense. The former is located on the antennæ, and the sense organ consists of a flask-shaped cluster of sense cells which are exposed at the surface at the bottom of a pit in the cuticula. The organs of taste are similar, but are found on surfaces bounding the mouth cavity or on the mouth appendages.

370. In arthropods we first observe a decided limitation of the chemical sense organs to the region of the mouth and in the air breathers, the first differentiation of the senses of taste and smell. In some fishes, organs of taste are found on the surface

FIG. 77.—Sense organs. A-E, General sense organs; F-H, organs of taste; I, olfactory organ; J-O, eyes. A, General sense organs of nereis; B, general sense organs of Arthropods; C, free nerve terminations in the epidermis of Vertebrates; D, sensory corpuscles in the dermis of Vertebrates; E, same, enlarged; F, diagram of human tongue showing distribution of fungiform (1) and circumvallate papillæ; G, section through a circumvallate papilla showing position of the taste buds; H, section of a taste bud, showing two sensory cells, one supporting cell (c) and a nerve fibre (g); I, section of the olfactory epithelium; J, outline of a small "gliding worm" with two simple eyes; K, anterior end of another "gliding worm" with a number of simple eyes arranged along the edge of the body; L, eye of a "gliding worm" consisting of a single cell with a sensory brush partly surrounded by a pigment cell; M, eye of a snail (Patella); N, eye of nereis; O, part of N, on a larger scale. c, Supporting cell; Cu, cuticula; D, dermis; $Ep.$, epidermis; g, fibre from a ganglion cell; h, sensory hair, or bristle; $N.C.$, nerve cell; $N.F.$, nerve fibres; $O.N.$, optic nerve; P, pigment; S, sense cells.

158   ANIMALS

of the body, more particularly in the region of the mouth, but with this exception we can say that for all vertebrates the organs of taste and of smell are limited to the surface of the cavities of the mouth and nostrils, respectively.

371. The organs of taste are called taste buds, because the sense cells are grouped in small cask-shaped clusters. The taste buds may occur in various parts of the mouth, but in mammals they are chiefly found on the sides of the fungiform and circumvallate papillæ (and the foliate papillæ, where they are found) of the tongue. The bud consists of two kinds of cells, both very much elongated. One of these, the supporting cells, taper to a point at the free end while the deeper end is very irregular in outline. The sensory cells are more slender and end at the free extremity in a short cuticular hair. At the other end they broaden out into a slight enlargement. They have no fibre processes. Nerve fibres from deeper lying nerve cells form a network of numerous branches, which enclose the bud and penetrate between the cells which compose it.

FIG. 78.—Antennæ of a moth, Samia cecropia. *A*, Of male; *B*, of female. (From Folsom.)

372. In man there are four kinds of taste sensations: sweet, sour, salt and bitter. At the tip of the tongue sweet is most readily detected, sour along the edges, salt at the tip and edges, and bitter at the base of the tongue. We conclude, therefore, that these four sensations are yielded by as many different kinds of organs which, however, are not distinguishable anatomically.

373. The sensations yielded by the olfactory organ are much more various than those of the sense of taste, but at the present no satisfactory analysis of olfactory sensations is possible. So far as can be seen under the microscope, however, the sense organs are very simple and all of the same kind. They present very much the same appearance as the sensory cells of the epidermis of nereis. The olfactory organ forms a small part of the mucous epithelium, lining the nasal cavity at its upper angle. The epithelium here consists of columnar cells of two kinds. The first are the sensory cells which are very slender and end in a group of six to eight short bristle-like tips. Below the nucleus the cell narrows to a very slender nerve fibre which goes to the brain. Between the sensory cells are the somewhat stouter "supporting" cells. The superficial ends of these are quite regularly prismatic in form, but below the nucleus they are very irregular in form. A third type of cells, called "basal cells," form the deeper layer of the epithelium.

THE ORGANS OF SIGHT

374. Mention has already been made of the fact that sensitiveness to light is exhibited by protozoa, which have no sense organs. There are some protozoa, however, which have an "eyespot," a small speck of red pigment embedded in the protoplasm. These eyespots are found to be especially sensitive to light, and must, therefore, be regarded as an exceedingly simple type of light sense organs.

375. Hydra is sensitive to light, but has no organs specially for light perceptions. In some other Cœlenterates, as some of the free swimming medusæ, true light-sense organs are found.

376. Among worms, again, sensitiveness to light does not always indicate the presence of well-defined sense organs especially constructed for this function. The earthworm is more or less sensitive to light over the entire body surface, but

this is more marked at the anterior end of the body. It is possible that some of the sense organs scattered over the surface of the body are light-sense organs, but there is no direct evidence that such is the case. In many other worms, however, there are organs which are unquestionably eyes. They are usually on the head, but may be found elsewhere, and they vary greatly in number.

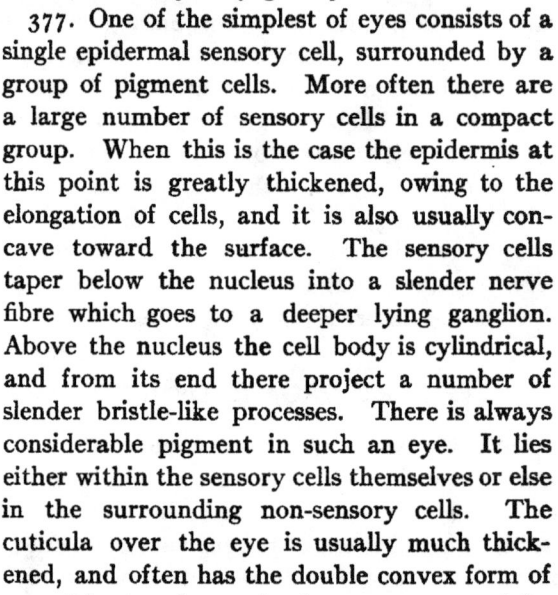

377. One of the simplest of eyes consists of a single epidermal sensory cell, surrounded by a group of pigment cells. More often there are a large number of sensory cells in a compact group. When this is the case the epidermis at this point is greatly thickened, owing to the elongation of cells, and it is also usually concave toward the surface. The sensory cells taper below the nucleus into a slender nerve fibre which goes to a deeper lying ganglion. Above the nucleus the cell body is cylindrical, and from its end there project a number of slender bristle-like processes. There is always considerable pigment in such an eye. It lies either within the sensory cells themselves or else in the surrounding non-sensory cells. The cuticula over the eye is usually much thickened, and often has the double convex form of a condensing lens. Often, as in nereis, the sensory area sinks in so deeply that it approaches a complete sphere in form. It may then also separate entirely from the epidermis.

FIG. 79.—Diagram of an ommatidium. *a*, Cuticular cornea; *b*, corneal cells; *c*, cone cells; *d*, retinal cells; *e*, rhabdom; *f*, fibres of the retinal cells.

378. In Arthropods the optic apparatus attains a much higher degree of functional perfection, and at the same time becomes much more complex. Its development, however, proceeds along very different lines. An eye similar in structure to that described for worms is found in many crustacea, and the ocelli of insects are also much the same, but the com-

THE EYE 161

pound eyes of the higher groups of both Crustacea and Insects are of a different type. The compound eye is convex and it is made up of a large number of units called ommatidia. The surface of the cuticula is divided into numerous polygonal areas, the "facets," each of which corresponds to an ommatidium. The ommatidium is made up of the following cells: two superficial cells which secrete the lens-shaped cuticula; below these,

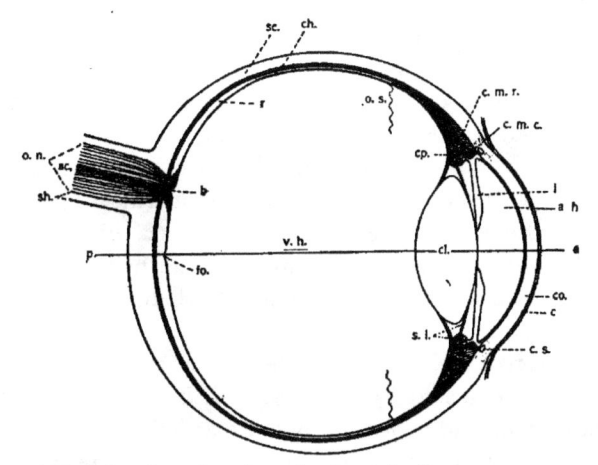

FIG. 80.—Horizontal section through the right human eye. *a-p*, Axis of vision; *ac*, central artery; *ah*, aqueous humor; *b*, blind spot; *c*, conjunctiva; *ch*, choroid layer of the eyeball; *cl*, crystalline lens; *cmc*, circular fibres of the ciliary muscle; *c.m.r.*, radial fibres of the ciliary muscle; *co*, cornea; *cp*, ciliary process; *cs*, canal of Schlemm; *fo*, fovea centralis; *on*, optic nerve; *os*, ora serrata, the anterior limit of the sensory portion of the retinal layer; *r*, the retina; *sc*, the sclera; *sh*, sheath of the optic nerve; *vh*, vitreous humor. (From Galloway).

four cells which form an egg-shaped lens, and below these, again, seven or eight sensory cells, so arranged as to form a single sensory unit. Around the whole is a cylindrical curtain of pigment cells. From the sensory cells, nerve fibres pass downward to a deeper ganglion.

379. The sensory portion of all invertebrate eyes is developed from the epidermis, but the retina of the vertebrate eye and all

the connected nervous elements are developed from the brain. The vertebrate eye is exceedingly complex, and only the more essential features will be called to mind: 1. The sclera is a hollow shell of approximately spherical form, composed of a thick and dense layer of connective tissue. It is the protective and supporting framework of the eye. The cornea is the transparent, more convex portion of the sclera on the side where the light enters the eye. 2. The choroid layer is a layer of blood vessels and capillaries, which lines the inner surface of the sclera. In front it forms the iris, and an opening in the latter is the pupil. 3. The retinal layer is double. Against the surface of the choroid layer there is a layer of pigment cells, which extends from the point where the optic nerve enters the eye to the pupil. The retina proper is the innermost layer and extends from the optic nerve to within about 60° of the centre of the pupil, where it thins out into an endothelium, and as such, continues on to the edge of the pupil, where it merges into the pigment layer.

380. The nervous elements of the retina are arranged in three layers: 1. The sensory layer, proper, is composed of two types of cells, rods and cones, as they are called. The rods are much more numerous than the cones, except at the point of most distinct vision—the fovea centralis—where the rods are entirely wanting. The "rods" consist of a slender cylinder, which tapers at one end into a short fibre. The latter is more or less beaded and ends in a small knob. The cones are shorter and thicker than the rods and, as the name signifies, are conical in form. From the base of the cone a rather stout fibre proceeds, but ends shortly in a broad disc. The nuclei of the "cones" are rather large and located at the base of the cone. The nuclei of the rods are smaller and lie somewhere along the course of the fibre. The cylindrical and conical portions of the rods and cones, respectively, project into the pigment layer in such a way that their ends are completely surrounded by

processes of the cells of the pigment layer. The fibre ends of the rods and cones project toward the centre of the eye. 2. The bipolar cells of the second layer are short nerve cells which end at either extremity in a tuft of branches. They seem to connect the first and third layers. 3. The ganglion cells of the

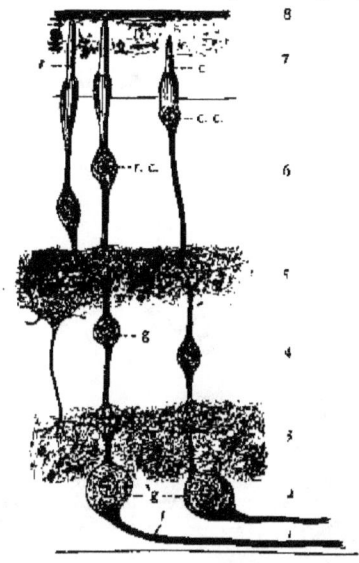

FIG. 81.—Diagram showing some of the retinal elements. Layer 1 is nearest the centre of the eye and consists of nerve fibres (*f*) which enter the optic nerve at the blind spot; 2, the ganglionic-cell layer, made up of nerve cells from which the fibres (*f*) arise; 3, the inner molecular layer made up of the minute branches arising from the cells of layers 2 and 4; 4, the inner nuclear layer, containing the nuclei of the short elements which connect layers 3 and 5; 5, the outer molecular layer which is similar to layer 3; 6, the outer nuclear layer —contains the nuclei of the rod and cone elements; 7, the layer of rods (*r*) and cones (*c*); 8, the pigment layer. The rods and cones are the sensory elements. They project into the pigment layer. (From Galloway.)

third layer are large cells with a bush of protoplasmic processes and a long fibre. The fibres form a layer on the surface of the retina next the centre of the eye. They all converge to the point where the optic nerve enters the eye. It is these fibres with their medullary sheaths that constitute the optic nerve.

381. Just inside the pupil lies a double convex lens. It originates from the epidermis by an infolding. It is the densest organic structure of the body. It is fibrous in structure and of glassy transparency. The lens is enclosed in a capsule, which is attached by means of fibres to the muscular ciliary body, a portion of the choroid layer.

382. The large central cavity of the eye is filled with a transparent jelly, the vitreous humor. The smaller space in front of the iris contains a more fluid, aqueous humor.

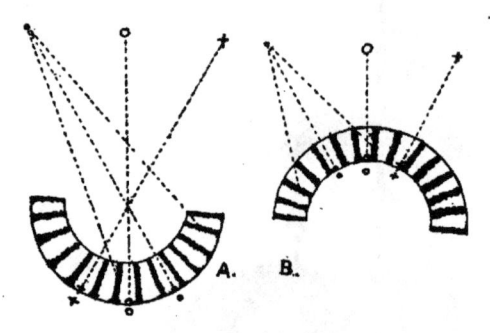

FIG. 82.—Diagrams to show how the concave and convex arrangement of the sensory elements in invertebrate eyes serves to indicate the direction of the light rays. *A*, The concave eye, like that of Patella; *B*, the convex eye, like that of the compound eyes of Arthropods.

383. **Vision.**—The simplest type of eye described doubtless enables the possessor to distinguish more readily differences in the intensity of light, such as a passing shadow. The animal would not be able, however, to distinguish one object from another by its form, since the eye is not so constructed as to form an image. Where there are a number of such eyes so placed on the body that they "look" in different directions, the stimulation of one more than another would be an indication of the direction of the source of light. In the slightly more complex eye, where the elements are arranged radially on a concave surface, there is formed a crude image, because the

arrangement of the pigment and the sensory elements determines that each element is stimulated from a particular direction. The image in this case is formed by projection. If there is a cuticular lens it is too close to the retina to form an image; it only serves to concentrate the light.

384. When the sensory elements are arranged on a convex surface as in the insect eye, an image is also formed by projection, but in this case the image is erect while in the concave eye it is inverted. However, the cuticular lens and the cone of the ommatidium are so placed that an image is formed in the plane of the retinal cells. There is, therefore, a combination of image by projection and image by refraction. This type of eye is comparatively efficient. Form is distinguished with considerable detail, and colors are recognized, but there is still a deficiency which makes the insect eye decidedly inferior to the vertebrate eye. There is no provision for focusing. It is possible that the great depth of the sensory element (the rhabdom) is in some measure a compensation; the multiplicity of eyes is another. In some cases a single eye is so constructed that one part is adapted for far vision, the other for objects near at hand.

385. In some Vertebrates (fishes) the eye is focused by moving the lens toward or away from the retina. A more refined method is adopted by the higher Vertebrates. The lens is elastic and is continually flattened somewhat by the pressure of the capsule on the anterior and posterior surfaces of the lens. By the contraction of the ciliary muscles this pressure is somewhat removed and the lens, by elasticity, assumes a more convex form.

386. In many eyes the quantity of light admitted to the sensory elements is controlled by movements in the pigment cells. When the light is too intense the pigment advances and cuts off some rays. In weak light the pigment recedes, thus admitting a broader beam of light. This adjustment is

well developed in the insect eye. In the vertebrate eye this adjustment is supplemented by a change in the size of the pupil. A circular muscle in the iris causes the pupil to contract while a set of radial muscles cause it to expand.

HEARING AND EQUILIBRATION

387. Statocysts.—Many of the lower animals have been credited with a sense of hearing, but it is very doubtful whether any aquatic invertebrate has really an organ for perceiving sound. That many aquatic animals may "feel" and respond to vibrations set up in the water is quite probable. But this may be due to the stimulation of other organs, such as the tactile sense organs. The organs found in jellyfishes, worms, crustacea, and many other aquatic invertebrates, which have been called "ear sacs," are well understood and are more properly called statocysts.

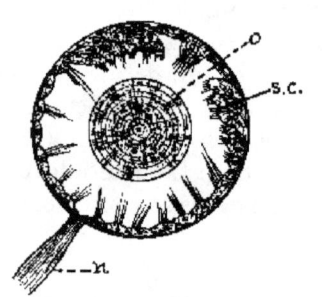

FIG. 83.—Statocyst of a Mollusc. *n*, Nerve; *o*, otolith; *s.c.*, sensory cells. (From Galloway, after Claus.)

388. In hydra there are no statocysts, nor are they found in any other fixed forms. In the hydromedusæ, however, they are very common. They consist, typically, of a deep sack-like depression of the ectoderm, which contains sensory cells and a statolith. The sack may be open or closed, but in either case is filled with a fluid. The sensory cells are provided with bristle-like processes which project into the cavity of the statocyst. The statoliths are heavy concretions of inorganic matter which stimulate the sensory cells by contact with the bristles. When the animal turns over in swimming, the statoliths, by their weight, always settle to the lower side

of the statocyst and stimulate the cells in that region. By this means the organism is informed of the orientation of its body in space.

389. No statocysts are found in either nereis or the earthworm, but they are present in some other Annelids.

390. On the upper surface of the basal portion of the antennules of the crayfish there is a small opening which leads into a statocyst. The inside of the sack is lined with sensory hairs, upon which rests the statolith. In this case the statolith is composed of grains of sand cemented together by a secretion

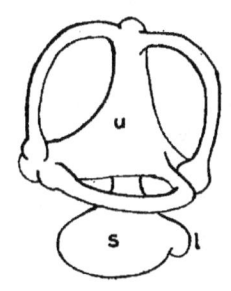

FIG. 84.—Diagram of the internal ear (labyrinth) of one of the lower vertebrates. *u*, Utriculus with three semicircular canals; *s*, sacculus; *l*, lagena.

FIG. 84*a*.—Diagram of the labyrinth of a mammal showing the cochlea.

of the epidermis. The sand is introduced into the sack by the animal itself after each ecdysis, for the lining of the sack "sheds" like the remainder of the cuticula, and its contents are cast out at the same time.

391. Statocysts are practically wanting in insects.

392. **The Vertebrate Organ of Equilibration.**—The internal ear of vertebrates consists of a membranous sack, the labyrinth, which is lined internally with a layer of cells of ectodermal origin. At certain places in this lining there are groups of sensory cells, which have a close resemblance to the sensory cells of the statocysts just described. The labyrinth is filled with a fluid and

contains a large calcareous concretion, the "ear stone," or numerous smaller particles which are called ear sand.

393. The labyrinth of the round-mouth eels is a simple ovoidal sack, but in the higher fishes the sack is partly divided into two chambers, a utriculus and a saculus, and connecting with the utriculus are three semi-circular canals, two of which are in vertical planes but at right angles to each other, while the third canal is horizontal.

394. In the higher vertebrates the utriculus with the three semi-circular canals, and the sacculus are also found, and, in essential features, the same as in the higher fishes.

395. The function of this part of the vertebrate ear is the same as that served by the statocyst of the invertebrates. It has nothing to do with hearing. It is an organ of orientation and equilibration. If the organ is destroyed or the nerve leading to it severed, the animal has difficulty in maintaining its normal upright position. A fish, for example, which has lost the use of this organ no longer swims in its normal way. It turns over and over, or may swim with its back downward.

396. **The Auditory Organ.**—The sense of hearing seems to be primarily developed in connection with voice, and it is doubtful whether there is any species in which one occurs without the other. Within the class Insecta we find the only invertebrates having sense organs for the perception of sound, and the species in which they occur best developed are our singing insects, the grasshopper, katydid, cricket, and cicada ("locust," "harvest fly," "jar fly"). The singing in these cases is usually done by the male, and is intended for the "ears" of the female. Many sounds are produced by animals, which are accidental, and cannot be called voice, as in most cases the buzzing produced by the wings in flight. At the same time the buzz of the wings may, in some cases, be used as a means of communication between individuals, in which case it would have to be regarded as voice. On the other hand, sound vibrations may be per-

ceived by sense organs other than that of hearing, hence a response to a sound is not necessarily an indication of the presence of an organ of hearing. It must also be kept in mind that other animals may make and hear sound vibrations of so high a pitch as to be inaudible to the human ear.

397. The ear of the grasshopper is called a tympanum, because of its resemblance to a drum head. It is, in fact, a thin membrane stretched over a large respiratory cavity, and is located on the side of the first abdominal segment. The katydid and cricket also have tympanums, but they are located on the tibia of the anterior legs. But in the essential points these organs are similar in structure. The sensory apparatus consists of groups of sensory cells, intimately connected with the inner surface of the tympanum. The tympanum is highly responsive to vibrations of the air, and by its own vibrations the connected sensory cells are stimulated.

398. At one side of the sacculus, in frogs and reptiles, there is a small pocket which is not found in fishes. In birds this pocket becomes a long tube, and in mammals it is very long and coiled. This is the cochlea and is the true organ of hearing. On one side of the cochlea the lining epithelium is composed of peculiarly arranged columnar cells, which form what is known as the organ of Corti. The cochlea is filled with a fluid, endolymph, like the other parts of the labyrinth. In a cross section of the organ of Corti there are several supporting cells and about four sensory cells, but in a longitudinal section there would be from 4,000 to 5,000 sensory cells, covering a space of more than 25 mm. The sensory cells are rather stout and rounded at the lower end. At the free end they each bear about twenty rod-like processes, which project into the endolymph. This organ rests on a membrane of fibres (the basilar membrane) which stretches across from the bony wall of one side to that of the other. Above the sensory cells, suspended in the endolymph, is a thick cuticular membrane (membrana tectoria),

which almost touches the processes of the sensory cells. This membrane is free at one edge, but attached at the other to a non-sensory portion of the cochlea. The nerve fibres supplying this organ end in free nerve terminations around the sensory cells. The basilar membrane becomes wider toward the apex of the cochlea, and the fibres of the basilar membrane become correspondingly longer.

399. The entire labyrinth lies in a cavity of approximately the same shape, in the petrosal portion of the temporal bone. This is the bony labyrinth. It is considerably larger than the membranous labyrinth, and the space between is filled with perilymph. A small opening in the wall of the bony labyrinth is covered by a membrane, and a small, movable bone, the stapes. By the vibrations of these parts the perilymph is disturbed and through it the fibres of the basilar membrane and thus the cells in the organ of Corti are stimulated. It is supposed that the difference in the lengths of the basilar membrane fibres corresponds to differences in the lengths of sound waves, and that, therefore, sounds of a given pitch stimulate only that part of the organ of Corti in which fibres of a corresponding length occur.

400. Certain accessory organs, by which the sound waves in the air are transmitted to the fluids of the labyrinth are found in all animals having a well-developed sense of hearing, and the condition of these organs is a very good index as to the degree of perfection of the sense itself.

401. The auricle, or shell, of the outer ear is found only in Mammals. Its function is manifestly to gather the sound waves and direct them to the auditory meatus, the tube which leads to the ear drum. The external auditory meatus is also found in Birds and some Reptiles. But in the frogs the ear drum is on a level with the surface of the head. Some Reptiles (snakes), some Amphibia (salamanders) and Fishes have neither outer nor middle ear.

THE EAR

402. The ear drum is a tightly stretched membrane, which is so constructed that it vibrates equally well with sounds of different pitch.

403. Between the ear drum and the inner ear there is a small cavity which communicates with the pharynx through the

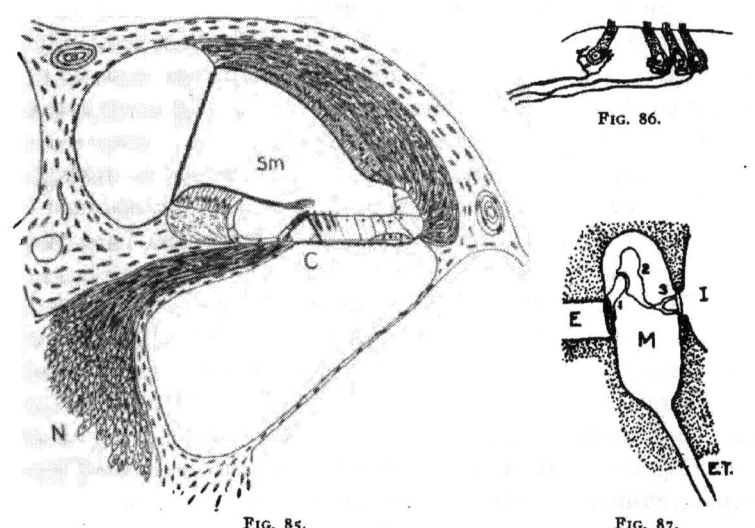

FIG. 85.

FIG. 86.

FIG. 87.

FIG. 85.—Cross section of one turn of the cochlear spiral as it lies in position in the long labyrinth. The organ of Corti (above the letter *C*) rests on the basilar membrane and nerve fibres run out to the spiral ganglion *N*.

FIG. 86.—Part of the organ of Corti, to show the sensory cells and the nerve fibres leading to the spiral ganglion.

FIG. 87.—Diagram of the middle ear of a mammal. *E*, External auditory passage, ending at the ear drum; *I*, internal ear; *M*, middle ear, opening into the pharynx by the Eustachian tube *E.T.*; 1, malleus; 2, incus; 3, stapes, fitting into the oval window.

Eustachian tube. This cavity is the middle ear. Its most important parts are three small bones, the hammer, the anvil and the stirrup, through which the vibrations of the ear drum are transmitted to the perilymph. The hammer is attached to the ear drum, the stapes fits over the opening in the bony labyrinth, and the two are connected by the anvil. In Birds and those Reptiles and Amphibia which have an ear drum the bones of the middle ear consist of one piece only, the columella.

404. **Caution.**—Our knowledge of the senses of animals is still far from complete. Since we cannot experience the sensations of another human being we can only, in a general way, infer what they are by supposing them to resemble our own. Such an assumption, with regard to the lower animals, is of little value. We have senses of which we are unconscious (the sense of the organ of equilibration and the senses of the deep lying organs mentioned above), and the lower animals may have senses which we do not have. The lateral line of Fishes, for example, is a system of sense organs by which the animal is informed of movements of the water. Many other sense organs have been found whose function is unknown.

405. **Function of the Senses.**—Concerning sense organs in general, it may be said that animals are provided with sense organs for perceiving those **changes** in the environment which might operate either to the advantage or detriment of the organism, and to which the organism is capable of making an effective response. Within the meaning of the term as used here, we are insensible to those constant elements of the normal atmosphere, oxygen, carbon-dioxide and nitrogen, although oxygen is absolutely and constantly necessary to life, while carbon-dioxide in large quantities is fatal. Nor do we possess organs for dectecting changes in the force of gravity, of atmospheric pressure or of electrical conditions, for the evident reason that either the welfare of the organism is not affected by the changes which normally occur or else that no effective response is possible.

ORGANS OF RESPONSE

406. When an animal is sufficiently stimulated a response occurs. This is usually in the form of a contraction or expan-

sion or a combination of both. Very often, however, response takes the form of glandular activity. Some times light is produced and some times an electrical discharge. The latter responses are relatively rare. We will now consider the organs of response; and first the muscles.

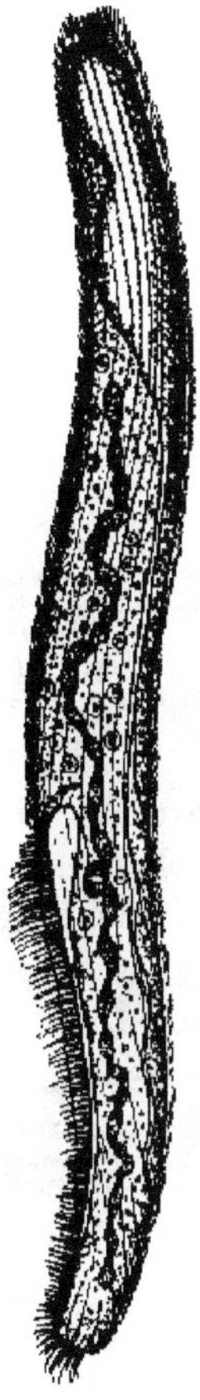

407. When an expanded amœba is strongly stimulated it contracts into a spherical mass. How this is done we do not know. It is a property of undifferentiated protoplasm in which no contractile elements of any kind can be distinguished. In some other protozoa (paramœcium and stentor) there are distinct contractile elements in the form of slender fibrils (myonemes), which traverse the ectoplasm in a longitudinal, slightly spiral direction. By their contraction they also cause the animal to assume a more nearly spherical form. Such cells contract more energetically than does the amœba.

408. In hydra, the contractile fibrils of each cell are grouped into a bundle, the muscle fibre, which is much longer than the body of the cell and projects on either side. This gives the cell the form of a T with a very short stem, representing the cell-body and the cross bar representing the fibre. The fibres of the ectoderm cells run longitudinally, while those of the entoderm run circularly around the body. In this case part of the cell remains undifferentiated and continues to form part of an epithelium. This condition is also met with in others of the lower phyla, but in the Annelids and higher forms the differentiation proceeds farther and involves the entire cell. So we find

FIG. 88.—Spirostomum, a large ciliate protozoan with longitudinal contractile fibrils (myonemes).

174   ANIMALS

that besides the epithelial layers which cover the exterior of the animal and line the internal cavities, there are also other tissues like the muscles which lie between the ectoderm and entoderm. These other tissues constitute a third layer, which is called

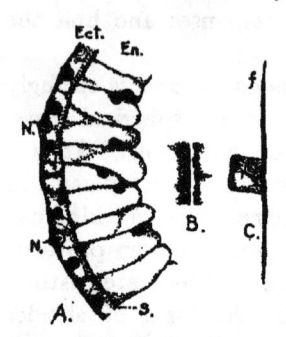

FIG. 89.—Structure of the body-wall of hydra. *A*, Part of a cross section of the column; *B*, the region between ectoderm and entoderm, more highly magnified to show the longitudinal and circular muscle fibres; *C*, diagram of an ectoderm cell with a muscle-fibre process. *Ect*, ectoderm; *En*, entoderm; *f*, muscle fibre; *N*, nematocysts; *s*, supporting layer between ectoderm and entoderm.

mesoderm (in the embryonic stage of development). This layer is entirely wanting in hydra and is not well developed in any of the Cœlenterates.

409. The muscles of the Annelids are composed of fibres, and each fibre consists of a bundle of muscle fibrils. Each

FIG. 90.—A branched muscle fibre from the wall of a blood-vessel (Nereis).

fibre has a nucleus and represents an elongated cell. The fibres taper to a point at each end and are arranged parallel in masses called muscles. In the worm the principal muscles are arranged in two sets. Just beneath the epidermis there is a thin layer which runs circularly around the body, and beneath this there are four large masses which run longitudinally, two on the dorsal side and two on the ventral.

410. The muscle systems and the integument form a hollow cylinder, which is closed at both ends and filled with a fluid, the body fluid. This constitutes a locomotor mechanism, which operates as follows: When the circular muscles contract the body becomes more slender, and must, therefore, elongate, which causes the longitudinal muscles to expand. When the longitudinal muscles contract the body is shortened and must become correspondingly thicker, which causes the circular muscles to expand. The activity of a muscle is always expressed by contraction. When it expands it is passive, the action being due to the contraction of other muscles. The worm is provided with groups of

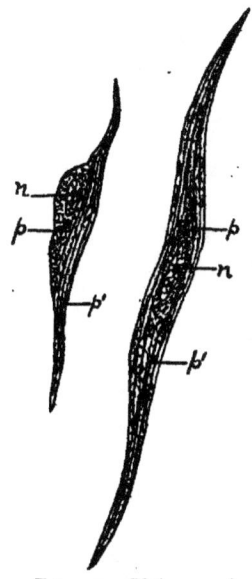

FIG. 91.—Plain muscle fibres. n, Nucleus; p, protoplasm; p', muscle fibrils.

FIG. 92.—Three muscle cells of nereis in cross section. The dots on the periphery of the cell are the muscle fibrils in cross section.

bristles (setæ) on either side of each segment. These bristles can be set forward or backward by means of small muscles connected with them. The setæ prevent slipping of the body in the direction in which they are set. If now the setæ are set backward and the circular muscles contract, the anterior end of the animal moves forward, the posterior end remaining fixed. Then, when the longitudinal muscles contract, the posterior end moves forward, and the anterior end remains fixed. A repetition of these events causes another hitch forward, and so the worm progresses by a process called inching.

411. If the setæ are set forward and the muscular contraction repeated in the same sequence as before, the animal inches backward, and practically with equal facility. This is the chief method of locomotion of the earthworm, but nereis, by wave-like contractions of the longitudinal muscles, alternately right and left, causes a serpentine movement of the body by which it creeps along. A similar mode of contraction, alternating between the dorsal and ventral muscles, causes an undulatory up and down motion by which nereis swims. The leech swims in the same way.

412. In Arthropods, the method of locomotion is totally different. Here the animal, both body and appendages, is encased in a series of rings or cylinders composed of the stiff cuticula and permitting of practically no change of form within the individual segments. However, the segments are flexibly connected with each other and provided with muscles attached in such a way that the segments may be moved with respect to each other. Thus the ambulatory appendage of the crayfish consists of six segments, connected with each other and with the body by six hinge-like joints. The muscles lie inside the cylindrical segments of integument to which they are attached and extend across the joint from segment to segment. When a muscle contracts, it flexes the appendage at the joint between the two points of attachment. The muscles are arranged in pairs at each joint, and the two muscles of a pair move the appendage in opposite directions. The appendages operate purely as levers, and locomotion is wholly due to leverage action. This is true also of the action of the tail fin, which by its powerful strokes causes the body to shoot backward. The wings of insects likewise operate as levers. In these cases the fulcrum of the leverage action is the water or air instead of the earth.

413. Locomotion in Vertebrates is similar to that of Arthropods in principle, with this important difference: The levers occupy the axis of the appendage while the muscles are attached to the surface and lie outside. A mechanical advantage is here obtained by the greater flexibility of the joints. The hinge joint, which is the only one possible in Arthropods, permits of motion in one plane only, while the ball and socket joint, which is found at many points in the vertebrate skeleton, gives universal motion.

414. The muscular tissue of the body-wall and the organs of locomotion, is composed of fibres of a complex structure. Almost the entire substance of the cell is transformed into muscle fibrils, of which there are a large number. There is also a fibre sheath which binds the fibrils together, and among the fibrils are a number of nuclei. This type of fibre is, therefore, not a uninuclear cell. The most striking characteristic of these fibres is the banded appearance which they present under the microscope. The light is affected differently at different points in the fibre so that some appear light and others dark. These points alternate regularly and give the fibre the appearance of being crossed by alternating dark and light bands. Such muscular tissue is called cross striped or striate and distinguishes the skeletal muscles of Vertebrates and Arthropods from the muscles of Worms and most other invertebrates. The heart of Vertebrates is also composed of striate muscle, but the muscles of the digestive tract and many other parts of the body are more like those of the Annelids. They are called smooth muscle fibres. Generally the cross-striped muscles are more quick and vigorous in action than the smooth muscle fibres. See Fig 101.

SKELETON AND CONNECTIVE TISSUE

415. Between the ectoderm and entoderm of hydra there is a thin layer called the supporting lamella. It is secreted by the cells of the ectoderm and entoderm, and is, therefore, not a

cellular layer. It is of a firm gelatinous substance, which probably adds to the rigidity of the body. In other Cœlenterates this layer is much thicker, and especially in jelly fishes it forms the major portion of the mass of the animal. In these cases it may contain cellular elements of various kinds, which have moved into it from the ectoderm and entoderm.

416. Worms generally have no skeleton, but special tissues are sometimes developed in connection with certain organs. The nervous system of nereis is enclosed by a thick covering of a non-cellular connective tissue.

417. The chitinous cuticula of the Arthropods forms a highly efficient exoskeleton. To this the muscles and other internal organs are attached through the medium of the epidermis and basement membrane. The latter is a thin non-cellular layer secreted by the epidermis on its inner surface.

418. In the Mollusca, also, the exoskeleton is usually extremely well developed. In this case it consists chiefly of thick layers of limey salts, deposited between the cuticula and the epidermis. This "shell" is formed only by the epidermis of a special fold of the skin called the mantle.

419. An exoskeleton is rather exceptional among Vertebrates. The scaly covering of the body of most Fishes is an excellent protective structure, but is rather too flexible to be called an exoskeleton. In the head region, however, the scales are often so intimately united as to form a real supporting shell. In special cases this shell is extended over a large portion of the body, as in the gar pike and trunk fishes.

420. The shell of the turtles is composed partly of the expanded ribs of the endoskeleton and partly of bony plates formed in the skin. The whole of the bony portion is covered by horny plates developed by the epidermis.

421. The jointed shell of the armadillo is made up of bands of dermal bone, while the covering of the scaly ant-eater is composed of large, horny scales.

THE ENDOSKELETON

422. A well-developed endoskeleton is found only in Vertebrates, but the notochord of the lancelet may be regarded as an endoskeleton of the simplest form. It is simply a rod of large turgid cells with strong cell membranes. This rod extends lengthwise of the body, immediately under the spinal cord. It is also found well developed and functional in the round-mouth eels, but in other fishes the vertebræ are

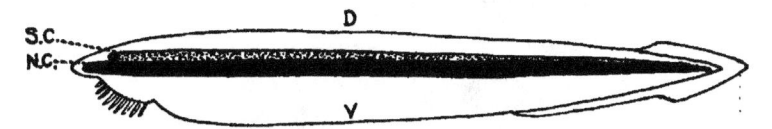

Fig. 93.—Outline drawing of the lancelet (Branchiostoma) to show the position of the notochord (*N.C.*) and the spinal cord (*S.C.*).

formed around it and take its place, though traces of it remain in the adult. In the higher Vertebrates it is formed in the embryo, but all evidence of it disappears with the development of the spinal column.

423. The first evidence of a true internal skeleton occurs in the round-mouth eels. Here small pieces of cartilage are formed around the notochord and spinal cord. These pieces do not unite to form vertebræ, but they are arranged in a series segmentally. Beneath the brain and around the pharynx a large number of similar cartilages occur. In the sharks and rays and some other fishes like the sturgeon, the skeleton is also cartilaginous, but better developed. There is a continuous column of vertebræ and a skull.

424. In the higher Fishes and all the higher classes of Vertebrates the skeleton is also, at first, cartilage, but this is gradually transformed into true bone. Certain parts of the skeleton remain cartilaginous throughout life, even in the highest forms.

425. Cartilage is composed of cells which secrete an extremely firm gelatinous substance. This substance is secreted

in such large quantities that the cells themselves come to lie far apart in the jelly. Cartilage is sometimes semi-transparent. Sometimes it contains fibres, and very often it is hardened by deposits of lime salts.

426. When true bone is formed, it either takes the place of cartilage or else is formed where no cartilage had previously existed. In the first case, the cartilage is first dissolved and in its place solid masses of lime salts are laid down, layer upon layer, by special bone-forming cells. Some cells become embedded in the bone and these are connected with each other by slender protoplasmic threads. The cells and their connecting threads form the lacunæ and canaliculæ of the dry bone. Around the blood vessels the bone is deposited in concentric layers, but elsewhere the layers are parallel with the surface of the bone. The layers are called lamellæ; the spaces occupied by the blood vessels, Haversian canals.

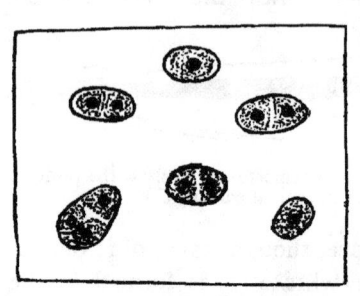

FIG. 94.—Cartilage cells lying singly, or in small groups of two or three, in the cartilage jelly which is secreted by them.

427. When the bone does not take the place of a cartilage, it is formed in connective tissue. Such bone is called membrane bone.

428. The skeleton is bound together by bands of exceedingly strong, elastic connective tissue called ligaments. They are found at the joints, binding bone to bone, so as to keep each in its place. They are not connected with the muscles.

429. The muscles are sometimes connected directly with the bones, sometimes indirectly through the medium of tendons, which are bands of inelastic connective tissue. The muscles which produce motion at a given joint must be connected

across the joint from bone to bone. But a mass of muscle around a joint would impede motion. The tendon of a muscle is not nearly so thick as the muscle, consequently where freedom of motion is important, the muscle is frequently connected

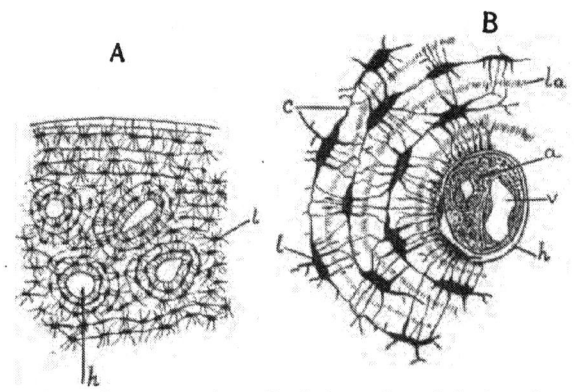

FIG. 95.—Bone, in cross section. In *A* the surface of the bone is uppermost; *B*, an Haversian system more highly magnified. *h*, Haversian canal; *l*, lacuna—the lacunæ connected by canaliculi; *a*, artery; *v*, vein; *la*, bony lamella. (From Galloway.)

at a distant point and only the tendon crosses the joint. Note, for example, that the muscles of the fingers are located in the forearm, and the tendons can be traced across the wrist and knuckle joints. The proximal point of attachment of a muscle is its

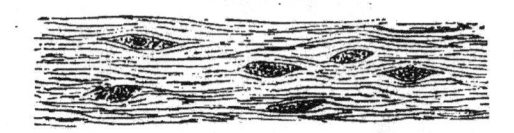

FIG. 96.—Connective tissue, showing fibrous structure and a few scattering cells.

"origin," the distal point of attachment the "insertion." The middle, thicker portion of a typical muscle (like the biceps) is the "belly." The muscle is composed of muscle fibres, arranged in bundles. The fibers of each bundle are bound together by connective tissue, and the bundles are bound in the same way to form the muscle as a whole.

430. When a muscle contracts it becomes shorter but proportionally thicker, so that its volume is not changed. At the time of contraction it also undergoes electrical and chemical changes, and heat is evolved. These subjects are discussed elsewhere.

431. The cause of a muscular contraction is in every case a stimulus. Chemical stimuli, like salts and acids, applied to the muscle, will cause a contraction. The electric current will do the same. But the normal stimulus for the body musculature of the higher animals is a nerve impulse originating in some other part of the body. The origin of this impulse is in every case to be traced to some peripheral sense organs. In some cases the impulse may seem to arise in the central nervous system, but a careful analysis will show that even in these cases the impulse can be traced backward to some sense organ.

432. The glands, luminescent organs and electrical organs are discussed elsewhere.

433. We will next consider the means by which connection is made between the sense organs and the organs of response.

THE NERVOUS SYSTEM

434. In no respect do the highest animals diverge so greatly from the lowest as in the way they respond to stimuli. This difference is due, not so much to the differences between the sense organs or the organs of response, as to the way in which the two sets of organs are related. In amœba the organs of sensation and response are identical, and no system of communication is required, but in mammals the organs of communication, the brain and spinal cord, exceed in complexity all other organs of the body combined.

435. We have seen that the muscle fibres of hydra are parts

of cells which are otherwise undifferentiated and exposed at the surface. Here, then, the stimulus received by one part of a cell is transmitted to another part of the same cell. In other Cœlenterates, some of these epithelial cells are prolonged at the deeper extremity into slender fibres, which are regarded as nerve fibres instead of muscle fibres. In this case the entire cell is nervous in function, it receives and transmits stimuli. Again, cells are found which do not reach to the surface of the epithelial layer to which they belong, and are, therefore, probably not sensory. These cells, however, are multipolar nerve cells. They serve only to transmit stimuli. We have, therefore, three types of nerve cells:

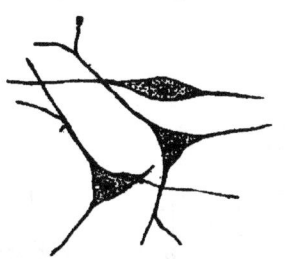

FIG. 97.—Diagram of nerve cells found beneath the ectoderm of a jelly-fish.

    1. Sensory—Transmitting—Motor.
    2. Sensory—Transmitting.
    3.   Transmitting.

While in the taste buds are found:

    4. Sensory.

436. The first class is an extremely low type of differentiation, and is not found in the sensory-motor mechanism of the higher animals.

437. In the jelly-fish many cells of type three are found, and they are largely grouped in a circle of ganglia around the edge of the umbrella. This circle of ganglia constitutes a simple central nervous system, arranged with reference to the radial organization of the animal.

438. In Annelids, the central nervous system is bilaterally arranged. There is a double ganglion in each segment, and all the ganglia are connected longitudinally by a double nerve.

184   ANIMALS

This chain of ganglia lies on the ventral side, just on the inside of the epidermis. The fibres of the sensory cells enter the ganglia through the paired lateral nerves, which spring from each ganglion and pass out to all parts of the corresponding

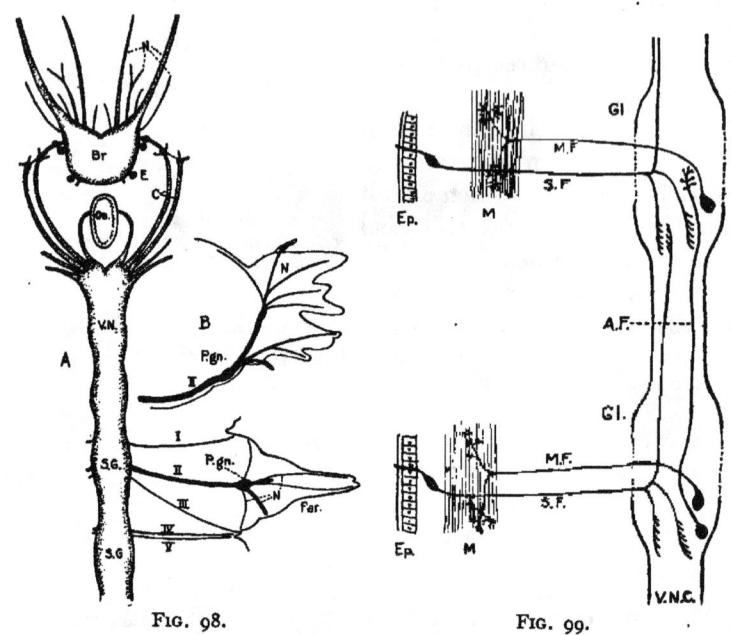

FIG. 98.   FIG. 99.

FIG. 98.—Diagram of the nervous system of nereis. *A*, The brain, ventral nerve cord, and the five nerves of a metamere; *B*, diagram of a parapodium to show the chief branches of nerve II. *Br*, Brain; *C*, circum-œsophageal connectives; *E*, eye; *N*, nerves; *Oe*, œsophagus; *Par*, parapodium; *P.gn*, parapodial ganglion; *S.g.*, segmental ganglion; *V.N.*, ventral nerve cord.

FIG. 99.—Diagram to show the relation of sensory fibres (*S.F.*), motor fibres (*M.F.*) and association fibres (*A.F.*) in a simple type of central nervous system. *Ep*, epidermis; *Gl*, ganglion; *M*, muscle; *V.N.C.*, ventral nerve cord.

segment. The ganglia contain two classes of cells: 1. Those which send fibres up and down the chain to other ganglia, but do not pass out of the central system, and 2, those which send fibres out to the other organs through the lateral nerves. In addition to the ventral nerve chain, the worm has a ganglion which is not duplicated and which serves as a centre for the entire system. This ganglion is located in the cephalic lobe, on the dorsal side of the œsophagus. It is called the brain or supra-œsophageal ganglion. It is connected with the ventral chain by a pair of connecting nerves, which pass around the œsophagus and unite with the first ventral, or sub-œsophageal ganglion. The nerves from the eyes, tentacles, cirri and other special sense organs of the head region, connect with the brain. The central nervous system of Worms is usually sharply marked off from surrounding tissues, and is enveloped in a special protective connective tissue.

439. The nerve elements are well differentiated and fall naturally into three distinct classes: 1. The sensory cells (see page 360), which are called receptors, always lie outside the central nervous system, and send a fibre into the ganglion of the corresponding segment. 2. The connecting fibres, called also association fibres, lie wholly within the central nervous system and serve as a connection between the cells of the first and third classes. The cells of these fibres lie in the ganglia. 3. Cells of the third class lie in the ganglia, but send fibres out to the muscles, glands and other organs of response. These cells are called effectors.

440. Where the receptor fibres end in the ganglia, they divide into a tuft of small branches, which end in contact with similar branches of other elements or with the body of another cell. The fibres of related cells are also often intimately connected where no branches occur. In this way, physiological connection is made between nerve cells and the stimulus transmitted from one to another. The effectors, where they end on muscles or glands, also break up into numerous small branches, which terminate in small disc-like enlargements in contact with the response organs.

441. The mechanism of response is then as follows: When a

186   ANIMALS

sense organ is sufficiently stimulated a process is set up which travels along the receptor element to the central nervous system. Here connection may be made directly with an effector element, and the stimulus pass out on another fibre to a muscle or other response organ and bring the latter into action. Or, the stimulus may be taken up by an association element,

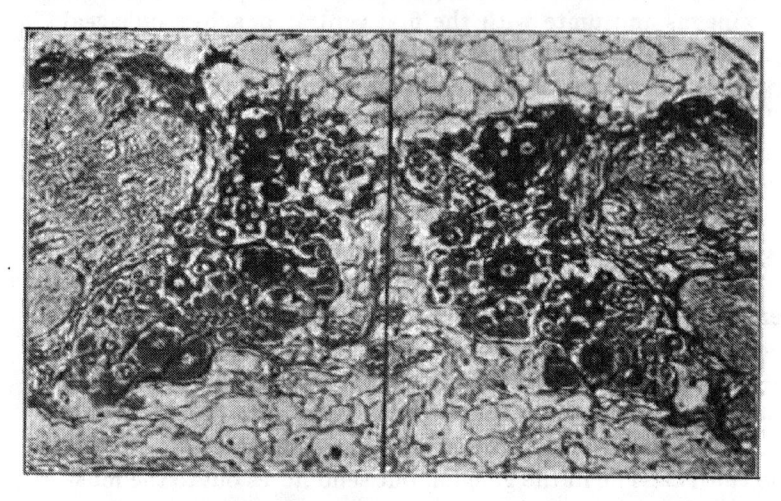

FIG. 100.—A photomicrograph of a section through the ventral edge of the brain of the crayfish. The black line represents the plane of symmetry. On either side of it are groups of ganglionic cells and, farther out, part of the circumœsophageal connectives in cross section. Among the larger cells may be distinguished at least six pairs of cells. The two cells of each pair are alike in size and exactly symmetrical in position and presumably their functions are identical with regard to the corresponding side of the body. This example seems to indicate that within the nervous system differentiation may extend to individual cells.

and through it transferred to an effector of the same or a distant ganglion. Thus a response may occur in a distant portion of the body. A stimulus originating in the periphery may first pass to the brain, and from there return to the organs of response.

442. The superiority of the nervous system of the worm over that of the Cœlenterate is evident in the more complete dif-

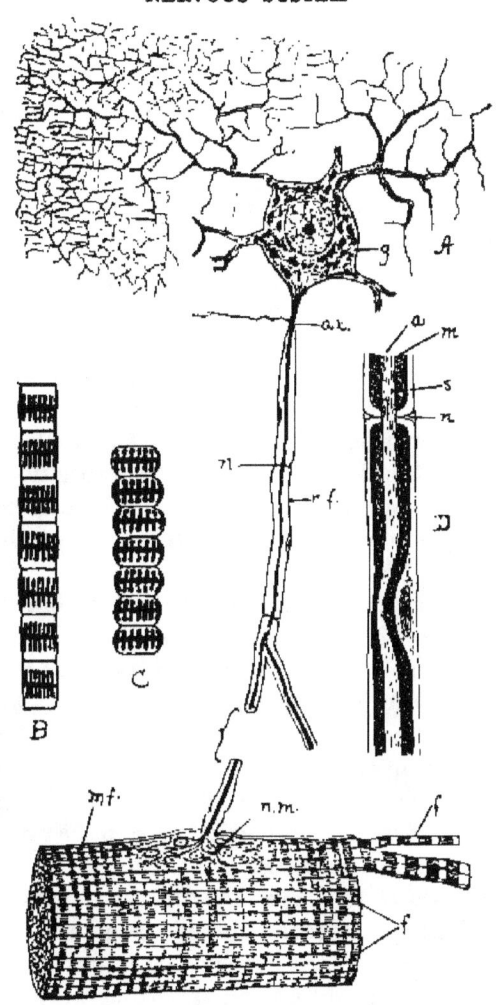

FIG. 101.—Nerve cell and striate muscle fibre. *A*, Nerve cell; *g*, the body of the cell—a ganglionic cell; *d*, dendron or dendritic process; *a.x.*, axis cylinder process or nerve fibre. At *n.f.* the fibre is covered by a medullary sheath; *n.m.*, the ending of the nerve fibre on a muscle fibre. *D*, Part of nerve fibre highly magnified; *a*, axis cylinder; *m*, medullary sheath; *s*, sheath of Schwann; *n*, node; *m.f* muscle fibre; *f*, muscle fibril. *B*, Muscle fibril highly magnified; *C*, the same in contracted condition. (From Galloway.)

ferentiation of the elements, but the more significant difference is the centralization. The brain of the worm has no counterpart in the medusæ where there are a number of centres of coordinate rank.

443. The central nervous system of Arthropods is, in most respects, much like that of Worms. The most significant difference is the better development of the brain, which results largely from the better development of the special sense organs. The differentiation of body segments and of the appendages also makes possible a much greater number of movements, and, therefore, demands greater complexity in association elements of the nervous system. Besides, the nervous system is itself subject to independent differentiation, and this manifests itself in the increased complexity of the association elements. This takes place especially in the brain or highest centre, and it is in this respect especially that the brain of the crayfish and insect is in advance of that of the worm.

444. The central nervous system of the Vertebrates is wholly dorsal and consists of the brain and spinal cord. It originates from the ectoderm as a tube, but the cavity of the tube remains extremely small, except in the region of the brain, where a series of chambers of considerable size are developed. The nerve elements develop in the walls of this tube and form a continuous ganglionic mass. The nerves are arranged segmentally, but there is little evidence of segmentation in the brain or spinal cord. In a cross section of the spinal cord the nerve cells are seen to be massed in the central portion in an area resembling a letter H. The space around this is made up of longitudinal nerve fibres, which are each one encased in a thick sheath of a fatty substance, which gives them an opaque white appearance when seen in mass. The central gray area contains naked fibres as well as cells. In the central parts of the brain there are also large masses of the cellular gray matter, but a still larger quantity of the gray is distributed over the surfaces of the folded

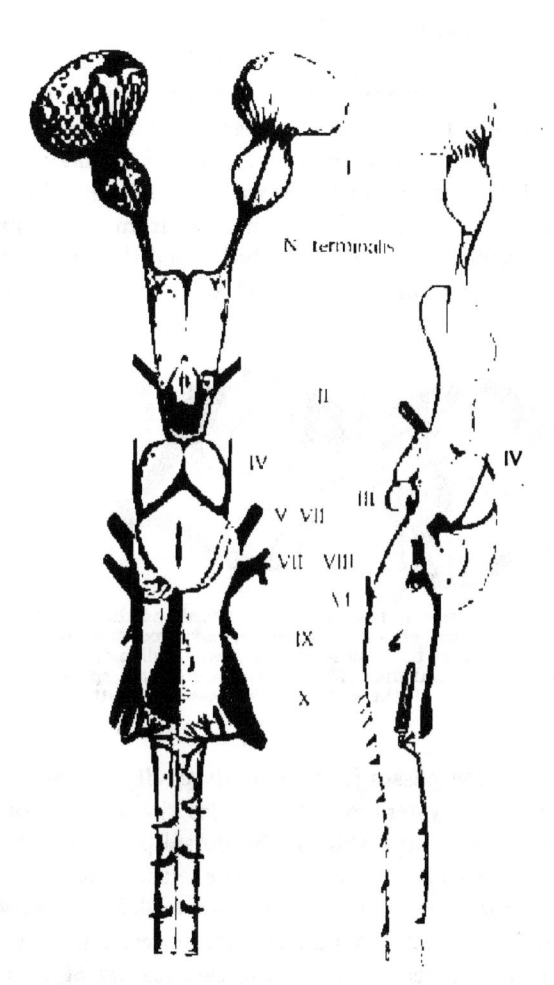

FIG. 102.—Brain of a shark, Notidanus. *A*, Dorsal view; *B.* lateral view. The roots of the nerves are represented in black. (From Johnston.)

cerebral and cerebellar regions. Hence, the surface of the brain is largely composed of the gray matter, while the fibre tracts are wholly beneath the surface. In the human body there are forty-three pairs of nerves, twelve connecting with the brain and thirty-one with the spinal cord. A typical spinal nerve is connected with the spinal cord by two "roots," one dorsal and one ventral. On the dorsal root, not far from the spinal cord, there is a ganglion, and immediately beyond the two roots unite to form the spinal nerve. The latter then divides into

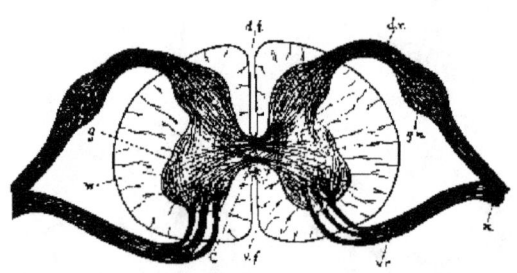

FIG. 103.—Diagram of a cross section of the spinal cord and the roots of the spinal nerves. *C*, Central canal; *df*, dorsal fissure; *dr*, dorsal root of spinal nerve, arising from the dorsal horn of the gray matter (*g*); *gn*, ganglion on the dorsal root; *n*, spinal nerve; *vf*, ventral fissure; *vr*, ventral root of the spinal nerve, arising from the ventral horn of the gray maater; *w*, white matter. (From Galloway, by Folsom.)

three main trunks; one passes into the body cavity to connect with the sympathetic system which supplies the viscera, one passes up to the muscles and skin of the dorsal portion of the body, and the last turns downward to the muscles and skin of the ventral portion of the body. Both dorsal and ventral branches contain both receptor and effector fibres, but at the juncture of dorsal and ventral roots the two classes of fibres separate, the effectors pass over the ventral root and the receptors pass over the dorsal root. The cells of the receptors lie in the spinal ganglion of the dorsal root, while the cells of the effectors lie in the ventral horn of the gray matter in the cord.

445. The spinal nerves are quite uniform in their relations so far as described above, but the cranial nerves are considerably modified. The olfactory (I) and optic (II) nerves are not comparable with spinal nerves at all. The III, IV, and VI go to the muscles of the eye ball and contain no receptor elements. The VIII nerve is the auditory and is purely receptor. The V and VII nerves supply the skin and muscles of the face and lower jaw, and are mixed in function. The IX nerve supplies the muscles and sense organs of the tongue (taste) and pharynx, and is also mixed. The X nerve supplies the viscera from the pharynx to the liver, including larynx, lungs, œsophagus and stomach and heart. It is also a mixed nerve. The XI and XII are chiefly effector in function; they supply chiefly muscles of the neck region.

ENERGY RELATIONS OF THE ANIMAL

446. When an animal puts itself in motion, work is being done, as is the case when any other body is being moved, and when work is being done there is an expenditure of energy. However, throughout its life the animal is continually moving itself as well as other bodies, and hence, as constantly expending energy. And for a considerable portion of its life its capability of expending energy increases, even though energy is constantly being spent. Now, a fundamental postulate of physics says that energy is never created, but that wherever it appears it has merely been transformed or transferred from some other source. The animal may be exhausted temporarily and yet after a while its power of expending energy is renewed. And we know that the condition upon which this renewal of energy depends is the supply of proper food to the organism. Thus the food is apparently the energy source for the animal.

447. If we analyze the foods of animals we find that the most important by far, for their energy-yielding value, as food, are

the carbohydrates and fats. We also know that these substances may be readily made to yield energy by heating them in the presence of oxygen. The carbohydrates are then decomposed and their constituents unite with oxygen to form carbon-dioxide and water. This union produces heat, which is a form of energy.

448. The wood in the firebox of an engine is a case where $C_6H_{10}O_5 + 6O_2 = 6CO_2 + 5H_2O$. The heat liberated in this process is taken up by the water, which, because of the added energy, expands into stem. The energy of the enclosed steam is evident in the pressure which it exerts, and by means of the mechanism of the engine, the pressure energy is transformed into the motion of piston, crankshaft and wheels. Thus the oxidation of the fuel releases the energy which causes the engine to move and do work. Fats and oils, $C_mH_n(O)$ when burned yield CO_2 and H_2O and energy is also set free in the same way.

449. That in these processes it is a question of liberation rather than the creation of energy becomes clear if we consider the origin of the substances. The carbohydrates, we will recall, were formed in the leaf from CO_2 and H_2O, through the agency of chlorophyll and light. But light is a form of energy whose source is the sun. In some way the energy of the ether vibrations breaks up the CO_2 molecule and the carbon atom unites with the H_2O molecule, producing, as a final result, starch ($C_6H_{10}O_5$), sugar, cellulose, oil, proteid or other carbon compound. These substances remain stable at ordinary temperature, but when slightly heated they break down, and the C then unites with the O and the energy which was stored up in photosynthesis is again set free. In physical terms, the energy of the light becomes potential energy in the chemical compound, and again kinetic energy of heat in combustion.

450. The processes by which the food yields energy to the animal are closely analogous to the case of the fuel in the

steam engine, but it will be necessary to point out some differences and show how the animal engine works.

451. In the first place, the animal "fire box" is not the stomach or lungs or any similar organ. The combustion takes place in the cells and each individual cell of the animal body is a unit so far as this process is concerned. Some cells require more fuel than others in proportion as some are greater workers than others. Consequently the muscle cells require much fuel. But how does the food get to the muscle cells? That is another question, and to make it clear we will return to the case of the amœba.

452. **Digestion.**—When the amœba comes in contact with a particle of food its protoplasm flows around the particle until it is entirely enclosed and lies embedded in the protoplasm, but with the particle there is also engulfed a droplet of water. This is called a food vacuole. The water in which the amœba lives is always slightly alkaline and the protoplasm of the amœba is also alkaline, but if delicate test is made it is found that the water or fluid of the food-vacuole becomes slightly acid and soon changes may be observed in the food particle. If it was a living object it soon dies; if it was a blue green alga, the blue color is rapidly diffused into the surrounding medium. The vacuole becomes alkaline, and the food substance becomes translucent as though it were being dissolved, and gradually it disappears. Probably some portions remain unchanged. The vacuole grows smaller until the unchanged portions of the ingested object are closely surrounded by protoplasm. Finally, what remains in the food vacuole is ejected. While this has been going on, other food vacuoles have been formed and the same series of phenomena take place in each. All the while the animal is growing larger at the expense, evidently, of the substance of the food-vacuoles. It is important to note that the food substance of the vacuoles disappears and later reappears as protoplasm. Between these

two stages there is a stage when this substance is invisible in solution, and it is during this stage that it passes from the vacuole into the protoplasm.

453. Let us recall the phenomena of fermentation as exhibited by the yeast plant or bacteria. Here we have living cells enclosed in a membrane, through which no visible particle is known to pass. The bacteria live in a watery medium surrounded by solid substances, upon which they are nourished. In the medium there appear substances which are secreted by the living cells and which act upon the food substances in such a way as to cause them to go into solution. This process may come about in many different ways, but the result is always a solution which may be absorbed by the cell through the membrane. The chief difference between the bacteria and the amœba, with respect to the way in which the food is prepared, so that it may be absorbed, is this: The bacteria fill the surrounding medium with an enzyme which dissolves the food substances there. The amœba takes into its body a droplet of the medium containing a particle of food, and into this droplet of the medium it secretes a digestive fluid. We may transpose terms and say that the bacteria digest the food before it is taken into the body and the amœba carries on a process of fermentation within its food-vacuoles. That is to say, digestion is a matter of fermentation.

454. The term gastro-vascular cavity applied to the central cavity of hydra indicates that it is analogous to the stomach, and hence, concerned in digestion. The food unquestionably passes into this cavity, but to what extent it is there digested is uncertain. Small particles are known to be captured by the flagellate cells of the entoderm and engulfed by the protoplasm. So that in this case as well as in Sponges and some Flat-worms the digestion resembles that of amœba. In this case the function of the gastro-vascular cavity would be to serve as a sort of trap for the food particles. But frequently objects are captured

and swallowed which are much too large to be taken up by a cell. In the sea anemone such objects undergo partial disintegration in the gastro-vascular cavity, and the fragments are taken up by the cells. The hydra lacks the organs by which this is accomplished by the anemone, but it is still probable that the close application of the walls of hydra to the prey may accomplish the same end. The undigested portions of the food are cast out at the mouth.

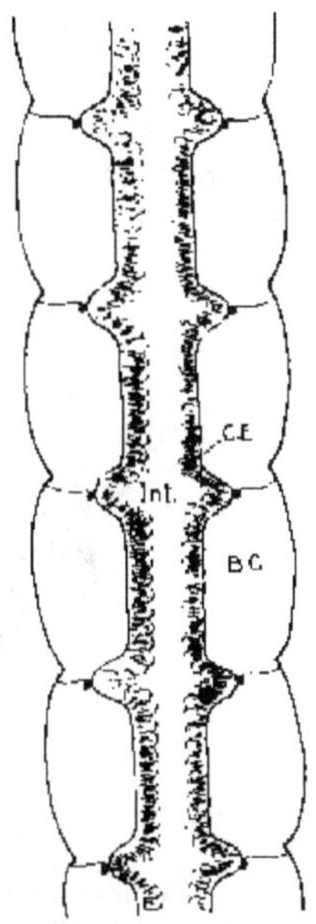

455. The elongated form of the body of the worm makes possible a considerable advance in the digestive system. The digestive cavity is a slender tube opening to the exterior at each end. The food is taken in at the mouth, and as it passes slowly along the narrow channel it is gradually digested and absorbed. The parts that remain undigested are cast out at the vent. The elongated form makes possible the successive application of different agencies of digestion to a given particle and the simultaneous operation of these agencies in different parts of the canal. In nereis there are jaws and denticles by which the food is captured and forced into the mouth, and perhaps, to some extent, lacerated. There is a pair of "salivary" glands which open into the anterior end of the digestive tract and throughout the remainder of its length the intestinal epithelium is thickly studded with unicellular glands, which also pour a secretion into the digestive cavity. In the earthworm the digestive canal is more differentiated.

FIG. 104.—The intestine of a worm (nereis) showing segmentation and folding of the glandular epithelium. The body-wall is represented in outline. B.C., Body cavity; C.E., glandular epithelium; Int, intestine.

456. In Worms we have unquestionably a case of a true

198   ANIMALS

digestive cavity, into which the digestive enzymes are secreted, in which digestion takes place and from which the soluble products are then absorbed. The long digestive tube gives a large absorbing surface, but in some cases, as in the earthworm, the surface is further increased by a longitudinal fold which hangs from the dorsal side of the canal and gives the lumen of the canal a crescentic form in cross section. The

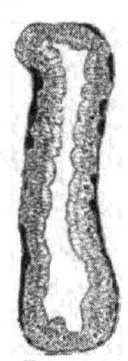

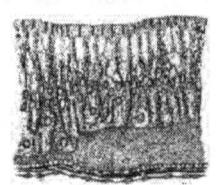

Fig. 105. Fig. 106. Fig. 107.

Fig. 105.—Cross section of the intestine of nereis showing the glandular epithelium and blood capillaries (black).

Fig. 106.—A part of the preceding figure enlarged. The upper two-thirds of the figure is the epithelium. Below that is a blood capillary. Then follows a layer of longitudinal muscle fibres cut across and a layer of circular muscle fibres lying in the plane of the section. The lower layer is an extremely thin epithelium lining the outer surface of the intestine.

Fig. 107.—A surface view of the inner surface of the intestinal epithelium. The cells are outlined by a network of supporting fibres.

salivary glands are a simple type of a compound gland. The glandular epithelium is pushed outward into the body cavity and is greatly folded so that a large glandular surface occupies a small space. The part by which the gland is connected with the intestine forms a duct through which the secretion is poured into the digestive cavity. In nereis the greater part of digestion is doubtless due to the activity of the unicellular glands.

457. The glandular intestinal epithelum is only a lining of a

tube which is composed largely of muscle fibres. The muscles by peristaltic contraction force the contents of the canal slowly backward. They also regulate the size of the canal as the volume of the contents may demand.

Fig. 108.—Wall of the intestine in a small aquatic Annelid, Chætogaster. There are only two thin layers of cells, one (*a*) which forms the lining of the body cavity and (*b*) the intestinal epithelium.

458. The separation of the digestive processes advances a step farther in Arthropods and the digestive tract is divided into well-defined regions. In the crayfish there are, in the immediate region of the mouth, six pairs of segmental appendages which are modified for grasping and tearing up the food.

Fig. 109.—A section through one of the folds of the intestinal epithelium of nereis, showing a few of the glandular cells. The inner ends of the greatly elongated cells are filled with a granular secretion. The accumulation of the secreted substance in the ends of the cells causes them to swell and hence throws the surface into folds.

From the mouth a short œsophagus leads into a large muscular stomach, which consists of two divisions. The first is lined with chitin and is provided with a mechanism consisting of several chitinous hooks or teeth and a set of muscles for operating them. By means of this the food is still further broken up. A pair of large digestive glands lying in the body cavity

200   ANIMALS

communicate with the second smaller portion of the stomach by means of short ducts. Digestion proper takes place in this portion of the digestive tract. A narrow intestine of simple structure leads to the vent at the posterior end of the abdomen.

459. The function of salivary glands is primarily to moisten the food preparatory to swallowing. Consequently they are only necessary in terrestrial animals. The so-called salivary glands of nereis owe their name to their position and

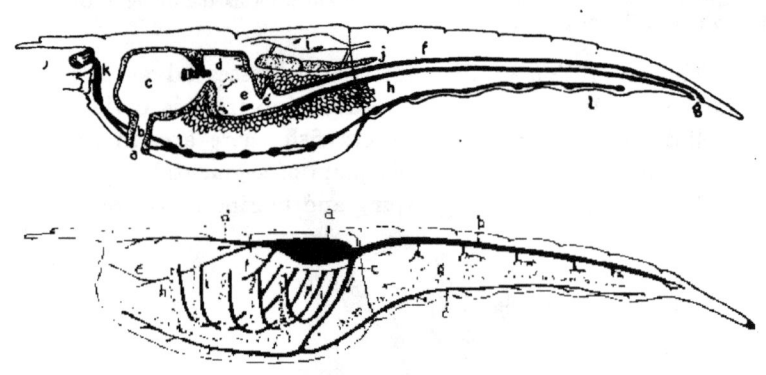

FIG. 110.—Digestion and circulatory systems of the crayfish. Upper figure: *a*, Mouth; *,b* œsophagus; *c*, cardiac portion of stomach; *d-ê*, pyloric portion of stomach; *e*, opening of digestive gland; *f*, intestine; *g*, vent; *h*, digestive gland ("liver"); *i*, heart; *j*, gonad; *k*, brain; *l, l*, ventral nerve cord. Lower figure: *a*, Heart; *b*, dorsal abdominal artery; *c*, sternal artery which branches into the ventral abdominal and the ventral thoracic arteries; *d*, ophthalmic artery; *e*, antennary artery; *f*, hepatic artery; *g*, blood sinuses; *h*, afferent branchial vessels; *i*, efferent branchial vessels.

must not be supposed to be in any sense true salivary glands. No such glands occur in the crayfish, but in the terrestrial Arthropods, the Insects, they are generally found. The mouth parts in Insects consist of three pairs of appendages. There is an œsophagus, into which the salivary glands open. Sometimes the œsophagus is enlarged to form a crop. Sometimes there is also a gastric mill analogous to that of the crayfish. Then follows the true stomach which has numerous small glands embedded in its thick walls or else there are larger glands lying outside the stomach wall, but connected with it by ducts. From the stomach the digestive tract continues, first as a slender "small intestine" which farther on expands into a wider "large intestine." The latter ends at the vent.

460. Quite generally the digestive tract of Vertebrates is differentiated into the following series of parts; buccal cavity, œsophagus, stomach, small intestine, and large intestine. Its walls are very muscular, especially those of the stomach and small intestine. The internal surface area is greatly increased by folds and countless minute thread-like elevations, the villi. The teeth with which the mouth is usually armed serve either for seizing and swallowing the prey or for mastication.

461. The digestive glands are numerous and large. In man there are three pairs of large salivary glands, besides a number of smaller ones, which open into the buccal cavity. But for Vertebrates the general statement also applies, that salivary glands are characteristic only of terrestrial forms. Besides moistening the food for swallowing it the saliva also sometimes seems to soften it preparatory to digestion (birds). In herbivorous animals the saliva often contains an amylolytic ferment, ptyalin. Embedded in the thick walls of the stomach are numerous small tubular glands which secrete gastric fluid. This contains hydrochloric acid and a proteolytic ferment, pepsin.

462. A gland of considerable size, the pancreas, opens into the intestine near the stomach. Its secretion contains three ferments, one, amylopsin, is amylolytic; another, trypsin, is proteolytic, and a third, steapsin, decomposes fats into glycerine and fatty acids. There are also numerous small glands embedded in the wall of the intestine, which are said to secrete the ferment, invertin, which is found in the intestine and which inverts maltose into glucose.

463. Amylolytic ferments are not all alike. That is, there are

202 ANIMALS

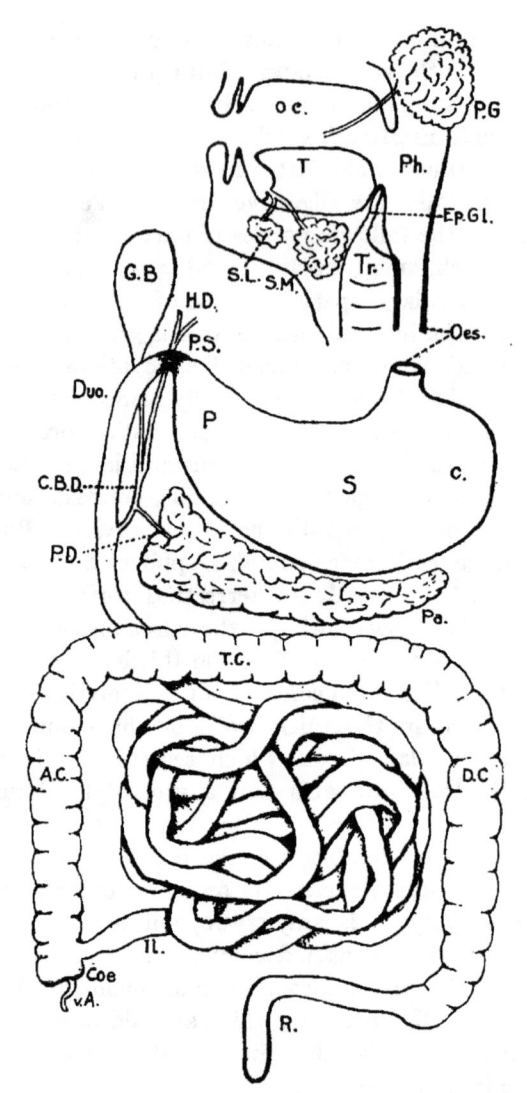

Fig. 111.—Diagram of the digestive tract of man. *A.C.*, Ascending colon; *C*, cardiac portion of the stomach; *C.B.D.*, common bile duct; *Cæ*, cæcum;

a number of substances, derived from different sources, which have the power of changing starch into sugar, but produce this result under different conditions. This indicates a difference in constitution of the ferments. The same is true of the proteolytic ferments, for example, pepsin and trypsin are both proteolytic, but the one in acid media, the other in alkaline, and in Cephalopods there is a ferment which resembles both of these. Generally, in higher animals, there are more kinds of ferments, but each is more circumscribed in its action. Conversely, in the lower forms, the ferments are fewer in kind but more general in action. So there is apparently in the higher animals a differentiation of ferments to correspond with the structural differentiation of the digestive tract.

464. In the food vacuole of amœba the medium first becomes acid but later, at the time when the food particles are disintegrating, the reaction is alkaline. Proteolytic and amylolytic ferments are present, and these seem to vary with different types of Protozoa and the exact nature of those found in amœba is not certainly known.

465. The fluid of the gastro-vascular cavity of Cœlenterates has no amylolytic powers. There is a slight proteolytic action which probably serves to dissociate large objects so that the particles may be ingested by the entodermal cells.

466. The digestive fluids of the earthworm and nereis are both tryptic and diastatic. The earthworm covers leaves it means to swallow with saliva and allows them to digest for some time before swallowing them.

467. The digestive gland of the crayfish has strong proteolytic and amylolytic action in both acid and alkaline media. Hence, it resembles both gastric and pancreatic digestion of

---

D.C., descending colon; *Duo*, duodenum; *Ep. Gl.*, epiglottis; *G.B.*, gall bladder; *H.D.*, hepatic duct; *Il*, ileum; *OC*, oral cavity; *Oes*, œsophagus; *P*, pyloric portion of the stomach; *Pa*, pancreas; *P. D.*, pancreatic duct; *Ph*, pharynx; *P.G.*, parotid gland; *R*, rectum; *S*, stomach; *S.L.*, sublingual gland; *S.M.*, submaxillary gland; *T*, tongue; *T.C.*, transverse colon; *Tr*, trachea; *v.A.*, vermiform appendix.

Vertebrates. In the cockroach the salivary glands have an amylolytic action. The intestinal fluids have amylolytic, proteolytic and inverting action, and the reaction is neutral and alkaline.

468. **Circulation.**—However simple or complicated the digestive processes may be, the result is essentially the same. The end finally attained is food substances prepared for absorption. This is a function entirely distinct from digestion, and since each cell must absorb food for itself, little differentiation is to be looked for in connection with this function. However, only those cells can absorb which are in contact with the food, i. e., the cells lining the digestive tract. Those farther removed must receive their portion from those nearer the source. In hydra no cell is more than one cell removed from the seat of digestion, for the gastro-vascular cavity extends to all parts of the body, even to the tips of the tentacles, and whether digestion takes place in the gastro-vascular cavity or in the entodermal cells the ectoderm cells are only one cell layer removed.

FIG. 112.—A view of the outer surface of the intestine of nereis, showing a network of blood capillaries and two sets of slender muscle fibres crossing each other at right angles.

469. In the smallest Annelids the intestinal wall is very thin. The same is true of the body wall, and the two are separated by a space, the body cavity, which is filled with a fluid ("body fluid"). This body fluid nourishes the tissues bathed by it and it is constantly replenished by the substances absorbed by the intestine. The movements of the animal force the body fluid about so that it becomes throughly mixed and freshly absorbed matter is thus directly brought to the farthest tissues of the body.

470. In the larger worms, however, the tissues are often so

CIRCULATION

thick that the deeper lying cells would be starved by such a method of food distribution. Moreover, the wall of the digestive tract is so thick that it would greatly impede the transfer of absorbed food to the body fluid. There is, therefore, necessary a system of channels by which the food may more readily be transferred from the seat of digestion to the place of assimila-

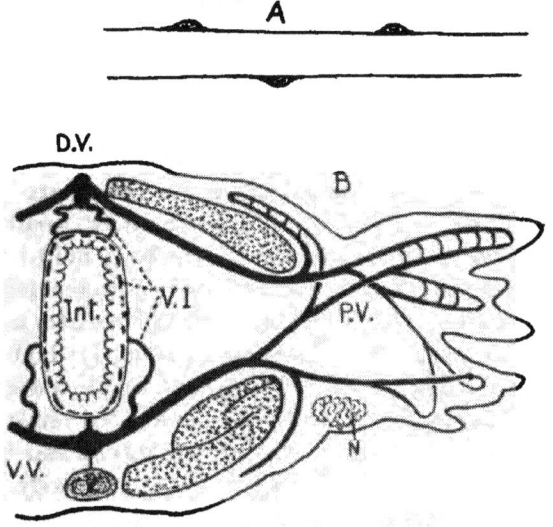

FIG. 113.—The circulatory system of annelids. *A*, A longitudinal section of a blood-vessel of a small fresh-water annelid (Chætogaster) showing extremely thin walls. *B*, Cross section diagram of nereis to show the arrangement of the vessels; *D.V.*, dorsal vessel; *Int*, intestine; *N.* nephridium; *P.V.*, parapodial vessels; *V.I.*, intestinal vessels and capillaries; *V.V.*, ventral vessel. All vessels black.

tion. These channels consist of a network of tubes of extremely small calibre, which penetrate to every part of the intestinal wall, immediately outside the intestinal epithelium. Larger vessels lead from this network of capillaries to a much larger vessel which runs longitudinally along the mid-dorsal line of the body. In each segment branches of the dorsal vessel lead out laterally to the muscles, epidermis and all other organs of the body, where they divide into another network of capillary vessels, through which the blood is distributed to all the tissues. From this second system of capillaries larger vessels lead to another large, longitudinal vessel lying between the ventral nerve cord and the intestine. This vessel is connected with the intestinal system of capillaries, and thus a complete circuit is formed. The larger vessels are muscular, and by their rhythmical contraction the blood is forced along. This is especially true of the dorsal longitudinal vessel, in which a continuous series of contractions pass forward from posterior to anterior, forcing the blood along in the same direction. In the ventral longitudinal vessel the blood flows from anterior to posterior.

471. In the system just described the vessels are "closed"; that is, they do not open into the body cavity, and they contain blood, which is not the same as the body fluid. In many invertebrates, however, the body cavity forms a part of the system of spaces through which the blood circulates and in this case there is no distinction of blood and body fluid. This is the type of circulatory system found in Crustacea and Insects. A part of the dorsal vessel is much enlarged and very muscular. By its contraction the blood is forced forward and backward through branching vessels to all parts of the body. On its return the blood enters large spaces, which represent the body cavity and thus it reaches a space immediately surrounding the heart, the pericardial cavity. The heart is pierced by six or eight pairs of openings guarded by valves. When the heart expands the blood enters by these openings (ostia), but when it contracts the closing of the valves prevents the return of the blood through the ostia. It is therefore forced out through the vessels. (See Fig. 110.)

472. In Vertebrates the circulatory system is always closed and the heart is developed into a powerful pumping organ with two, three or four chambers. From the intestine the absorbed food is first carried to special organs in which it undergoes

CIRCULATION 207

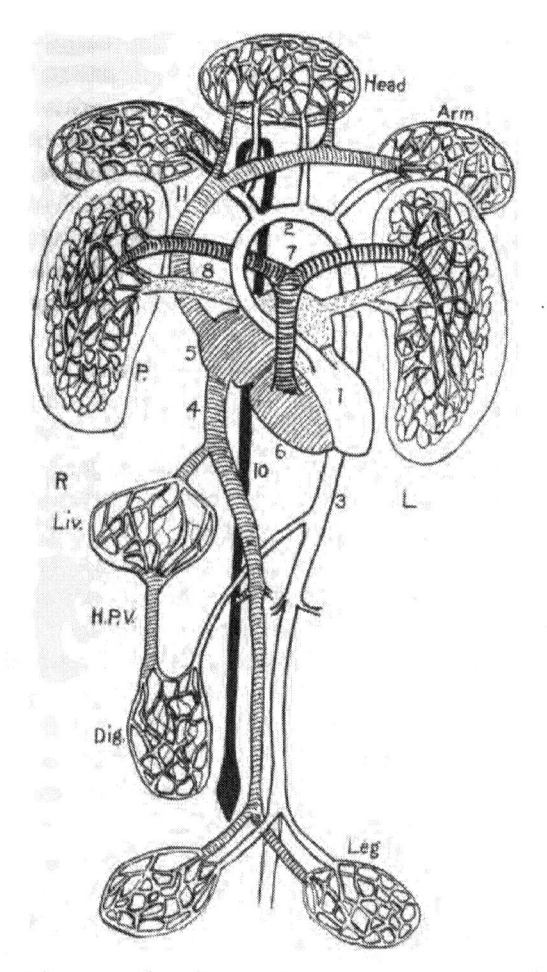

Fig. 114.—Diagram to show the general plan of the circulation in mammals. 1, Left ventricle; 2, aortic arch; 3, dorsal aorta; 4, postcaval vein; 5, right auricle; 6, right ventricle; 7, pulmonary artery; 8, pulmonary veins (the pulmonary veins open into the left auricle which in turn opens into the left ventricle). The order of the numbers 1–8 indicates the course taken by the blood in completing a circuit of the systemic and pulmonary circulations. 10, the thoracic (lymphatic) trunk; 11, precaval vein. *Dig.*, The digestive tract; *H.P.V.*, hepatic portal vein; *Liv*, liver; *P*, lung.

further changes before it is admitted to the general circulation. The carbo-hydrates and peptones are collected by the hepatic portal vein and carried to the liver, where certain substances are absorbed and ultimately pass back into the intestine. This occurs in the case of some substances which would be deleterious if permitted to pass into the general circulation. Excess carbo-hydrates are also stored temporarily in the liver and other organs in the form of glycogen. The fats are broken up into fatty acids and glycerine, and then, after absorption, resynthesized as fats of a different kind in the cells of the mucous epithelium. They finally appear as globules in the lacteal capillaries of the villi and thus come into the blood through the thoracic duct.

473. Fats are also stored, sometimes in large quantities, and represent a large reserve of energy. They are usually found in the connective tissues, under the skin, among the muscles, covering the visceral organs and elsewhere. From the liver the absorbed food materials get into the circulation through the inferior vena cava, while the lacteals pour their contents into the thoracic duct and thus into the left sub-clavian vein.

474. So long as the nourishing fluids remain in the blood vessels they can be of no service to the tissues. But the walls of the capillaries are so thin that the fluid portion of the blood can seep through. In this way the lymph arises which is found in all the living tissues of the body, filling the minute spaces between the cells. Fresh supplies of lymph are continually escaping from the capillaries and the impoverished lymph drains off out of the lymph spaces into the lymph vessels, which finally empty into the thoracic duct. Thus the lymph enters the circulation agin.

RESPIRATION

475. When the fuel is consumed in the firebox, to return to the analogy of the steam engine, there must be free access of

air, specifically the oxygen of the air. Otherwise the combustion will not continue, the fire will die out, and the engine finally come to a standstill. An animal also, when deprived of air, soon goes into a quiescent state, and when active, the amount of air required varies with the energy expended. The living animal is also continually evolving CO_2, and that, too, in proportion to the energy expended. It is evident, therefore, that there is combustion, or oxidation of carbon, going on in the organism. It is known that this process takes place in the tissues, i. e., in the cells, and we must, therefore, account for the presence of oxygen in the tissues.

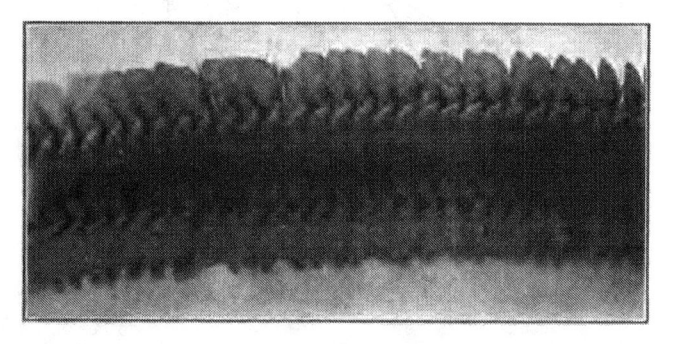

FIG. 115.—Part of the body of nereis, showing the respiratory organs. The broad superior ligula of the dorsal ramus of each parapodium has a thin integument and is richly supplied with blood-vessels.

476. Amœba and many other organisms can absorb enough oxygen through the general surface of the body. Even comparatively large animals, because of their form and peculiarity of structure, can obtain enough oxygen in this way. The sea-anemone, for example, though comparatively large, exposes not only the external surface of the body and tentacles, but the much larger folded surface of the gastro-vascular cavity is exposed to the water, which is being continually renewed by currents passing in and out of the mouth. Even the frog, when

210   ANIMALS

quiescent, may have its demands for oxygen satisfied by absorption through the skin. But the more compactly built animals, even when not large, are provided with special organs for the absorption of oxygen. The earthworm is among the largest of animals destitute of such organs. But the earthworm is unable to absorb enough oxygen when in water and will ultimately drown. Nereis possesses a pair of flat plates in

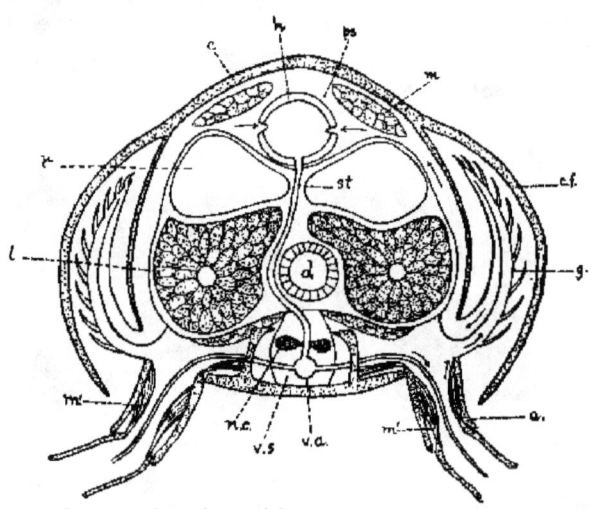

FIG. 116.—Cross section of crawfish in the thoracic region. *a*, Appendage; *c*, carapace; *cf*, part of carapace covering the gill chamber; *d*, digestive tract; *g*, gill; *h*, heart; *l*, liver; *m*, *m'*, muscles; *n.c.*, nerve cord; *p.s.*, pericardial sinus; *r*, gonad; *st*, sternal artery; *va*, ventral artery; *vs*, ventral blood sinus. (From Galloway, after Lang.)

each segment, one on each parapodium, which are richly supplied with capillaries lying very near the surface. These supplement the general body surface in the absorption of oxygen. Even here the worm feels the necessity of keeping the water in motion in order to bring in fresh supplies of oxygen. When the animal is at rest the body keeps up a rhythmical undulating movement by which the water is kept in motion.

477. The crayfish bears under a fold of the carapace, on either side, a large number of brush-like gills, composed essentially of numerous slender thin-walled filaments, through which the blood constantly circulates. There is also a special structure in the form of a curved paddle or spoon, which by its motion keeps the water constantly moving through the gill chamber. This highly efficient set of organs evidently makes good the deficiency in absorbing power of the body surface resulting from the impervious cuticular integument.

478. In Insects, a unique method of aerating the body has developed. The air is carried to all parts of the body by an intricate system of slender tubes, tracheæ, which open on the surface through small pores in the integument, the stigmata. The air is forced into and out of these tubes by a telescoping action of the rings of the abdomen.

479. In Fishes, the gills are not unlike those of the crayfish, but the water current is produced in a different way. The water is first taken into the pharynx through the mouth, and from the pharynx it passes through a series of slits between the arches which bear the gills. A pair of delicate membranes at the mouth serve as valves and cause a flow of water, always in the same direction, to result from merely opening and closing the mouth.

FIG. 117.—Diagram of a feather-like gill. This type is found in the crayfish.

480. In a few fishes and in the adult stage of all other Vertebrates, a pair of air sacks or lungs take the place of the gills of the fish. In the lower forms the lungs are comparatively simple, the inner surface of the air sacks being, at most, somewhat folded. In the birds and mammals, however, they become exceedingly complex, through the folding of the walls to increase the absorbing surface. The lung first appears as a

pocket in the ventral wall of the digestive tract in the region of the pharynx. This pocket divides into two branches which develop into the right and left lungs. Each branch divides many times so that a very complicated system of tubes is formed. The air tubes are thin walled and a network of blood capillaries closely surrounds them.

481. **Inspiration in the Amphibia and a few Reptiles is a process analogous to swallowing.** But in most Reptiles and in

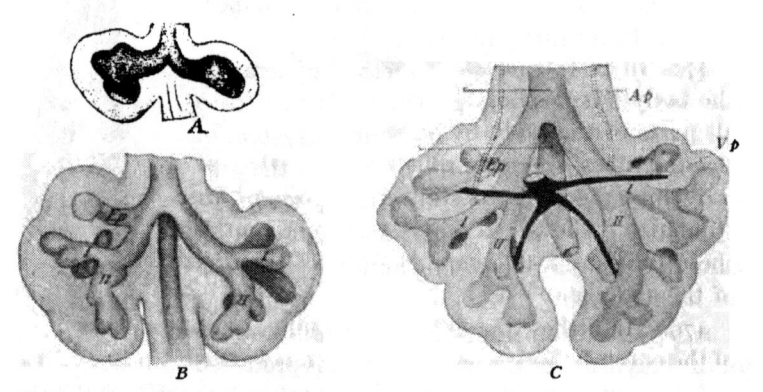

FIG. 118.—Three early stages in the development of a mammalian lung. In B the alimentary canal is shown extending upward directly above the letter B. Ep, I, and II, the bronchial tubes. Ap, pulmonary artery; Vp, pulmonary veins. (McMurrich, after His.)

Birds and Mammals the air is forced into the lungs by atmospheric pressure upon muscular expansion of the thoracic cavity. The latter is brought about by elevation of the ribs and, in Mammals, by depression of the dome-shaped diaphragm.

482. **The course which the blood takes may or may not have a fixed relation to the respiratory organs.** In Worms and Crustacea some blood is continually being oxygenated, and this, mingling with the rest, is sufficient for the needs of the animal. In Fishes, all the blood passing through the heart is forced through the gills and then passes on to the tissues of the body.

In Frogs and Reptiles the oxygenated blood coming from the lungs and that coming from the other tissues of the body mingle to some extent in the heart, and this mixed blood is then supplied to the tissues of the body. In Birds and Mammals again, through the complete separation of the respiratory and systemic circulation, all blood passes alternately through the lungs and the body tissues.

483. Oxygen is taken up by the blood as air is absorbed by water, but in most animals, excepting Insects, there is a substance present in the blood which has a special affinity for oxygen. In some cases, especially among invertebrates, this substance forms part of the blood plasma; in others, including all Vertebrates, it resides in certain cells floating in the blood, the red blood corpuscles. In either case it gives the characteristic color to the blood. In some invertebrates, the earthworm, for example, and all Vertebrates, the substance is red and contains iron. In other cases, some Crustacea and some Mollusca, the substance is blue and contains copper. The first is called hæmoglobin, the latter hæmocyanin. There are also some others, more rare. These substances have an affinity for oxygen, so that the blood is enabled to carry more oxygen than it otherwise could. In passing through the respiratory organs the oxygen carriers become charged with oxygen and assume a brighter color. In passing through the tissues where oxygen is needed the hæmoglobin, or hæmocyanin, again assume a darker color because of the loss of oxygen to the tissues. The red corpuscles originate in the red marrow of the bones. They are short lived and disintegrate in the liver and form the red and green pigments of the bile.

METABOLISM

484. In green plants, the protoplasm takes up inorganic substances, such as water, carbon-dioxide, nitrates and other mineral salts containing sulphur, phosphorus, iron, calcium,

magnesium, potassium, and others. From these the simpler organic compounds, such as the carbohydrates, are formed, also more complex nitrogenous substances like aleurone and finally protoplasm itself. Animals, however, lack the power of building up protoplasm from its inorganic constituents. They require food containing organic nitrogenous compounds like aleurone, albumen and protoplasm. These may be supplemented by the simpler carbon compounds, like the carbohydrates, fats and oils. The nitrogenous substances are necessary wherever growth or repair are taking place, i. e., wherever protoplasm is being formed. The carbon compounds may be used as well as the nitrogenous where there is merely an evolution of energy demanded, as in locomotion and the production of heat. The details of the processes which take place in the cell are not known. But when foods are assimilated, growth takes place and the cell becomes energized so that it is capable of performing the functions peculiar to it.

485. The results of the activities of the cell may be briefly summarized:

486. Growth is the most general result of assimilation, but need not be further discussed here.

487. In glandular cells, activity results in the formation of the special secretions which are characteristic of the gland. These may be used in the building up of permanent structures of the organism, such as bone or cartilage, or the secretions may have only a temporary value, and after they have served their purpose, be eliminated from the body as slime and oil from the glands of the skin. With this class may be included those cells which produce substances by the transformation of protoplasm, although in the true glandular cell the secretions have probably not reached the complexity of structure of protoplasm. Cuticular and epidermal structures are of the transformed protoplasm type.

488. The activity of muscle is manifested primarily by a

contraction and secondarily by the production of heat, but at the same time, substances are formed and set free, which show that chemical processes are at work and which give a clue as to the nature of those processes. The oxygen and food substances, $C_6H_{12}O_6$, let's say, make their appearance again, but in an altered form. Carbon dioxide is produced in large quantities together with other substances which must be eliminated from the body, or else serious disorders occur. Nitrogen waste compounds are also formed, and like the CO_2, they have a lower energy value than the substances from which they were derived.

EXCRETION

489. The waste matters produced by metabolism are soluble in the body fluids and in water. Hence, small animals like amœba and hydra can eliminate them from the body surface by

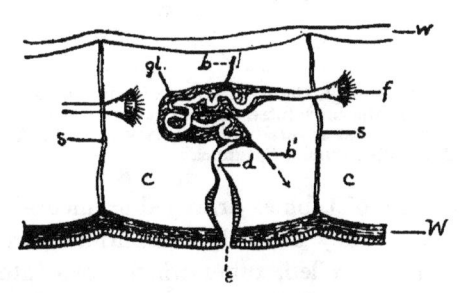

FIG. 119.—Diagram of a nephridium of an Annelid. b, b', blood-vessels; c, cœlom; d, duct; e, opening through the epidermis; f, funnel; gl, glandular portion; s, mesentery; W, wall of body; w, wall of intestine. (From Galloway.)

diffusion. In larger animals the substances excreted by the cells pass out into the body fluid or the blood current and are thus carried to the place of elimination. The CO_2 being a gas is chiefly given off from the organs of respiration, following the path of the oxygen, but in the reverse direction. The volume of oxygen absorbed in the human lung is about 5 per cent. of the inspired air. The volume of CO_2 given off is a little over 4

216   ANIMALS

per cent. on the average. If only carbohydrate foods were assimilated the percentage of these gases should be equal, but the oxygen consumed with hydrocarbon and proteid foods in part leaves the body by another path.

490. The nitrogenous waste matters are not gaseous and, therefore, cannot be eliminated by the lungs, and in fact, we find in all the higher animals a special set of organs for this function. The organs which presumably perform this function

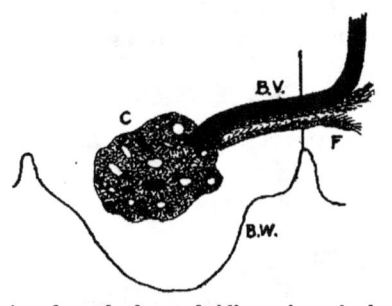

FIG. 120.—A section through the nephridium of nereis showing the funnel in longitudinal section and the convoluted tubule cut across at many points. The blood-vessels are also cut at several points (black). *B.W.*, The body wall; *B.V.*, blood-vessel; *c*, coiled tubule; *F*, funnel.

in Worms are pairs of tubules arranged segmentally, one pair in each segment. They are called nephridia and consist of slender, more or less coiled, tubes which open into the body cavity by a ciliated funnel-like opening. The other end of the tubule opens by a pore on the surface of the body.

491. In the crayfish there are organs, the "green glands," which are probably homologous to nephridia, but there is only a single pair, located at the base of the antennæ. They are comparatively large organs and more complicated in structure.

492. The single pair of kidneys of Vertebrates are much more complicated excretory organs and yet the uriniferous tubules of the kidney resemble the nephridia of the worm and are probably homologous organs. The kidney tubule is a long,

slender convoluted tube which in the primitive condition has a funnel like the nephridium, but in the mature condition of the mammal it is closed. Instead, however, a considerable part of its wall is closely applied to complex knots and networks of blood capillaries from which the secreting cells of the tubule extract the nitrogen waste matter. The kidney tubules all open into a common chamber from which a duct, the ureter, leads to a reservoir, the urinary bladder. The nitrogenous wastes leave the tissues with the lymph and thus are carried back into the general circulation. In this way they reach the kidneys. The chief waste drawn from the blood by the kidneys is urea, CON_2H_4, but there are a number of other substances eliminated in much smaller volume.

493. The liver of the higher animals seems to have several functions, one of which is excretion. The bile secreted by the liver is a complex substance and its significance is not fully understood. Its function in digestion is probably only a secondary one. It contains waste matters taken from the blood and these are eliminated through the intestine.

494. The white blood corpuscles also assist in ridding the body of useless or deleterious substances.

REPRODUCTION

495. Under favorable conditions an amœba will occasionally divide into two similar parts. These parts then continue to grow and after a time they also divide. This phenomenon is one of the characters of the living cell. The impulse to divide does not seem to depend upon any special external stimulus. It is the normal consequence of growth under favorable conditions. The process of division requires from a few minutes to an hour from beginning to completion, and may be repeated after a number of hours to several days.

496. With regard to the details of the process of division there are two types. In one case it is much more complicated than

in the other. In the simpler type the first evidence that division is about to take place is seen in a slight elongation of the nucleus. This proceeds until the nucleus assumes the shape of a dumb-bell. The two halves continue to draw apart until only a slender strand connects them and this finally breaks. As the division of the nucleus proceeds the body of the cell also elongates. The pseudopodia are formed only at the two ends. The cell becomes constricted in the equatorial plane and this cuts deeper into the cell until the latter is finally cut into two approximately equal parts. The two daughter nuclei have by this time assumed the normal rounded form and there are then two amœbæ. In the division the contractile vacuole remains in one of the daughter cells, but before division is complete a new vacuole has been formed in the other one.

497. In other cases, division comes about through a complicated process known as mitosis or karyokinesis. This process is described below. No significance is known to attach to the difference in method. The results are apparently the same.

498. In many Protozoa, another interesting phenomenon has been observed which should be mentioned here, although it has not been observed in amœba. This is the phenomenon of conjugation. Two similar animals unite, either partially and temporarily or else completely, so as to form a single cell. In the latter case the two nuclei fuse into one. When the union is only temporary the nuclei of both cells divide and a part of the nuclear matter from each cell is transferred to the other cell, where it unites with the nucleus of that cell. By either of these processes cells are formed with nuclei composed of material derived in equal parts from two individuals. The details of this process will be discussed more fully in Part III. Its significance will be better understood when compared with the sexual method of reproduction of the metazoa.

499. Hydra reproduces by budding and by development of eggs. Budding is a process found among other metazoa as

REPRODUCTION 219

well as among the Cœlenterata. The process is well exemplified by hydra. The bud which is eventually to form a new polyp is first seen as a slight protuberance of the lower part of

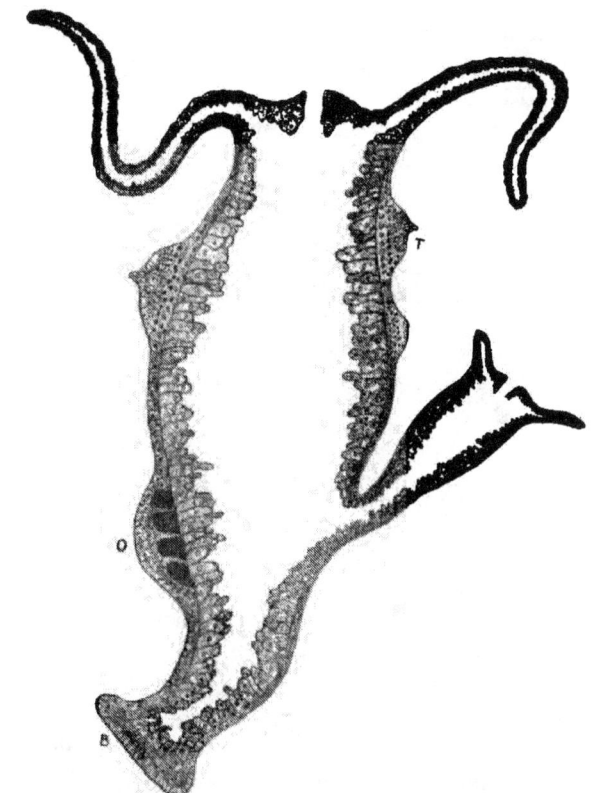

FIG. 121.—Diagram of hydra in longitudinal section. *A*, Well-developed bud is shown on the right; *B*, base; *o*, ovary; *T*, testis. (From Korschelt and Heider, after Aders.)

the wall of the column. This is caused by the more rapid growth of the tissues in this region and involves both ectoderm and entoderm. The bud grows larger, becomes cylindrical, and finally a circle of tentacles forms around the distal end.

The bud resembles the parent polyp in form and may be half as large. With the opening of a mouth in the centre of the circle of tentacles the animal is complete. Up to this time the gastro-vascular cavity of the bud has been in communication with that of the parent, but the base of the bud becomes gradually more constricted until finally the bud is cut off entirely and is then an independent organism. Several such buds may be in process of development at one time and by this means the number of individuals rapidly grows.

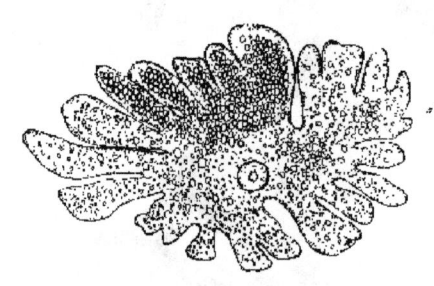

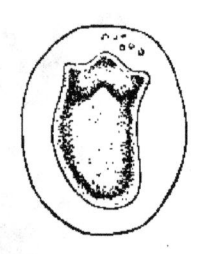

FIG. 122.—The egg cell of hydra, in amœboid form. (After Kleinenberg.)

FIG. 123.—A hydra embryo. The first four tentacles just beginning to develop. (After Kleinenberg.)

500. Less frequently another type of protuberance may be observed on the column of the hydra. Just below the circle of tentacles may be found a conical eminence which affects only the ectoderm. Lower down on the column, frequently on the same individual, a somewhat similar, though more rounded, protuberance may be found. These are the gonads. The upper ones are testes and in them are developed the sperm cells, which are very small and provided with a flagellum. These are produced in large numbers. The lower gonads are the ovaries and contain finally a single large cell, the ovum. Both ova and sperm cells are derived from the ectoderm, but they recede from the surface and are covered by the ectodermal epithelium during the period of development. When the egg is mature it

becomes exposed by the breaking of the ectoderm, but it still remains attached by a stalk. At this time the sperm cells are liberated from the testis in large numbers. They swim about in the water and by some means, probably a chemical stimulus originating in the egg, they are attracted to the egg. One of the sperm cells penetrates the protoplasm and fuses with the egg nucleus. This "fertilizing" process initiates the developing process. A membrane is first formed around the egg and by repeated cell division a cylindrical embryo is developed. The membrane then breaks and the ciliated larva is set free at the

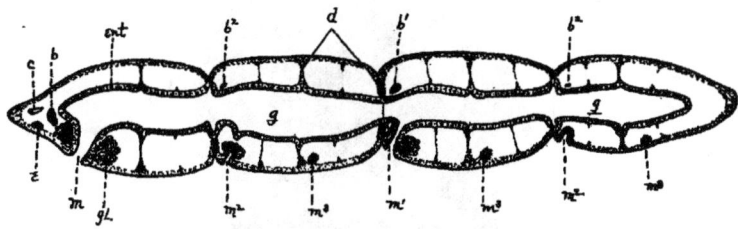

FIG. 124.—Longitudinal section of small Turbellarian, Microstomum, which multiplies asexually by strobilation. *b*, Brain; *c*, ciliated pit; *d*, planes of division; *e*, eye-spot; *ent*, entoderm; *g*, intestine; *gl*, gland cells; *m*, mouth (original); *m'*, mouth of second zoöid; m^2, m^3, mouths of offspring of second and third orders. The strobila consists of a chain of four nearly completed zoöids. (From Galloway).

time when four tentacles are just beginning to develop. After swimming for a time the larva becomes attached and a mouth is formed. From three to five more tentacles appear in the spaces between the others and the young hydra is complete. After maturing a number of ova the parent hydra dies.

501. Some annelid worms also reproduce by asexual methods, but among the higher forms like nereis and the earthworm reproduction is wholly by the sexual method. In nereis the sexes are distinct; each individual produces either eggs or sperm, but not both. The reproductive cells are differentiated in size and form, very much as in hydra. They are developed from cells of the mesodermal epithelium lining the body cavity (on the

222   ANIMALS

wall of the digestive tube). When they are mature they lie free in the body cavity, from which they escape into the water by the breaking of the body of the worm. The sperm and ova escape into the water at the same time. After fertilization a larva is developed which has no resemblance to an Annelid but is much more like a rotifer. This is called a trochophore larva and is regarded as indicating relationship between the Rotifers and Annelids. From one end of the trochophore larva

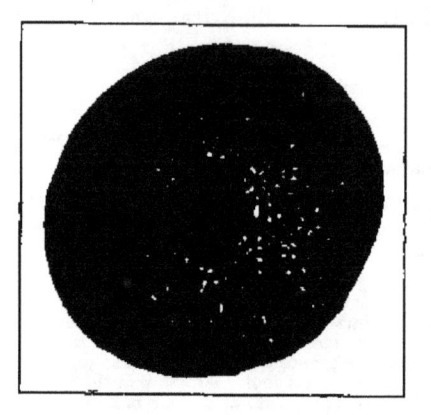

FIG. 125.—The ovum of nereis. Photomicrograph; greatly magnified.

the body of the worm is developed segment after segment. The development of nereis is, therefore, by metamorphosis.

502. The earthworm is hermaphroditic, i. e., both sexes are united in one individual, and development is direct.

503. In the crayfish the reproductive cells are developed in special sack-like organs lying in the thoracic part of the body cavity. The sexes are separate. There is a single ovary, consisting of a pair of lateral lobes connected by a single median lobe. A pair of ducts lead from the ovary to the basal joints of the eleventh appendages where they open to the exterior. The testis of the male is similar in position and composition,

but the ducts open at the bases of the appendages of the thirteenth segment.

504. The eggs are fertilized at the moment of their escape from the oviducts and are then cemented to the hairs of the abdominal appendages of the female. In this way they are protected from other animals; care is taken that they have the necessary supply of aerated water and they are not carried away by currents of water toward the sea. Even after the young are hatched they continue to cling for some time to the appendages of the female.

505. It happens that development is direct in the case of the crayfish, though in many Crustacea there is a well marked metamorphosis. In some Insects development is also direct, as, e. g., in the grasshopper, but in several orders of Insects there is a complete metamorphosis. From the egg of the butterfly is hatched a small caterpillar. This grows into a large caterpillar. Then a metamorphosis occurs. The caterpillar becomes a quiescent pupa and remains such for a time; then another change gives birth to the imago butterfly.

506. A few fishes are hermaphroditic. In all other Vertebrates the sexes are distinct. The gonads are developed from the mesoderm. They have no ducts primarily, but certain tubules which belong primarily to the excretory system become specially modified and assume the function of genital ducts. In some aquatic Vertebrates the eggs are fertilized in the water, but in all reptiles, birds and mammals fertilization takes place in the oviduct and development begins before the escape of the egg from the body of the parent. In the highest Mammals this intra-uterine development continues for weeks, months or even, in the case of the elephant, to nearly two years. In some fishes, and especially in frogs and toads, there is a marked metamorphosis, but in the higher groups the development is direct.

APPENDIX TO PART II

CLASSIFICATION OF ANIMALS

507. **Phylum I.** *Protozoa.*—Protozoa are found in nature practically everywhere where there is moisture; in the soil, in fresh and salt waters and even, as parasites, in the tissues of higher animals and plants. They may even be found in practically dry situations, as in dust, but then only in a resting or spore condition. When Protozoa in this state are moistened they absorb water, the protoplasm swells, the enclosing membrane is broken and the organism resumes an active existence. This is why they always appear when a little dry soil, a few dry leaves or any other organic matter is placed in a dish of water. Many species are found the whole world over, others are more limited in distribution. For example, some of the parasitic forms are limited to one, or a few related species of host and consequently are limited to the range of the host. Some groups are peculiar to fresh waters while others are marine.

508. The number of species of Protozoa is very great and there is great diversity in size, form and habits. Many are easily visible to the unaided eye. Many others approach the limit of visibility but most can only be seen with the aid of the microscope. The phylum is very difficult to classify but most forms can readily be placed in one or the other of the following five classes, viz., Rhizopoda, Mastigophora, Sporozoa, Ciliata and Suctoria.

509. **Class I. Rhizopoda.**—This class is characterized by the temporary root-like processes of the naked protoplasmic body, by which locomotion is effected and food ingested. A common example is amœba.

510. In the order *Amœbina*, to which amœba belongs, there is no fixed form of body; there is no membrane, shell or skeleton of any kind. Representatives of this order are found in both fresh and salt waters and many are parasitic. Entamœba coli is a common harmless parasite in the human intestine and Entamœba histolytica is the cause of tropical dysentery. The order *Heliozoa* comprises rhizopods which have a spherical central body from which radiate numerous long, slender, ray-like pseudopodia. The body may be either naked or surrounded by a gelatinous or silicious capsule perforated by numerous pores through which the pseudopodia project. Sometimes the cell is attached to other objects

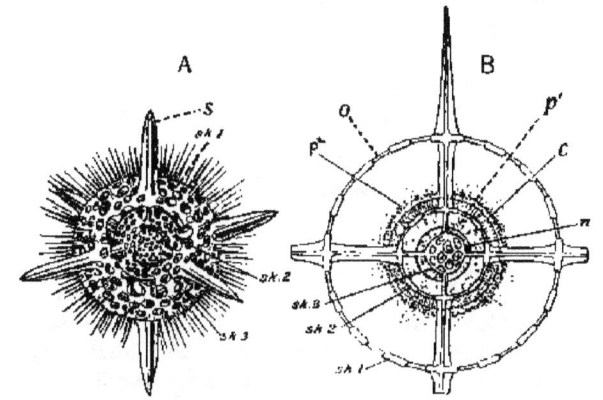

FIG. 126.—Actinomma, a Radiolarian. *A*, Whole animal with a portion of two shells removed to show the interior. *B*, section, showing concentric shells, radial spines and central capsule (*c*); *n*, nucleus; *p*, protoplasm. (From Galloway, after Parker and Haswell.)

by a slender stalk. Heliozoa are found in fresh and salt water. They are never parasitic. The order *Foramenifera* includes fresh- and salt-water rhizopods which have a shell composed of gelatinous or horny matter, to which may be added calcareous or silicious secretions deposited by the protoplasm, or minute foreign particles like grains of sand. The pseudopodia may be amœboid in form or long and slender like those of the heliozoa but differing from the latter in the less regular arrangement and constantly changing form. Many species add successively larger chambers to the first shell. These are often in a spiral arrangement. In the order *Radiolaria* there is found a peculiar structure called the central capsule which encloses the nucleus and the central part of the protoplasm. Outside the capsule is another layer of protoplasm which contains large quantities of a gelatinous secretion. Besides the central capsule there is a skeleton, usually of silica, composed of radial spines and concentric shells. This skeleton is often of a very intricate and beautiful design. The pseudopodia are slender and branching and are sometimes supported by a slender axial filament. The Radiolaria are marine.

511. **Class II. Mastigophora.**—The Mastigophora are distinguished by the flagellum, a whip-like vibratory appendage by which locomotion is effected. There may be two or four or even a circlet of these flagella but more often there is only one. Flagella also occur in other groups of animals and also in plants but only as temporary structures. In the Mastigophora they are always present during the active life period of the organism. The body has usually a definite form though it is often capable of great contortion. There is a nucleus and a contractile vacuole. The class may be divided into three sub-classes, Flagellata, Dinoflagellata and Cystoflagellata.

512. The *Flagellata* are widely distributed and there is extreme diversity of form and habit so that the group is difficult to characterize and classify. Many contain chlorophyll and are holophytic, some contain chlorophyll but also ingest particles of food. Some are holozoic, some saprozoic and many parasitic. Special examples of the latter are described in Part III. Those forms which ingest solid food may do so either through a definite oral opening or the food may be engulfed at the surface where no preformed mouth occurs. In one group, the Choanoflagellata, the base of the single flagellum is surrounded by a collar-like membrane. The flagellum jerks the food particles against the outside of the collar and from there they pass into the cell-body. Undigested fragments of food substances are ejected at the base of the flagellum, within the collar. Some of the Flagellates form swimming colonies by the adhesion of a group of cells to each other. Others are stalked and adhere in groups to form fixed colonies The *Dinoflagellata* are highly specialized fresh-water or marine Mastigophora. The cell has two flagella, usually placed at right angles to each other, and hidden in deep grooves on the surface of the cell wall. The cell often has a very odd form and is covered with cellulose plates which are fancifully ornamented. Many species contain chromatophores of yellowish, brownish or greenish color. The *Cystoflagellata* are another small group of

PROTOZOA 227

Mastigophora. They have one flagellum and locomotion may be assisted by rhythmical motions of the protoplasm. They are large and contain considerable gelatinous matter enclosed within the strong pellicula. One species, Noctiluca miliaris, which is found in all seas is largely responsible for the phosphorescence of the water.

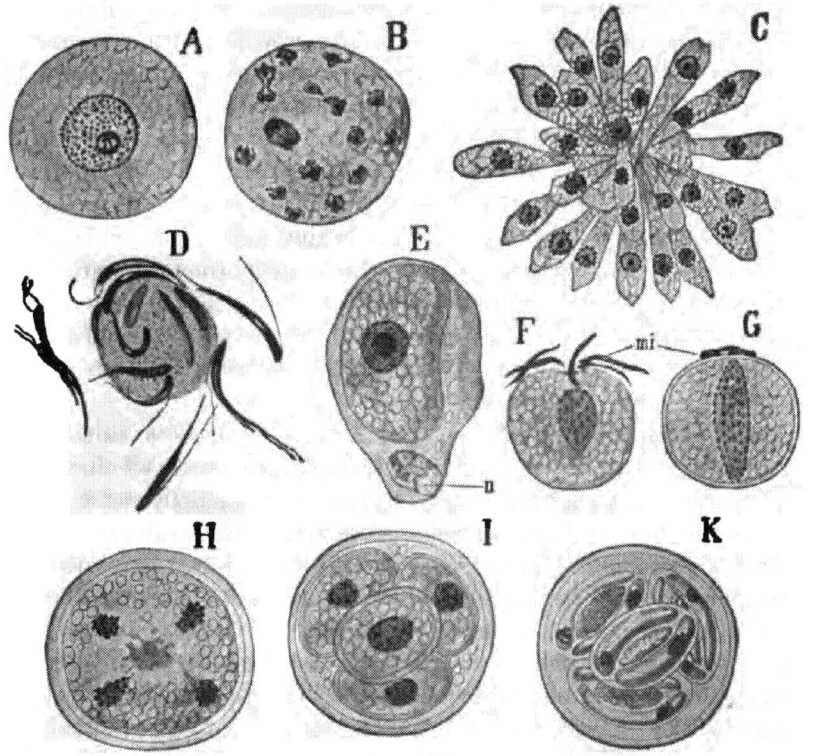

FIG. 127.—Eimeria Schubergi, a sporozoan parasitic in the intestinal epithelium of Lithobius. *A–C*, Three steps in the formation of sporozoites (asexual); *D*, microgametes; *E*, macrogamete; *F–G*, fertilization; *H–K*, three steps in the formation of spores (sexual).

513. **Class III. Sporozoa.**—The class Sporozoa includes those protozoa which at one time in their life cycle multiply by the formation of spores. The spores are usually enclosed in

a spore case but this may be wanting, as, e. g., when there is an alternation of hosts. The number of spores in a case is usually numerous but sometimes they are few or only one. All Sporozoa are parasitic. They are very commonly cell parasites, either in the young stages or permanently. They absorb fluid food by osmose. The Sporozoa are widely distributed and infect all groups of the higher animals, especially worms, arthropods, tunicates, molluscs and vertebrates. Most species are limited to one or a few host species. The passage from one host to another similar (not alternate) host is effected in the spore stage. There is frequently another method of reproduction which takes place wholly within a single host. This may alternate with the spore-producing generation thus giving rise to a regular alternation of generations. Many Sporozoa are comparatively harmless parasites but among them are also some of the most dangerous. Several examples are described under the head of parasitism.

514. **Class IV. Ciliata.**—The Ciliata all possess as locomotor organs, numerous minute vibratile processes called cilia. They are widely distributed. Very few are parasitic, some are saprozoic, but most are holozoic. A few even are carnivorous. They are generally free-swimming but some attach themselves temporarily to other objects and some are permanently fixed by a stalk. The cilia serve for driving currents of water containing food particles to the mouth and in the fixed forms this is the chief function of the cilia. The form of the body is definite but the animal often has the power of considerably changing the form by contraction. The cell is covered by a dense protoplasmic layer called a pellicula. There are usually two nuclei, a large macronucleus and a small micronucleus. Multiplication is effected by division or by budding. Sometimes this is accompanied by the formation of a protecting membrane or cyst. Cysts are also formed when conditions are unfavorable and represent a resistant condition.

PROTOZOA · 229

515. The Ciliata are classified on the basis of the arrangement of the cilia. The *Holotricha* have no special zone of cilia in the region of the mouth. The *Heterotricha* have a left-hand spiral of larger cilia around the mouth. The *Oligotricha* have a spiral or circle of cilia around the peristome which is anterior and at right angles to the axis of the body. Elsewhere the body is almost or wholly destitute of cilia. The *Hypotricha* are flattened dorso-ventrally. The adoral spiral is on the ventral side and the dorsal side is without motile cilia. The *Peritricha* have the adoral spiral right-handed, otherwise the body is not ciliated, many are stalked and colonial.

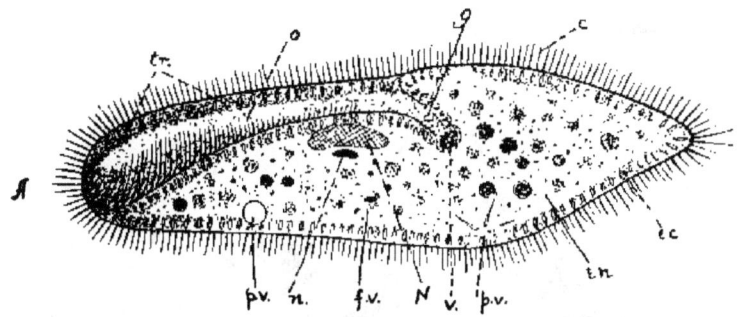

Fig. 128.—Paramœcium. *A*, Anterior; *c*, cilia; *e.c.*, ectoplasm; *e.n.*, endoplasm; *f.v.*, food vacuole; *g*, gullet; *N*, macronucleus; *n*, micronucleus; *o*, oral groove; *p.v.*, contractile vacuole; *tr*, trichocysts; *v*, food vacuole.

516. **Class V. Suctoria.**—In this group there are no organs of locomotion in the adult and consequently all are sessile or at least motionless. They are provided with long tubular processes by which they catch their prey. Through these tubes they then suck the protoplasm of the small animals they have caught. The young are formed by budding. They are provided with cilia by which they swim about for a time before becoming attached. Some suctoria are parasitic. The group is not large and is comparatively unimportant.

Metazoa

517. The Metazoa are multicellular animals. In the embryo the cells are arranged in three distinct layers, an outer ectoderm, an inner entoderm

230 CLASSIFICATION OF ANIMALS

and a middle mesoderm. In the cœlenterates the mesoderm is only incompletely developed and in some cases entirely wanting. Reproduction is generally of the sexual type though in the lower phyla asexual methods often occur in addition to the sexual.

518. PHYLUM II. *Cœlenterata.*—In the Cœlenterates the mesoderm is represented usually by a gelatinous matrix containing various cellular elements which are derived either from the ectoderm or entoderm. There is no body cavity or vascular system. The gastric cavity is extended by canal-like prolongations into all parts of the body.

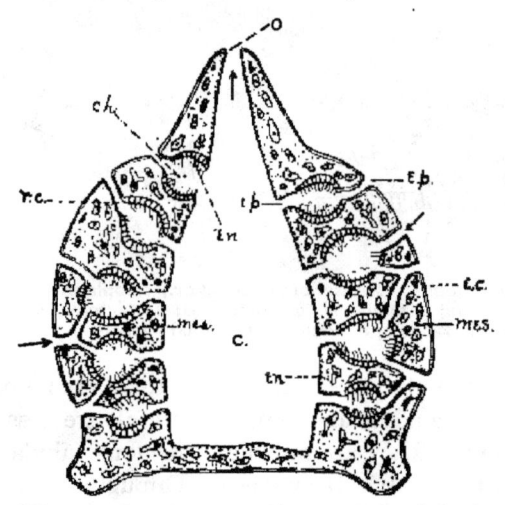

FIG. 129.—Diagram of a sponge. *c*, Cloaca; *ch*, flagellale chambers; *sp*, incurrent pores; *ip*, excurrent pores; *mes*, mesenchyme; *o*, osculum; *r.c.*, radial canals. (From Galloway.)

519. **Class I. Porifera.**—Sponges are all marine with the exception of a single fresh-water genus, Spongilla. They are always attached to some object and sometimes bore into shells or calcareous rocks. They vary greatly in form; sometimes covering the substratum like a thin velvety crust, sometimes rising into conical, spherical, cylindrical or vase-shaped masses.

PORIFERA 231

They are often branched, especially the cylindrical ones and the more massive forms may become very irregular in shape through the development of new parts by irregular budding. Some are very delicate and fragile while others are very firm, even stony. The color is as variable as the form; they are often

FIG. 130.—A large cup-shaped sponge (Poterion?) from the Philippine Islands. × 1/8.

a dull gray but highly colored species are very common. Orange, sulphur yellow, violet, purple and green sponges often give color variety to the sea bottom. The fresh-water Spongilla is usually green; the color in this case being due to the presence of minute algæ imbedded in the tissue of the sponge in a symbiotic relationship. In size sponges vary from a fraction of an inch to several feet in diameter.

FIG. 131.—Stylotella heliophila, a typical sponge. Beaufort Harbor, N. C. × 1/2.

520. A sponge is essentially a tubular structure, the walls of which consist of three layers, an outer thin epithelium, the ectoderm, an inner epithelium of collared flagellate cells, the

entoderm, and a middle gelatinous connective-tissue matrix in which are embedded branched connective-tissue cells, calcareous or silicious spicules, primitive muscle cells and reproductive cells. Through the walls of the sponge numerous fine pores or slender canals penetrate from the exterior to the central larger canal or cloaca. In the simpler sponges the

FIG. 132.—A Niaxon sponge (Pheronema?). Philippine Islands. × 1/2.

surface of the cloaca is lined with the collared flagellate cells. These have a marked resemblance to the protozoan Choanoflagellata and are not found in any other metazoa. The lashing of the flagella creates a current in the water which flows inward at the pores and outward at the osculum, the large opening of the cloaca. The flagella and collars together serve for the capture of food particles as in the Choanoflagellata and digestion is likewise intra-cellular.

521. In more complex sponges the flagellate epithelium is limited to certain depressions of the cloacal surface which form chambers radiating from the cloacal cavity. These are called flagellate chambers or radial canals. In many cases the flagellate chambers are so far removed from the cloaca that another system of canals results, the excurrent canals, which connects the flagellate chambers with the cloaca. In still more complex forms the incurrent and excurrent canals are branched.

522. Sponges have no power of locomotion and only in some cases can any evidence of contraction be observed directly. However, the minute pores can be closed by the contraction of the muscle cells of the mesoglea. Some sponges are quite soft, almost jelly like, but usually the mesoglea is so filled with calcareous or silicious spicules as to render the sponge firm or even hard. In some sponges the mesoglea contains a skeletal structure composed of horny fibres, in addition to the spicules. This is notably the case with the common bath sponge in which the spicules are not well developed.

523. Sponges reproduce by a process similar to budding. A fragment of the sponge separates, is carried away by water currents, becomes attached and develops into a new sponge. The sexual method is, however, the more frequent. The eggs and sperm are developed in the mesoglea, where the egg becomes fertilized and begins its development. It escapes as a ciliated larva, swims away and becomes attached with the gastrula mouth down. The gastrula cavity becomes the cloaca and an osculum is formed by thinning of the wall at the end opposite the point of attachment. The incurrent pores are formed in like manner.

Order 1.—The Calcispongiæ have calcareous spicules of one, three or four rays. Grantia.

Order 2.—The Triaxonia are sponges with large flagellate chambers, a thin mesenchyme layer and triaxial silicious spicules. The latter may be replaced by horny fibres or, occasionally, skeletal structures are wanting.

Order 3.—The Tetraxonia have a complicated system of canals, small flagellate chambers and a thick mesenchyme layer. The skeleton consists of tetraxial or monaxial silicious spicules sometimes combined with, or replaced by, spongin fibres. Euspongia is the commercial sponge and Spongilla the fresh water sponge.

524. *The Cnidaria.*—A great many Cœlenterates are characterized by the possession of peculiar organs, the cnidoblasts or nettling cells. These occur in both ectoderm and entoderm but are often aggregated in certain regions, as on the tentacles. The nettling cell contains a small capsule which is filled with a fluid and contains a spirally wound thread. A sensory point projects at the surface. When this is stimulated the capsule bursts, the nettling thread is turned inside out and with it the fluid content of the capsule is also ejected. The effect of this discharge is to paralyze or kill the prey. Even the human skin is strongly irritated by the nettling discharge of the larger Cnidaria and from this fact arose the name. The Cnidaria are the Hydrozoa, Scyphozoa and Anthozoa.

525. **Class II. Hydrozoa.**—This class is named after the genus Hydra which is found in fresh waters very widely distributed. Practically all other Hydrozoa are marine. The individual animals of this class are always small but many species are colonial and the colony may attain to considerable dimensions. There is usually a remarkable alternation of generations in which an asexual, fixed polyp form alternates with a sexual free-swimming medusa. The polyp is in most essential features like the hydra in form but the lower part of the column is much elongated and slender thus forming a stalk. When budding occurs the buds are not set free but remain attached to the parent stem and thus is formed a colony. At certain times another type of bud is formed. It differs in form from the parent polyp and is usually set free. This is the medusa. Its principal axis is shorter than the radial axes so that it assumes the form of a saucer or bell with a fringe of tentacles around the edge. Near the margin of the bell on its concave

surface a thin fold of the ectoderm projects inward toward the principal axis, forming a circular shelf. This is the velum, which serves to distinguish the medusæ of this group from the Scyphomedusæ.

526. From the gastric cavity four radial canals run out to the margin of the bell and there join a canal which runs circularly along its edge. In some cases there are six, eight or more radial canals. The gonads are developed from the ectoderm somewhere along the course of the radial canals or on the manubrium. Special sense organs, eye spots or statocysts, may occur along the edge of the bell and there is also a ring of nerve fibres. The animal has a feeble power of locomotion, effected by a rhythmical contraction of the edge of the bell. The hydromedusæ vary in size from a small fraction of an inch to two inches. In one group they are somewhat larger. Although so different in appearance the medusæ are in reality of essentially the same structure as the polyps. They are a little more highly developed in accordance with the free life habit.

527. When the eggs are fertilized a free-swimming ciliated larva is produced. This becomes attached by the aboral pole, develops tentacles and thus forms a polyp and by budding of the polyp a colony is developed. There is frequently more than one kind of polyp found in a colony. In this case there is a division of function so that there may be feeding polyps which are of the typical form; protective polyps, without tentacles and mouth but well supplied with nettling cells; reproductive polyps which produce the medusa buds for the colony. Sometimes the medusæ remain attached to the parent colony and there mature the reproductive cells. In this case the medusa is more or less rudimentary. Such medusæ are then another type of polyp and the alternation of generations resolves itself into a special case of polymorphism.

Order 1.—The Hydroidea comprise solitary polyp forms which have no medusa stage, like Hydra; the Trachymedusæ which have no polyp stage;

HYDROZOA

the colonial millepore corals; and the colonial campanularian and tubularian hydroids. The colonial forms are all fixed and usually have a free medusa stage with alternation of generations.

Order 2.—The Siphonophora are swimming colonies in which there is a highly developed stock polymorphism in which certain individuals form floats or swimming bells. The sexual generation is either a free medusa or an attached medusoid bud. Physalia, the "Portuguese Man of War," is a well-known example.

FIG. 133.—A hydroid colony. × 1.

528. Class III. Scyphozoa.—The Scyphozoa are the common jellyfishes. They are usually larger than the medusæ of the Hydrozoa, varying from four inches to a yard in diameter. The bell is usually strongly convex and is made up of four antimeres though most of the organs occur in multiples of four. The margin of the bell is lobed, with as many sense organs

warmer seas where they often occur in vast numbers. Some forms are widely distributed. To the Anthozoa, sponges and sea weeds, is chiefly due the brilliant coloration so often found in the sea bottom of tropical and sub-tropical seas. Most anemones are attached to some firm object such as rocks, sea

FIG. 136.—A whip coral (Gorgoniidæ). × 1/2.

weeds, shells or even the surface of other animals. This attachment is effected by a sucking action of the basal disc and permits the animal to move by a slow creeping motion. Some anemones lie partly embedded in the sand into which they can completely withdraw by longitudinal contraction. Others form a leathery tube by a secretion of the column, still others secrete calcareous matter, especially from the surface of the basal disc. This is notably the case with the corals. Through this secretion the animal becomes immovably fixed. The basal disc of the

FIG. 137.—A branching madrepore coral, Astrangia. Slightly reduced.

coral polyp secretes more rapidly along its edge so that a cup is formed into which the animal can more or less completely withdraw. Within this cup there are also vertical plates and pillars built up by the unequal secretion of the various parts of the base. To this is due the beautiful structure of many

242   CLASSIFICATION OF ANIMALS

kinds of coral. Some corals secrete a horny skeleton and in some there is a mixture of the horny and calcareous substances.

530. The larger anemones are considerably more complex

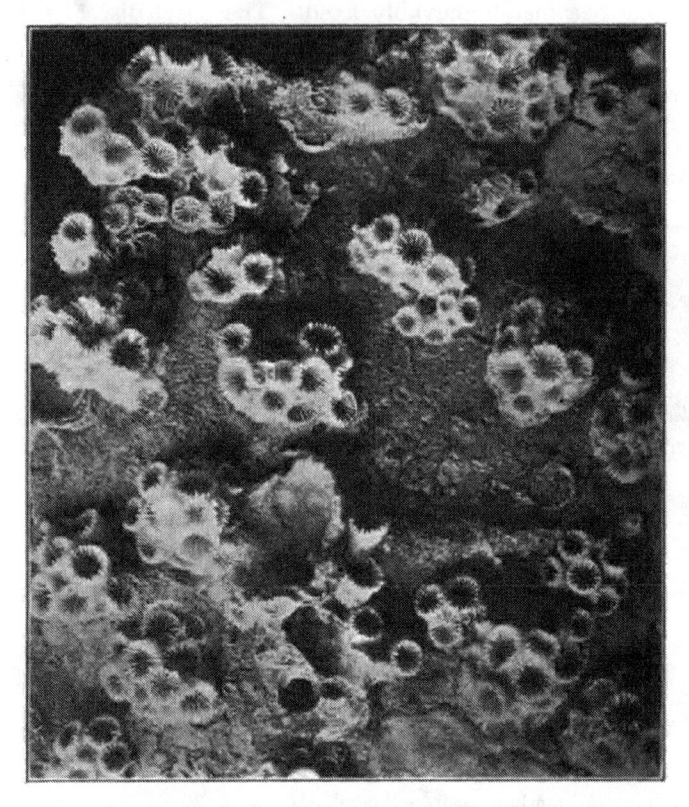

FIG. 138.—Coral colonies developing on a shell. Various steps in the process are shown.

than the smaller corals but certain important characters are common to all and serve to distinguish this type of polyp from that of the Hydrozoa. The Anthozoan polyp is distinguished by the œsophagus and mesenteries. The mouth does not open directly into the gastro-vascular cavity as it does in the Hydrozoan polyp. There is a long œsophagus which extends from the edge of the mouth to the centre of the gastric cavity. It is in reality a cylindrical continuation of the oral surface and is lined with ectoderm. The gastric cavity is incompletely divided into chambers by folds of the entoderm supported by layers of mesoglea. Some of these mesenterial folds extend from the wall of the column to the œsophagus. These are said to be complete. Others do not reach the œsophagus and are therefore known as incomplete mesenteries. On the free edge of some of the mesenteries there is a thick muscular cord, the mesenterial filament, which is richly supplied with gland and nettling cells. There are no special sense organs and nothing that can be called a central nervous system, though beneath the ectoderm of the oral disc the network of nerve fibres is better developed than elsewhere. A strong circular muscle is usually found just below the edge of the oral disc and in the mesenteries there are strong longitudinal muscle bands. The gonads lie embedded in the mesoglea of the mesenteries along the free border. The sexes are usually distinct. The larva develops for a time within the body of the parent and escapes as a ciliated planula which becomes fixed and develops directly into the polyp.

Order 2.—The Octactiniaria are chiefly colonial. The polyp has eight pinnately branched tentacles and eight mesenteries. There is frequently a skeletal structure of horny or calcareous matter. The whip corals, sea fans, organ pipe corals, etc.

Order 3.—The Ceriantipatharia include the anemone Cerianthus and some colonial forms with a horny skeleton and polyps with six tentacles.

Order 4.—The Zoanthactiniaria comprise the sea anemones and the madrepore corals. The mesenteries are grouped in pairs.

531. **Class V. Ctenophora.**—The Ctenophora are another group of jelly fishes. They are more transparent and watery then the medusæ and exceedingly fragile. A common type is

the pear-shaped Pleurobrachia which is also comparable to a pear in size. The mouth is located at the small end and opposite it there lies a single statocyst. Extending about two-thirds of the distance from pole to pole and at about equal distances from the two poles are eight bands of vibratile plates which are regarded as rows of cilia fused together. These are the locomotor organs. In place of nettling cells the two long tentacles are covered with adhesive cells to which the prey adheres.

532. *The Cœlomata.*—In none of the Cœlenterates are the fundamental animal characteristics strongly developed. Sense organs and the organs of locomotion are in no case highly developed and the symmetry of the body is always primarily radial though in some cases a tendency toward secondary bilateral symmetry may be observed. In the Cœlomata there is always a well-developed mesoderm. This makes possible a more highly developed muscular system and consequent greater locomotor activity. With this go also more highly differentiated sense organs and bilateral symmetry. The mesoderm is derived from the entoderm and encloses a paired series of cavities, the cœlomic, or body, cavity.

533. PHYLUM III. *Scolecida.*—Several classes of animals more or less resembling worms in the form of the body but with no evidence of metameric segmentation are often called the unsegmented worms. In this group the true body cavity is limited to small spaces connected with the excretory and reproductive organs.

534. **Class I. Platyhelminthes.**—The animals of this group have a flattened body. The digestive tract is sack-like, without vent, or wholly wanting. The space between the intestine and body-wall is filled with a parenchyma of contractile fibres. The nervous system consists of a paired supra-œsophageal ganglion and a pair of ventral longitudinal nerves. Two other pairs of longitudinal nerves are sometimes present. The excretory system consists of a branched system of protonephridia, also called a water vascular system. The proximal

end of the protonephridium is closed by a so-called flame cell. This is a large cell provided with long vibrating cilia which project into the proximal end of the canal. The flat worms are usually hermaphrodyte and the reproductive system is highly complicated.

535. *Order* 1.—The *Turbellaria*, or gliding worms, are usually small, very much flattened, aquatic animals. The name refers to the method of locomotion which is effected through the cilia by which the surface of the body is covered. The mouth is on the ventral side and is usually provided with an eversible proboscis. The digestive tract is a simple blind sack in the smallest microscopic forms, but in the larger ones it is divided into three main trunks which have numerous branches. This form of digestive tract is a substitute for a circulatory system. There are usually 2-many simple eyes at the anterior end and over the brain.

536. *Order* 2.—The *Trematoda* are parasites and consequently show more or less evidence of degeneration. In the form of the body they resemble the Turbellaria, but the surface of the body is destitute of cilia in the adult. The animal is provided with hold-fast organs in the form of hooks and suckers. Commonly there are two suckers, one at the anterior end enclosing the mouth and another further back on the ventral side. The digestive tract is usually two forked but may be more complexly branched. Eyes are only found in the ectoparasitic forms and in some free-living larval stages of endoparasites. The life history of a trematode is described in Part III. Page 366.

537. *Order* 3.—The *Cestoda* are all endoparasites and in the adult stage are found only in the digestive tract of higher animals. Special sense organs and digestive tract are both entirely wanting. The digested food of the host is absorbed through the surface of the body. In place of a head there is a hold-fast organ called a scolex which in the most common forms has a circle of four suckers and sometimes also a circlet of hooks. In a narrower region just below the scolex a process of strobilation takes place by which the body of the parasite is formed. This is usually composed of a long series of proglottides, the ones farthest from the scolex being the oldest. The last segments may be "ripe" while new ones are forming below the scolex. A pair of lateral nerves extend through the body from segment to segment. There is also a pair of longitudinal excretory tubes which are connected by transverse canals in each proglottis. Each proglottis contains also a complete set of reproductive organs highly

developed, of both sexes. A "ripe" proglottis contains a large number of fertilized eggs. It is cut off from the main chain and passes from the host with the fæces. The embryonic stages develop in a second host as is described in the case of a typical example in Part III. Page 367.

538. **Class II. Aschelminthes.**—The animals comprised in this class have usually a cylindrical body and a simple tubular digestive tract opening posteriorly by a vent. A false body cavity originating from the blastula cavity is often of considerable size. The sexes are usually distinct.

539. *Order 1.*—The *Rotatoria* are small, mostly microscopic, free-living animals. They are found chiefly in fresh waters. The anterior end of the body is provided with a contractile crown of cilia by which locomotion is effected. At the posterior end there is usually a stalk-like "foot" which is provided with adhesive glands. By means of this foot the animal attaches itself temporarily. The name Rotifer has reference to the apparent revolution of the crown when the cilia are in motion. The currents produced by the cilia carry food particles to the mouth which lies in the centre of the crown. The œsophagus opens into a stomach which is provided with a set of cuticular teeth. A pair of excretory tubules opens into the posterior end of the intestine.

540. *Order 4.*—The *Nematoda* are in part free living, in part parasitic. They are often called thread worms or round worms. The mouth is at the anterior end. There is then a sucking œsophagus and a simple tubular intestine which opens on the ventral side near the posterior end. Special sense organs are practically wanting. There is a nerve ring around the mouth and from this a pair of nerves, one dorsal, one ventral, extend the length of the body. There is a pair of excretory tubules, one on either side, which extend from end to end of the body. The life histories of several parasitic forms are described in Part III.

541. **Class IV. Nemertini.**—This group is composed chiefly of free-living marine forms. The body is much elongated and muscular. The epidermis is ciliated. There is a long eversible proboscis and the intestine opens posteriorly by a vent. Eyes are often present and in large number and there is a pair of sensory grooves on the head. The nervous system consists of a supra-œsophageal ganglion and a sub-œsophageal ganglion.

These are connected around the œsophagus and give off three longitudinal nerves, one dorsal and two ventral. There is a pair of branched protonephridia which open on the side of the body. The sexes are usually distinct.

542. PHYLUM IV. *Annelida.*—The true worms are free living, aquatic or, if terrestrial, at least confined to moist situations. The body is usually much elongated, bilaterally symmetrical and segmented, and the segments are similar (homonomous). The intestine is usually a straight tube with a vent at the posterior end of the body. There is a true body cavity completely lined with mesoderm. Eyes and other sense organs are often present. The nervous system consists of a supra-œsophageal ganglion, a pair of circum-œsophageal connectives and a ventral chain of ganglia arranged metamerically and connected by a pair of longitudinal nerves. In each segment there is a pair of nephridia.

543. **Class II. Chætopoda.**—The Chætopoda include the typical worms, such as nereis and the earthworms. They are distinguished by the cuticular bristles or setæ with which each segment of the body is armed.

544. *Order 1.*—The *Polychæta* are marine annelids. They have two bundles of setæ on each side of each segment. The setæ are borne by short, unjointed appendages (parapodia) which are divided into two branches, each branch having a bundle of setæ. They usually live on the sea bottom in burrows or tubes but some are pelagic. Many are active predatory animals and have well-developed sense organs. Others live in leathery or calcareous tubes formed by secretions of epidermal glands. These never leave the tubes voluntarily. Only the anterior end is in most cases protruded for the purposes of feeding and respiration. In many cases a circle of feather-like tentacles covered with cilia produce currents by which food is carried to the mouth. The sexes are usually distinct and there is a metamorphosis in development.

545. *Order 3.*—The *Oligochæta* are the small fresh-water worms and the earthworms. They lack parapodia and the bristles are few in number, usually eight in each segment, two groups of two each on a side. They are hermaphrodytic and the development is direct.

546. Class III. Hirudinea.—The leeches differ considerably from the Chætopoda. The external segmentation does not correspond to the metamerism. There are usually three or five external rings to one segment. There are 34 metameres. The body cavity is almost obliterated by parenchymatous tissue. They are all external parasites and are provided with suckers for holding to the host and for locomotion. There are two suckers, a small one at the anterior end enclosing the mouth and a large one on the ventral side at the posterior end. There are neither parapodia nor bristles. Series of lateral pouches render the digestive tract very capacious. The leeches are hermaphrodyte. They are found only in the water, or in moist places.

547. PHYLUM V. *Molluscoidea.*—Under this head are grouped several classes which are sometimes placed under the heading worms. They are aquatic, usually fixed and provided with a cuticular covering in the form of a tube or a two-valved shell. They are unsegmented. The mouth is surrounded by a circle of tentacles covered with cilia. The intestine is usually U-shaped so that the vent lies near the mouth.

548. Class II. Bryozoa.—The Bryozoa, or Polyzoa, are all minute aquatic animals. Most are marine but there are also a few fresh-water forms. They are usually colonial and the colony may spread over considerable areas though the individuals are barely visible to the unaided eye. There is a gelatinous, horny or calcareous test into which the animal may completely withdraw. The tests of a colony often form an incrustation over the surface of other objects and again they form branching plant-like structures comparable to moss plants in size and general appearance, hence the name. The test is secreted by the epidermis and forms part of the animal. A pair of strong retractor muscles cause the rapid withdrawal of the body completely within the test on the slightest irritation. The mouth is surrounded by a crown of ciliated tentacles, sometimes

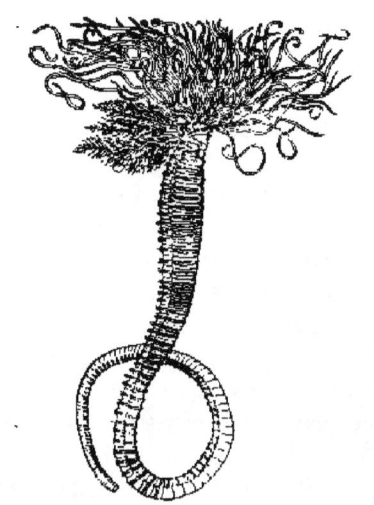

FIG. 139.—Amphitrite ornata, a marine Polychæte. (From Galloway, after Verrill.)

FIG. 140.—Cirratulus grandis, a marine Polychæte. (From Galloway after Verrill.)

borne on a horseshoe-shaped disc, the lophophore. The vent lies just outside the tentacles. There are no special sense organs. The nervous system consists of a single ganglion and a few nerves leading from it. The nephridia are very rudimentary or entirely wanting. The colonies are often polymorphic; certain individuals being specialized receptacles for eggs while others form slender, jointed, vibrating whips or a pair of jaws which open and close like the beak of a bird.

549. **Class III. Brachiopoda.**—The Brachiopods are not generally well known, although they are not at all rare and are widely distributed. They live only in salt water and may be found not far from shore. They have a shell somewhat like that of a clam but the plane of symmetry cuts the hinge at right angles and one of the valves is dorsal and the other ventral. They are usually unlike. The shell is composed either of chitin or calcareous matter. The animal is attached by a stalk-like extension of the posterior end of the body or by the cementing of the ventral valve to the substratum. On either side of the mouth the body is prolonged into a pair of coiled arms which bear numerous ciliated tentacles. There is a true body cavity in which lie the simple U-shaped digestive tract with a digestive gland, the heart, the gonads, one or two pairs of nephridia and a dorsal and a ventral ganglion.

550. PHYLUM VI. *Echinodermata.*—This is a well-defined group of animals. They are all marine, without exception. The larvæ are bilateral but by a metamorphosis the adult becomes radially symmetrical and the number of rays is usually five. The name, Echinoderm, means spiny skin and refers to the calcareous bars and plates embedded in the integument. These are not equally well developed in the various classes but they serve in varying degree as an exoskeleton and in most forms some pieces project beyond the general surface in the form of spines. The ambulacral system is the most distinctive anatomical character of the group. It consists of a

system of tubes filled with water which enters through the sieve-like madreporic plate near the aboral pole of the animal. From here a "stone canal" leads to a ring canal which circles the mouth and gives off five radial canals to the five rays of the body. Each radial canal has numerous lateral branches which end in tubular processes of the integument, called tube feet.

FIG. 141.—Starfish, oral view showing tube feet. (From Galloway, after Leuckart and Nitsche.)

At the base of each foot there is a bladder-like lateral enlargement of the foot canal, the ampulla. By its contraction the ampulla forces the water into the foot causing it to elongate. When the foot contracts the water is forced back into the ampulla. The end of the foot is provided with a sucking disc by which it may be attached to an object. By this mechanism,

252   CLASSIFICATION OF ANIMALS

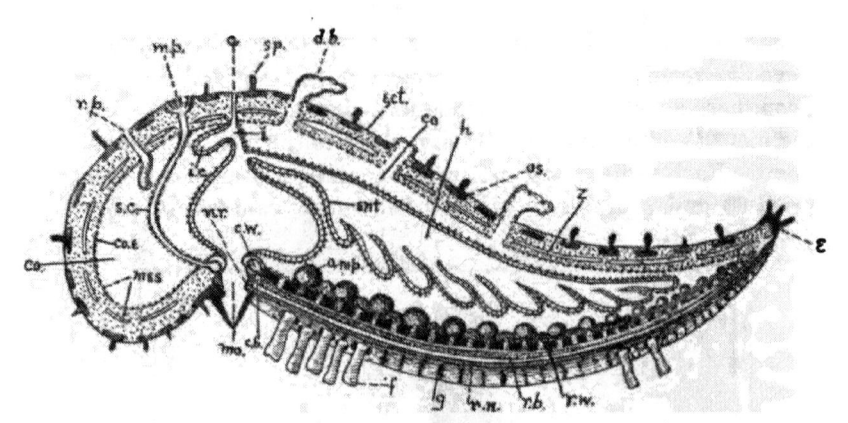

FIG. 142.—Section through the arm and disc of a starfish. *A*, Anus; *amp*, ampulla; *cb*, circular blood-vessel; *cw*, circular water canal; *co*, cœlom; *co.e.*, cœlomic epithelium; *d.b.*, dermal branchiæ; *e*, eye-spot; *ect*, ectoderm; *ent*, entoderm; *f*, ambulacral foot; *g*, ambulacral groove; *h*, hepatic cæca; *i*, intestine; *i.c.*, intestinal cæca; *mes*, mesoderm; *mo*, mouth; *mp*, madreporic body; *nr*, nerve ring; *os*, ossicles; *rn*, radial nerve; *rb*, radial blood-vessel; *rp*, genital pore; *rw*, radial water canal; *sc*, stone canal; *sp*, spine. (From Galloway.)

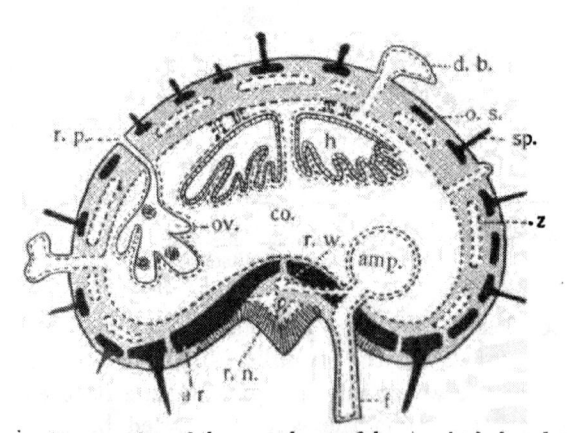

FIG. 143.—Cross section of the arm of a starfish. *ar*, Ambulacral rafter; *ov*, ovary containing ova. Other lettering as in preceding figure. (From Galloway.)

the numerous feet acting in unison may slowly pull the animal along. The spines frequently assist in locomotion, in which case they are long, jointed at the base and operated by special muscles. In some cases the tube feet lack the sucking disc and serve either as sense organs or organs of respiration.

There is a body cavity in which the digestive and reproductive organs are freely suspended. The circulatory system is not well developed. Special sense organs of a simple type sometimes occur. The nervous system is also poorly developed, consisting chiefly of a ring of nerve fibres encircling the mouth and sending a radial nerve into each ray of the body.

551. **Class I. Pelmatozoa.**—The crinoids or "sea lilies" are the only living representatives of this group. The body is attached by a stalk-like development of the aboral pole. In a few forms this is true only in the young stages but for most families the stalked condition is permanent. The skeletal elements are highly developed. The stalk, body and arms are largely composed of calcareous joints and plates. The five rays are usually repeatedly branched. The ambulacral system consists of ciliated tentacles which serve for respiration and to maintain the currents by which food is carried to the mouth. In connection with the latter function, ciliated grooves on the

FIG. 144.—Antedon, a Crinoid. × 1/2.

254   CLASSIFICATION OF ANIMALS

oral surface of the arms are also important. The digestive tract opens by a vent on the oral surface in an eccentric position.

552. **Class II. Asteroidea.**—The starfishes lie on the sea bottom with the mouth or oral side down. The ambulacral feet

Fig. 145.—A starfish, Astropecten. × 3/4.

serve for locomotion. The oral-aboral axis is shorter than a radius and the five radii are longer than the inter-radii so that the body assumes the form of a five-rayed star. The skeleton consists of small rod-shaped pieces attached to each other by muscles in such a way as to form a network. This skeleton is very flexible and by means of the muscles the arms may be slowly bent through an arc of 180° or more. Short spines, more or less movable, project beyond the general surface. Each radial canal ends at the tips of the arm in a tentacle and at its base there is an eyespot.

553. The starfish is carnivorous, living largely on shell fish. The mouth is located at the centre of the disc and is capable of opening to an enormous size so that large objects can be taken into the stomach. After digestion the insoluble part is ejected at the mouth. The animal also attacks larger prey than it can swallow. By attaching some of the tube feet to the solid substratum and others to the two valves of a shell fish the shell may be pulled open. Then another remarkable feat is performed: The stomach is everted though the mouth and its rather voluminous folds are thrown around the soft parts of the prey. Digestion then takes place outside the body of the animal. Five pairs of long retractor muscles connect the wall of the stomach with the interior of the arms; their function is to draw the stomach back into the body. The stomach is connected with a vent at the aboral pole by a small intestine. But intestine and vent are largely functionless and are often rudimentary. Connected with the stomach are five long tubes which project into the cavities of the arms. The walls of these tubes are glandular and secrete a digestive fluid. These glands are called hepatic cæca. The sexes are distinct and the five pairs of gonads lie in the body cavity, a pair in each arm.

554. **Class III. Ophiuroidea.**—The serpent stars, or brittle stars, have the general form of the starfish but are more distinctly divided into disc and arms. The arms are proportionately longer and more slender and also more actively movable and it is entirely by the sweeping movement of the

arms that locomotion is effected. The ambulacral "feet" are without sucking discs and ampullæ and do not assist in locomotion. The arms are almost solid, that is, the digestive and reproductive organs do not extend into them. The skeletal parts are better developed than in the starfish. In the "basket fish" the arms are branched.

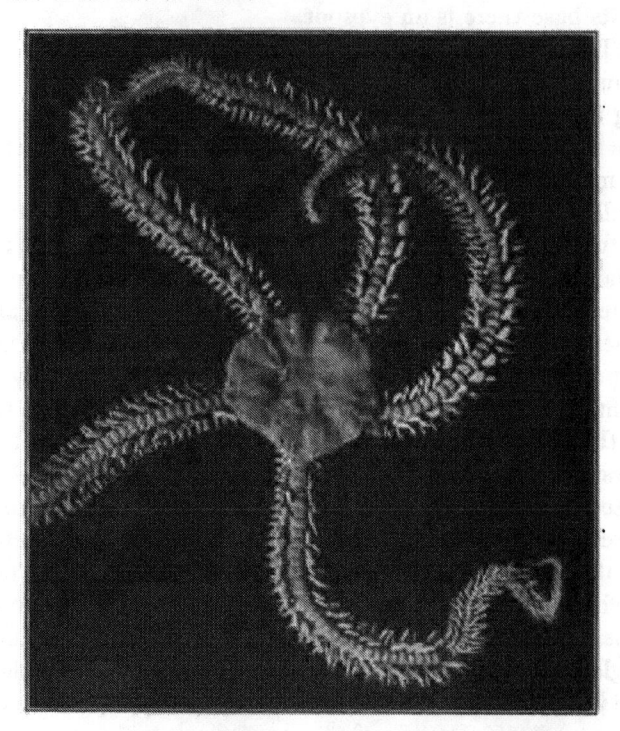

FIG. 146.—A brittle star (Ophiuroidea). × 3/4.

555. **Class IV. Echinoidea.**—In the sea urchins the radii and inter-radii are almost or quite equal and hence there are no "arms." The skeletal parts are broad plates which fit together so as to form a single piece, the shell or test. The oral surface

ECHINODERMATA 257

is down and the oral aboral axis is often nearly equal to a horizontal diameter so that the body is nearly spherical. The spines are often long and are movable and are important in locomotion. The tube feet are much as in the starfish. The true sea urchins are vegetable feeders and the mouth is provided with a set of five jaws which form a complicated apparatus known as Aristotle's lantern. The intestine is long

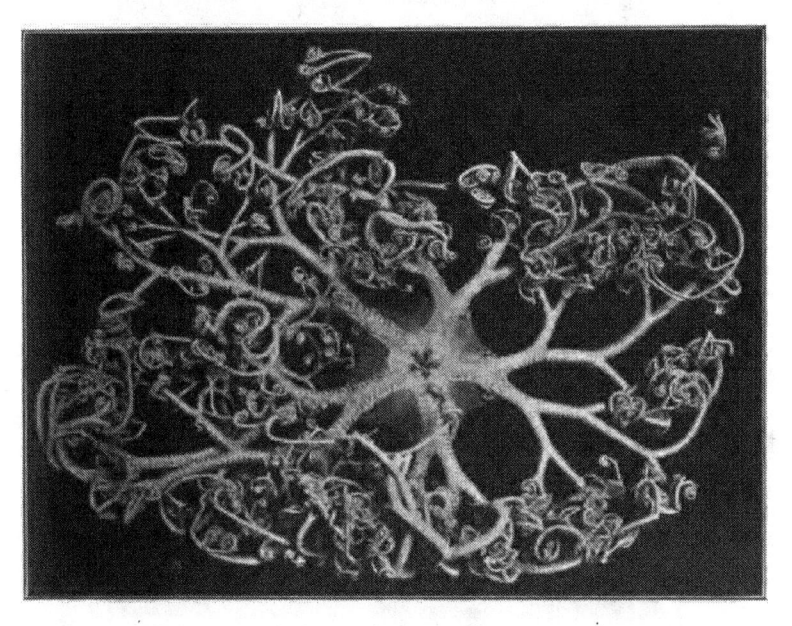

FIG. 147.—The basket fish, Astrophyton. × 1/2.

and coiled and opens by a vent on the aboral surface. In some groups of Echinoidea a secondary bilateral symmetry appears and in these the vent is at the posterior margin of the oral surface.

556. **Class V. Holothuroidea.**—The sea cucumbers have the principal axis horizontal so the oral-aboral axis is at right

258   CLASSIFICATION OF ANIMALS

angles to that of the other Echinoderms. The principal axis is also much longer than the radii. The skeletal parts are reduced to minute hooks and plates, but the integument is very thick and leathery. The animals feed on organic detritus which they collect by means of a circle of branching tentacles

FIG. 148.—A sea-urchin (Clypeaster). The spines have been removed. The five ambulacral areas are clearly shown. The test shows marked bilateral symmetry.

surrounding the mouth. The intestine is a coiled tube and ends at the aboral pole of the animal in a large cloacal cavity. Lying in the body cavity and connected with the cloaca is a very peculiar organ called the respiratory tree. It is a tubular structure and is many times branched. The main stem opens into the cloaca. The respiratory tree is filled with water which is regularly renewed from outside through the cloacal vent. This is brought about in the following way. Numerous small muscles connect the outside of the cloacal chamber with the body wall. When these contract the cloaca expands and fills with water. The cloacal aperture then closes, the walls of the cloaca contract and the contents are forced into the respiratory tree. The tubes of the respiratory tree also have contractile walls and these by contraction again force the water out. In some of the small Holothuria, which do not possess such an impervious integument, the respiratory tree is absent. The ambulacral system is variously developed within the group. In several families the tube feet are entirely wanting. Locomotion is chiefly effected by worm-like movements of the body.

557. PHYLUM VII. *Arthropoda.*—The Arthropoda are bilaterally symmetrical, segmented animals. They are distinguished from the Annelida by their jointed appendages. The number of segments is usually not more than twenty, and they are not alike (heteronomous). The body is always covered with a cuticula of chitin, secreted by the epidermis. One or more pairs of appendages are modified to serve as mouth parts for the ingestion of food. The blood vessels open into the body cavity which is also connected with the cavities derived from the primitive blastula cavity. The body is typically divided into three regions, head, thorax and abdomen. The nervous system consists of a brain and ventral nerve cord as in the Annelids. In point of numbers the phylum includes two-thirds of the animal kingdom.

558. **Class I. Branchiata.**—As the name implies the Branchiata are the Arthropods which are provided with gills. But this is true only of the larger forms and even in some of these the gills have been lost. With a very few exceptions, however, the Branchiata are aquatic. The term Crustaceæ

is also frequently applied to the group because the chitinous cuticula is impregnated with salts of lime which render it very hard. The appendages are forked (biramous) and at least three pairs are modified as mouth parts and two pairs, the antennæ, have a sensory function.

559. The orders Phyllopoda, Ostracoda, Branchiura and Copepoda comprise only small forms, seldom more than an inch in length and usually minute. The *Phyllopoda* are characterized by their broad, leaf-like swimming appendages. The *Ostracoda* have a carapace in the form of two valves, like the shell of a clam, which can be opened and closed. The *Copepoda* are cigar shaped and have a single median eye. The Ostracoda and Copepoda are very common in our fresh-water ponds. The *Branchiura* are parasitic in the gill chambers of other crustacea and on fishes. There are also many parasites among the Copepoda.

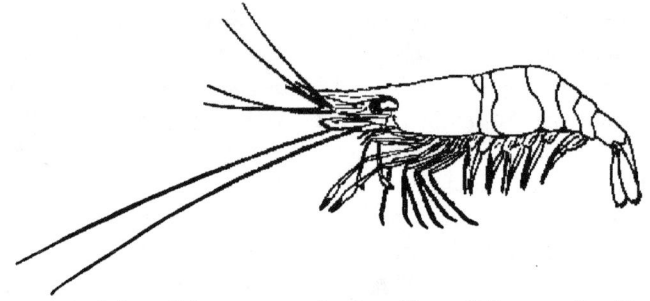

FIG. 149.—A shrimp, Palæmonetes vulgaris. (From Galloway, after Verrill.)

560. *Order 5.*—The *Cirripedia* are the barnacles. They are all marine. The young are free swimming but they come to rest and attach themselves to some object. A series of calcareous plates are formed by folds of the skin. Some of these are hinged and can be moved by muscles. The animal may be entirely enclosed by the shell. The appendages are long and slender and are fringed with hairs. These organs are thrust out into the water and by a sweeping motion currents carrying food particles are directed toward the mouth. The eyes are degenerate in the adult but the reproductive organs are highly developed. The barnacles are usually hermaphrodytic. Several families belonging to this group are parasitic. The sacculina described in Part III is a notable example.

561. *Order 6.*—The *Malacostraca* are a large group, comprising all the larger crustacea. The head and thorax together are composed of thirteen segments and the abdomen of six. There are always two pairs of antennæ, a pair of mandibles and two pairs of maxillæ. In most cases several more pairs of appendages function as mouth parts. This order is very large and includes shrimps, prawns, crayfish, lobsters, crabs, sand fleas and "wood-lice." Of the five great divisions of the group the following are the most important. Legion 2. Thoracostraca. The compound eyes are on movable stalks and the head and most or all of the segments of the thorax are covered by a single cuticular shield. The gills are usually attached to the basal joints of the thoracic appendages or to the adjacent parts of the body-wall and are covered by the cephalo-thoracic shield.

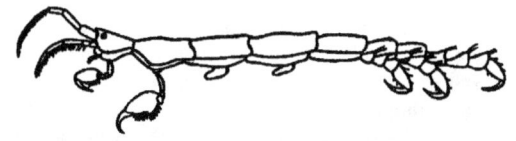

FIG. 150.—Caprella geometrica, an Amphipod. (From Galloway, after Verrill.)

The sub-order Decapoda comprises the most important families. In this group the five pairs of appendages from the 9th to 13th segments inclusive are ambulatory appendages. Those of the 3rd to 8th are mouth parts. The following analysis of the classes of the malacostraca will show the relation of the groups mentioned.

Order, Malacostraca.
    Legion 1. Leptostraca.
    Legion 2. Thoracostraca.
        Sub-order 1. Schizopoda.
        Sub-order 2. Decapoda.
            Section 1. Macrura natantia, shrimps, pawns.
            Section 2. Macrura reptantia, crayfish, lobster.
            Section 3. Anomura, hermit crabs.
            Section 4. Brachyura, crabs.
        Sub-order 3. Cumacea.
    Legion 3. Stomatopoda.
    Legion 4. Anomostraca.
    Legion 5. Arthrostraca.
        Sub-order 1. Anisopoda.
        Sub-order 2. Isopoda, "pill bug"="wood-louse."
        Sub-order 3. Amphipoda, sand fleas.

562. The Macrura natantia (swimming large tails) are generally compressed laterally, the ambulatory appendages are slender and the animal depends chiefly on the backward stroke of the strong abdomen for locomotion. The Macrura reptantia (crawling large tails) are not compressed and the thoracic appendages are strong as is also the abdomen. The section Anomura includes the hermit crabs which live habitually with the abdomen thrust into an empty snail shell. For this reason the abdomen is twisted, the posterior thoracic appendages reduced and the caudal fin transformed into an unsymmetrical hold-fast organ. The Brachyura are the true crabs in which the abdomen is much reduced and turned forward under the cephalo-thorax.

563. The Arthrostraca have sessile eyes and the thoracic shield is almost or wholly wanting. In the Isopoda the body is flattened dorso-ventrally and there are no gills on the thoracic appendages. The Amphipoda are compressed laterally and gills are present on the thoracic appendages. The body is curved with the abdomen turned down and forward. The last appendages of the abdomen are turned backward and are used in connection with the backward stroke of the abdomen to spring the body forward analogous to the movement of a flea, hence the name. Most of the Malacostraca are marine. The crayfishes are fresh-water representatives of the order. A number of crabs live on land though usually in the vicinity of water. The wood-louse is also a familiar terrestrial form, though it is also at home only in damp places. The terrestrial crabs have rudimentary gills and the gill chamber takes on the function of a lung.

564. **Class II. Palæostraca.**—These arthropods have only one pair of appendages anterior to the mouth and five pairs surrounding the mouth. Those around the mouth serve both for the ingestion of food and for locomotion.

565. *Order 2.*—The *Xiphosura* have a broad horseshoe-shaped cephalothorax, an unjointed abdomen and a long spine-like terminal appendage, to which the name "sword tail" refers. There are a pair of ocelli and a pair of compound eyes on the dorsal surface of the cephalothorax. The first pair of appendages are chelate but are not used in locomotion. The following five pairs are locomotor but their basal joints are spiny and serve for the trituration of the food. The abdominal appendages are broad leaf-like structures which protect the "book gills" which are attached to them. There is only one genus of Xyphosura, the horseshoe crab, Limulus.

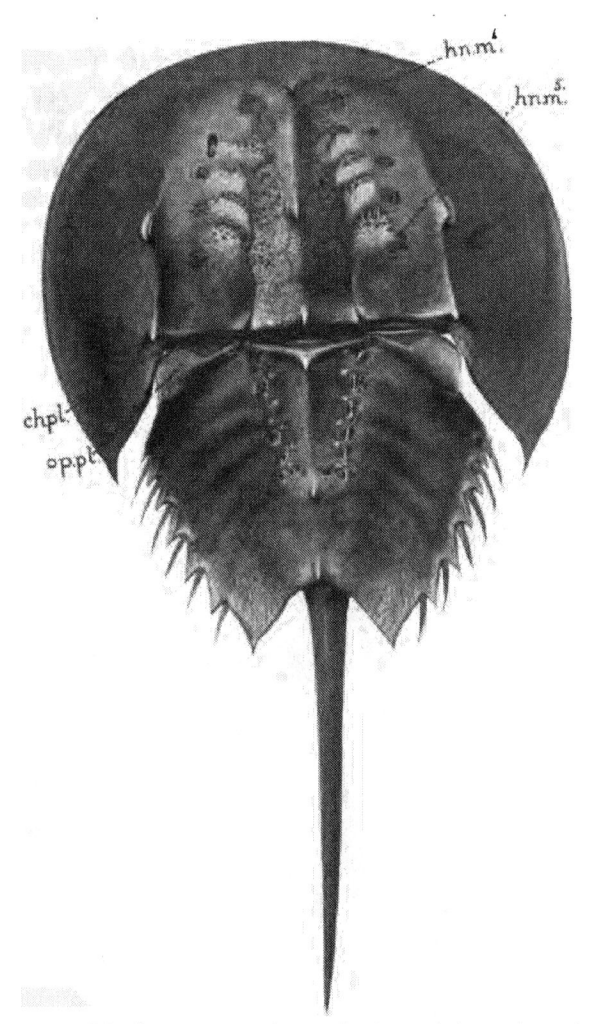

FIG. 151.—Limulus, the horse-shoe crab. Dorsal view. (From Patten.)

566. Class III. Arachnoidea.—The Arachnoidea are air-breathing Arthropods, with a cephalothorax, two pairs of mouth appendages and four pairs of locomotor appendages. The abdomen has no appendages. There are from 2 to 12 eyes.

567. Order 1.—The *Scorpionidea* are large Arachnoidea with a long segmented abdomen consisting of a preabdomen of seven segments and

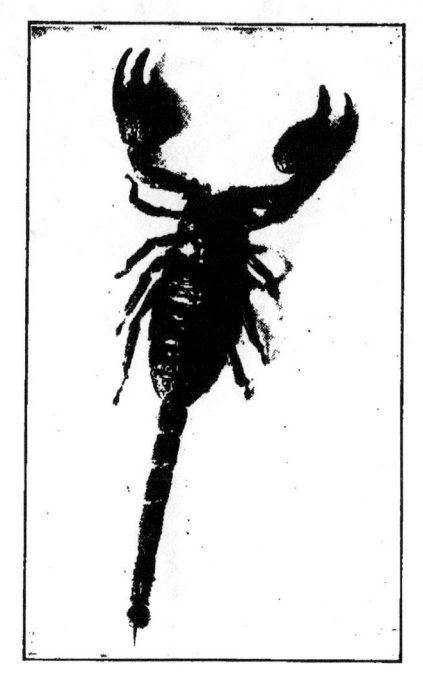

FIG. 152.—A Scorpion, Buthus afer. × 1/2.

a postabdomen of six segments and ending in a spine and poison gland. The first and second pairs of appendages, the chelicerae and maxillary palps are chelate. The respiratory organs consist of four pairs of book lungs which open on the ventral side of the preabdomen.

568. Order 2.—The *Pedipalpi* have clawed chelicerae, clawed or chelate

ARACHNOIDEA 265

maxillary palps, and the third pair of appendages are whip like. The abdomen is 11-12 jointed. There are two pairs of book lungs.

569. *Order 3*.—The *Araneida*, or true spiders, have the abdomen connected with the cephalothorax by a narrow waist. The abdomen is usually unsegmented. The cheliceræ are chelate and the maxillary palps are similar to the ambulatory appendages. There are four book lungs or, two book lungs and two tracheæ or, four tracheæ. On the ventral surface of the abdomen is a group of four or six glands from which the

FIG. 153.—The great bird-killing spider, Mygale, of South America. × 5/8.

web is spun. The web is a fluid secretion which sets on exposure to the air. It is used to build and line the nest, for building traps by which the prey is caught, for winding about the egg masses, for locomotion and a variety of other purposes. The cheliceræ are provided with a poison gland.

570. *Order 6*.—The *Opilionidea* are the "harvestmen" or "daddy-long-legs." The abdomen is broadly connected with the cephalo-thorax so that the whole forms apparently one continuous body. The cheliceræ are chelate and the maxillary palpi are like the legs. The legs are often very long. The respiratory organs are tracheæ.

266   CLASSIFICATION OF ANIMALS

FIG. 154A.—Home of the trap-door spider. Door closed.

FIG. 154B.—Home of the trap-door spider. The door propped open with a straw. × 1.

571. Order 8.—The *Acarina* are the mites and ticks. Many of the members of this group are parasites. The body cannot be divided into cephalo-thorax and abdomen as all evidence of segmentation is lacking. The mouth parts are often adapted for piercing and sucking. The legs

FIG. 155.—The home of the trap-door spider laid open. The door is held open with a pin. × 3/4.

are often merely hold-fast organs. The parasitic forms are often much degenerate.

572. Order 9.—The *Linguatulida* are parasitic forms especially notable

268   CLASSIFICATION OF ANIMALS

for the degenerated condition of many organs. The body is worm-like and the appendages are reduced to two pairs of hooks.

573. **Class 6. Protracheata.**—This group is of interest as forming a connecting link between the annelids and insects.

Fig. 156.—The trap-door spider. × 1.

There are only a few species, which are not common but are found in widely separated parts of the globe. The animals are small, worm-like, and are found in damp places under stones, decaying wood or other similar situations. The body is worm-

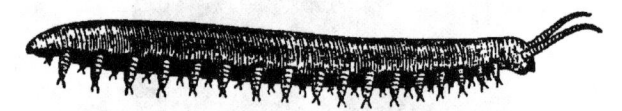

Fig. 157,—Peripatus capensis, an example of the class Protracheata.
(From Galloway, after Moseley.)

like and provided with short feet somewhat like the false feet of a caterpillar but provided with claws. There is one pair of tentacles and a pair of eyes. There are two pairs of appendages in the region of the mouth. The respiratory organs are tracheæ with stigmata scattered irregularly over the surface of the body.

MYRIAPODA

574. Class 7. Myriapoda.—The "thousand legs" have a worm-like body divided into similar segments, a distinct head with one pair of antennæ, usually one pair of maxillæ and with one or two pairs of appendages on each body segment. Respiration is by tracheæ and the stigmata are arranged segmentally.

575. *Order 3.*—The *Diplopoda* are the common "thousand legs." The body is cylindrical or half-cylindrical and is covered with a chitinous cuticula hardened by deposits of carbonate of lime. All the segments except a few of the most anterior and the last one bear two pairs of appendages. The animals are vegetable feeders and harmless.

576. *Order 4.*—The *Chilopoda* bear some resemblance to the preceding group but

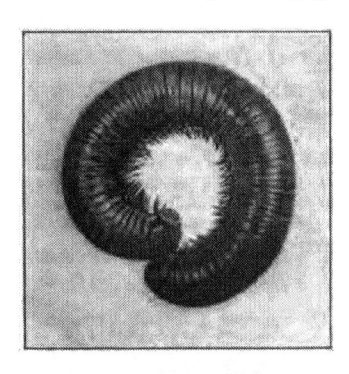

FIG. 158.—Spirobolus, a Diplopod. (From Folsom.)

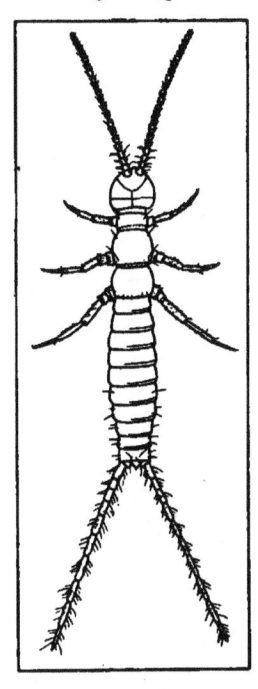

FIG. 159.—Campodea, an example of the class Apterygogenea. (From Folsom.)

the body is usually flattened and no segment bears more than one pair of appendages. There is a pair of mandibles, two pairs of maxillæ and one pair maxillipeds. The maxillipeds belong to the first body segment. They are stout claws and contain a poison gland. The centipede of the south is an example of this order but a more familiar one is the long-legged Cermatia often seen in our dwellings where it preys upon other insects.

270   CLASSIFICATION OF ANIMALS

577. Class 9. Apterygogenea.—This class is often grouped with the insects as the lowest order. They have many characters in common with insects and are doubtless closely related.

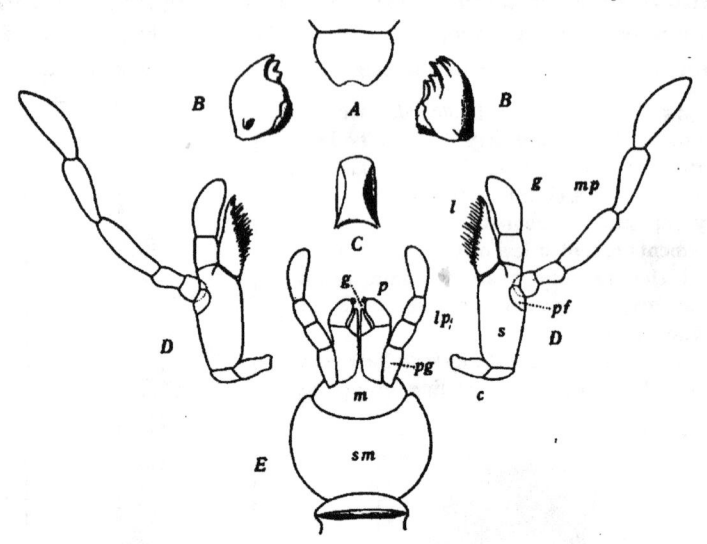

FIG. 160.—Mouth parts of a cockroach, Ischnoptera pennsylvanica. *A*, labrum; *B*, mandible; *C*, hypopharynx; *D*, maxilla; *E*, labium; *c*, cardo; *g* (of maxilla) galea; *g* (of labium) glossa; *l*, lacinia; *lp*, labial palpus; *m*, mentum; *mp*, maxillary palpus; *p*, paraglossa; *pf*, palpifer; *pg*, palpiger; *s*, stipes; *sm*, submentum. *B*, *D* and *E* are in ventral aspect. (From Folsom.)

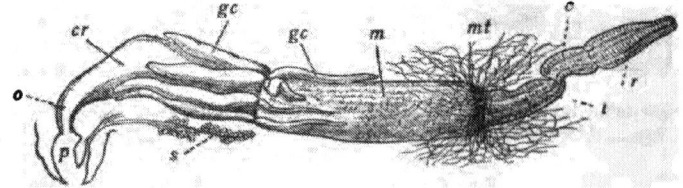

FIG. 161.—Alimentary tract of a grasshopper, Melanoplus. *c*, Colon; *cr*, crop; *gc*, gastric cæca; *i*, ileum; *m*, midintestine, or stomach; *mt*, malpighian tubules; *o*, œsophagus; *p*, pharynx; *r*, rectum; *s*, salivary gland. (From Folsom.)

There is a distinct head, a thorax of three segments and an abdomen of 6–11 segments. The head bears a pair of antennæ and sometimes compound eyes. An ocellus may also be present. There is a mandible and two pairs of maxillæ. Each segment of the thorax bears a pair of appendages. The only evidence of abdominal appendages to be found are a pair of stiff bristles attached to the ventral surface of the fifth segment and projecting forward beneath the body, and a pair of hooks beneath the third segment. By means of this apparatus the animal makes springing movements. Hence they are called spring tails. The respiratory organs are tracheæ except in some groups where respiratory organs are wanting.

578. **Class 10. Insecta.**—In the Insects the body is divided into head, thorax of three segments (prothorax, mesothorax and metathorax) and an abdomen of 9–10 segments. The appendages of the head are a pair of antennæ, a pair of mandibles, a pair of maxillæ and a labium which represents a second pair of maxillæ. Each segment of the thorax bears a pair of legs and in addition the meso- and metathorax also each have a pair of wings. The abdominal segments bear no appendages.

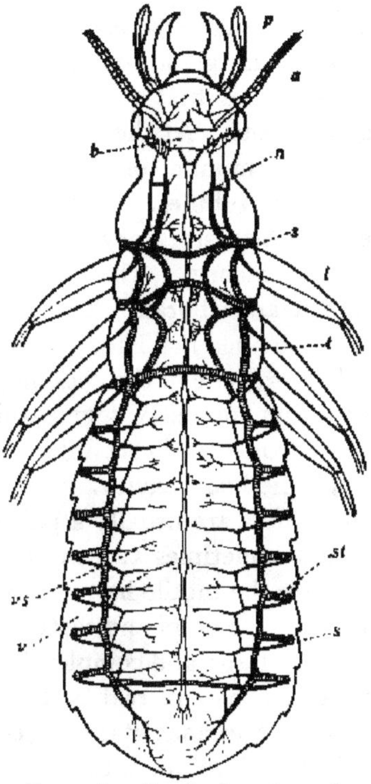

FIG. 162—Tracheal system of an insect. *a*, Antenna; *b*, brain; *l*, leg; *n*, nerve-cord; *p*, palpus; *s*, spiracle; *st*, spiracular, or stigmatal branch; *t*, main tracheal trunk; *v*, ventral branch; *vs*, visceral branch. (From Folsom, after Kolbe.)

579. The mouth opens into a narrow œsophagus with which

several salivary glands are connected. The œsophagus is often enlarged to form a crop. In several orders there is also a gizzard between the crop and the stomach. The stomach is the true digestive portion of the alimentary canal. It is larger in diameter than œsophagus or intestine and usually has sack-like or tubular glands opening into its anterior end. Following the stomach is first a narrow small intestine and then a wider large intestine. At the junction of stomach and small intestine there are a number of long and very slender tubes, known as Malpighian tubules. These are the excretory organs of the insect. The respiratory system consists of a greatly branched system of tracheæ. These open on the surface at the side of the abdomen and thorax. The tracheal capillaries extend to all parts of the body. The heart is a long contractile vessel lying on the dorsal side of the abdomen. The blood enters it through eight pairs of ostia segmentally arranged. A vessel leads forward from the heart into the head. The blood circulates through the body cavity.

580. There are usually a pair of highly developed compound eyes and sometimes two or three ocelli. Other special sense organs are the tactile hairs on the antennæ, the olfactory cones and pits of the palpi and taste cells of the mouth cavity. The "brain" is large and complex in structure. The ventral ganglionic chain may in reality be a chain of as many as twelve ganglia, but various stages of concentration occur even to the fusion of all into one mass.

581. The gonads open by a pair of ducts at the posterior end of the abdomen. The sexes are separate and usually dimorphic. In some orders polymorphism is not uncommon. The eggs, in many cases, develop without fertilization (parthenogenesis). In most orders there is a marked metamorphism.

582. *Order* 1.—The *Orthoptera* are insects with biting mouth parts, two pairs of wings which are unlike, and development by an incomplete metamorphosis. The order includes, earwigs, cockroaches, the praying-

mantis, "devil's horse" or "darning needle," grasshoppers, katydids and crickets,

583. *Order* 3.—The *Corrodentia* have biting or rudimentary mouth parts, wings alike, and development without or with little metamorphosis. The group includes the highly interesting "white ants" or termites and the less interesting body lice, ectoparasitic on mammals. The latter are degenerate, lacking wings and having rudimentary mouth parts and eyes greatly reduced. The termites are colonial and polymorphic. The sexually perfect males and females are winged but the wings are later cast off. A third form called a worker and sometimes another form called a soldier may also be found. These are individuals in which the reproductive system remains undeveloped.

584. *Orders* 6 *and* 7.—The *Odonata*, "damsel flies," dragon flies, and *Ephemeroidea*, "day flies," are found only in the vicinity of fresh-water ponds or streams in which the larval development takes place.

585. *Order* 8.—Some of the *Neuroptera*, "lace wings," also develop in the water as for example Corydalis whose larva is the "hellgrammite." The ant lion ("doodle bug") is the larva of another "lace wing." The Odonata have an incomplete, the Ephemeroidea and Neuroptera a complete metamorphosis. All the remaining Orders except the last, Rhynchota, also undergo complete metamorphosis.

586. *Order* 11.—The large order *Lepidoptera*, butterflies and moths, is perhaps the most readily distinguished of all. Here the maxillæ are modified for sucking and form a proboscis. The two pairs of wings are similar and covered with scales. The prothorax is united firmly with the mesothorax. The larva is a caterpillar with distinct head and jaws developed for biting. The head also bears two antennæ and two or three pairs of simple eyes. The first three segments behind the head have jointed appendages and there are besides on the segments of the abdomen from two to five pairs of false feet. After a time of voracious feeding and rapid growth the larva attaches itself in some sheltered place or spins a cocoon of silk fibres. It then undergoes a complete change of form, metamorphosis, becoming a quiescent pupa in which condition it continues for a short time if it is in the summer or through the winter if pupation takes place in the fall. Finally another transformation takes place, the integument of the pupa bursts and the imago emerges in all respects a mature insect. The life period of the imago is usually brief; the female is fertilized, deposits a single brood of eggs and dies.

587. *Order* 12.—The *Diptera* or two wings include the flies, gnats, and mosquitos. They have mouth parts developed for sucking or piercing.

The anterior wings are membraneous, the posterior pair reduced to "balancers" or halteres. The body is usually compact with the ventral chain of ganglia united into a single mass. The abdomen consists of 5-9 segments. The larva is a footless and often headless grub (maggot) and in the process of metamorphosis is transformed into a pupa and finally the imago. The larvæ of the mosquitos are aquatic, those of most of the true flies live in decaying organic matter but many are parasitic. In a number of cases the adult is also parasitic.

588. *Order* 13.—The *Siphonaptera* or fleas. In this group the wings are wanting through degeneration. Compound eyes are also lacking. The body is laterally compressed. The mouth parts are for piercing and sucking. The third pair of legs are used for springing. The larvæ are usually free living, the adult an external parasite.

589. *Order* 14.—The *Coleoptera*, or beetles, are a very large order. The mouth parts are constructed for biting. The anterior pair of wings are horny, the second pair membraneous. The first pair are called elytra. They fit together to form a shield over the abdomen and at rest the second pair of wings are folded under them. The larvæ have a distinct head with simple eyes and a soft body—("grub worms"). The feet may be wanting. The grub lives in protected situations, underground, under the bark of trees or boring into wood or in other similar places. Metamorphosis includes a pupa stage.

FIG. 163.—The Lantern-fly of Brazil. Fulgora lanternaria. This odd example of the Rhynchota is said by the natives to carry a light in the peculiar appendage borne on the head. This statement is seriously questioned, however, and the function of the "lantern" is not known. × 5/4.

590. *Order* 16.—The *Hymenoptera* include the ants, bees and wasps. The mouth parts are adapted for biting. The wings are two pairs, of a membraneous texture. There are two compound eyes and three ocelli. The females are provided with a sting of a complex structure and located at the posterior end of

the abdomen. This may be used for depositing eggs or for defense. The brain is highly developed. Some larvæ feed on leaves, others are parasitic in the tissues of other insects or of plants while others are fed by the adults with either animal or vegetable food. The larvæ usually spin a cocoon in which the pupa stage is passed. Some of the most important forms are: The gall wasps which deposit the eggs in the tissues of plants whereby a gall develops and forms a shelter and source of food for the larvæ; the ichneumon flies which sting the larvæ of other insects and deposit their eggs there, the larvæ then developing as internal parasites; the ants with their complex social organization, polymorphism, consisting of three or four types of individuals, and division of labor, keeping of slaves, cultivation of plants and fostering of aphids for economic purposes; the common solitary wasps and social wasps with the more or less artfully constructed nests of mud or "paper"; the social and polymorphic honey bee and the bumble bees with their combs and honey. This interesting order merits a special treatise.

591. *Order* 17.—The *Rhynchota* or bugs. These insects are provided with a protruding snout and piercing mouth parts. Metamorphosis occurs in some cases, in variable degree. The wings are sometimes wanting but there are usually two pairs. The anterior pair may be partly horny. They are all ectoparasitic on other animals or plants. Included in this group are the bed bugs, the plant bugs, such as the squash bug, chinch bug and cicada, the water bugs, water-boatmen, water-striders and electric-light bug, and the "plant lice" and scale insects.

592. PHYLUM VIII. *Mollusca.*—The Molluscs are the highest group of unsegmented animals. The group is pretty well defined but there is a great difference in the scale of organization between the lowest and highest orders. The most marked anatomical character of the phylum is the mantle, which is a single or paired fold of the integument of the dorsal side of the body. This mantle is usually of sufficient extent to entirely enclose the body of the animal, and on its external surface it secretes a hard shell composed of horny and calcareous matter deposited in layers. There are no paired appendages. A ventral muscular portion of the body is called the foot and sometimes serves for locomotion. The nervous system con-

sists of three ganglia called the cerebral, pedal and visceral ganglia. These are connected by paired nerves. The cœlomic cavity is almost obliterated by a mesenchymatous parenchyma. A pair of nephridia connect the remnant of the body-cavity with the exterior. There is also a pair of gonads. The body is fundamentally bilaterally symmetrical but in one large group a twisting of the visceral mass results in more or less asymmetry. The mollusca are primarily aquatic animals but a large number have become adapted to a terrestrial life.

593. **Class I. Amphineura.**—This is a small class and only one example need be described. Chiton is bilaterally symmetrical and flattened dorso-ventrally. There is a partially differentiated head but the mantle fold includes the head as well as the body. On its dorsal surface the mantle forms a single series of eight plates. The foot is very broad and muscular and is used for locomotion and as a sucking disc for a hold-fast. In the groove between the mantle and the side of the body is a series of ctenidia, or comb-like gills. The digestive tract consists of a mouth cavity with radula and a pair of "salivary" glands, an œsophagus, stomach with a pair of digestive glands and a coiled intestine. The vent is at the posterior end, opening into the mantle cavity. The nervous system consists of an œsophageal ring or nerve collar and two pairs of longitudinal nerves, one ventral and one lateral. Besides, there are several smaller ganglia and numerous connectives between the longitudinal nerves. There is a pair of nephridia and a double gonad with paired ducts. All the Amphineura are marine.

594. **Class II. Conchifera.**—This group is distinguished from the preceding by the fact that the mantle fold does not include the head and by the way in which the shell is formed. The latter consists of numerous spine-like pieces in the Amphineura while in the Conchifera it is formed in layers as a single structure.

MOLLUSCA 277

595. *Order* 1.—The *Gastropoda* have a distinct head, a twisted visceral sack, a single shell and a creeping foot with, sometimes, lateral swimming lobes. The head usually bears two or four tentacles and a pair of eyes. The visceral organs are chiefly contained in a dorsal conical sack-like development of the body-wall which is more or less coiled in form of a spiral. The lower edge of the mantle forms a collar-like continuation of the ventral edge of the visceral sack. The entire surface of the visceral sack down to the edge of the collar is covered with a calcareous shell into which the head and foot may also be withdrawn. Between the surface of the mantle and the body there is a space of considerable size. This is called the mantle cavity. In it lie two feather-like gills, ctenidia, which are developed from the body-wall. Because of the twisting of the visceral mass the gills become shifted in position and one is frequently reduced.

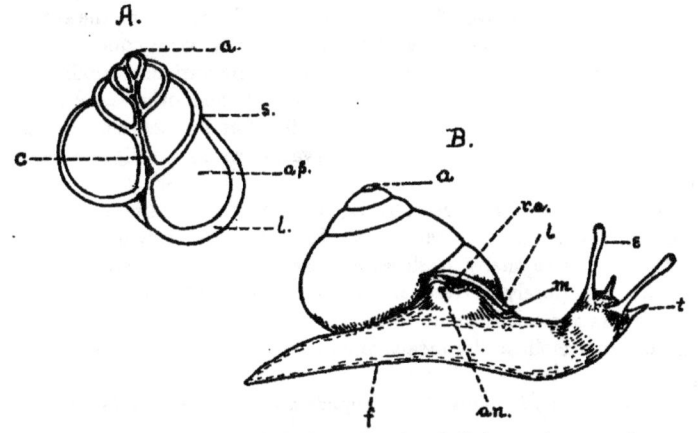

Fig. 164.—The garden snail, Helix. A, The shell in section. *a*, Apex; *an*, anus; *ap.* aperture; *c*, columella; *e*, eyestalk; *f*, foot; *l*, lip; *m*, edge of mantle (collar); *ra*, respiratory aperture; *s*, suture; *t*, tentacles. (From Galloway.)

596. In the mouth cavity there is a horny jaw and a tongue covered with a rough, file-like cuticular ribbon. This as called a radula. The digestive tract is rather long and coiled. There are a pair of "salivary" glands with ducts opening into the buccal cavity. The œsophagus is enlarged into a crop. Another enlargement of the canal forms a stomach into which the ducts of a large digestive gland ("liver") open. The coiled small intestine opens into a shorter and wider large intestine.

The vent is usually on the right side anterior to the visceral mass. The heart consists of a ventricle and one or two auricles. It lies in a small body cavity called a pericardial chamber. The kidney communicates with the pericardial chamber by a nephridial funnel and opens into the mantle chamber through a duct—the ureter.

597. The nervous system consists of a pair of cerebral ganglia, pleural ganglia and pedal ganglia which are all closely connected into a nerve collar. There are also parietal and buccal ganglia. From these ganglia nerves are supplied to the sense organs and muscles of the head, to the mouth, to the foot, to the gills, olfactory organs (osphradia) and a part of the mouth, and to the buccal mass and intestine respectively. The sense organs usually present are tentacles, eyes, a statocyst which is usually close by the pedal ganglion though it is innervated from the brain, and chemical sense organs, called osphradia, located on or near the gills.

598. Some of the Gastropods are hermaphroditic, in others, the sexes are separate. The reproductive system is frequently very complicated for besides the gonads and their ducts which may be variously modified, there may be two, three or more kinds of glands and other accessory reproductive organs. Development is either direct or by metamorphosis. The embryo is at first symmetrical. A larva known as a veliger occurs in many forms.

599. The Gastropods are typically aquatic but there are many forms in which the mantle chamber serves as a lung, no gills being developed. This is the case with many fresh-water forms and a large number of forms which are purely terrestrial. Many Gastropods are vegetable feeders. Others are carnivorous, some have the power of boring through the shells of other molluscs by means of an acid secretion, and thus killing their prey.

600. The numerous families of Gastropods are classified as follows:

    Legion I. Streptoneura
        Sub-order 1. Aspidobranchia
        Sub-order 2. Ctenobranchia
        Sub-order 3. Heteropoda
    Legion II. Euthyneura
        Sub-order 1. Opisthobranchia
        Sub-order 2. Pulmonata.

601. The Streptoneura have the visceral nerves crossed like a figure 8 because of the twisting of the visceral mass. For the same reason the gills lie in front of the heart. The sexes are generally distinct. The

MOLLUSCA 279

Aspidobranchia have feather-shaped (double) gills which are free at the tips. The Ctenobranchia have a single comb-shaped (single) gill. The Heteropoda are pelagic. The foot forms a flat fin. The visceral mass is small and the shell poorly developed or wanting.

602. The Euthyneura have the visceral nerves parallel. They are hermaphrodytic. The Opisthobranchia are marine forms with the gills usually behind the heart. The Pulmonata are chiefly terrestrial and fresh water snails without gills. The mantle cavity serves as a lung. In the slugs the shell is greatly reduced or wanting.

603. *Order 2.*—The *Solenoconchæ* have a horn-shaped shell and body and a cylindrical foot. The group is small and the animals are also small. They are marine and live in the mud of the bottom.

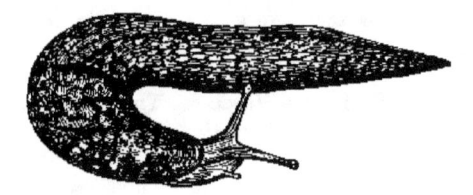

FIG. 165.—A slug, Limax. (From Galloway, after Binney's Gould.)

604. *Order 3.*—The *Lamellibranchiata* are compressed laterally. The head is rudimentary. The mantle is large and double, right and left. The shell is also double and the two valves are connected by a dorsal ligament. The foot is usually wedge shaped. There are two pairs of plate-like gills. The animal is usually bilaterally symmetrical but there may be considerable deviation from this rule.

605. The shell is secreted by the mantle and is composed of three layers. On the surface is a thin layer of a horny cuticula (periostracum) which is formed by the extreme edge of the mantle. The hinge ligament is of the same substance but forms a very thick layer. The hinge is elastic and causes the shell to gape when the adductor muscles are relaxed. Beneath the cuticula there is a thick layer of calcium carbonate deposited in a matrix of organic matter (conchiolin). The limey portion of the shell consists of two layers, an outer "prismatic" layer and an inner layer of "mother of pearl." The prismatic layer is so called because of the columnar or prismatic arrangement of the substance. The prisms stand perpendicular to the surface. The "mother of pearl" is in layers parallel to the

surface. The mantle lines the entire inner surface of the shell. Sometimes the edges of the mantle are partly united. There are always two points, however, where they are not united. One is at the posterior border and one is ventral anterior, opposite the foot. The posterior opening is frequently double and the edges of the mantle are then often extended so as to form a pair of tubes or siphons, or one double siphon. Through the ventral siphon the water enters the mantle cavity and escapes by the dorsal siphon.

606. The flattened body is suspended from the dorsal border of the mantle lobes. At its anterior and posterior ends are two strong muscles which connect the two valves of the shell. These are the adductors which close the shell. The gills are suspended from the dorsal border of the body in the mantle cavity. Each gill consists of two series of parallel vertical bars or filaments which are connected by short longitudinal and transverse bars. The gill is therefore a sort of double grating. On either side of the mouth are two triangular lappets, the labial palps. The surface of the gills and palps is covered with cilia which induce the currents in the water for respiration and feeding. The minute particles of food are carried toward the mouth along the edge of the mantle and thence between the palps. The mouth is a simple opening into the short œsophagus. The stomach is rather large and receives several ducts from the large digestive gland. From the stomach the intestine makes a number of loops and passes out of the visceral mass dorsally and posteriorly to a point above and behind the posterior adductor muscle into the mantle cavity.

607. The heart lies on the dorsal side of the visceral mass and consists of a ventricle and two lateral auricles. It is enclosed in a pericardial chamber which represents the body cavity. A nephridial funnel opens into the pericardial chamber on each side and this connects with the kidneys, or organs of Bojanus. The kidneys open into the mantle cavity on the side of the visceral mass. The sexes are usually separate. The gonads are large paired organs embedded in the visceral mass and opening with or near the kidney openings.

608. The nervous system consists of a cerebral ganglion which lies above the œsophagus, a visceral ganglion below the posterior adductor muscle, and a pedal ganglion embedded in the foot. These ganglia are connected by pairs of nerves. Sometimes there is also a separate pleural ganglion. The special sense organs are not well developed. There is a double statocyst near the pedal ganglion. Eyes are seldom found on the body but in a number of forms they occur on the edge of the mantle

and on the siphon. Tentacles, or special tactile organs are common on the siphon and mantle edge.

609. Fertilization of the eggs takes place in the mantle cavity where the early stages of development also take place in many cases. In the fresh-water clams especially, the larvæ remain for a long time attached to the gills of the parent. The marine forms have a trochophore larva. In the fresh-water forms the metamorphosis is more complete and in some cases the larvæ live for a time as parasites attached to the gills and fins of fishes.

610. All Lamellibranchs are aquatic and chiefly marine. Most live free on the bottom but some are attached by byssus threads which are formed by the secretion of a byssus gland in the small foot. Others are attached by the cementing of one valve to the substratum. Some bore into wood and others into calcareous rocks.

611. *Order 4.*—The *Cephalopods* are the most highly organized of all molluscs and in some respects of all invertebrates. All are marine and some attain great size. Some species are known to attain a length of 50–60 feet including the long arms.

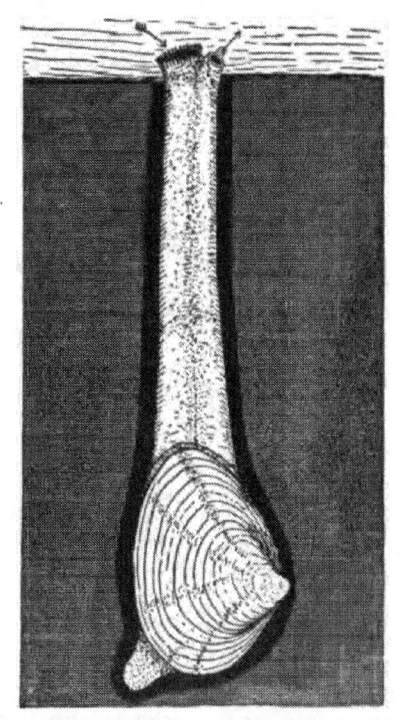

Fig. 166.—The "soft shell" clam, Mya arenaria. Showing the position when buried in the mud with the siphons extending to the surface. (From Galloway after Kingsley.)

The squid, cuttlefish, nautilus, and octopus are some of the best-known examples. Except in the pearly nautilus the shell is always rudimentary, and completely overgrown by the mantle. The visceral mass is elongated, conical in form, and lies in a much larger mantle chamber. There are two or four plume-like gills. The

282   CLASSIFICATION OF ANIMALS

mantle is very thick and muscular. The foot is shaped like a funnel and projects somewhat beyond the edge of the mantle. By the strong contraction of the mantle a stream of water is shot out through the funnel which causes a backward movement of the animal. Less vigorous contractions of the mantle produce respiratory currents. The large head is produced into eight or ten long arms which encircle the mouth. The oral surface of the arms is covered with numerous suckers which are purely hold-fast organs. The mouth opens into a buccal cavity and is provided with two strong jaws which together have the form of a beak. The buccal cavity contains a radula, and into it open four large salivary glands. The

FIG. 167.—The Devil-fish (Octopus), a dibranch Cephalopod. *A*, At rest; *B*, swimming. *a*, Arms; *e*, eye; *s*, siphon. (From Galloway after Merculiano.)

long œsophagus is sometimes enlarged into a crop. The stomach consists of two sacks into one of which two large digestive glands open. A large gland secreting ink opens into the rectum near the vent. The vent opens into the mantle cavity. The ink is discharged when the animal is pursued and serves to cover its flight. The heart lies in the upper side of the visceral mass. It consists of a ventricle and as many auricles as there are gills, 2 or 4. The arteries entering the gills are enlarged, muscular and rhythmically contractile. They are called branchial hearts. There are one or two pairs of kidneys intimately connected with the circulatory system and also connected with the body cavity by nephridial funnels. The kidneys open into the mantle cavity.

MOLLUSCA

612. The cerebral, visceral, pedal, pleural and buccal ganglia are all grouped in the region of the buccal mass. Other ganglia occur at the bases of the arms and in other parts of the body. The sense organs consist of a pair of eyes, a pair of statocysts and a pair of chemical sense organs below the eyes. The eyes are usually very highly developed and have a remarkable resemblance to the vertebrate eye, though fundamentally very different.

613. An internal skeleton of cartilage supports and protects the eyes and central nervous system. Other cartilages are found at the bases of the arms, at the edge of the mantle and in the funnel and in the fin. The rudimentary shell in most cases serves as a supporting structure. It may be either horny or calcareous.

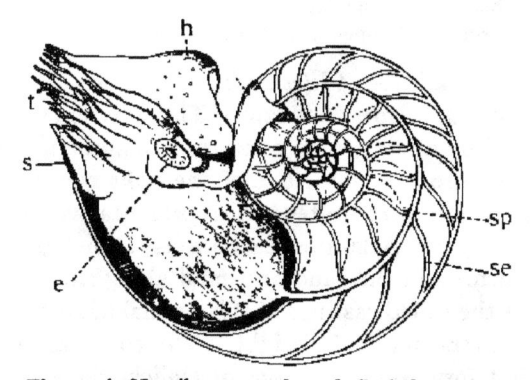

FIG. 168.—The pearly Nautilus, a tetrabranch Cephalopod. *e*, Eye; *h*, hood; *s*, siphon; *se*, septa forming the chambers of the shell; *sp*, siphuncle; *t*, tentacles. (From Galloway after Nicholson.)

614. The sexes are separate and dimorphic. The single gonad lies in the end of the visceral sack and its products are emptied into the cœlomic cavity. A pair of complicated ducts with associated glands lead from the body cavity to the mantle cavity. One of these ducts is frequently rudimentary or wanting. Development is direct.

615. The cephalopods are carnivorous, using their arms for catching their prey. When on the bottom the arms are also used for locomotion. By means of the mechanism already described a strong swimming stroke which carries the animal backward is performed. Some species are habitually swimming, others keep close to the bottom.

616. The sub-order Tetrabranchiata is characterized by the four gills, numerous tentacles in place of the arms and a large many-chambered shell of which only the last, largest chamber is occupied by the animal. The ink bag is wanting. There is only one living species, the pearly Nautilus. The Dibranchiata have only two gills and a rudimentary shell. In the section Decapoda there are eight arms and two longer tentacle arms. The suckers are stalked and have a horny rim. There are two lateral fins. In the section Octopoda the tentacles are wanting, the suckers are sessile and without a horny rim. There are usually no fins.
Cephalopoda:

> Sub-order. Tetrabranchiata, Nautilus.
> Sub-order. Dibranchiata.
> > Section. Decapoda, Squid.
> > Section. Octopoda, Octopus.

617. PHYLUM IX.—*Adelochorda*.

618. **Class I. Enteropneusta.**—This phylum and class are represented by a few genera of worm-like animals which are of interest because they form one of the links connecting the invertebrates and vertebrates. A representative of the group common on our Atlantic seashore is Dolichoglossus. The animal burrows in the sand and mud along shore. When the tide is out the coiled castings of this animal are often seen forming piles several inches in height. The coiled castings and an odor of iodoform are indications of Dolichoglossus. The body is composed of a conical proboscis, a broad band-like "collar" and a long tapering trunk. Only three points in the anatomy need be mentioned. 1. The mouth lies in front of the collar and from here the digestive tract extends directly to the posterior end of the body. The anterior part of the digestive tract is differentiated for respiration. It is connected at regular intervals with the body-wall and at these points there are openings which form a passage from the enteric cavity to the exterior. These openings are called gill slits. The respiratory current enters the mouth and passes out through these slits. 2. The nervous system consists of two ganglionic chains, one

dorsal and one ventral. These are connected by a nerve ring in the region of the collar. The dorsal nerve chain is tubular in front of the nerve ring. 3. The dorsal wall of the digestive tract is prolonged forward into the proboscis as a stiff tube of cells which forms a supporting axis for the proboscis. Neither of these features are found in any of the phyla so far described but they are regarded as the homologues of the pharyngeal gill slits, dorsal tubular nervous system, and notochord, respectively, of the Vertebrates. The validity of the third homology may be seriously questioned.

619. PHYLUM X. *Urochorda.*—The Urochorda are also called Tunicata because of the tunic or test, a thick integumentary structure formed by the mantle in many forms. This test is remarkable because it contains cellulose, which is otherwise found only in plants. The test is sometimes gelatinous but is often extremely tough and resistant. Many Tunicata are fixed but there are also free swimming forms. In the adult, the animals are usually markedly degenerate. The body is often sack-like in form. There is a large pharynx with gill slits, a dorsal tubular nervous system and a notochord. The food in minute particles is collected from the respiratory current and directed to the œsophagus by the action of ciliated grooves in the pharynx. The Tunicata are all marine.

620. **Class I. Copelata.**—This class comprises free swimming forms in which the notochord persists in the adult. The gill slits open directly to the exterior. The body is cask-shaped and there is a flat tail. The mantle is readily cast off and reformed.

621. **Class II. Tethyodea.**—The Ascidians or sea squirts are for the most part fixed. The gill slits and vent open into a chamber, "atrium," formed by folds of the integument. The atrial opening is usually near the mouth. Both mouth and atrial opening can be closed by muscular contraction. The whole body can also be greatly contracted. From the pharyn-

geal chamber a short œsophagus leads to a stomach into which the ducts of a digestive gland open. There is then a short coiled intestine which opens into the atrium. There is a heart but the vascular system is not well developed. The nervous system consists of a single ganglion lying between the mouth and atriopore. The sense organs are not well developed. All Tunicata are hermaphroditic. The larva develops into a "tadpole" which shows marked vertebrate affinities. Extending through the tail and for some distance into the body of the "tadpole" is a rod of large cells which forms a supporting axis. This is the notochord. On its dorsal side is a long tubular nervous system which ends in front in a vesicle containing an eye and a statocyst. At the anterior end of the body there are three glandular papillæ by which the tadpole finally attaches itself. A metamorphosis then takes place in which the chorda entirely disappears and the nervous system is reduced to the single ganglion. The entire tail is resorbed and by a twisting of the body in the further process of development the mouth comes to lie opposite the point of attachment.

622. Reproduction also takes place asexually and in many forms colonies are formed by budding. The colonies may be free swimming.

623. **Class III. Thaliacea.**—The Thaliacea are free swimming, transparent, colonial forms with an alternation of generations. Solitary individuals give rise to a colony of sexual individuals by budding and the colonial individuals produce eggs which develop into the sexless solitary form.

624. PHYLUM XI. *Acrania.*—This phylum has so much in common with the vertebrates that the absence of a skull was considered of sufficient note to be indicated in the name of the phylum. The body is elongated, flattened laterally and pointed at both ends. There is a persistent notochord, a long series of gill slits and a dorsal tubular, nervous system. The body is segmented but there are no paired appendages.

625. **Class Leptocardia.**—There is only one class represented by a few species. The form of the body has given rise to the common name "lancelet." The integument of the lancelet consists of a single layered epidermis. The gill slits open into a peribranchial chamber formed by folds of the skin. This chamber opens to the exterior by a pore at its posterior end. The mouth is surrounded by a circle of cirri. The animal lies on its side partly buried in the sand and collects its food from the respiratory current which is produced by ciliary action. The intestine is a straight tube opening by a vent on the left side of the tail. A long glandular pocket connected with the intestine probably represents a digestive gland. There is no heart but the larger vessels drive the blood by pulsating contraction. There is a ventral vessel (truncus arteriosus) which carries the blood forward. From this lateral branches pass over the gill arches to unite above in another vessel through which the blood flows back toward the posterior end of the body. A portal vein connects the intestine and digestive gland (liver), and other veins from the body-wall and digestive gland unite in the truncus arteriosus. In the region of the gills there is a paired series of nephridia which begin with funnels in the cœlomic cavity and open into the peribranchial chamber. The lancelet cannot be said to have a brain. The anterior end of the nerve tube (spinal cord) is slightly enlarged and contains a vesicular enlargement of the central canal. Connected with this is a single eyespot and an olfactory groove. Numerous other eyespots lie scattered along the spinal cord. The gonads lie against the wall of the peribranchial chamber which breaks to permit the reproductive cells to escape. The development of the lancelet is by a metamorphosis. The early stages are described in Part III.

626. PHYLUM XII. *Vertebrata.*—The Vertebrates all have a series of gill slits. In the terrestrial forms these are only present in the larval stages. The nervous system arises as a

tubular infolding of the ectoderm of the dorsal side. The axial skeleton consists primarily of a notochord which persists in the lower forms but is only found in the larval stages of the higher forms. In addition a vertebral column and a skull supplement or replace the notochord. The vertebral column consists of a series of segmentally arranged vertebræ with dorsal arches protecting the nervous system and ventral arches protecting the viscera.

627. **Class I. Cyclostomata.**—The round mouth eels. This class comprises only a few species of eel-like animals which are destitute of a lower jaw. The skin is smooth, i. e., there are no scales. There are no paired appendages. There is a median dorsal fin which is continued around the tip of the tail forming a tail fin. The mouth forms a circular sucking disc which is covered with hard epidermal tubercles by which the animal bores through the skin of the host to which it attaches itself. The Cyclostomes are ectoparasites and some even make their way for some distance into the host. The alimentary canal is practically a simple tube, though some forms have a spiral valve; and there is a large liver which opens into the digestive tract by a duct. There are also glands in the wall of the intestine. There are 6–14 pairs of gill slits which open directly to the exterior. The skeletal system consists of a well-developed notochord with a thick fibrous sheath, and a number of cartilages. The brain is enclosed in a skull composed partly of cartilage, partly of membrane. To this are attached the two cartilaginous ear capsules and a cartilaginous nasal capsule. There is also a network of cartilages surrounding and supporting the mouth and pharyngeal regions. The vertebræ consist only of neural arches with intercalary pieces, and of hæmal arches in the tail region. There is a heart similar to that of fishes. The olfactory organ is a single sack with a median opening. The eyes are of the typical vertebrate type but in some cases more or less reduced. The ear is a simple

statocyst-like sack. The brain is well developed, but lacks cerebral hemispheres and cerebellum. The ten cranial nerves are of a simple type and the spinal nerves do not unite dorsal and ventral roots.

628. **Class II. Pisces.**—The Fishes are a large group in which are included animals of very diverse character. The skin is

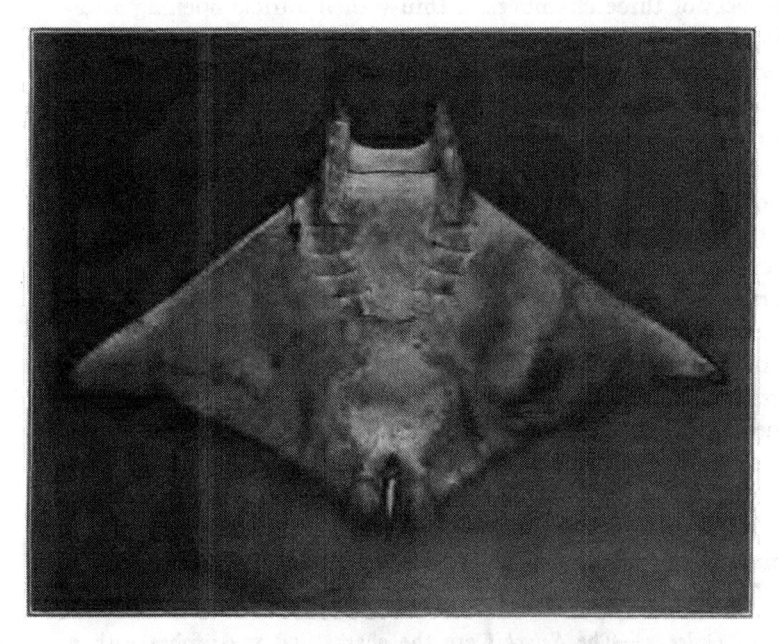

FIG. 169.—The Devil-ray, Manta. The lateral expansions are developed from the pectoral fins. This is a ventral view and shows the five pairs of gill slits, the odd shaped head with the eyes on the sides of the horns, the wide, straight mouth, and the whip-like tail. Taken at Beaufort, N. C. Much reduced.

usually covered with bony scales. There is a median fin which may be divided into several parts. There may be one or more dorsal fins, a tail fin and a ventral fin. There are usually two pairs of appendages which also have the form of fins. The fins are all dermal expansions supported on cartilaginous rays and bony spines. Fishes are all aquatic and respiration is by means of gills. There are often accessory respiratory organs— the swim bladder and true lungs. The swim bladder is an unpaired sack filled with air which serves to give the body of the fish the same specific gravity as the water. The heart consists of three chambers, a thin-walled auricle opening anteriorly into a very strong thick-walled ventricle which in turn is continued anteriorly by the conus arteriosus. In the bony fishes the latter is wanting and in its place the truncus arteriosus is enlarged into a bulbus arteriosus. The vessels have practically the same arrangement as in the lancelet. The organs of special sense are two nasal chambers which do not communicate with the mouth but have each two openings on the surface, one incurrent, one excurrent orifice; two eyes; two statocysts with utriculus and sacculus and three semicircular canals; and the lateral line system. The lateral line organs line depressions or tubes which communicate with the surface. These organs are arranged in a line along each side of the body and other shorter lines along the side and over the dorsal surface of the head. The sensory cells are clustered and their sensory bristles project into the canal of the lateral line. The function is to sense the currents in the water. The cerebral hemispheres are small, the cerebellum comparatively well developed.

629. *Order* 1.—The *Selachii* are the sharks and rays; fishes with a cartilaginous skeleton, placoid scales, 5–7 gill clefts with separate openings, a spiral valve, and upper jaw not united with the skull. The body is spindle shaped in the sharks and flattened dorso-ventrally in the rays. The spiral valve is a much enlarged posterior portion of the intestine with a spiral shelf-like fold projecting inward from the wall. These fishes are chiefly marine.

630. *Order* 2.—The *Holocephali* are not numerous in point of genera. They have a cartilaginous skeleton with the upper jaw articulated with the skull. The notochord persists and the vertebræ are represented only

by thin calcareous rings in the chorda membrane. There is only one pair of external openings of the gill clefts.

631. *Order 3*.—The *Dipnoi* or lung fishes. In this group there are four pairs of gills which are covered by an operculum. The tail is diphycercal i. e., the tail fin is symmetrical around the straight spinal axis. The chorda persists. The skeleton is cartilaginous and partly bony. There is a spiral valve and a pair of lungs. These fishes live in tropical regions in rivers and ponds which dry up in the dry season. During the dry season the animals bury themselves in the mud.

632. *Order 4*.—The *Brachioganoidea* also have gills covered by an operculum and a diphycercal tail. The skeleton is bony. The body is covered with thick rhombic scales covered with ganoin, a kind of enamel. There is also a spiral valve.

633. *Order 5*.—The *Chondroganoidea* or sturgeons have the gills covered by an operculum; a persistent chorda and cartilaginous skeleton; the head prolonged into a snout; the skin is naked or with bony plates; the tail fin heterocercal, i. e., the axis is bent up and the fin is unsymmetrical; a spiral valve and a conus arteriosus. The number of genera is small. The fishes are found chiefly in fresh waters.

634. *Order 6*.—The *Rhomboganoidea* or gar pikes have gills covered by an operculum; a bony skeleton; a long snout; body covered with rhombic ganoid scales; tail heterocercal; rudimentary spiral valve and a conus arteriosus. A few species only; found in the rivers and lakes of North America.

635. *Order 7*.—The *Cycloganoidea* have operculum, bony skeleton, cycloid scales, tail heterocercal, rudimentary spiral valve and a conus arteriosus. There is only one species, Amiatus calvus. This is found in the streams of North America.

636. *Order 8*.—The *Teleostei* or true bony fishes are very numerous. They have an operculum, bony skeleton, ctenoid or cycloid scales or large bony plates, a bulbus arteriosus, no spiral valve. The order is divisible into twelve sub-orders with many families. Some of the families are the herrings, salmon, electric eel, carp, catfish, eels, pike, sea horse, mullet, perch, mackerel, flat fishes, toad fish, trunk fish, etc.

637. **Class III. Amphibia.**—In this group of animals the larva is typically aquatic, the adult terrestrial. This is primarily evident in the respiratory organs though in many cases a marked metamorphosis occurs which involves other organs. The Amphibia have two pairs of pentadactyl appendages, a

292   CLASSIFICATION OF ANIMALS

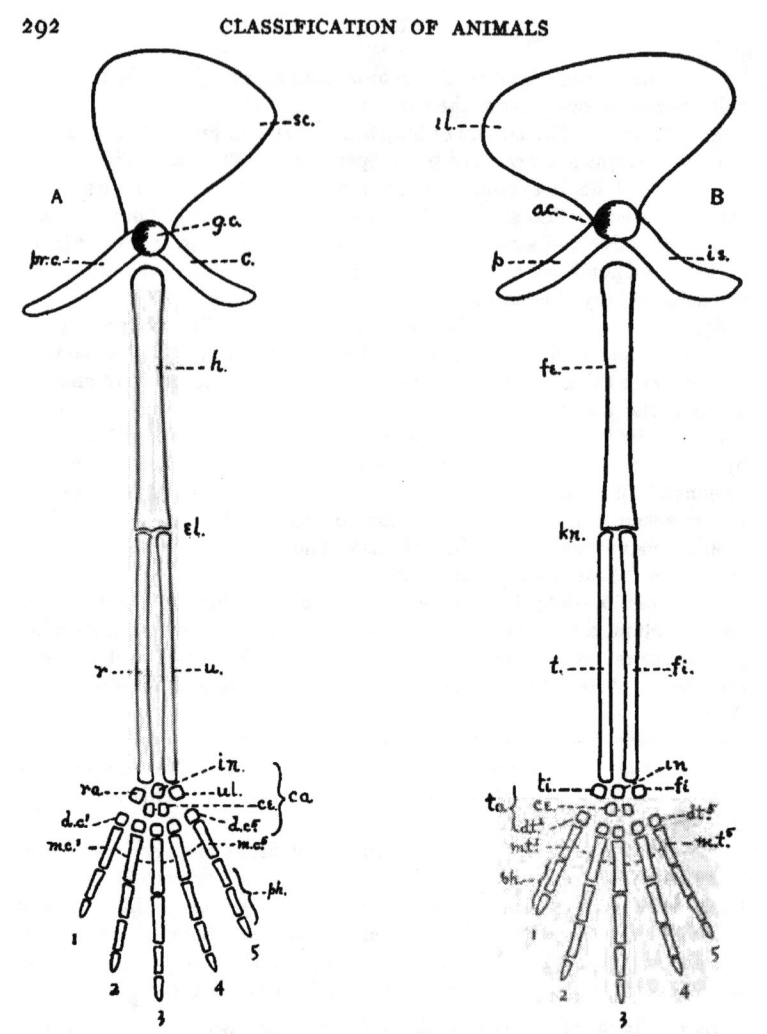

FIG. 170.—Diagrams of the girdles and appendages of a typical Vertebrate. *A*, Anterior; *B*, posterior; *ac*, acetabulum; *c*, coracoid; *ca*, carpals; *ce*, centralia; *d.c.*, distal carpals; *d.t.*, distal tarsals; *el*, elbow-joint; *f*, fibula; *fe*, femur; *fi*, fibulare; *g.c.*, glenoid cavity; *h*, humerus; *il*, ilium; *in*, intermediale; *is*, ischium; *kn*, knee-joint; *m.c.*, metacarpals (1–5); *m.t.*, metatarsals (1–5); *p* pubis; *ph*, phalanges (1–5); *pr.c.*, pre-coracoid; *r*, radius; *ra*, radiale; *sc*, scapula; *t*, tibia; *ta*, tarsals; *ti*, tibiale; *u*, ulna; *ul*, ulnare. (From Galloway.)

naked skin, gills in the larval stages, lungs in the adult, a three-chambered heart of one ventricle and two auricles. The larva is a tadpole with a broad tail but no paired appendages. It is a vegetable feeder and has a long coiled intestine. In metamorphosis the tail shrivels as the legs develop. At the same time the gills are also resorbed and the lungs are developed and be-

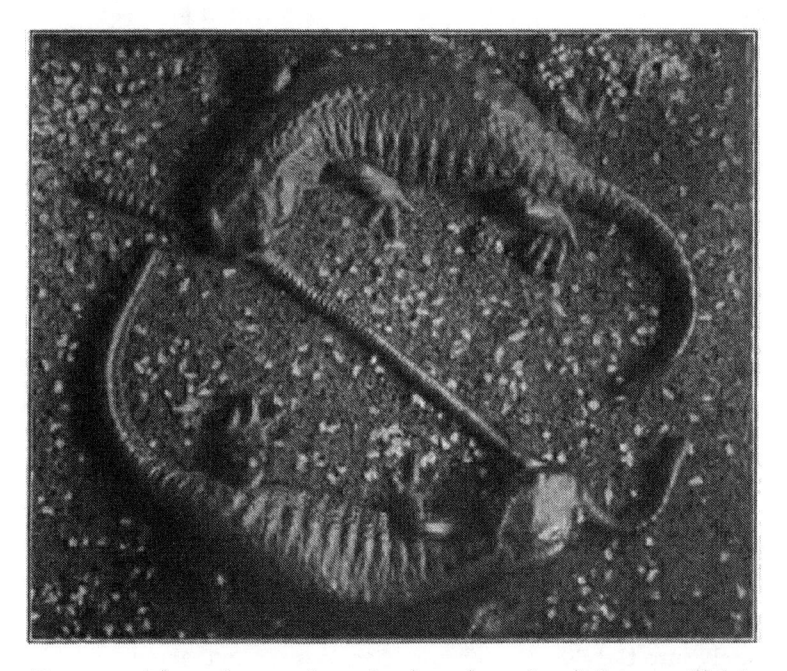

FIG. 171.—Salamandra maculosa, the fire salamander of Europe. Slightly reduced.

come functional as respiratory organs. The adult is carnivorous and the digestive tract is relatively shorter in correspondence to the character of the diet. This is the type of metamorphosis which occurs in the frogs and toads. The newts and salamanders undergo a less radical transformation. The skeleton is bony, though parts remain cartilaginous in the adult. The skeleton is so much like that of the higher vertebrates that most parts can be accurately homologized. The same is true of the digestive tract. There is a cloaca into which the intestine, the ureters and the genital ducts open. On its ventral wall there is a large pocket, the urinary bladder. The lungs are simple sacks with the walls usually more or less folded like a honey comb. The thin skin also acts as a respiratory organ.

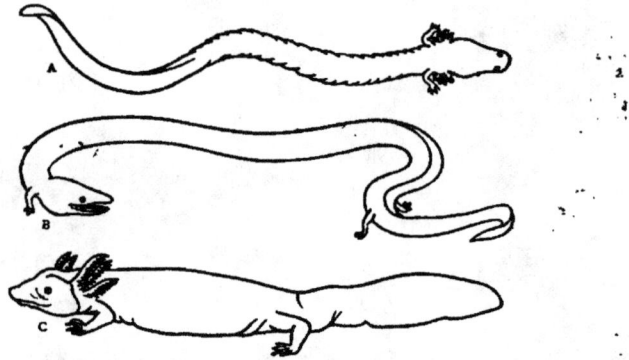

FIG. 172.—Outline drawings of three urodele amphibians showing successive stages in degeneration of the appendages. *A*, Siren; *B*, Amphiuma; *C*, Necturus. (From Galloway, after Mivart.)

The kidneys open into the cloaca by a pair of ureters. The oviducts are two long convoluted tubes beginning in the anterior part of the body cavity by large funnel-like openings and leading separately into the cloaca. The male gonads are connected with the kidneys and the sperm reaches the cloaca by way of the urinary tubules. The nostrils have an opening into the anterior part of the mouth. The brain is well developed but the cerebellum is small.

638. *Order* 1.—The *Gymnophiona* are worm-like Amphibia, without appendages. The trunk is elongated and the tail rudimentary. The skin is filled with small scales. The chorda is persistent. The eyes are

AMPHIBIA

not well developed and the ear drum and middle ear are wanting. This is a small group, found in tropical regions living underground.

639. *Order 2.*—The *Urodela* have an elongated body with a tail and usually weak legs. In one family (Sirenidæ) the posterior legs are wanting. In some families the gills are retained in the adult and in others the gills are lost but the gill slits are retained. In most cases, however, the gills and slit both disappear. The eyes are small and the ear

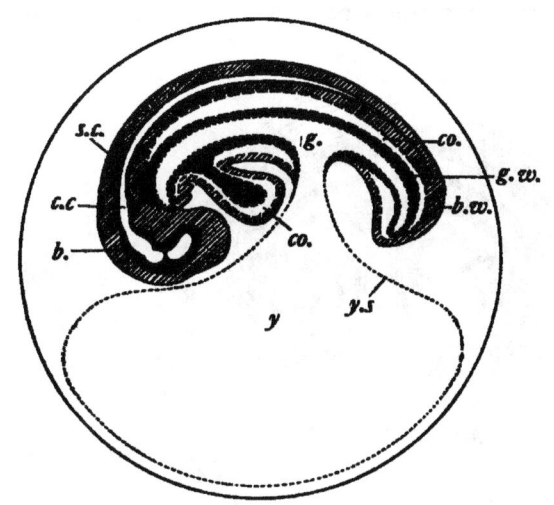

Fig. 173.—Diagram of a bird embryo within the egg membrane. The fœtal membranes are omitted (see next figure). *b*, Brain; *b.w.*, body wall; *c.c*, central canal of spinal cord; *co*, cœlom; *g*, intestine; *g.w.*, wall of intestine; *s.c.*, spinal cord; *y.s.*, yolk-sac.

drum and middle ear are absent, To this order belong newts, efts, "spring lizards," "mud puppies" and salamanders.

640. *Order 3.*—The *Anura* comprise frogs, toads and tree toads. The body is short and tailless. The posterior pair of appendages are usually long and strong. The eyes are large; there is usually an ear drum with a middle ear communicating with the mouth cavity.

641. **Class IV. Reptilia.**—The Reptiles are typically terrestrial though many live in the water. They never have gills. The skin is covered with horny scales or plates formed by the

296   CLASSIFICATION OF ANIMALS

epidermis. There are typically two pairs of appendages but these have been lost in many of the Squamata. The heart has two auricles and the ventricle is partly divided by an incomplete partition. The lungs are spongy in structure. There are twelve cranial nerves. This comprises the ten cranial nerves of the amphibia and the first spinal nerve as well as a spinal accessory nerve not represented as a separate nerve in

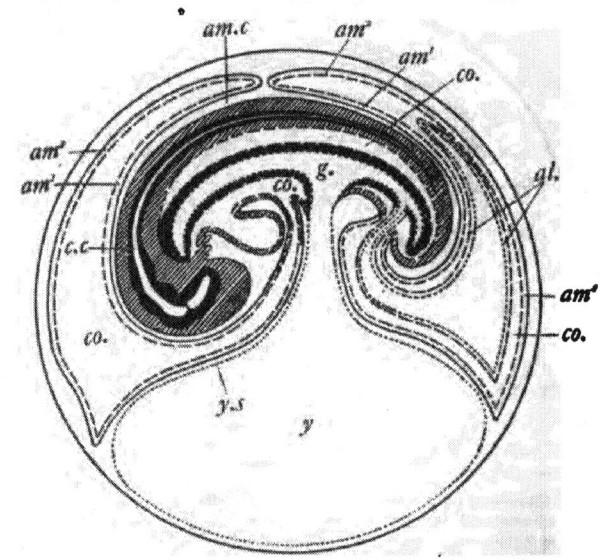

Fig. 174.—Diagram of a bird embryo with the fœtal membranes, the amnion and the allantois. am^1, inner or true amnion; am^2, outer or false amnion; $am.c$, amniotic cavity; al, allantois. Other lettering as in the preceding figure.

Amphibia. The cerebral hemispheres are well developed. The intestine, ureters and genital ducts open into a cloaca. The eggs are fertilized in the oviduct. They are very large and are covered by a tough shell secreted by the oviduct. The eggs are generally not brooded but are buried in the earth and allowed to develop at atmospheric temperature. The embryo is provided with the fœtal membranes, the amnion and allantois.

642. *Order 1.*—*Rhynchocephalia* are represented by a single species living on islands off the coast of New Zealand. The animals are lizard-like, but more primitive in a number of ways.

643. *Order 2.*—The *Testudinata* or turtles have a very compact form with bony dorsal and ventral shields, the carapace and plastron. The jaws are covered with a horny sheath forming a beak. Teeth are wanting. The carapace is formed by the broad dorsal spines and the much expanded ribs together with a series of marginal plates of dermal bone. The plastron is chiefly composed of plates of dermal bone. The shell is covered with thick horny scales, the "tortoise shell." Most of the Testudinata are aquatic. Snapping turtle, terrapin, tortoise, and sea turtles.

644. *Order 3.*—The *Emydosauria* are large aquatic lizard-like reptiles. The alligator, crocodile and gavial are well known. There are only a few genera. The skin contains bony plates as well as horny scales. The teeth are set in sockets. The ventricle is completely divided into two chambers.

645. *Order 4.*—The *Squamata* comprise both lizards and snakes. Usually the lizards have two pairs of appendages while the snakes have none, but among the lizards are found various stages of degeneration of the appendages even to forms in which no evidence of limbs is discernible externally. On the other hand among snakes rudiments of appendages are also found. The Squamata are distinguished from the other reptile orders by the movable quadrate bone. In the sub-order Lacertilia, the lizards, the upper jaws are not movable. The tongue is flat. There is a urinary bladder. In the sub-order Ophidia, the upper jaw is movable, the tongue is forked and enclosed in a sheath and there is no bladder. The ear drum and middle ear are also wanting. Another small sub-order of lizard-like forms, including the chameleon, are tree dwellers and as a special adaptation to such conditions the toes are opposable for clasping, and the tail is prehensile.

646. **Class V. Aves.**—The Birds are in many respects the most highly specialized of all animals. The feathers, which are characteristic of the class, are specialized epidermal structures and are very remarkable. The skin is comparatively thin but the feathers more than compensate as protective structures. For resistance to mechanical injury, or protection from cold, or heat, or wetting, or adaptation to thermal control, or for the

possibilities of ornamentation either in form or color, it is difficult to find within the entire range of the animal kingdom more efficient structures. In their ability to fly we have another evidence of high specialization. Both pairs of appendages are fundamentally pentadactyl but the anterior pair has undergone a profound modification. The bones of the upper arm and fore arm are of the typical pentadactyl type but the hand is reduced to the three matacarpals of the 1st, 2nd, and 3rd digits and two, three, and one phalanges respectively. The muscular development is concentrated in the muscles which move the wing as a whole, viz., those connecting the wing with the sternum. This requires a great development of the surface of the sternum and its keel to which these muscles are attached. The other muscles of the wing are greatly reduced. Another anatomical peculiarity which is thought to be an adaptation to flight is the comparatively small head of the bird. This is due chiefly to the absence of the organs for mastication, teeth, heavy upper and lower jaws and heavy masseter muscles. The absence of these organs is compensated for by the crop in which the food is softened, and the gizzard in which it is triturated. By this substitution the weight of the body is concentrated and the centre of gravity lowered. The posterior appendages are also peculiar. The pelvic girdle is attached to at least six vertebræ but is open below, that is, there is no symphisis pubis. This condition of the pelvic girdle allows of the passage of the relatively very large eggs of the bird. The fibula is rudimentary and the proximal tarsals are fused with the tibia forming a single bone, the tibio-tarsus. The distal tarsals are fused with the metatarsals to form a tarso-metatarsal. The fifth, and sometimes the first, digits are wanting.

647. The heart is completely divided into four chambers as in the Crocodilia and Mammals but the blood from the left ventricle goes to the lungs while that from the right goes to the general systemic circulation, reversing the order as found in Mammals.

The lungs are connected with an extensive system of air spaces which penetrate far into other parts of the body, even penetrating the bones and replacing the marrow. The vocal cords are located at the junction of the bronchi in an organ, the syrinx, which takes the place of the larynx. The right ovary is wanting and the corresponding oviduct is rudimentary. The eggs are fertilized in the upper part of the oviduct and are then surrounded by layers of albumen, membraneous shell and calcareous shell in succession, as they pass down the oviduct.

648. The eyes and ears are highly developed. There are two eyelids and a nictitating membrane. The ear is without a concha. The brain shows a considerable advance over that of Reptiles, especially with regard to the development of cerebrum, optic lobes and cerebellum.

649. In many points Birds differ radically from Mammals and at the same time show a strong resemblance to Reptiles.

650. In a comparatively small group of birds the wings are not used and are consequently rudimentary. These are the running birds or Ratitæ—ostrich, emeu and cassowary, the almost extinct apteryx of New Zealand and the recently extinct moa of New Zealand. With the disuse of the wing the muscles have degenerated and with them the keel of the breast bone, their point of attachment. Other birds are called Carinatæ because of the keel of the breast bone. They are divided into seventeen orders as indicated in the following synopsis.

Ratitæ.
1. *Struthiomorphæ.* Ostrich, rhea, cassowary.
2. *Dinornithes.* The recently extinct gigantic Dinornis.
3. *Aepyornithes.* The recently extinct Æpyornis.
4. *Apteryges.* The Kiwi Kiwis of Australia and New Zealand.

Carinatæ.
5. *Tinamiformes.* South American fowl-like birds.
6. *Gallinacei.* Pheasants, turkey, fowl, quail.
7. *Columbæ.* Pigeons, doves. The extinct dodo.
8. *Lari.* Gulls.
9. *Grallæ.* Rails, cranes.
10. *Lamellirostres.* Geese, ducks, flamingo.
11. *Ciconiæ.* Ibis, storks, herons.

300 CLASSIFICATION OF ANIMALS

12. *Steganopodes.* Pelican, frigate bird.
13. *Tubinares.* Stormy petrel, albatross.
14. *Impennes.* Penguin.

FIG. 175.—The kiwi, Apteryx. ×1/4. The outline in the background represents the size of the wing.

15. *Pygopodes.* Divers, grebes.
16. *Accipitres.* Condor, vultures, eagles, hawks, falcons.
17. *Striges.* Owls.

18. *Psittaci*. Parrots.
19. *Coccygomorphæ*. Cuckoo.
20. *Pici*. Woodpeckers.
21. *Cypselomorphæ*. Whip-poor-will, bull bat, humming birds.
22. *Passeres*. The song birds; a very large order.
    Sub-order 1. Clamatores. King bird.
    Sub-order 2. Oscines. Swallows, fly catchers, warblers, thrushes, black birds, mocking bird, cat bird, larks, titmouse, crows, ravens, finches, sparrows.

651. **Class VI. Mammalia.**—The Mammals are typically covered with hair. In several cases the hairs are scattered or limited to the "whiskers" as, e. g., in some marine mammals—the sea cow and whale. The function of the hair is primarily to retain the heat of the body. When the hair is wanting the function may be performed by a thick layer of fat beneath the skin. The name mammal refers to the mammary glands in the skin of the ventral surface of the body. There are usually two sets of teeth, first a milk dentition which is later replaced by a permannt dentition. The latter consists of four kinds, incisors, canines, pre-molars and molars. The heart consists of four chambers; the red blood corpuscles are without a nucleus; the temperature of the body is constant. The lungs and heart are separated from the abdominal viscera by a muscular membrane, the diaphragm, which thus divides the body cavity into thoracic and abdominal cavities. There is no cloaca, the vent and the openings of the urino-genital systems are separate. The eggs are fertilized in the oviduct and development continues for a variable period, up to two years in the elephant, in an enlargement of the oviduct called the uterus. The embryo is provided with the fœtal membranes, amnion and allantois. The sense organs are usually highly developed and the brain, especially the cerebral and cerebellar parts, is much in advance of those of all other animals.

652. The thirteen orders belong to three sub-classes as follows:
Sub-class Monotremata. Spiny ant-eater, duck mole.

302 CLASSIFICATION OF ANIMALS

Sub-class Marsupialia.
    Order 1. *Polyprotodontia* (carnivorous or omnivorous). Opossum.
    Order 2. *Diprotodontia* (herbivorous). Kangaroo.
Sub-class Monodelphia.
    Order 1. *Insectivora.* Moles, shrews, hedgehog.
    Order 2. *Chiroptera.* Bats.

FIG. 176.—The spiny ant-eater, Tachyglossus. ×1/4.

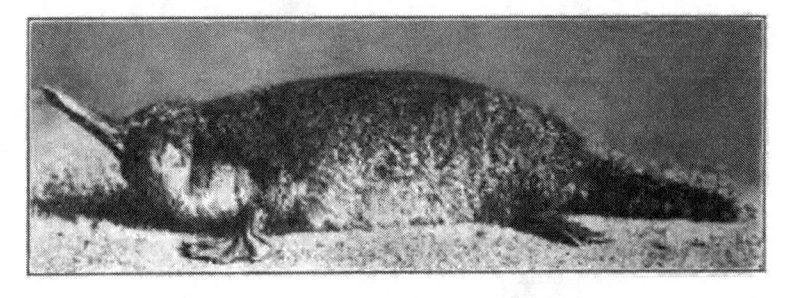

FIG. 177.—The duck-bill, Ornithorhynchus. ×1/4.

Order 3. *Rodentia.* Rats, mice, rabbits, squirrels, beavers.
Order 4. *Edentata Nomarthra.* Scaly ant-eater.
Order 5. *Edentata Xenarthra.* Sloth, armadillo.
Order 6. *Carnivora.* Dogs, bears, cats, seals.
Order 7. *Cetacea.* Whales, porpoises, dolphins.

Order 8. *Ungulata.* Hoofed animals.
Order 9. *Sirenia.* Manatee and dugong.
Order 10. *Primates.* Monkeys, apes, man.

653. The Monotremata are the most primitive mammals. The embryo is not nourished in a uterus. An egg is laid from which the embryo hatches in a very immature condition. It is then nourished from the mammary glands. The long snout is covered by a horny sheath like a duck's bill. There are no teeth in the adult. The mammary glands have no nipple. Many reptilian characters are presented as, e. g., in the presence of a coracoid bone, a cloaca, a variable body temperature, the slightly developed corpus callosum, the condition of the reproductive organs, etc. The Monotremes are found only in Tasmania, Australia and New Guinea.

654. The Marsupialia, with exception of the American opossum, are also confined to Australasia. There is no placenta and the young are born in a very immature stage. They are then placed in a sack formed by a fold of the skin covering the region of the mammary glands. Here the young attach themselves to a nipple and continue their development. The pouch is supported by two bones.

655. The Polyprotodontia are carnivorous or omnivorous Marsupials. They have a well-developed set of teeth of the four kinds.

656. The Diprotodontia are vegetable feeders and the teeth are not developed as a full set.

657. The Monodelphia have no pouch. The foetal membranes form a placenta which becomes attached to the wall of the uterus thus forming an organic connection between the embryo and the tissues of the mother. By means of the placenta the embryo is nourished for a period within the uterus. After birth it is nourished from the milk of the mammary glands.

658. The Insectivora have a full set of pointed teeth. The feet usually are five toed and the toes clawed. The foot is plantigrade.

659. The Chiroptera have wings formed by a membrane of skin stretching between the greatly elongated fingers and the side of the body. In some cases the eyes are large and the ears small, in others the eyes are small and the ears large. Some are fruit eaters, others catch insects. A few are blood sucking.

660. The Rodentia are characterized by the long, sharp, chisel-shaped incisors. There are no canines. Rabbits, squirrels, beaver, pocket gopher, mice, rats, guinea pig.

661. The Edentata are either without teeth or have poorly developed teeth without enamel. Scaly ant-eater, armadillo, ant bear.

662. The Carnivora are flesh-eating mammals with a characteristic dentition. The clavicle is rudimentary or wanting. The toes are clawed.

663. Sub-order Fissipedia.—Terrestrial carnivores with molar teeth unlike. Canidæ; dogs, wolves (digitigrade). Ursidæ; bears, (plantigrade). Procyonidæ; raccoon, (plantigrade). Mustelidæ; weasel, ferret, mink, pole cat. Viverridæ; civet cat (ichneumon). Hyænidæ; hyæna. Felidæ; cats, lions, tigers, leopards, panther.

664. Sub-order Pinnipedia.—Aquatic carnivores with webbed feet and molar teeth alike. Anterior and posterior appendages well developed. Otters, walrus, seals.

665. The Cetacea are aquatic mammals with anterior appendages in form of paddles, the posterior ones only represented by internal rudiments. There is a broad horizontal tail fin. In the baleen whale the teeth are wanting; a curtain of fringed horny plates suspended from the roof of the mouth acts as a strainer to collect the food. Whales, narwhal, dolphins.

666. The Ungulata have broad toes covered with a horny hoof. Sub-order Proboscidia; elephants, 5 toes, thick skin, long proboscis. Sub-order Perissodactyla; number of toes odd. Tapir, 4 toes on anterior appendages, 3 on the posterior. Rhinoceros, 3 toes. Horse, 1 toe. Sub-order Artiodactyla, even number of toes. Section 1. Non-ruminants: Hippopotamus, 4 toes; swine, 2 long, 2 short toes. Section 2. Ruminants: Tribe 1. Tylopoda; camel, dromedary, llama, toes 2, no horns or antlers. Tribe 2. Traguloidea; toes 2 long, 2 short (small, hornless, deer-like animals of West Africa). Tribe 3. Pecora; usually with horns or antlers, toes 2 long, 2 rudimentary. Deer family with antlers. Cattle family with horns; antilope, buffalo, cattle, goats, sheep. Giraffe family with two toes, horns covered with skin.

Order *Ungulata*:
    Sub-order 1. Condylarthea. Phenacodus, extinct.
    Sub-order 2. Hyracoidea. Hyrax—the coneys of Africa and Arabia.
    Sub-order 3. Proboscidea. Elephants.
    Sub-order 4. Perissodactyla (odd-toed). Tapirs, rhinoceros, horse.
    Sub-order 5. Artiodactyla (even-toed).
        Section 1. Non-ruminantia. Hippopotamus, swine.
        Section 2. Ruminantia:
            Tribe 1. Tylopoda.
            Tribe 2. Traguloidea.
            Tribe 3. Pecora.

667. The Sirenia are herbivorous marine mammals. The anterior appendages are paddle like, the posterior rudimentary. Manatee, dugong, sea cow.

668. The Primates have a heterodont dentition, all appendages have five digits. The nails are flat. The eyes are directed forward. Sub-order Prosimiæ; the teeth similar to those of Insectivores, the wall of the orbit incomplete laterally. Lemurs. Sub-order Simiæ; the incisors are chisel shaped, the orbit wall complete. Monkeys and apes.

Section 1. Platyrhina; the flat nose monkeys of South America.

Section 2. Catarrhina; the monkeys, mandrels, gibbons, orang-utan, chimpanzie and gorilla.

669. Finally the genus Homo is placed by some authors in an order by itself, the order Bimana. Others place this genus in a family, Hominidæ, under the order Primates. The genus is regarded as containing only one living species, Homo sapiens, which is sub-divided into races.

PART III.—GENERAL PRINCIPLES

THE CELL AND THE INDIVIDUAL

670. **Spontaneous Generation.**—It was at one time held that some animals originate spontaneously. In the middle of the seventeenth century the great anatomist, Harvey, expressed the view that all living things spring from eggs (Omne vivum ex ovo). But this opinion was not generally accepted. A quarter of a century later another anatomist, Redi, showed that the maggots which develop in decaying flesh are bred from the eggs deposited by flies. But for two centuries more spontaneous generation was thought to account for the appearance of many living things, though it came gradually to be limited to the microscopic organisms, like the bacteria and protozoa. Finally, in the latter half of the nineteenth century the experiments of Pasteur and others definitely established the view that even for these microscopic forms a living germ is necessary to development of a living organism. It was shown that if the germs of the organisms which produce fermentation and decay were carefully excluded from the substances in which they usually occur, that the processes of fermentation and decay would not take place and the associated organisms would not appear.

671. **Continuity of the Living Substance.**—At the present time the term egg is applied only to special cells produced by multicellular organisms, from which new individuals develop, but the unicellular organisms produce spores which are, in this sense, the counterpart of eggs. Another objection to Harvey's phrase may be made on the ground that new individuals may be produced by methods, such as budding, fission,

308 GENERAL PRINCIPLES

etc., in which neither eggs nor spores occur. Still, in essence, it is now generally accepted as true that all living things originate from eggs, and in this statement is expressed one of the most remarkable attributes of the living substance, that of its continuity.

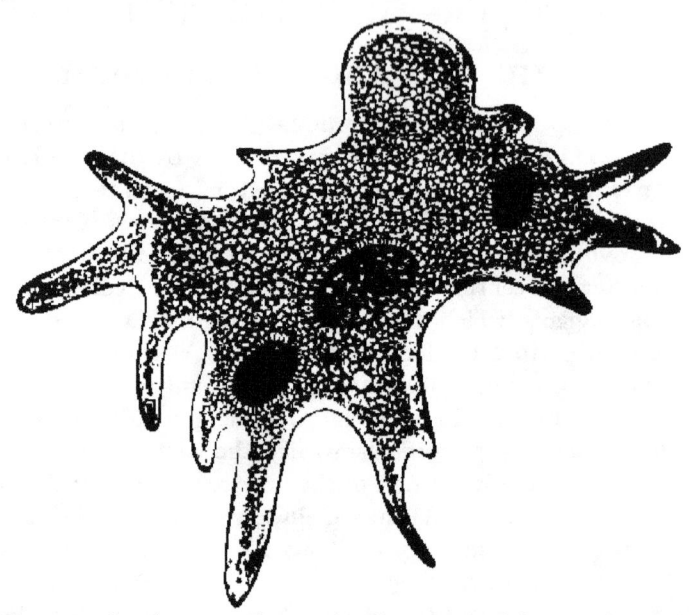

FIG. 178. Amœba vespertilio, showing the structure of the protoplasm. The outer layer is denser and more homogeneous, and is called ectoplasm. The central part, called endoplasm, has the appearance of foam. (From Marshall after Doflein.)

672. Structure of Protoplasm.—Much has been learned concerning the physical and chemical properties of protoplasm, but even our best microscopes and most refined chemical methods still leave much more to be determined. As seen through the microscope the cytoplasm seems to consist of: (1) a ground substance of a transparent, colorless, homogeneous fluid, and (2) a network of a more viscid and more highly refractive and sometimes granular substance. This network may be either the sectional view of a sponge-like structure or of an emulsiform structure or of true fibres interlaced. The granules, which are called microsomes, vary greatly in size and number and are frequently absent or too small to be seen. They are often less conspicuous in the peripheral layers of the cytoplasm, which is therefore distinguished as ectoplasm.

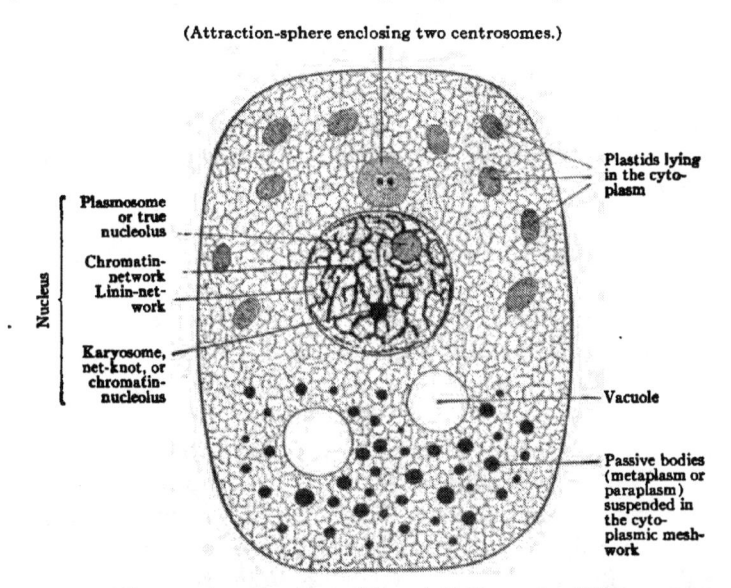

FIG. 179.—Diagram of a cell. (From Hegner's Zoölogy, after Wilson, published by the Macmillan Co.)

Beside these constant constituent elements of the cytoplasm there are also a large number of structures, which occur only in certain cells or at certain times. Among these may be mentioned here the chromoplasts and amyloplasts, the vacuoles filled with cell sap, the ingested food particles, the reserve elaborated food substances, such as starch, oil, aleurone, and the secretions and other like substances resulting from the activity of the protoplasm. With the last named class of cell constituents may be included the cell membrane or cell wall. This is usually present in plants and usually absent in animal tissue, though many exceptions occur to both rules.

673. **The Nucleus.**—The nucleus must be regarded as an essential part of the cell. It is true there are certain lowly organisms, such as the bacteria, blue green algæ and related forms, in which there is no such distinct, highly complex structure as the typical nucleus; but even in these forms there are found scattered in the protoplasm of the cell minute bodies which have properties recognized as belonging to constituents of the nucleus. These are generally regarded as representing the nucleus.

674. The typical nucleus is a round or oval body, but it may also be greatly elongated or even branched. It is usually single, but sometimes it consists of two parts, a large macronucleus and a small micronucleus. Sometimes there are several or even many nuclei in one cell. Usually the nucleus is provided with a membrane, but this disappears at certain times, and in some cases is entirely absent. Like the rest of the protoplasm, the nucleus is transparent and colorless, and in the living condition appears homogeneous. But if the cell is treated with certain "fixing" and staining reagents, the nucleus becomes deeply colored, due to the affinity of one of its constituents for the dye. Because of its tendency to stain, this substance is called chromatin. In the "resting" nucleus the chromatin assumes a great variety of forms; sometimes it is in the form of granules of various sizes, more often it is best described as a mass of knotted and tangled threads. The chromatin is apparently a very important constituent of the cell, and in it centre many most interesting phenomena. Another element of the nucleus which may be stained is the nucleolus. There is often only one, but there may be more. They are usu-

ally spherical masses and, therefore, distinguishable from the chromatin. But a better means of distinguishing between these is given by the fact that they are not stained by the same dyes.

675. The linin is a part of the nucleus which does not stain at all by ordinary methods. It also assumes various forms, but when most evident it is as a system of fibres, or a network of threads by which the other elements of the nucleus are bound together.

676. The interstices of the nucleus are filled with a nuclear sap.

677. There is one other structure in the cell which must be mentioned, though there is some doubt whether it should be classed with the cytoplasmic or nucleoplasmic structures. This is the centrosome. It is generally found in the cytoplasm close by the side of the nucleus, but sometimes it is far removed, and again it seems to be enclosed by the nuclear membrane. The centrosome is excessively small, scarcely more than a point, even with the highest powers of the microscope, but it may be stained by certain methods, and is further distinguished from other minute protoplasmic structures by the radial arrangement of the surrounding protoplasm, for which it forms a centre. Something concerning its significance will appear in the discussion of cell division.

678. In this brief description of the protoplasm, only the most important constant structures have been mentioned. These have each their optical, physical, and chemical peculiarities. The list of substances which have been recognized might be greatly extended and yet, because of our imperfect instruments and methods we are far from having made a complete analysis of the protoplasm. It seems probable that further investigation will show that among the innumerable minute particles which at present are indistinguishable one from another are many chemically and otherwise distinguishable kinds.

679. **Chemical Structure of Protoplasm.**—Protoplasm contains a very large percentage of water, 70 per cent or more; it is alkaline in reaction in the living condition and contains many mineral salts, which, however, vary greatly with the kind of protoplasm. Among the chemical elements which may be found are phosphorous, manganese, magnesium, calcium, sodium, chlorine, and iron. It does not necessarily follow that these substances form an integral part of the protoplasmic molecule. They may be present as inorganic salt dissolved in the cell sap or even in crystalline form. Chemically, the living substance is classed with the albumens, but it were perhaps better to say that on analysis it decomposes into a series of albuminous compounds. These are themselves extremely complex organic bodies, and as yet lie somewhat beyond the range of the chemist's power of analysis. An analysis of egg albumen yielded the result, $C_{72}H_{106}N_{18}SO_{22}$, though this cannot be regarded as a correct chemical formula. Nucleoplasm is distinguished from the cytoplasm by the presence of phosphorous. From all that we know regarding protoplasm we are led to regard it as an aggregate of many highly complex organic compounds.

680. **Function of Cytoplasm and Nucleus.**—Much light has been thrown on the question of the function of cytoplasm and nucleus by a series of simple experiments. If a unicellular organism is cut into two parts, so that the nucleus is also divided, the wound immediately "heals," and each half regenerates the part cut away so that eventually there are two complete organisms. The operation does not itself greatly injure the cell. If the cell is divided so that all of the nucleus remains in one part, the part without nuclear matter, even though it is the larger part, does not regenerate. It may remain alive for weeks, but ultimately dies. If the nucleus is completely removed from the cytoplasm, both nucleus and cytoplasmic parts die. The death of enucleated portions is

evidently due to the lack of nutrition. The cytoplasm retains its irritability and responds to stimuli; the pseudopodia may still be formed or the cilia continues to move, as the case may be, but food particles are no longer ingested, and those contained in the food vacuoles are no longer digested. The cytoplasm seems to have lost the function of assimilation and consequently starves.

681. These experiments indicate that the animal functions, irritability and contractility, are functions of the cytoplasm.

682. On the other hand, from what has just been said, it is seen that the nucleus has to do with the function of assimilation. This is further evident in many cases in which cells are especially active in the absorption of food. In such cases the nucleus is prolonged into curious finger-like processes on the side of special activity. In other cases the nucleus shows evidence of special activity where secretory processes are prominent. Here its surface also projects toward the point of activity. Since assimilation and secretion are two phases of metabolism it is natural that both should be controlled from the same source, and that the nucleus should present similar appearances in both cases. In addition to the control of metabolism the nucleus also has the function of cell division or reproduction..

683. **Cell Division.**—The process of cell division is such a complicated one, and with it are connected so many important biological phenomena that it demands careful study. The first evidence of preparation for cell division is seen in the rearrangement of the chromatin. This gradually assumes a more regular form. The irregular clumps and strands take on the form of one or more coiled bands. These have at first an irregular outline, which gradually becomes smoother. The bands become thicker and shorter and finally are seen to consist of a limited and definite number of V-shaped bodies, to which the name chromosomes has been given. During these changes of form the affinity of the chromatin for the stains increases. At about

this time two centrosomes make their appearance close beside the nucleus. They are connected by a number of slender fibres, which curve outward in the middle so that all together form a spindle-shaped figure. The centrosomes gradually recede

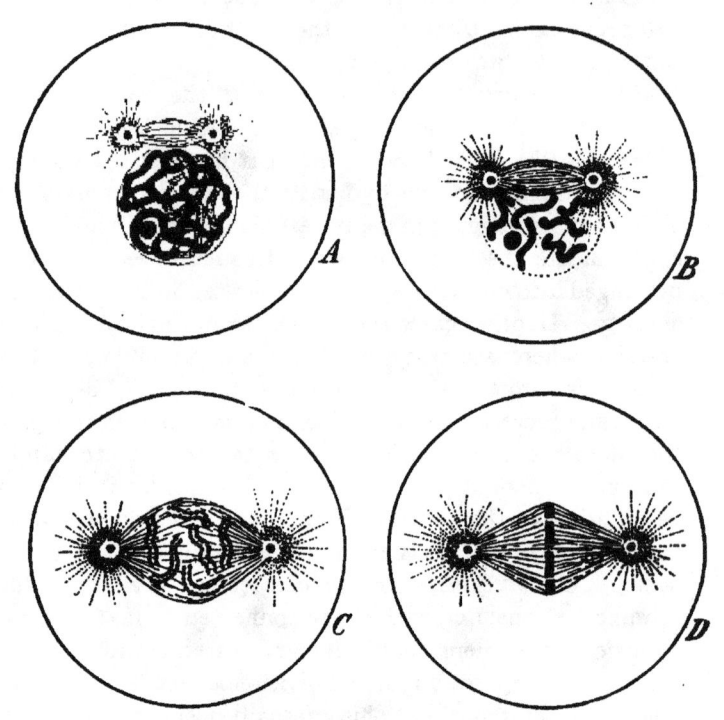

FIG. 180.—Diagrams illustrating the prophases of mitosis. *A*, Beginning of formation of the spindle. *B*, chromosomes formed. *C*, Chromosomes approaching the equator of the spindle. *D*, Chromosomes ready to divide. (See next figure.)

from each other until they come to lie at opposite poles of the nucleus. During these changes the nucleoli have gradually disappeared and the nuclear membrane also becomes indistinct and fades away. The spindle fibres now traverse the nucleus

CELL DIVISION 315

and some are attached to the chromosomes. Other fibres extend from the centrosomes outward into the cytoplasm, and the constituents of the cytoplasm take on a radial arrangement with the centrosomes as centres. The chromosomes lie regularly arranged around the spindle in its equatorial plane.

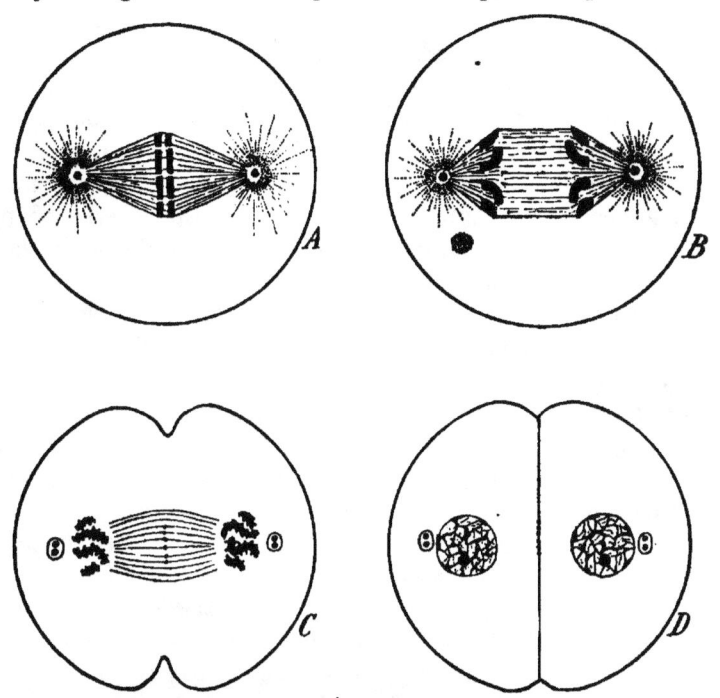

FIG. 181.—Diagrams illustrating the metaphase and anaphases of mitosis. *A*, Chromosomes divided; *B*, chromosomes approaching the centrosomes; *C*, cytoplasm beginning to divide, the centrosomes also divided; *D*, cell completely divided and nuclei in resting condition. (This and preceding figure from McMurrich, adapted from E. B. Wilson.)

684. The process of division begins with the splitting of each chromosome lengthwise into two equal and similar parts, whereby the number of chromosomes is doubled. The two halves of each original chromosome separate and move in

opposite directions, each one approaching one of the centrosomes. In this way two groups of chromosomes of equal numbers are formed at opposite ends of the spindle. At about this time a groove appears in the surface of the cytoplasm in the equatorial plane of the spindle. This groove cuts deeper into the cell until it is divided into two equal masses. Thus the nucleus and cytoplasm are divided.

685. The process of division is concluded by the formation of a nuclear membrane around each group of chromosomes and the rearrangement of the chromatin. The chromosomes lose their individuality again in a tangle of chromatin and the nucleoli reappear. The spindle fibres and attraction sphere disappear and the centrosomes may also be lost among the other granules of the cytoplasm.

686. This process of cell division is called mitosis or karyokinesis. It is the normal method of cell division, but under certain conditions a simpler process occurs. This has been described elsewhere. With slight modification the description just given of the mitotic method will apply generally to both animals and plants. Several additional points may be mentioned.

687. **Number of Chormosomes.**—The number of chromosomes is constant for any given species. For different species the numbers observed vary from two in the Nematode, Ascaris megalocephala, to 168 in Artemia, a genus of Crustacea. The most common numbers recorded are 12, 16 and 24.

688. **Nucleoli.**—The fate of the nucleoli during mitosis is in question. There is some reason for believing that in some cases at least they take part in the formation of the chromosomes. More often they seem to disintegrate, and then new ones are formed on the organization of the new nucleus.

689. **Centrosomes.**—The centrosomes are apparently permanent cell structures which propagate themselves by division. At the close of cell division the centrosome of each

daughter cell often divides before it is lost in the granular protoplasm of the resting cell. In many cases the centrosome or centrosomes can be found in the resting cells. In other cases, division of the centrosome occurs just previous to cell division.

690. **Spindle Fibres.**—The spindle fibres are achromatic substances, i. e., they do not stain like the chromatin. They are probably derived in large part from the linin network of the nucleus. The astral figures and, perhaps, the spindle in part, are cytoplasmic.

691. **Resting Nucleus.**—Ordinarily, after division, the cells remain quiescent for a time; that is, so far as any apparent changes in the nucleus are concerned. This is called the resting state, although growth and other processes may be actively going on.

692. **Conjugation.**—Another very important process in which the nucleus is especially concerned is the reverse of cell division. Cell division is ordinarily followed by a period of growth, then another cell division and another period of growth. This constitutes the ordinary daily routine of cell life. At comparatively long intervals this chain of events is broken by the fusion of one cell with another. This may take place in a great variety of ways, which, however, are apparently fundamentally the same, and the significance of the process may best be explained by the description of a number of examples.

693. Mougeota is a filamentous alga, which consists of a series of similar cells adhering to each other in a row. At certain times two such filaments, lying side by side, become connected by a series of tubes in such a way that each cell of one filament is connected with a similar cell in the other filament. Then the protoplasm of each cell flows into the tube where the two masses unite into a single body. In some other algæ swarm spores are formed and set free in the water. Each spore is pear-shaped and has two flagella by which it actively swims about. They are all of the same size and cannot be

distinguished one from the other. These swarm spores unite in pairs, and from each pair a single protoplasmic mass is formed, which is, in fact, a single cell. Spirogyra is another filamentous alga similar to Mougeota, but when two filaments unite by tubes the protoplasts of one flow completely across to the other, where the union takes place; the protoplasts of the second cell remaining passive. In another example of swarm spores, two kinds of spores are produced. The difference is not great, but

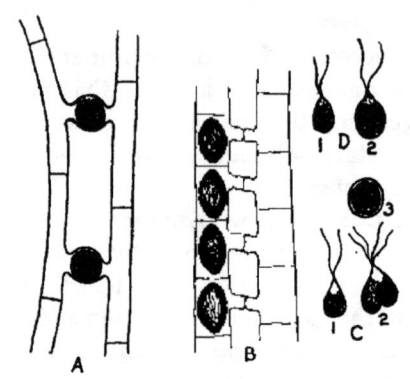

FIG. 182.—Conjugation and differentiation of sex. *A*, Conjugation in Mougeota; *B*, conjugation in Spirogyra; *C*, conjugation in Hydrodictyon (isogamous); *D*, conjugation in Chlamydomonas (heterogamous). In *C*: 1, a gamete; 2, conjugation; 3, zygote. In *D*: 1, a male gamete; 2, female gamete.

one is somewhat larger than the other. Here the union takes place between individuals of different kind. In Fucus, a brown sea weed, the two kinds of cells differ greatly in size. The large one is motionless, while the small one has two flagella and is very active. In all the higher plants and animals the difference in size is enormous, and in animals especially, the smaller motile cell consists of little more than a small and compact nucleus with a single flagellum.

694. **Fertilization.**—In the lower forms, where the two uniting cells are equal in size or nearly so, the process in question is

called conjugation; in those instances where there is a great difference in size, it is called fertilization. The conjugating elements are called gametes. In case of fertilization the large cell is called a macrogamete or egg, while the small one is called a microgamete or sperm. Further, the individual giving origin to a macrogamete is called female, and the one from which the microgamete springs is a male. A further comparison between male and female will be made a little later.

695. **Maturation.**—In every case of conjugation or fertilization the nuclei of the two cells sooner or later unite, and the real significance of the process centres in the nuclei. The statement has already been made that the number of chromosomes is fixed for a given species, a condition that is maintained by the splitting of the chromosomes at each cell division. On the fusion of the nuclei, however, the number would be doubled were it not for the preliminary process by which both nuclei are prepared for the approaching fusion. To explain this process we will take as an example the sperm cells of Ascaris megalocephala. The typical number of chromosomes in this species is four, and this is also the number in the cell divisions which lead up to the formation of the sperm mother cells. The latter remain for an unusually long period in the growing, resting condition and attain unusually large size. When mitosis begins it is seen that the four chromosomes have already split into eight which, however, still remain paired. The four pairs ararnge themselves in two groups of four (tetrads) in the equator of the spindle, and the cell divides into two halves, after the usual method. Then the centrosomes immediately divide and form new spindles, so that a second division occurs before the nucleus has entered the resting condition. In this second division the four daughter chromosomes do not split, but one chromosome from each of the original two tetrads moves toward each pole of the spindle. There are thus formed four similar cells, each with two chromosomes. These are the sperm cells.

actually takes place in many animals, but the polar bodies undergo no further development and are to be regarded as parts ejected from the maturing egg cell as useless. It is also reasonable to regard the first polar body of Ascaris as potentially equivalent to two second polar bodies. This leads then to the conclusion that the egg nucleus and the nuclei of the polar bodies are the equivalents of the four sperm nuclei which developed from one sperm mother cell.

697. The essential difference between the ripe egg cell and the sperm lies in the great size of the egg and the motility of the

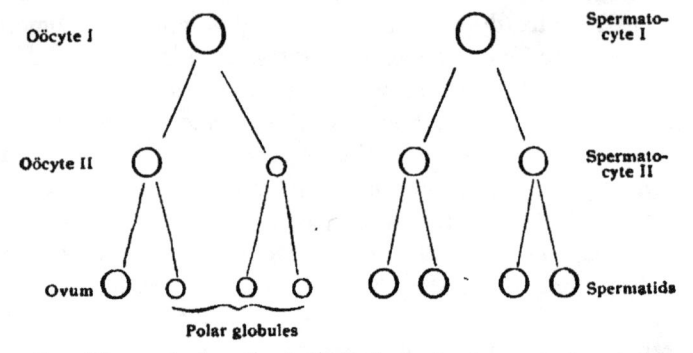

Fig. 185.—Diagram to show the similarity in the development of ova and sperm cells. (McMurrich.)

sperm. The great size of the egg is due in part to the prolonged growth period, during which the quantity of protoplasm is greatly increased and reserve food in the form of yolk granules is stored up within the cell, and in part to the formation of two (three) rudimentary cells (polar bodies) in the process of maturation instead of four equals cell, which leaves one with the developmental material which would otherwise be divided among the four. These are evidently provisions for the early developmental period of the embryo.

698. The consequences of these preparatory processes are now readily seen. The second maturation division is called

the reduction division, because it leaves the nucleus with half the normal number of chromosomes. When now fertilization takes place the sperm nucleus and the egg pro-nucleus fuse, and there results therefrom a new egg nucleus with the normal number of chromosomes. In many ways minor variations occur, but the essential features seem to hold throughout the animal and vegetable kingdoms. Only one variation will be described.

699. **Conjugation in Potozoa.**—In many protozoa conjugation occurs in a peculiar form. The cells do not fuse and only the nucleus is greatly affected by the process. In Paramœcium, for example, two individuals adhere to each other by their oral surfaces and remain in this condition for some time. Finally, they separate, the same two individuals, at least in external appearance. However, radical changes have occurred in the nuclei, which are briefly as follows: The macronucleus disintegrates and finally disappears without apparently having taken any part in the process of conjugation. The micronucleus forms a spindle and divides. This is repeated so that four daughter nuclei are produced. Three of these also disintegrate while the fourth divides again. There are now two active nuclei in each cell, and one of these passes out of one cell to the other through the cell mouths, which are placed one over the other. These nuclei are regarded as the equivalents of sperm nucleus and egg pro-nucleus, and each is said to have approximately half the usual chromatic substance. From the fusion of the two nuclei, the receptive nucleus and the wandering nucleus, a new nucleus is produced, from which the new macronucleus and the new micronucleus are both developed.

700. **Fertilization.**—The approach of the sperm to the egg cells is not a matter of accident. Observation of the movement of the active sperm in the presence of a ripe egg is sufficient to persuade one that there is a positive stimulus which directs them to the egg. In a short time large numbers are swarming about the egg and apparently endeavoring to penetrate its surface.

324   GENERAL PRINCIPLES

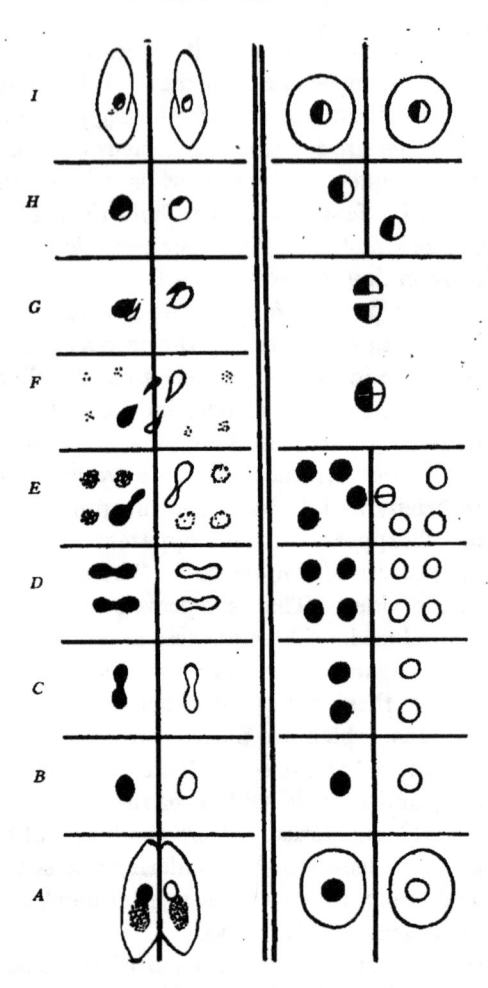

Fig. 186.—Diagram of the process of conjugation in Paramœcium (on the left), and of maturation and fertilization (on the right). In A and I the outlines of the cells are represented and the condition of the nuclei before and after the changes they undergo. In each case white and black are used to distinguish between the nuclear material of the two parent cells. In B–H the cell outlines are omitted.

In Paramœceum (on the left); A and B, temporary union of the two cells; C,

By experiment it can be shown that the sperms of mosses are attracted by solutions of cane sugar and fern sperms are attracted by solutions of malic acid. These or similar substances are probably excreted by the egg and serve as a directing stimulus to the sperm.

701. Many eggs are enclosed in a gelatinous envelope, which is readily penetrated by the sperm. In eggs which have a firmer covering, or "shell," there are one or more pores (micropyles) through which the sperms enter. In most cases only one sperm cell enters the egg under normal conditions. This control is effected by the response of the egg to the first sperm. For no sooner has a sperm entered the egg than the latter develops a membrane which excludes all other sperms.

702. **Cleavage.**—After fertilization the eggs of higher plants and animals immediately begin segmenting (early cell division). Among the lower forms, on the contrary, a long "resting stage" often ensues after the zygote (conjugated gametes) or fertilized egg has formed a heavy membrane.

703. In some instances the chromosomes of the two gametes can be separately followed through the first cell division. In which case it is seen that the chromosomes of the first segmentation spindle come in equal numbers from the two gametes and that therefrom the daughter cells receive an equal number of chromosomes from each parent. This is an important point which will be discussed more fully at another place. The events which follow the first cell division vary greatly with the organ-

---

first division of the micronucleus; D, second division; E and F, three daughter nuclei disintegrate, the fourth divides into a migrating male element and a passive female element; F and G, the male element migrates into the other cell and fuses with the opposite female element; H, the process completed; I, the cells separate. In maturation and fertilization (on the right): A and B, the primary spermatocyte and the primary oöcyte; C, secondary spermatocyte and secondary oöcyte; D, mature egg and three polar bodies, and four sperms; E and F, sperm and egg unite and the nuclei fuse; G, the oösperm nucleus divides; H and I, the cell divides. A–D, maturation stages; E and F, fertilization; G–I, first cell division. In F–G the two cells are completely fused. Three of the sperms and the three polar bodies are not represented after stage E.

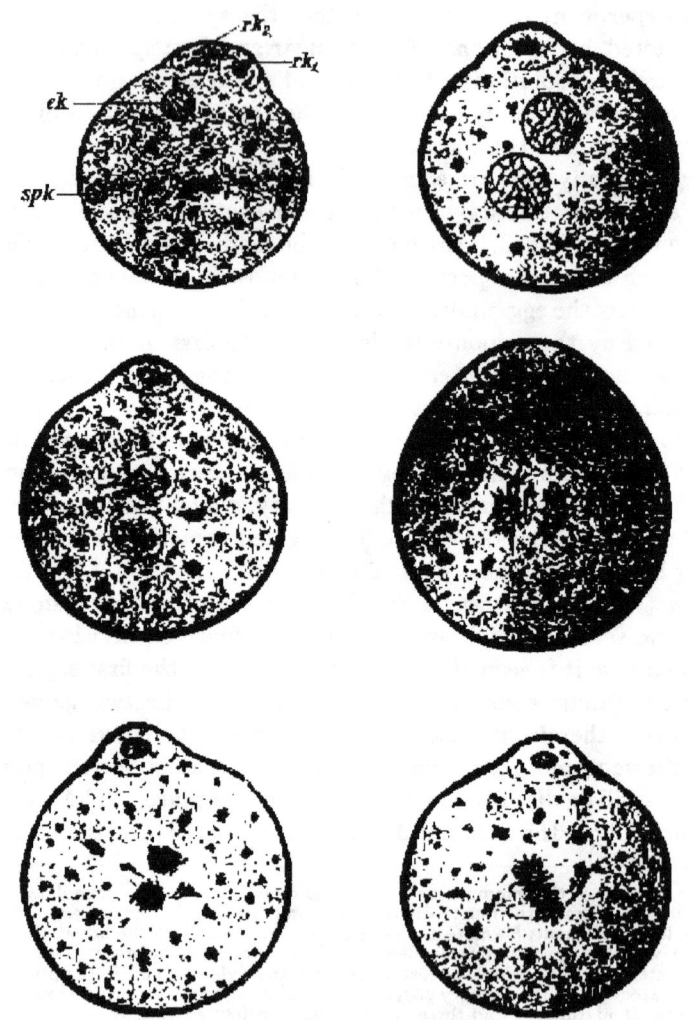

FIG. 187.—Six stages in the process of fertilization of the ovum of a mouse. After the first stage figured it is impossible to determine which of the two nuclei represents the male or female pronucleus. *ek*, Female pronucleus; *rk*₁ and *rk*₂, polar globules; *spk*, male pronucleus. (McMurrich from Sobotta.)

ism, whether it is a unicellular form or whether it is a higher plant or animal. Only a few typical cases will be outlined.

704. (1) When the cell has divided the daughter cells separate completely. On future divisions the same thing occurs and all the cells remain alike. This type includes the free protozoa and many unicellular plants. Sometimes a number of divisions occur before the cells separate, so that a group of eight, sixteen, etc., cells are produced. These then all become free at once and become independent organisms.

705. (2) The cells divide, but are held together by a gelatinous matter which they secrete (Fig. 60); or by their cell walls (Figs. 182 and 212), or by a connecting bridge which develops into a branching stalk. These are colonies, and the arrangement of the individuals in the colony depends largely on whether the planes of division are always parallel, forming filaments (Figs. 182 and 212), or at right angles in two planes, forming plates, or at right angles in three planes, forming cubical masses. (Fig. 60.)

706. (3) The cells divide structurally, but remain in functional unity. The resulting entity is not a colony, but still remains a single organism. Because of cell division the nuclear matter is distributed throughout the body of the organism, and the size of the body is not limited by the limited distance through which the nucleus acts on the cytoplasm, as would probably be the case if there were but a single central nucleus. The division of the body into cell units also permits differentiation to an unlimited degree, and with it division of labor and perfection of function. (See pp. 136, 338.)

707. Under this head two types of development occur which we may characterize as evolving and involving. In the former the cell mass is solid and leads to the diffuse, plant type of organization, while in the latter the cells are arranged in layers enclosing cavities, and through it the compact animal type of organization is attained. (See pp. 328, 331 ff.) This apparent

328 GENERAL PRINCIPLES

paradox disappears when we recognize that the "cavities" mentioned are not so much spaces as cleavage planes between organs, which permit the involution (growing inward) of other organs.

708. As examples of the first type we may take a fern and a dicotyledon. The fertilized egg cell of the fern divides into two cells, and these divide again, making four. These four cells continue to divide indefinitely, and the cells remain a

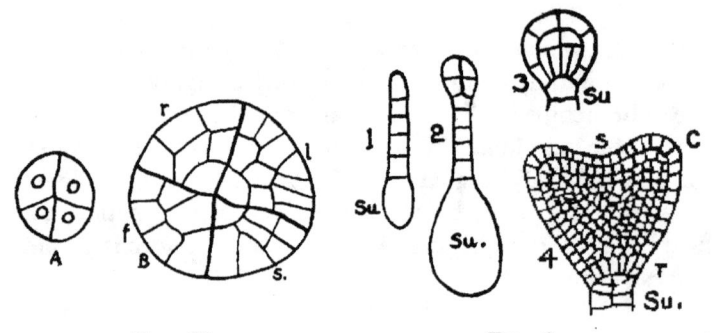

FIG. 188. FIG. 189.

FIG. 188.—Development of the fern embryo. *A*, The egg cell divided into quadrants; *B*, a later stage, the four quadrants still evident and from them develop the four parts of the plant as indicated. *f*, Develops the foot; *r*, develops the root; *s*, develops the stem; *l*, develops the first leaf.

FIG. 189.—Development of the dicotyledon embryo. 1 and 2, Early stages showing all of the suspensor; 3 and 4, only the end of the suspensor is shown. In 2 the embryo is marked off at the upper end of the suspensor. In 3 the embryo is farther advanced. In 4 the root (*T*), stem (*S*) and cotyledons (*C*) are distinguishable.

single solid mass. From each quadrant of the four-cell stage a definite part of the young plant develops; that is, from I develops the root, from II the stem, from III the first leaf, and from IV the foot, an organ by which the plantlet continues to draw nourishment from the mother prothallus. This foot is a type of structure which is very common among plants and animals; that is, of structures which are functional only in the embryonic period of the organism, and later disappear or remain only as rudiments.

709. In the dicotyledon embryo a similar embryonic structure is found. The suspensor is a row of cells which forms no part of the young plant. The terminal cell divides into two, four, eight, etc., cells, which at first form a spherical mass. This soon becomes heart-shaped and then the four parts of the dicotyledon embryo may be localized, viz.: I the caulicle, II the epicotyl, and III and IV the cotyledons.

710. In many of the higher cryptogams the new cells are all divided off from one terminal or apical cell. In some cases a few divisions may occur in segments cut off from the apical cell, but only the apical cell is capable of continued division. In the dicotyledon, cell multiplication takes place only in limited regions of the bud and root-tip and in the cambium. These have already been described (p. 48). (Growth in Monocotyledons, see p. 343.)

711. **Types of Cleavage.**—The course of segmentation of animal eggs is greatly modified by the quantity of yolk present in the egg, and in this respect animal eggs vary greatly. Some eggs contain little yolk (Cœlenterates, Worms, Echinoderms, the lancelet, Mammals), others have moderate quantities (many Molluscs, some Fishes, Amphibia), while in still others the quantity of yolk may be many times in excess of the protoplasm (Arthropods, Cephalopods, many Fishes, Reptiles and Birds). The effect of the yolk is to retard or even completely inhibit division. The simplest type of development occurs, therefore, in eggs with little yolk, and as an example of this type we will take the egg of the lancelet.

712. **The Blastula.**—The first cleavage plane of the egg of the lancelet is vertical, the second is also vertical and at right angle to the first. The third is horizontal and cuts the four segments slightly above the centres, so that the four lower cells are slightly larger than the four upper. This is due to the slightly

330 GENERAL PRINCIPLES

(Figures 190 to 210 represent the early steps in the development of Amphioxous Branchiostoma). According to the wax models of Ziegler, Freiburg, i. B.

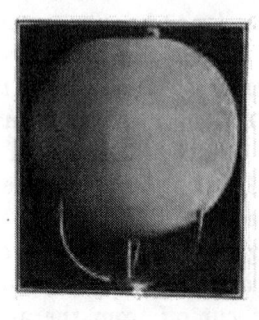

FIG. 190.—The mature egg with the polar body above.

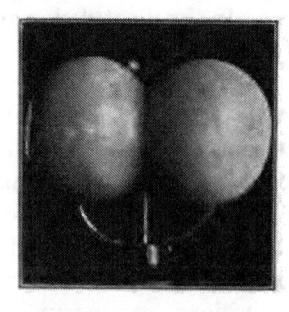

FIG. 191.—Two-cell stage.

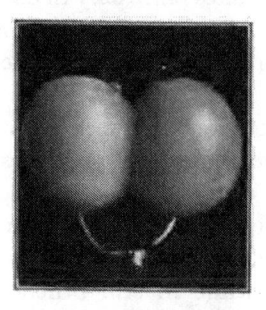

FIG. 192.—Four-cell stage.

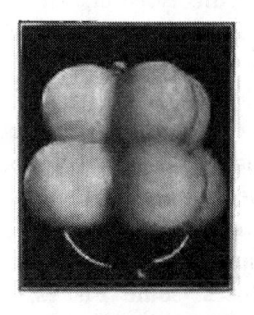

FIG. 193.—Eight-cell stage.

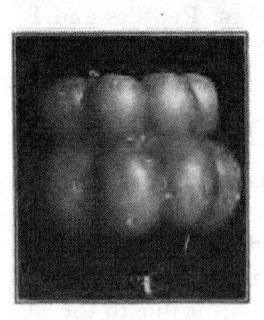

FIG. 194.—Sixteen-cell stage.

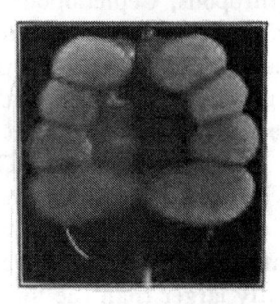

FIG. 195.—Thirty-two cell stage, in section.

BLASTULA, GASTRULA

larger quantity of yolk at the lower pole of the egg. For the same reason the succeeding divisions take place slightly more rapidly at the upper pole of the egg, and hence the cells

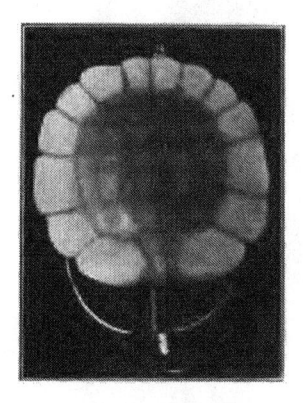

FIG. 196.—Blastula.

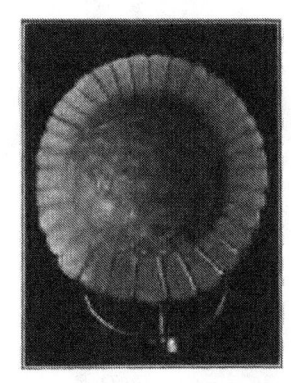

FIG. 197.—Blastula, later stage.

FIG. 198.—Gastrulation.

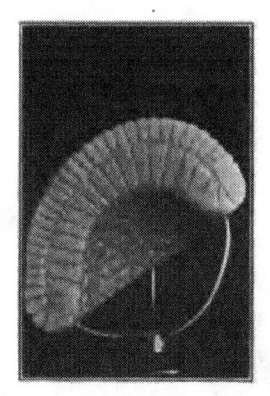

FIG. 199.—Gastrulation, later stage.

here are also somewhat smaller. The cells have a decided tendency to round up after division and so give the whole somewhat the appearance of a mulberry. Hence, this is called

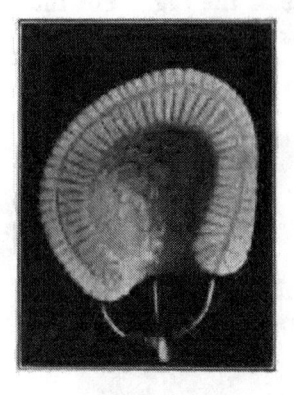

332 GENERAL PRINCIPLES

FIG. 200. 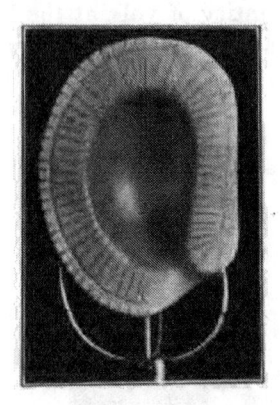   FIG. 201.

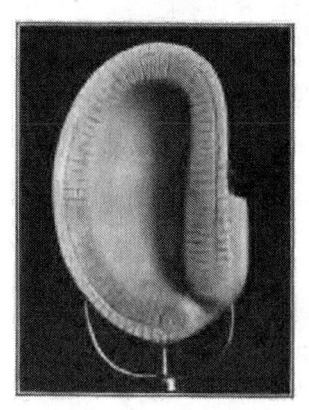

FIG. 202. 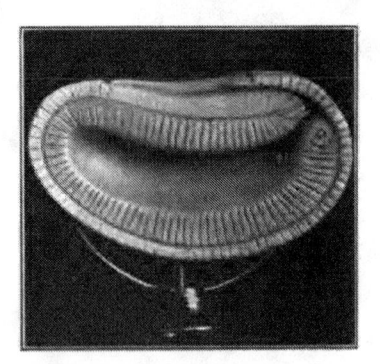   FIG. 203.

FIGS. 200 to 203 represent four steps in the development of the larva from the gastrula. The gastrula mouth narrows and is finally closed in by the ectoderm. The gastrula cavity elongates and becomes the primitive digestive cavity (archenteron).

the mulberry or morula stage. In the centre of the mass a space is formed between the rounded inner surfaces of the cells, and this grows larger as division proceeds. The free surfaces of the cells become flatter and they adhere more closely to their neighbors. By this way we arrive at a stage called the blastula, a hollow sphere, the wall of which is formed by a single layer of cells. The cavity of the sphere is the blastula cavity.

713. **The Gastrula.**—By the next series of changes the blastula is transformed into a gastrula. Cell division continues and the embryo increases in size, but we will fix our attention on another set of changes: First, the vegetative (yolk) pole of the blastula becomes flattened, then concave, as seen from the outside. This cavity deepens and thereby the blastula cavity grows smaller, until it is finally obliterated, when the inverted vegetative hemisphere comes in contact with the hemisphere of the animal pole. The embryo now has the form of a cup, with double walls. This stage is the gastrula. The new cavity which has been formed is the gastrula cavity (archenteron), and its opening to the exterior is the gastrula mouth. The two layers which form the wall of the gastrula are the ectoderm and entoderm. After a time the embryo has elongated, and by unequal growth its axis has been shifted so that now the gastrula mouth, which has become very small, lies at the posterior dorsal extremity.

714. **The Medullary Plate.**—From now on several important developmental processes occur simultaneously, but we will trace them one by one.

715. The dorsal surface of the elongated embryo becomes flattened and the cells of the ectoderm along the median line assume a columnar form, which results in a thickening of the ectoderm. The medullary plate thus formed curls up along its edges, forming a medullary groove. The edges of the groove approach above and fuse to form the medullary tube. This

334   GENERAL PRINCIPLES

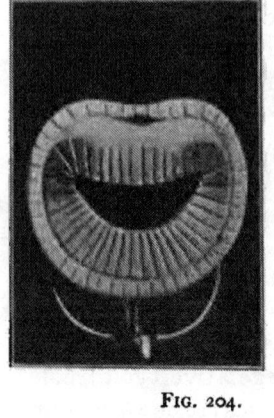

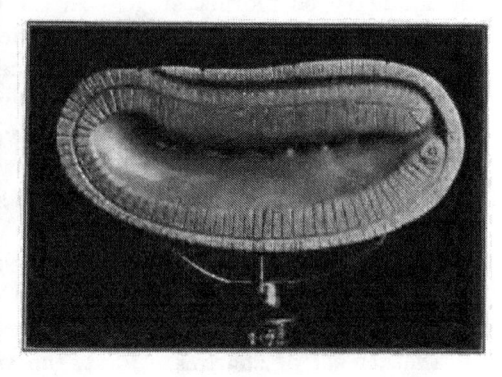

FIG. 204.   FIG. 205.

FIG. 204 is a cross section of the stage represented in Fig. 203. The medullary plate is shown above, between entoderm and ectoderm.

FIG. 205.—A later larval stage showing six mesodermic pockets, and the medullary plate completely covered by the ectoderm.

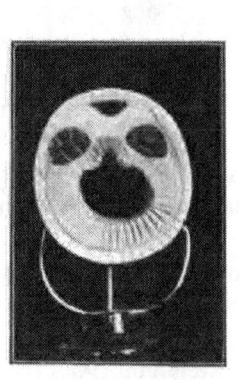

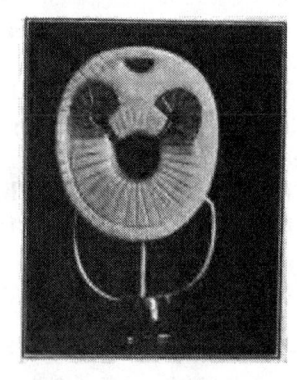

FIG. 206.   FIG. 207.

FIG. 206 is a cross section through the anterior (left in the figure) end of the stage represented by Fig. 205.

FIG. 207 is a similar section through the posterior end of the same stage. In both figures the medullary groove, the mesodermic somites and the first steps in the formation of the notochord are shown.

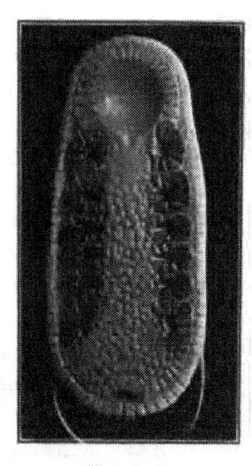

THE EMBRYO 335

FIG. 208. 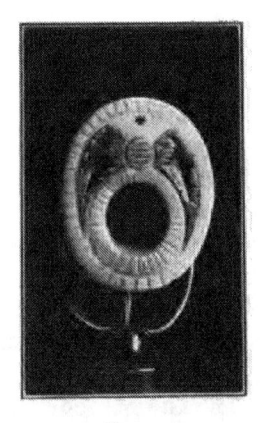 FIG. 209.

FIG. 208 is a horizontal section through the stage represented by Fig. 205, and shows the six pairs of mesodermic somites.

FIG. 209 is a section through a later stage (Fig. 210) and shows the medullary tube, the notochord, and the mesoderm pushing upward and downward between entoderm and ectoderm.

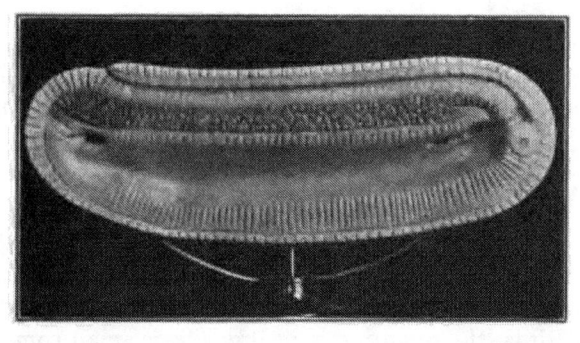

FIG. 210.—A later stage, showing most of the mesodermic somites completely cut off from the entoderm, the notochord, and the medullary tube.

tube ultimately gives rise to the central nervous system of the animal. Before the tube is completely formed the edges of the ectoderm slip over it from each side toward the median line and fuse. This superficial part of the ectoderm gives origin to the epidermis with its modifications, and the sense organs of the skin.

716. The Notochord.—While the medullary plate is forming in the ectoderm the notochord and mesoderm are also taking origin from the entoderm. A longitudinal inverted groove is formed by the bulging upward of the entoderm along the mid-dorsal line. The edges of this groove unite to form a tube, which is then cut off from the entoderm. This tube develops into the notochord.

717. The Mesoderm.—At the same time two series of pockets are formed by the bulging outward of the entoderm in the dorsal lateral quarters, i. e., on either side of the notochord. These pockets also close and are cut off from the entoderm. They are called mesodermic somites, and are the first evidence of the segmentation of the body. They gradually extend downward and upward till they finally completely surround the medullary tube, the notochord and the remaining entoderm. The cavities of the mesodermic pockets develop into the body cavity.

718. Other Types of Cleavage.—So far as the segmentation stages are concerned the chief deviations from the lancelet type may be ascribed to the quantity and disposition of the yolk. In the lancelet egg, cleavage is total and equal. In the frog's egg there is a large amount of yolk accumulated largely at the vegetative pole. In consequence cleavage, though also total, is unequal and at the first horizontal division the cells of the vegetative pole are many times larger than those of the animal pole. In the eggs of Cephalopods, many Fishes, Reptiles and Birds, the quantity of protoplasm is small compared with the yolk and forms a thin layer at the animal pole. When cleavage takes place the yolk does not divide and the cleavage only extends through the protoplasm, which is thus divided into a number of minute hummocks. From these, cells are later cut off by horizontal cleavage planes, and the same process extends outward and downward, continuously adding to the number of fully formed cells. This type of cleavage is called partial and discoidal, the latter referring to the disk-like form of the segmenting area. For most Arthropods cleavage follows still another course. Here the eggs are also laden with yolk, which is concentrated at the centre of the egg, while the protoplasm lies more equally distributed over the entire surface. When the nucleus divides there is at first no division of the cytoplasm. But after a time the nuclei arrange themselves near the surface in a single layer. The cytoplasm then divides partially as in the preceding case, but over the whole surface of the egg. This type is distinguished as partial and superficial cleavage.

719. **Origin of the Tissues.**—If allowance is made for the modification caused by the yolk, one may say that during the early stages of development all metazoa proceed along parallel lines. In all cases a blastula is formed, and this is followed by a gastrula stage. The formation of a distinct mesoderm, however, does not occur in the Porifera and Cœlenterates. These animals, even in the adult, consist only of two distinct cell layers, the ectoderm and entoderm, though there is usually a supporting layer between. This may be simply a structureless membrane or, in some cases, a thick layer composed chiefly of a gelatinous matrix. Some of the ectodermal and entodermal cells may send nervous or muscular fibre processes into this layer, and there may also be few or many cells of ectodermal or entodermal origin completely embedded in this layer. In the other phyla, where a true mesoderm is formed, there is considerable variation in the method. It is almost always wholly entodermal in origin, but some times it begins as a solid outgrowth,

which later splits to form the body cavity, and again it is gradually formed by cells which sink inward, one by one, from the entoderm and finally arrange themselves around the body cavity.

720. In general, after the mesoderm and notochord have been formed, the entoderm which remains forms the lining of the digestive tract; that is, the mucous epithelium with all the glandular organs connected with it, salivary, thymus, thyroid, gastric, hepatic, pancreatic and intestinal glands. The mucous epithelium lining the tracheæ, bronchi and lungs, is also of entodermal origin.

721. The mesoderm gives rise to all other parts of the body: the dermis, muscles, all connective tissues, including bones, cartilage, teeth (in part), ligaments, tendons, fascia; heart, blood vessels and blood; lymph, lymph glands, and spleen; the gonads and kidneys with their ducts; the pleura, pericardium, peritoneum and mesenteries.

722. **Indirect Development.**—The course pursued by the developing organism is not always the most direct. When the embryo gradually assumes the characters of the adult the development is said to be direct. Often, however, there is a sudden change in direction of development, so that the earlier steps seem to be directed toward a very different goal from that finally reached; so, for example, in most forms which are fixed, or very sluggish in the adult, there is an active free-swimming larva (Echinoderms, most Molluscs, Worms, Barnacles). This is called a dispersal larva because it seems to distribute the species partly by its own efforts, but more largely by the currents by which it is carried about. An interesting exception, which proves the rule, is that of the larvæ of the fresh-water clam. If this were to follow the rule the larvæ would be carried down stream by the currents much farther than the adult would be able to move upward during its entire existence. The result would be that the entire species would soon be carried to the

INDIRECT DEVELOPMENT

sea. But this larvæ attaches itself to the gills of fishes and may thus be carried up stream.

723. Another type of larva is the trophic larva, like those of many insects. These are characterized by their voracious appetites. The caterpillar, for example, consumes much more than is necessary for its daily needs. The excess is stored up in the tissues as fat. When a certain stage of development is reached, feeding ceases. The caterpillar finds a suitable place

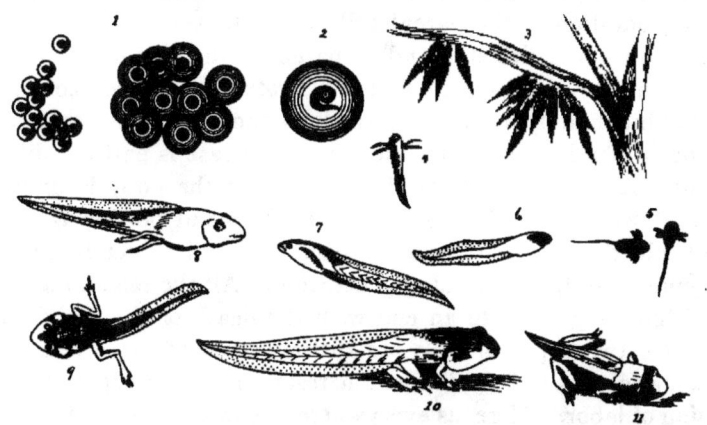

FIG. 211.—Development of the frog. An example of indirect development (metamorphosis). The gills have not disappeared in stage 6 but have been covered by a fold of the skin. (From Galloway after Brehm.)

in which to rest. Here a complete change takes place. The skin is cast and there emerges a quiescent pupa, without functional appendages, without mouth or eyes. In this form the animal remains for a shorter or longer time, a few days to many months. Then another radical change occurs. The pupa skin is cast and the winged adult emerges. In many cases the adult feeds very little. Some have no functional mouth parts and would be unable to take food. They live for a short time, mate, and deposit eggs. Here the adult is the dispersal stage. Its organs of locomotion, the wings, are not for the ordinary purposes of securing food or escaping enemies as much as to facilitate mating and the carrying of the species to new and favorable localities.

724. Differentiation of Germinal and Somatic Tissues.—Reproduction in the protozoa and most unicellular plants (all unicellular organisms are some times grouped together under the name Protista) means merely a division of the body of the organism. The two halves resulting from division reorganize themselves, and after a period of growth, each has attained to the condition of the parent cell before division. This process continues indefinitely, and apparently there is no inherent reason why the substance of the Protist should not continue thus indefinitely; that is, the Protist organism does not naturally end in death. With the metazoan the case is entirely different. At a certain stage of development the body is divided into two classes of cells. A relatively small portion consists of cells destined to develop into gametes and, therefore, to continue on in the succeeding generation. All the remaining cells of the body come to an end with the death of the individual. These two types of cells are distinguished as germ cells and somatic cells. This distinction rests on the principle of division of labor. Here, as everywhere else in the biological world, the chief end is the perpetuation of the species. This is secured more certainly if by unity of action but division of labor the life functions are performed in the most perfect manner. This seems to be the reason for the existence of the multicellular organism.

727. Division of Labor and Differentiation.—All the various types of aggregation of biological units are attempts to solve the same problem. The colonies of Protists, the hydroid colonies with polymorphism, the polymorphic societies of ants and bees, the various types of alternation of generation found among plants and animals are all devices to secure the most perfect functioning by dividing the functions. The metazoan individual is in one sense a colony of cells in which there is unity of action. But in order to secure the best results, the division of labor means differentiation, and differentiation carried very far means loss of power of recuperation and of cell division. Thus the functions of the somatic cells contribute to the perpetuation of the race by fostering the gametes and further nursing the embryo in many cases until it is well advanced in development.

726. **Regeneration.**—That the loss of the power of recuperation goes hand in hand with differentiation, appears from a study of the phenomena of regeneration. An egg has the power of regeneration like that of a protozoan, so that from a fragment of an egg a complete embryo may develop. This is true even of Vertebrate eggs. Among the lower invertebrates such power of regeneration exists even in the adult. An anemone or star fish may be cut in two, and the parts will regenerate all the organs that were removed. This is not possible with a crab or crayfish. But even the Crustaceæ will regenerate an appendage that was broken off. So as we pass to higher forms the power regularly decreases. In young Amphibia, appendages may still be regenerated, but in Birds and Mammals the power extends only to the healing of wounds, which is also a regeneration process.

727. **Mechanics of Growth.**—Differentiation begins at a very early stage. Even in the lancelet the entoderm is distinguishable from the ectoderm before gastrulation takes place, and the cells of the medullary plate are distinguishable from the rest of the ectoderm before the medullary groove is formed. But it will not be necessary to describe the individual types of tissues here, since this was done in connection with the anatomical description of types. There are, however, some points about the mechanics of growth which should be noted. A naked protoplasmic cell like Amœba expands freely with growth and often when there is a cell membrane it is elastic

enough to expand with the growth of its contents. But there are often rigid, supporting or protecting structures, which do not permit free expansion of the body. In such cases there are many interesting devices employed for securing expansion. The splitting bark of the exogen type of stem has been described, as well as the growing root-tip and the bud. If the position of the apical cell and the angles of the planes in which the successive segments are cut off from it are carefully considered it will be seen that we have here also a device for securing freedom for growth. Let us consider a few more cases among plants. The diatoms are always unicellular, and each cell is encased in a silicious capsule. The substance of which this capsule is composed is absolutely unyielding so far as the growth of the living contents is concerned. But the capsule is composed of two parts, which fit into each other like the parts of a common gelatin capsule or a pill box, and can slide apart as the protoplasmic contents increase in volume. At the time of division a new half capsule is formed inside each of the old half capsules. This means that each generation is confined in a slightly smaller compass than the preceding. Finally a limit is reached beyond which this decreasing size will not go. The shell is then cast off completely, a brief period of rapid growth as a naked cell ensues, and then a

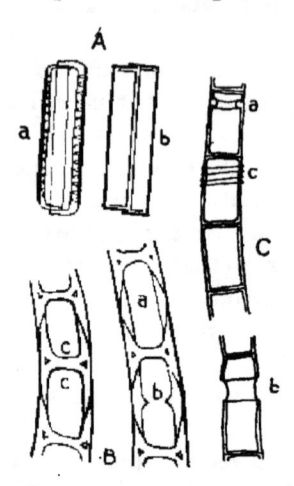

FIG. 212.—Mechanics of growth. *A*, A diatom; *B*, Microspora; *C*, Œdogonium. In *A*: *a*, the silicious "pill-box" shell of a diatom; *b*, a diatom dividing and forming two new half shells, back-to-back, within the old one. In *B*: *a*, *b* and *c*, three steps in the process of forming a new cross wall and elongating the side walls of a dividing cell. In *C*: *a*, the circular pad formed within the old wall preparatory to elongation; *b*, the old wall split under the pad and the pad stretching to form new wall; *c*, ridges left by a repetition of the process.

new and larger shell is produced as a starting point for a repetition of the process.

728. Sometimes cells adhering in filaments are encased in thick tubular sheaths, which become too unyielding to keep pace with the growing contents by stretching. In the case of Tolyptothrix the tube splits at a certain point, the chain of cells breaks, and one end pushes past the other and out through the opening. This produces what is called false branching. Again in Oedogonium the unyielding tube in which the cells are encased is made to expand in a curious fashion. Inside the cell a circular cushion of new cell wall substance is formed against the inner surface of the old wall. This cushion completely encircles the cylinder. Then the old wall breaks opposite the cushion, and this permits the latter to stretch and the cell to elongate, while at the same time maintaining the continuity of the cell wall. In Microspora the wall of the filament is made up of segments which are double-wedge-shaped in longitudinal section. These slip apart as growth proceeds and permit the insertion of new wedges by growth.

729. Among the Monocotyledons two methods of common occurrence are of special interest. In this group of plants we find the sheathing leaf base a very common type. The sheath completely surrounds and protects the stem for some distance upward from the node. Within this sheath the stem remains for a long time meristematic, after the upper part of the same internode has completed its growth. This device permits the stem to continue growth longitudinally for a long time, but growth in thickness is practically completed when the upper end of the node appears above its sheath. This type is especially characteristic of the long, slender, rapidly growing stems of grasses. A modification of this type occurs in the case of the perennial Monocotyledons like the palms. Here, the growth in height is very slow, and the short internodes are protected for a long time by the basal portions of the leaf stalks,

which often develop a very elaborate protective tissue. This often persists long after the death of the leaf as a thick interwoven mat of tough fibres. Protected in this way the stem slowly increases in thickness for several years. When the protective tissue finally rots away and exposes the stem the tissues of the latter have reached their final condition and the stem no longer expands in diameter. Thus the stem of this type soon reaches a limit in diameter while the growth in height may continue indefinitely, a condition which is decidedly inferior to that of the exogen stem, in which growth in thickness keeps pace with growth in height.

730. For animals, the question of growth mechanics is fundamentally not as difficult as for plants, because the tissues are generally more yielding in character. At the same time the problem has appeared in much greater variety and has been solved in more different ways. As soon as animals covered themselves with a protecting shell they learned the trick of making that shell conical in form, so that by adding to the edge or mouth of the cone it grew wider as well as longer. This type of shell is found in many forms, from the protozoa to the cephalopods. But a flat cone offers less protection, while a long one is awkward to handle. This difficulty was also soon solved by

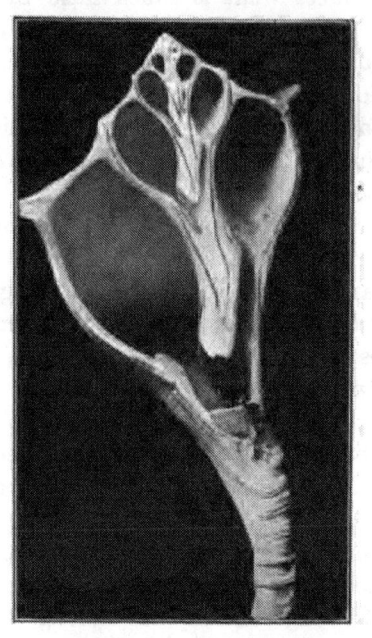

FIG. 213.—Section of a conch shell (Fulgur) to show that it consists of a spirally wound cone. ×1/2.

coiling the cone into a spiral by more rapid growth on one side. This device is also very generally employed wherever the cone is in use (many Protozoa, some Worms, Gastropods, Cephalopods, especially extinct forms).

731. One of the most distinctive characters of the entire phylum of Arthropods is the way the problem of growth mechanics is solved. The Arthropod is entirely enclosed in a sheathing of chitin, a substance which is very elastic but has very little power of stretching. In fact, the animal cannot grow while encased in this armor. Consequently, the armor is removed periodically and then a period of rapid expansion ensues until the new shell has hardened again. Among the Crustaceæ the casting of the shell (ecdysis) occurs frequently during the early periods of development (lobster 7-8 times in first year), later the moulting periods are less frequent (once per year, crab, lobster). During the soft-shell periods the animal remains concealed in some cranny, because it is then extremely helpless. Not only is it unprotected by a shell, but its "claws," at other times so formidable, are now useless. Nevertheless, the Crustaceæ as a class have been very successful, and we must conclude that the disadvantages of the period of ecdysis are more than compensated by the advantages of the chitinous armor.

732. The more primitive Insects follow in general the Crustaceæ in regard to the management of this armor, but most orders of Insects have adopted a different and probably a better plan. Diptera, Coleoptera, Hymenoptera and Lepidoptera, the most numerous orders, develop by metamorphosis. Their larvæ are soft-skinned and are in various ways enabled to dispense with the armor. During the pupal stage they are usually concealed in the earth or elsewhere, and after they emerge as completely armored insects, they no longer grow. Their growth is completed and no ecdysis is needed. Ecdysis occurs at the period of pupation, and again at the emergence of the imago, and at this time the insect is often concealed.

346 GENERAL PRINCIPLES

733. The development of an internal skeleton by the Vertebrates called for a new solution of these growth problems. But in the Vertebrates numerous integumentary structures, each with its peculiar method of growth, are also found. We will only consider the epidermis here. This layer of the skin is constantly growing in all the terrestrial Vertebrates and its dead,

FIG. 214.—Ecdysis of the blue crab. The animal (lower part of the figure) has almost freed itself of the shell from which it escapes by backing out. ×1/2.

outer layers are cast either at some intervals of time or as a continuous process. In the Amphibia, this layer is cast at intervals in large or small patches. In Snakes it often comes away in a single piece. In Birds and Mammals the epidermis is constantly shedding in minute scales, but in these two classes there is usually a well-marked period of moulting or shedding of feathers and hair. When the epidermis is cast it is, of course, not the

GROWTH 347

entire layer, nor even all the dead tissue. Only the hardened, more superficial part separates from the deeper, more flexible, layers. In some cases (Reptiles) a specially constructed layer of cells forms a cleavage plane. The process is comparable to the ecdysis in Arthropods, except that here we have to do with dead cells instead of formed substances.

734. The method of growth of the bones varies greatly. In the smaller bones with simple form, the process is not specially

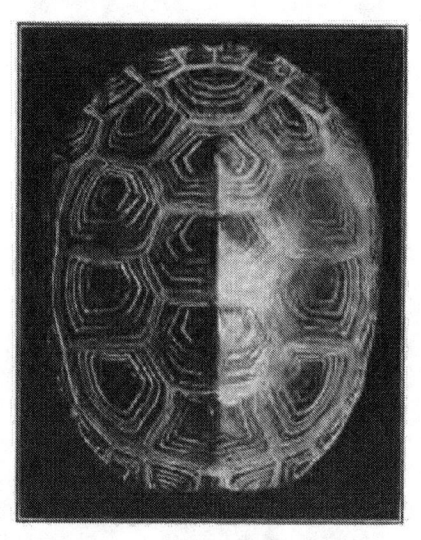

FIG. 215.—The carapace of the diamond back terrapin, Malaclemmys palustris. Note the concentric lines of growth in the horny plates. ×1/2.

noteworthy, but with the "long" bones and those of complicated figure, the enlargement of the bone, and at the same time maintaining its form, is often a complicated process. For example, the skull of the adult is practically a single piece. This condition could not have been reached by the addition of layers of bone to the surface, since this would not provide for the growth of the brain unless, at the same time, the cavity of the skull were enlarged by the removal of material from the inner surface of the skull bones. The end is accomplished in another way. The skull is composed of many pieces, which are fitted together in a peculiar way. The seam, or suture, along which two bones join is not an even line or smooth joint; it is an extremely sinuous line which effects a dovetailing of the two

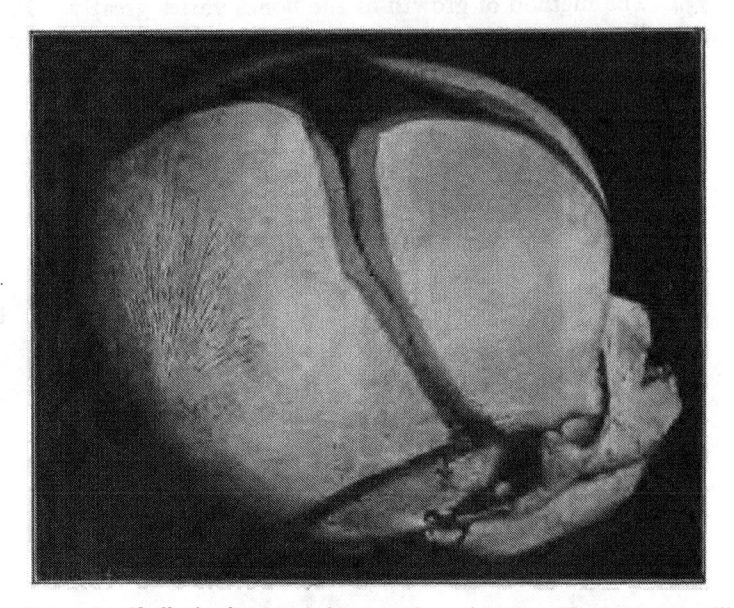

FIG. 216.—Skull of a human embryo at time of birth. The bones are still separated by seams of cartilage and membrane. The broad unossified space is called a fontanelle. In the figure the radiating lines on the parietal bone (large bone on the left) indicate the original centre of ossification and the direction of growth.

bones in a way to produce a very firm joint. The suture disappears at maturity by the complete fusion of the bones, but until the end of the growth period the suture is an open joint, in which material is being added to the bones of both sides. The skull, as a whole, therefore, expands by interstitial growth, while

GROWTH 349

each individual bone increases its dimensions by the addition of material along the sutural surfaces. In Reptiles the sutures tend to remain open throughout life.

735. In the ossification of the long bones like the femur, the bone is first deposited on the surface of the cartilage in its

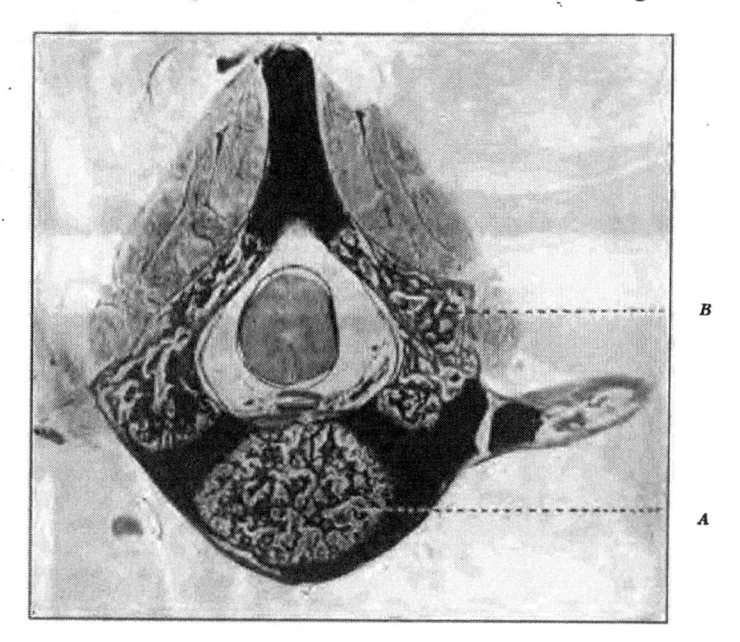

FIG. 217.—Cross section of a vertebra of an embryo (pig) showing centres of ossification. The parts in black are cartilage. At three points the cartilage is being replaced by bone; in the centrum (*A*) and in the two sides of the neural arch (*B*). As the bony parts grow outward into the cartilage the cartilage between them also grows. Thus the vertebra increases in size with the growth of the body. Finally, however, all the cartilage is replaced by bone and the parts unite to form a single body of bone.

middle region. The two ends remain cartilaginous for some time and grow by the growth of the cartilage. In the middle region or shaft the growth of bone continues by the addition of new layers to the outside, and the new layers extend gradually

350   GENERAL PRINCIPLES

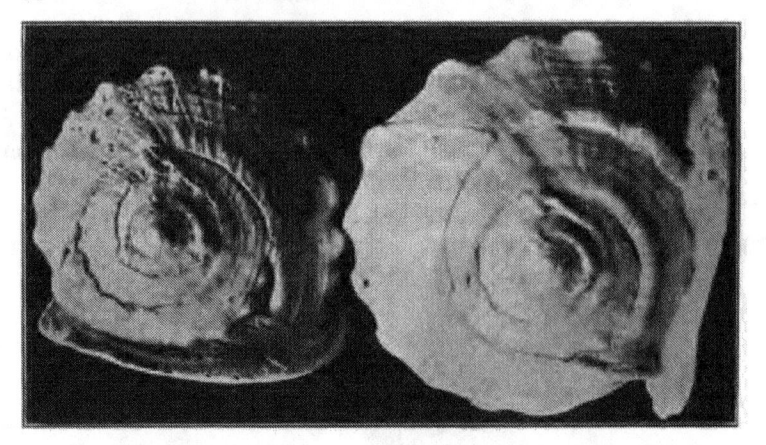

A   B

C

further toward the two ends. After a time new centres of ossification occur at each end. These form bony discs, which are later separated from the shaft only by a thin seam of cartilage. In this seam there are, however, three zones of growth; a middle zone, in which cartilage is rapidly forming, and on either side of this is a zone in which the cartilage is being eroded and replaced by bone. It is thus that the shaft increases in length, while the epiphysis is also increasing in thickness (compare with the growth in the cambium ring). When growth is complete the epiphysis unites with the shaft.

736. This method by which a complicated skeletal figure expands by interstitial growth through the growth of parts is also found among invertebrates. An excellent example is in the test of the sea urchin.

737. In cases where the proper form cannot be secured through growth by the addition of material to earlier stages, it often happens that parts of the earlier structure are actually removed, so that growth consists in a process of tearing down and building larger. This takes place, for instance, in many gastropod shells which form a thick rounded fold at the mouth of the shell at the close of the seasonal growth period. At the beginning of the next growing season this fold is removed by absorption before the edge of the shell is extended. (Ex.: The queen conch.) This also very often occurs in the development of the Vertebrate skeleton. The central cavity of the shaft of an adult femur, for example, is much larger than it was when the first layer of bone was laid down on the cartilage. Hence, the bone must have been removed at a later period. So also the lower jaw of the embryo, with its complex curvature, cannot be included within the outline of an adult jaw. There

Fig. 218.—Three successive steps in the growth of the queen conch (Cassia). The thickened lip of the shell (+) in A, is shown in B (+) partly absorbed and overgrown by the new growth. A new lip (o) is formed after a period of growth and this is again partly absorbed and overgrown (o, in C). In C, nine or ten successive stages of growth may be counted by the remnants of the lips. ×1/2.

352   GENERAL PRINCIPLES

must have been a process of absorption at work as development proceeded.

738. **Progressive and Regressive Development.**—Wherever development is direct the organization of the body is a continuous progressive process toward the final perfect adult. But when there is a change in the course of development, as in all

Fig. 219.—Sexual dimorphism in a beetle, Cladognathus. The difference appears both in size and in the peculiar development of the mandibles of the male. Male on the left. In many beetles the male is larger than the female. ×5/6.

cases of metamorphosis, or where there is a radical change in the life habits of the animal, there is also a break in the continuity of development, and to a greater or lesser degree a reversal of development. This is the case, for example, when a free-swimming larva becomes fixed in the adult, or when a holo-

REGRESSIVE DEVELOPMENT 353

zoic larva becomes paraistic in the adult. Such changes involve a loss of function, or at least a change of function of some organs, and hence a change in the organs themselves. This is called regressive development. When the tadpole develops legs and lungs and leaves the water, some of its organs have become useless. We need mention only the gills and the broad fish-like tail. These organs, being now no longer needed, undergo regressive changes, they are gradually resorbed, dwindle

FIG. 220.—Male (left) and female (right) of a fire-fly, Lampyris. The male has well-developed wings but the female is wingless. ×2.

and completely disappear. It must not be inferred, however, that if any tadpole were kept in the water that these changes would not occur. Indeed, these organs have become useless before the frog leaves the water. The position might be assumed that the change of habit occurs because of the change in organization. (See p. 339.)

739. **Sexual Dimorphism.**—In some species the adult individuals all strictly conform to one type. This is exceptional, however, and applies only to hermaphrodyte forms like the earthworms and some snails. The vastly more common condition is a sexual dimorphism; that is, two types of individuals

are regularly developed, male and female. The difference between the two is often indistinguishable except in the gonads, and it may require dissection to determine the sex. In other cases the gonads are visible through the transparent wall of the body, and a difference in color of those organs often distinguishes the sexes (jelly fish, some worms, etc.). More frequently there are secondary sexual differences, such as accessory sexual organs, egg-laying apparatus, or copulating organs or structures which are more remotely or not at all connected with the function of reproduction. The female is very generally larger than the male, a fact which is probably to be connected with her greater trophic functions. This is notably the case among insects. In a few remarkable instances the male is minute, compared with the female, and may even be attached to her as a parasite. (Ex.: Barnacles, Sacculina, Oedogonium.) Among Mammals the males often fight with each other for the possession of the females, and this has resulted in a greater development in size and strength of the males. The male of the fur seal is four times larger than the female. Among Birds the difference between the sexes is most conspicuous with regard to coloration and song, in which the males usually far excel the females. (See p. 423.) Among butterflies there are often remarkable differences in coloration between the sexes, and in a number of Insects the male is winged while the female is without wings (glowworm and Hibernia moth). Among plants, sexual dimorphism is usually evident only in the accessory reproductive organs (flowers).

740. **Polymorphism.**—There is also a manifolding of form types which has no direct relation to sex. It is best developed in lower forms, especially those which are colonial. Among the Hydrozoa there may be as many as four or five types of individuals. These may be classed as the trophic or feeding polyps, the budding polyps, the protective polyps, and the sexual medusæ. In the Siphonophores there are, in addition, the swim-

POLYMORPHISM

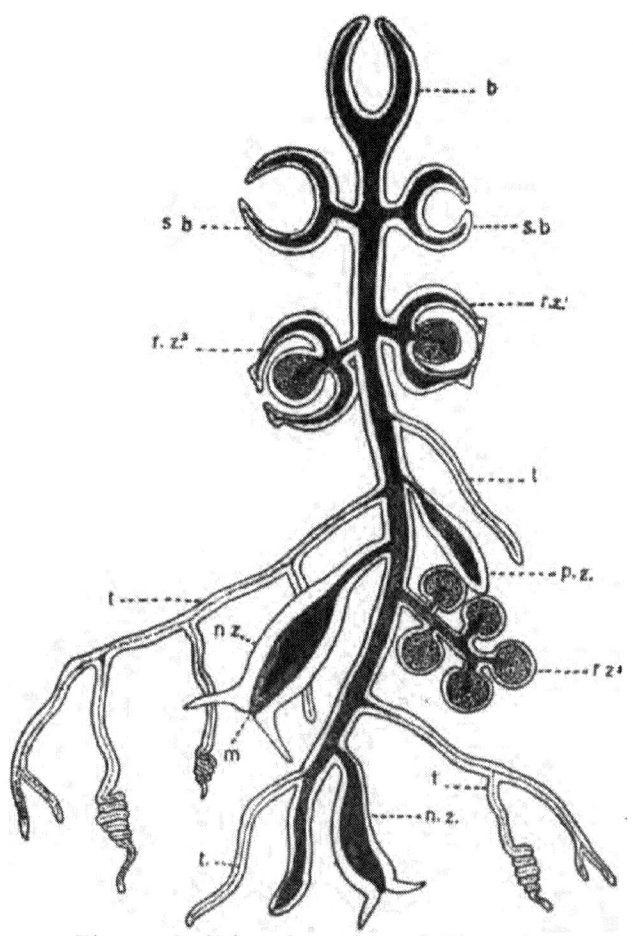

FIG. 221.—Diagram of a Siphonophore colony. b, Float; $s.b$, swimming bell; m, mouth; $n.s.$, trophic polyp; $p.s.$, protective zoöid; rz^1, rz^2, rz^3, reproductive zoöids; t, tentacles. (From Galloway, after Lang.)

356   GENERAL PRINCIPLES

ming bells. The vibraculæ and avicularia of the Bryozoa, are also modified zooids. In these cases, which are characterized as stock polymorphism, the differentiation of individuals occurs in connection with division of labor, and in this special type could only occur in a colony. An analogous kind of polymorphism occurs in the social Hymenoptera, the bees and ants, and the termites among the Corrodentia. In these societies there

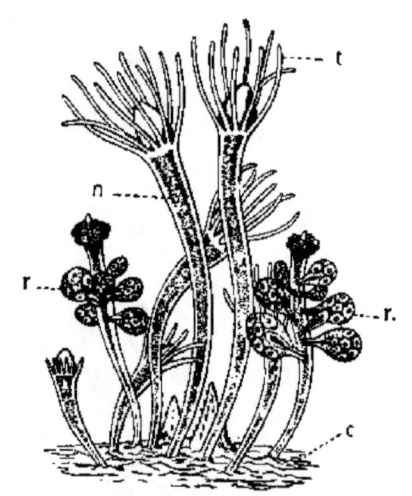

FIG. 222.—Hydractinia, a polymorphic hydroid. *C*, Cœnosarc covering the substratum; *n*, trophic polyps; *r*, reproductive polyps bearing buds containing ova; *t*, tentacles. (From Galloway after Hincks.)

are males, females and workers. The latter are undeveloped females. In some ants and termites there is also a fourth class, the soldier, individuals with exceptionally large heads and formidable jaw. The interdependence of the individuals of these societies is almost as great as that of polyps in a Hydroid colony.

741. **Alternation of Generations.**—When polymorphic types alternate with each other in successive generations we have the

ALTERNATION OF GENERATIONS

common phenomenon of alternation of generations. This occurs in the Hydroid colony when the free-swimming sexual medusa originates by budding from a colony, and itself gives rise to a new colony by a sexual method. This type of polymorphism is well exemplified by many of the trematodes (see p. 368), and is particularly widespread among plants. Indeed, all plants above the thallophytes undergo a regular alternation of generations. In the higher forms it is rather obscure and not easily

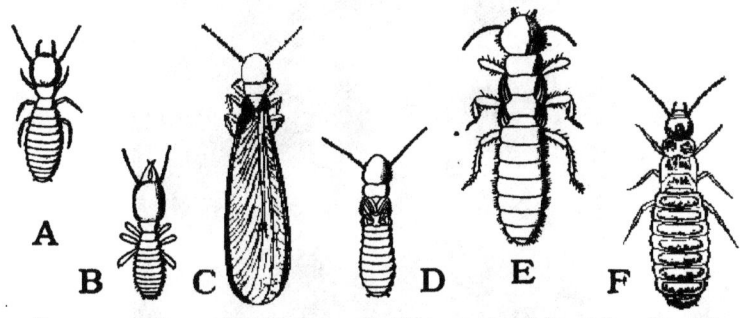

Fig. 223.—Polymorphism in Termes lucifugus. *A*, Adult worker; *B*, soldier. Both *A* and *B* are undeveloped males or females. *C*, Perfect insect (male or female); *D*, same after shedding the wings; *E*, young complementary queen; *F*, older complementary queen. Enlarged. (From Folsom after Grassi and Sandias.)

described. In Mosses it is most conspicuous. The leafy moss plant develops from a spore and is itself sexual and develops eggs and spermatozoids. From these are developed the spore capsule with its stalk. These remain connected with the sexual plant, but are themselves the asexual generation by which the spores are produced.

742. There are still other types of polymorphism of less common occurrence. Seasonal dimorphism occurs, for example, among some butterflies. In this the broods produced at different seasons are often very differently colored, so that there are summer and fall types or wet and dry season types.

743. The polymorphism found in many flowers, as a device for securing cross fertilization, has already been described. A

FIG. 224.—Passage ways of the "white-ants" in a post. The termites avoid the light, ordinarily, and hence construct tunnels of mud to cover their runways. These tunnels are often very extensive and much labor is involved in their construction. This is performed by the numerous small workers. ×1/2.

very peculiar type of polymorphism occurs among spiders and butterflies. A number of species of spider are known to pro-

HOLOPHYTIC ORGANISMS 359

duce two kinds of males, and among butterflies there occurs a duplication of types of females. In one case at least there are said to be five kinds of females. (See p. 430.)

744. Life Habits Depending on Food.—The character of the food and the method by which it is obtained exercises a

FIG. 225.—Seasonal dimorphism in a butterfly (Prioneris) from India. *A*, Wet season form; *B*, dry season form. ×3/4.

profound influence upon the organization of the body. The typical plant absorbs CO_2 and various mineral salts and through photosynthesis builds up its tissues. Such plants are said to be holophytic. The typical animal ingests organic matter and

360 GENERAL PRINCIPLES

prepares it for absorption and assimilation by digestion. Such an animal is said to be holozoic.

745. Some times two organisms of different kinds are found living together by mutual consent, apparently, and partake of the same food. The sea anemone, on the shell of the hermit

Fig. 226.—Seasonal dimorphism in a European butterfly, Araschnia levana. Both are females: A, the winter form; B, the summer form. ×2.

crab, is often quoted as an example of this kind. The anemone secures fragments of the crab's food, and the crab secures some measure of protection by the presence of the anemone. Such a relationship is called commensalism. More frequently the needs of two organisms are to some extent complementary, and one household may serve both to mutual advantage. This is

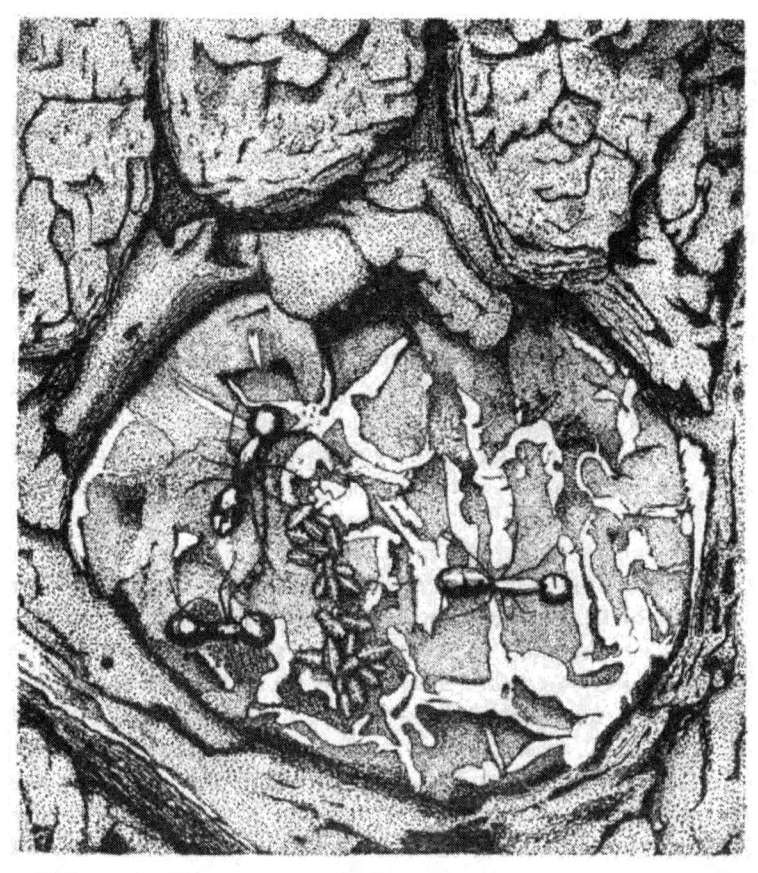

FIG. 227.—An example of a complex interrelationship of organisms. Three large brown ants (Camponotus?) are guarding a small colony of aphids from which they obtain honey-dew; the abdomens of these three ants being greatly distended with what they obtained in this way. The day after the above sketch was made the large ants had been driven away by a large band of small black ants, which then took possession of the aphid colony. The aphids in this case are feeding on a fungus (Peridermium?) which, in turn is parasitic in the bark of the trunk of a pine tree. Ants are known to care for the eggs of aphids during the winter, and carry the young to appropriate food plants, and then guard the aphid colony from the attacks of other predatory insects. For this service the aphids pay a tax in honey-dew. The honey-dew is a clear, sweet fluid secreted in drops from the anus (not from the tubules on the dorsal surface of the abdomen). The ants stimulate the aphids by stroking them with their antennæ; to this the aphids respond by voiding a droplet of the honey-dew.

symbiosis, and, as examples, we may refer to the green hydra, the green fresh-water sponge and some Protozoa in which cells of a unicellular alga have found the conditions of life favorable within the protoplasm of the animal host. The CO_2 eliminated by the animal tissues is food for the plant, while the O eliminated by the plant cells is equally useful to the animal. A similar relation exists between algæ and fungi of many kinds in the group of organisms called Lichens. Here the algæ are wound about by the mycelium of the fungus so that they seem to form a single organism. It has been found, however, that they may be separated and grown independently of each other, and in their structure they show their identity or near relationship with algæ and fungi which are found in nature unconnected. The mutual advantage here is probably like that in the case of hydra, and in addition the alga is protected from the dry air by the dense tissue of the fungus, and the fungus possibly secures soluble food from the alga.

746. It is difficult to judge of the degree of helpfulness or harm which one organism exercises over another in such a common household. A long list of examples like the following might be enumerated: The little oyster crab which is found at home within the shell of the oyster. A similar crab is found in the tube with certain marine annelids (Chætopterus). Certain ants capture the cocoons of other ants and rear the young as slaves. Among ant colonies are found a variety of other insects living in more or less harmony, though not always by the consent of the ants. Among the tentacles of certain jelly fish (Cyanaea) a small fish is usually found. Among higher animals a companionship between birds and mammals is often observed.

747. **Parasitism.**—More commonly the relationships of this sort are decidedly disadvantageous to the one party. This is then called parasitism, which in several respects is one of the

most important biological phenomena, and merits extended study.

748. The common mildews, lilac or grape mildew, which are seen in late summer as a whitish "fur" on the surface of leaves, is due to a mildew spore which, blown by the wind, falls upon the leaf and germinates. It puts out a slender tube which grows through a stoma into the mesophyll. Here it

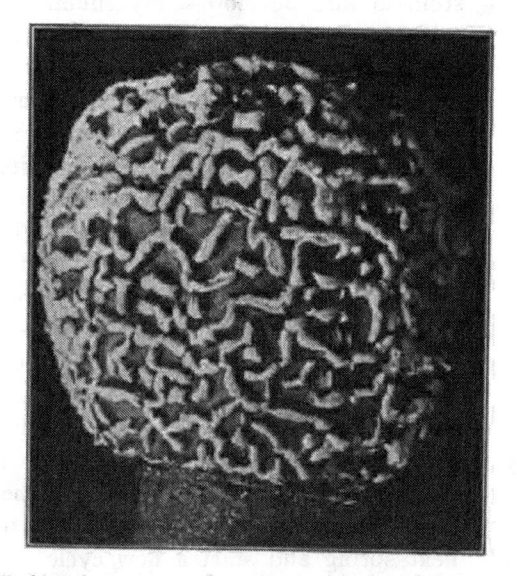

FIG. 228.—Peridermium, a rust fungus parasitic on pine trees. The white ridges are composed of masses of spores. ×2/3.

develops by absorbing its nourishment from the mesophyll cells, until finally it puts numerous branches out through the stomata, and on each of these are borne numerous spores. The orange-colored or black specks which appear later on the surface of the leaf are spore cases in which a second kind of spore is produced from the same mycelium.

749. The rusts which occur on our cereal grasses, wheat,

364 GENERAL PRINCIPLES

oats, etc., so much, have a complicated life history. One of the most complicated is that of the common wheat rust. In the spring the winter spores (teleutospores) germinate, produce a short mycelium on which four small spores of another kind (sporidia) are borne. These germinate on the surface of the barberry leaf, enter the mesophyll by the stomata and develop a mycelium. What is called a cluster cup is then formed just under the lower epidermis. This is filled with spores (æcidiospores), and when the epidermis finally breaks, the spores are set free. These then germinate on the wheat leaf and in its tissues a fourth kind of spore appears in such masses as finally to burst the epidermis and produce long, narrow orange-colored pustules filled with summer spores (uredospores). These may germinate in the same way and produce new generations of uredospores. Later in the season still another kind of spore appears among the summer spores, or in clusters by itself. These have thick, dark-colored walls, and make black patches on the leaf. These are the winter spores, teleutospores, which germinate in the next spring and start a new cycle.

Fig. 229.—A fungus, Cordyceps ravenelii, parasitic in the grub of a beetle, Lachnosterna. Two long stromata of the fungus are seen growing from the body of the grub. (From Folsom after Riley.)

750. The common cedar apple is the teleutospore-bearing stage of a rust which has its cluster cup on the leaves of the haw.

751. These parasites are fungi. They are typical plant parasites and often greatly damage the host, as, e. g., the wheat rust. Less important, economically, are the phenogamous parasites. The Indian Pipes are common flowering plants growing on the roots of other plants. The parasite has no

PARASITIC PHENIGAMS 365

chlorophyll and the leaves are scale-like. Only the flowers are like those of normal holoplytic plants. The dodder (love vine, golden thread) is a curious example. When the seed germinates on the ground a slender, leafless stem grows out. It does not root in the ground, but lies flat on the surface. In that way it continues to grow at one end, and if necessary, at

FIG. 230.—Dodder, or golden thread (Cuscuta). The weed host is completely overspun by the parasite. The flowers and seed pods of the dodder are seen in great numbers. ×1/2.

the same time, absorbs its substance at the other end, so that it grows along without having yet received any nourishment except what was contained in the seed. When by this creeping along the ground it comes in contact with certain green plants, it attaches itself to them. It sends little root-like structures (haustoria) into the stem of the host and from its tissues absorbs nourishment. Then it continues to grow, climbing upon the host and winding about from stem to branch, and from one plant to another, until a veritable tangle of golden threads is spun about the hosts. The leaves of the dodder are minute scales. It has no chlorophyll and its mode of nutrition is wholly parasitic. Small white flowers are finally produced and seeds as in normal holophytes. Our American "mistletoe" is only partially parasitic.

752. Among animals we likewise find parasitism more common among lower forms. Among Vertebrates only the roundmouth eel, the lowest of fish-like forms, deserves the name parasite. The sponges and Echinodermes contain no parasites; Cœlenterates and Molluscs very few. The unsegmented worms are the largest contributors to the list, and Insects follow closely. The Cestodes and Trematodes are the most common internal parasites, and to the order Hemiptera belong most of the external parasites.

753. The Trematodes are in some respects comparable with the rusts, especially with regard to the complicated life history, multiplicity of methods of reproduction and tendency to alternate hosts. As an example often described we may take the liver fluke.

754. The adult fluke lives in the liver of the sheep and matures many thousands of eggs, which pass down the bile ducts into the intestine, and thus to the exterior. From these eggs hatches a free-swimming larva, provided the eggs, washed by the rain, or by some other means, reach a pond or stream. The larva has a pair of eye spots, but is otherwise very simply organized. Its further development depends upon its coming in contact with a certain species of fresh-water snail. This provided, it attaches itself and bores its way into the interior of the snail, where it continues to develop as a parasite. It loses eyes and cilia (sense organs and locomotor organs) and is

little more than a sack (sporosac), in which, by a process of internal budding, a number of new individuals, rediæ, are produced. These are slightly more highly organized, but continue the process of internal budding for several generations. Then the rediæ, by a similar process, develop a new type of individuals called cercariæ. These are again a little more complex. They have two suckers, a forked intestine and a tail. The cercariæ leave the snail and become encysted on the grass. If now they happen to be ingested by a sheep with the grass they are set free from the cyst in the stomach of the host. The parasite may now be called a young fluke, for if it succeeds in finding the opening of the bile duct it works its way up into the liver and then develops directly into the fluke. The mature fluke is well organized as far as digestive tract and reproduction systems are concerned. The reproductive system especially is very highly developed.

FIG. 231.—The liver fluke, Fasciola hepatica, showing the arrangement of the reproductive organs. *Do*, Yolk, or vitelline glands; *Dr*, ovary; *Gp*, cirrus sac; *O*, mouth; *Ov*, oviduct, or uterus; *S*, ventral sucker; *Sg*, shell gland; *T*, testis; *U*, intestine; *V*, vitelline duct. (From Tyson after Sommer.)

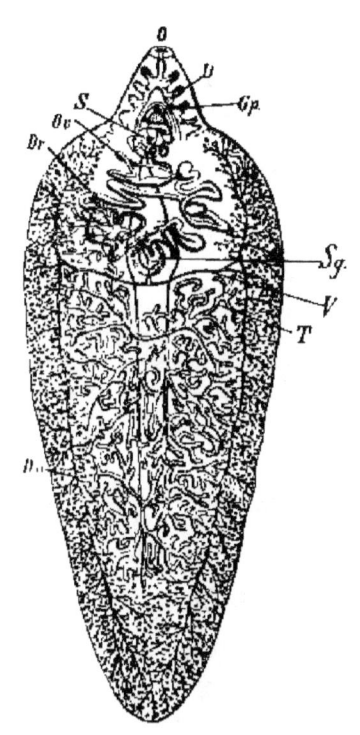

755. A common Cestode is the tapeworm. The one common in the dog may be taken as a type. The eggs originate in the intestine of the dog and reach the earth with the fæces. Either

through the drinking water or blown in the dust upon the food, these eggs find their way into the stomach of the rabbit.

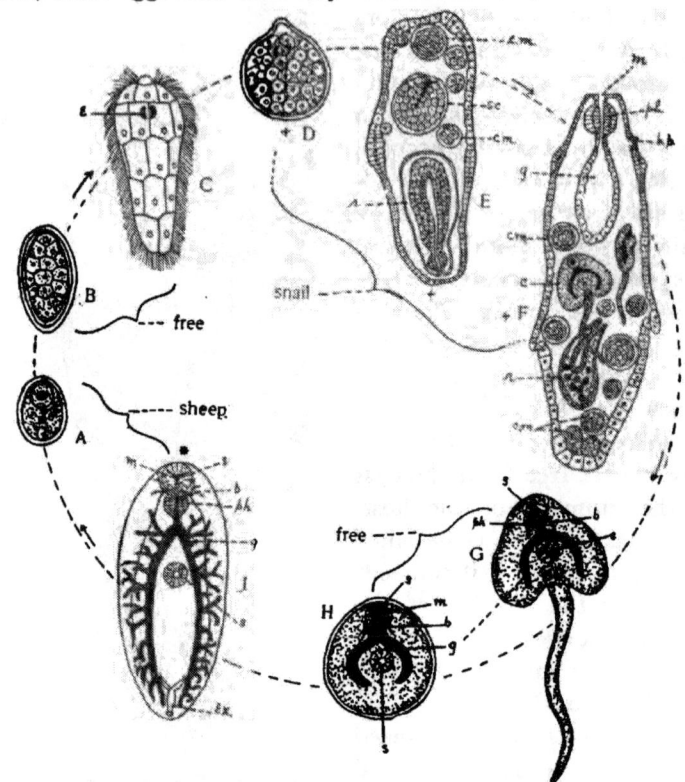

Fig. 232.—Diagram of the life history of the liver fluke (Fasciola). *A*, Egg; *B*, embryo; *C*, ciliated larva; *D*, sporocyst; *E*, sporocyst, later stage; *F*, mature redia containing young rediæ and cercariæ; *G*, cercaria; *H*, same encysted. *I*, young fluke; *b*, brain; *b.p*, birth pore; *c*, cercaria; *c.m.*, cell masses which develop into embryos; *e*, eye-spots; *ex.*, excretory tubules; *g*, intestine; *m*, mouth; *ph*, pharynx; *r*, redia; *s*, suckers; *sc*, sporocyst; +, stages at which non-sexual reproduction occurs; *, stage of sexual reproduction. (From Galloway after Thomas, Leuckart, and others.)

Here the larvæ are set free and bore their way into the tissues of the stomach, then get into the blood vessels and ultimately

THE TAPE WORM

become fixed in the muscle or other tissues of the body. The larva develops into a bladder-like, cysticercus, in which are formed one or more embryonic scoleces. In this condition it remains until the flesh in which it is embedded is eaten by a dog. Then the scoleces are set free. They attach themselves to the wall of the intestine by means of the suckers and hooks, and then develop the tapeworm strobila. In this case the develop-

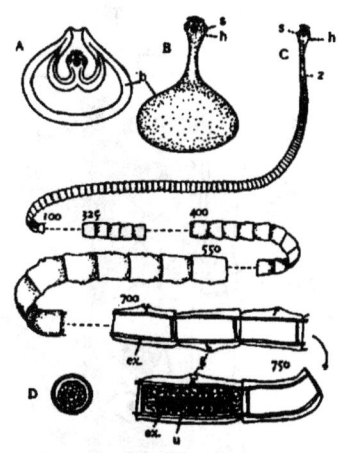

FIG. 233.—Diagram of the tapeworm, Tænia. *A*, Cysticercus or bladder-worm stage. *B*, later stage of same. *C*, Strobila. The last proglottis shows the uterus which is filled with embryos; *D*, one of the embryos in the egg shell; *b*, bladder; *ex*, excretory canals; *g*, genital pore; *h*, scolex with hooks and suckers (*s*); *u*, uterus; *z*, zone of strobilation. Some of the proglottides are numbered; many are omitted. (From Galloway.)

ment is simpler than that of the fluke, and asexual multiplication may be confined to the strobila, as when the cysticercus develops only one scolex. There is, however, always an alternation of hosts. There are many kinds of tapeworms, each with its specific two hosts. Thus, one tapeworm of the dog finds its other host in the dog flea. Others alternate between cat and mouse, goose and crayfish, man and fish, man and swine, man and dog, etc. The tapeworm is a dangerous parasite, not

370   GENERAL PRINCIPLES

so much in the adult stage as in the cysticercus. This, embedded in the brain or other organs of the body, sometimes reaches enormous size and destroys the surrounding tissues of the host.

756. As internal parasites the threadworms are very common. The famous "horsehair snake" (Gordius) is a parasite in the

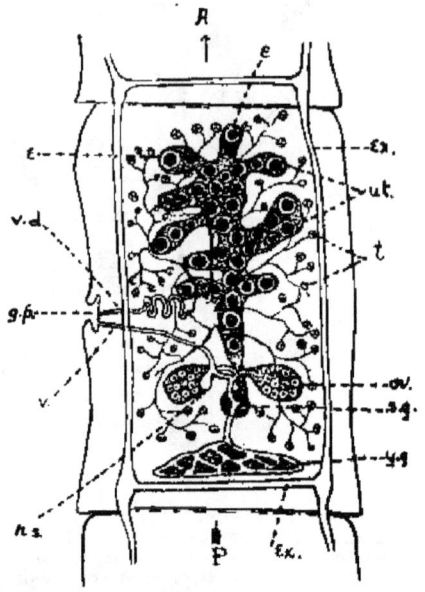

FIG. 234.—Sexually mature proglottis of Tænia. *ov*, Ovaries; *rs*, receptaculum seminis; *sg*, shell gland; *t*, testis; *v*, vagina; *vd*, vas deferens; *yg*, yolk gland. Other letters as in preceding figure. (From Galloway.)

cricket during the later developmental stages. At maturity it is free, living in the water.

757. Trichinella spiralis is the parasite which often infests the flesh of swine and is frequently transmitted to man by the eating of uncooked pork. The adult worm is 3–4 mm. long, and bores into the wall of the intestine, where the young are produced in large numbers. The young are only .1 mm. long,

and are carried by the lymph and blood to the muscle, where they remain and grow to a length of 1. mm., and become enclosed in a capsule. Unless flesh containing such encapsuled trichina is eaten by another mammal, the development of the worm proceeds no further. When such flesh is eaten the capsule is dissolved and the half-grown worm is set free. Thus it gets into the intestine and reaches maturity in the walls of the intestine. This parasite may infest any of the flesh-eating domestic mammals.

758. There are a large number of intestinal parasites belonging to the round worms which infest the intestine of all the domestic animals and man. Some of these (Ascaris) reach the size of an earthworm and are very prolific. The eggs find their way into the digestive tract of a host with the water and food, and their development takes place wholly within the intestinal cavity. These seldom produce an extreme pathological condition in the host.

759. Many smaller threadworms are parasitic in plants.

760. The parasitic Arthropods are chiefly found in two or three orders. Among the Entomostraca are the fish lice, chiefly external parasites, and the specially notable case of Sacculina. The adult Sacculina is found attached to the ventral surface of a crab. The portion of it, which is visible externally, is little more than a large sack containing an elaborately developed reproductive system. The sack is attached to the host by a process of its body, which penetrates the tissues of the host, and then branches and penetrates in all directions, like the root system of a plant. By this organ it absorbs nourishment from the host. It has no digestive system. The young of this strange organism are free-swimming nauplii with eyes and appendages of the typical nauplius. But when the larvæ attach themselves to a host, the appendages and eyes undergo degeneration until there remains only the organism as described.

761. Among Insects, the parasites are found chiefly among

372   GENERAL PRINCIPLES

the Diptera and Hemiptera. The larvæ of the Diptera are often parasites. The botfly, Hypoderma, develops under the skin of cattle. The botfly of the horse (Gastrophilus) deposits its eggs about the shoulders and head of the horse. The horse gnaws them off or they fall into his food, and thus get into the stomach, where the larvæ remain attached to the wall of the stomach.

762. The botfly larvæ of Cephalomyia ovis in the frontal sinuses of sheep produce blind-staggers. The larvæ of the

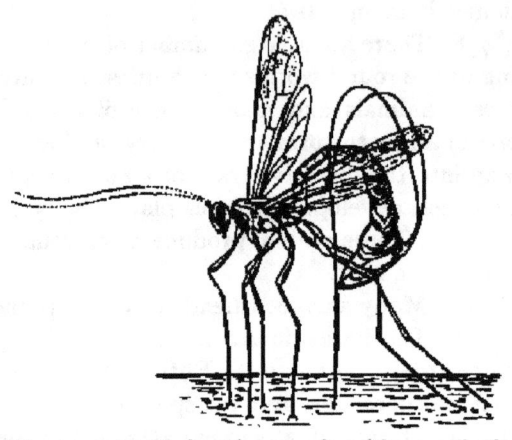

Fig. 235.—Ichneumon fly, Thalessa lunator, depositing eggs in the burrow of the wood-boring Tremex upon whose larvæ the larvæ of the Thalessa feed.

ichneumon fly, a Hymenopter, are parasitic in the caterpillars of various butterflies. The adults of a large number of flies are temporarily external parasites, as are also many mosquitoes. The flea is also closely related to the flies, and its wingless condition is probably the result of degeneration through parasitism.

763. The Hemiptera, or bugs, are, as a group, parasitic. They are often evil smelling because of the secretion of a peculiar gland. The bed bug and squash-bugs exemplify this point well. The plant lice, scale insects, the water striders, water boatmen

PHYLLOXERA

and electric light bugs (the last three are aquatic bugs), the cicadas (harvest fly and seventeen-year-locust), and chinch bugs, are all familiar parasites, largely on plant hosts. The Phylloxera is parasitic on the grape, and merits detailed description. In the spring the first generation of young hatch from eggs which were deposited the preceding fall under the bark of the vine. This generation is wingless and reproduces parthenogenetically. Successive generations of similar individuals follow.

FIG. 236.—A tomato worm covered with the cocoons of its parasite, Apanteles, which is also a Hymenopter. (From Folsom.)

These cause the galls on the leaves and the nodules on the roots, for they also attack the roots underground. In late summer another type appears. These are winged and serve to scatter the species. They lay two kinds of parthenogetic eggs on the underside of the leaves. From the larger eggs there develop females, and from the smaller ones males. These are both destitute of digestive tract. The females, after fertilization, deposit a single egg under the bark of the vine. These eggs remain over winter and hatch the first generation in the spring.

764. The galls so often seen on oak leaves and twigs, and also on many other plants, are abnormal developments of the plant tissue due to a stimulation produced by insect parasites. The female Cynips, a wasp-like insect, deposits her eggs in the tissues of the plant, and during the development of the young the tissues

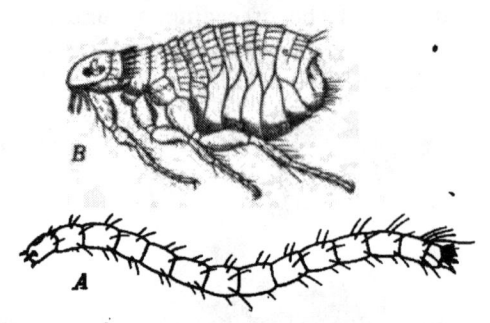

Fig. 237.—Dog flea, Ctenocephalus canis. *A*, Larva; *B*, adult. (From Folsom after Kunckel d'Herculais.)

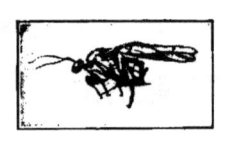

Fig. 238.—Oak galls (*A*) made by the gall wasp, Holcapsis globulus (*B*). *A*, natural size; *B*, magnified × 2. (From Folsom.)

are irritated in such a way as to cause the abnormal development of the surrounding tissues. The gall forms a shelter for the young brood and the juices of the plant provide food.

765. **Protozoa As Parasites.**—Many species of amœba (Entamœba) are found, as parasites, in the digestive tract and

in other organs of the body. They have been found in many mammals, birds, frogs, and insects. Some of these scarcely deserve the name parasite, since their presence in the digestive tract seems to cause the host no inconvenience. To this class belongs Entamœba coli, which is found in the human intestine in a large percent. of normal individuals. Entamœba histolytica, however, penetrates the wall of the intestine and causes the disintegration of the tissues, or ulceration. This is the cause of tropical dysentery, a serious and often fatal disease, which is quite common among the people of tropical countries.

766. Among the Flagellates the Trypanosomes are the most important group of parasites. They find their hosts among all

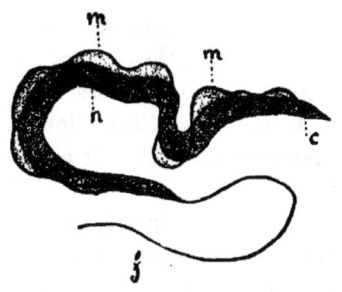

FIG. 239.—A Trypanosome. f, Flagellum; m, undulating membrane; n, nucleus. (From Marshall after Doflein.)

the classes of Vertebrates, as well as some invertebrates, but the Mammals are most seriously affected. The parasite is usually found in the blood and causes intermittent fever, swelling of the spleen and lymph glands, anæmia, eruptions of the skin and disorders of the nervous system. Trypanosoma gambiense is the cause of the terrible "sleeping sickness" of South Africa. It is apparently the toxic effect of the parasite on the nervous system that produces the later symptoms of the disease, a lethargic condition which slowly leads to a continuous sleeping and finally ends in death. In large parts of South Africa the cattle, horses, and in fact, all the domestic mammals, as well as wild mammals, are affected by a disease known as Tsetse fever. It is fatal to such a degree that "large areas are closed to colonization" where the disease is endemic. Trypanosoma Brucei is the cause of the fever, but Tsetse is the name of a fly. The natives have long known that the fever only occurs in districts in which the Tsetse fly is found, and there is now no doubt that this fly, in stinging affected cattle becomes itself infected and then carries the germs to uninfected cattle. There are several species of Tsetse fly (Glossinia), and of these, probably more than one is responsible for the spread of Tsetse fever. The sleeping sickness is also carried by Tsetse flies.

767. The domestic animals of South America, southern Europe and northern Africa, and the countries bordering on the Indian Ocean, are also affected by different types of Trypanosome diseases. In these cases other flies and mosquitos are the principal agencies of infection, but lice and fleas may perform the same office. The Trypanosomes of fishes are carried by leeches.

768. Of more direct interest to us is the parasite of malarial fever. There are at least three varieties of this, producing the "tropical," the "tertian," and the "quartan" fevers, respectively. At a certain stage there are found numerous minute bodies floating in the blood plasma of the host. These are the "spore" stage of a Sporozoan, Plasmodium. They are vastly smaller than a red blood corpuscle and are capable of amœboid motion. They attach themselves to a red corpuscle and work their way into it. Here they grow at the expense of the blood corpuscle, and at the end of 48 hours, in the case of the tertian parasite, they divide into a number of "spores." Hereupon the corpuscle goes to pieces and the spores are again floating in the plasma. These spores repeat the cycle just described and thus a new generation of "spores" is produced on each alternate day. This process may continue indefinitely,

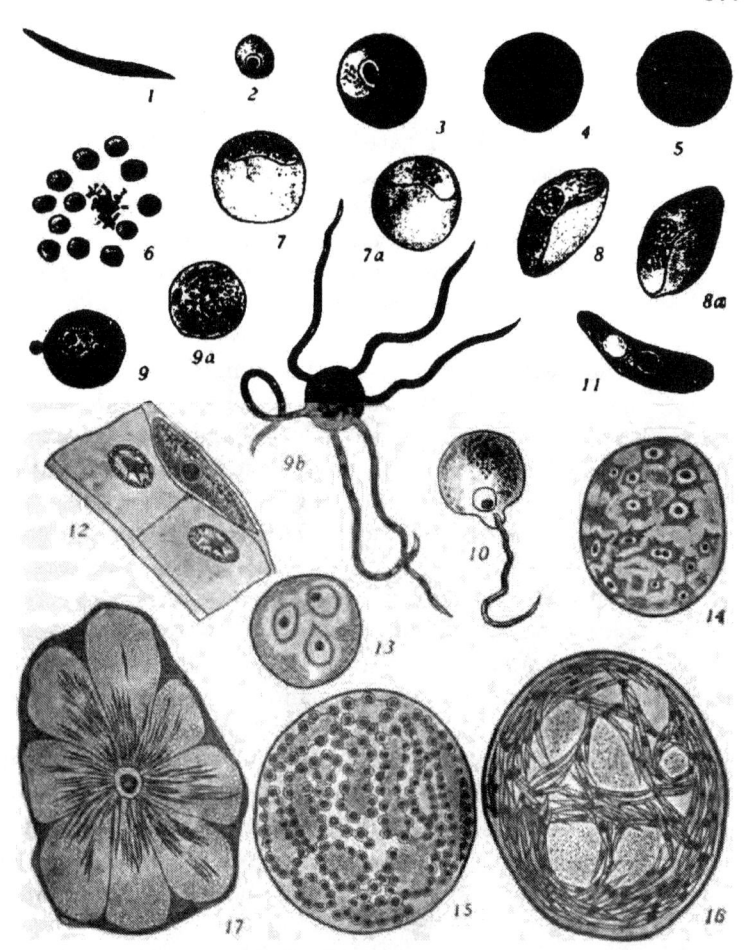

FIG. 240.—Life history of malarial parasite, Plasmodium. 1, Sporozoite introduced into human blood by bite of mosquito; 2, same a little later; 3 and 4, same growing in a red blood-corpuscle; 5, same dividing; 6, blood-corpuscle disintegrated and setting free the spores; 7, 8 and 9, a spore developing into a female gamete; 7a, 8a, 9a and 9b, a spore developing into a number of male gametes; 10, union of male and female gametes (fertilization); 11, motile zygote; 12, zygote embedded in the wall of the stomach of the mosquito; 13 to 16, stages in the development of sporozoites in the sporocyst; 17, sporozoites in the salivary gland of the mosquito. Stages from 1 to 8 in the human blood. Stages 8 to 17 in the mosquito. (From Folsom after Grassi and Leuckart.)

but at intervals another type of development occurs side by side with the spores. In this case the enlarged parasitic cell in the blood corpuscle does not divide into a number of spores, but becomes much elongated and cresent-shaped. Now, however, for further development a change of host is necessary and this host must be one of a few species of mosquitos (Anopheles). In the stomach of the mosquito the crescents just described become differentiated into two classes. In the one class the crescents become rounded and motionless, while in the other division occurs and a number of very long and slender motile bodies are formed. These are female and male gametes respectively, and a fusion takes place between them as in fertilization. The zygote now becomes motile. It works its way into the wall of the digestive tract where it remains for about eight days while undergoing further development. This is called the sporocyst stage. During this period it grows to an enormous size, it first divides into a number of cells and these then each develop a vast number of sporozoites, very long and very slender spindle-shaped motile spores. By the bursting of the sporocyst the spores escape into the body cavity and thus gain access to the salivary glands. For some reason they work their way into the salivary glands and their ducts, and hence, when the mosquito next punctures the skin of an uninfected person some of the sporozoites are carried with the saliva into the wound, and the victim is thus inoculated with malarial virus. The sporozoites are merely another type of spore. They attack the red blood corpuscles in the same way as in the stage with which we began.

769. We see that the malarial parasite completes its life history only by transferring from man to mosquito. Both hosts are necessary. This is probably also true of the trypanosomes, as is indicated by the more recent investigations.

770. The fever days of malaria are the days in which the new generation of spores are set free by the disintegration of the

blood corpuscles. This occurs every other day in tertian fever, and on every third day in quartan fever. A double inoculation may result in a more complicated succession of fever days.

771. The Apes, Bats and Birds are also subject to Plasmodium parasites. Texas cattle fever is caused by a elated Sporozoan (Babesia), which is transmitted by the cattle tick.

772. **Bacteria as Parasites.**—Most infectious diseases are caused by bacteria. This has been definitely established for many diseases, but the difficulties in the way of determining a causal relationship between such minute organisms and the diseases with which they are supposed to be associated are often very great, and in a number of cases the organism has not yet been identified, though the disease is almost certainly known to be bacterial. The part of the body infested by the parasites varies with the species; sometimes it is the mucous surfaces of the digestive tract or the respiratory passages, sometimes the tissues of certain organs, sometimes the blood vessels and lymph spaces of certain organs or even of the entire body. The mode of infection also varies with the disease. Sometimes the germs find their way to the host with the food, water or air of respiration, but they may also enter the body through the skin. The latter is not likely to occur except when the skin is broken.

773. The effect of the parasite on the host is sometimes limited to a disorganization of the tissues of a limited region. The result of this may not be serious, but if the destruction of the tissues goes far in a vital organ the function of the organ may be seriously impaired and result in the death of the host. In other cases no anatomical change can be observed in the tissues, and yet the function of some organs may be disturbed and consequently the life of the host threatened.

774. Bacteria vary like other classes of parasites with regard to the range of hosts in which they may be found. But this question has been studied more particularly from the point of

view of the host and has led to several very important general conclusions concerning the degree of susceptibility of species or of individuals to given bacterial diseases. From what is said concerning the physiological processes of bacteria in the Appendix to Part I, it may be suspected that the effect produced on the host by the bacterial parasite is due to substances secreted by the bacteria. As a matter of fact, it is found that if an extract from the bacterial cultures containing no living cells is introduced into the body of the host, the symptoms peculiar to the corresponding disease are produced. The bacterial products are similar to poisons in their effects, and are called toxins.

775. **Immunity.**—When an individual or a species is not susceptible to the attack of an infectious disease, it is said to be immune. The immunity may be a native character of the animal, it may be acquired during the life time of the individual through natural causes, or it may be induced artificially. These types are, therefore, designated natural immunity and acquired immunity, respectively, and of the latter there are two types, active and passive.

776. Natural immunity is due primarily to three kinds of defense, which the organism employs to defend itself against bacteria which have succeeded in entering the body. (1) Any foreign particles introduced into the tissues and causing irritation are attacked by the white blood corpuscles. These cells are capable of independent locomotion through amœboid movements. They escape from the blood vessels by penetrating the walls and move about in the lymph spaces in the tissues. They collect about foreign matter and engulf and digest particles as would an amœba. This process of phagocytosis is regarded as of great importance in keeping the body free of bacterial invasions. (2) The blood of a naturally immune animal contains a substance, alexin, which causes the death of the bacteria. This substance is probably formed by

the cells of the various tissues. (3) It is generally true that individuals are not equally susceptible to the same poisons and natural immunity rests, in part, on this fact. The immune individual is not affected by the bacterial products which act as toxins in other individuals. This is accounted for by the presence in the blood of the immune individuals of a substance, which neutralizes the toxins, and is, therefore, called antitoxin.

777. The animal organism is not passive to the attacks of bacteria. If the attack is not too sudden and violent the tissues respond by producing antitoxin, which neutralizes the effect of the toxin, and a lysin (alexin), which causes the dissolution of the bacteria. Another substance is also formed which causes the bacteria to adhere in clumps. This is called agglutinin. These substances (anti-bodies) produced by the tissues in response to the bacterial stimulus, may continue to be formed long after the exciting cause has disappeared and the body is therefore immune to a second attack. This is known as acquired immunity.

778. Bacteria are extremely variable. This is especially evident in the degree of virulence of different strains of what is apparently the same species. Immunity acquired from the attack of a mild form is also generally efficient against the more virulent types. This principle is employed to produce immunity by intentionally infecting or inoculating an individual with a mild type and thereby securing protection against more dangerous forms. Immunity secured in this way is active acquired immunity.

779. Passive immunity is secured by injecting into the animal a blood serum obtained from an immune animal. This serum-therapy is effective at the time, but the antibodies soon disappear from the blood and, since the tissues have not been stimulated to the formation of antibodies, the immunity is lost.

780. The various types of immunity may be illustrated by

a few familiar forms. Man is naturally immune to fowl cholera, though sometimes attacked by cattle fever, anthrax. The fowl is immune to rabies, to which both man and the dog are subject. The dog is immune to anthrax. By an attack of measles or smallpox man acquires immunity against subsequent attacks. By vaccinating man with the virus of cowpox, a mild disease is produced, which renders the individual actively immune against smallpox. Passive immunity against diphtheria is secured by the injection of an antitoxin serum taken from an actively immune horse.

EVOLUTION

781. Species.—The word species is one of the most important and most frequently employed of all biological terms, and yet it is impossible of exact definition. A species is a **kind** of a plant or animal, using the word kind in its most common sense. Thus the sweet-gum (Liquidambar Styraciflua), the persimmon (Diospyros Virginiana), and the tulip tree (Liriodendron tulipifera), are clearly defined species as are also, among animals, the turkey vulture, or buzzard (Cathartes aura) and the robin (Turdus migratorius). Any given example may immediately be recognized as sweet-gum or not-sweet-gum, as robin or not-robin. In other cases, however, difficulties may arise. Thus, among the oaks we have the willow oak, the blackjack, the white oak and the Spanish oak, all of which are distinct species and readily distinguishable. But it frequently occurs that the flowers of one species are pollinated by those of another and the resulting offspring is called a hybrid. It resembles both parent species to some extent, but belongs to neither. A much more important difficulty arises from individual variation, for the individuals of a species are never exactly alike. Even the individuals sprung from the same parents may vary greatly among themselves. Allowance must, therefore, be made for

VARIATION 383

individual variation within the species. Sometimes certain types of variation occur so constantly that the species may be subdivided into varieties. This is especially true where a species is widely distributed and thus lives under different conditions in the various districts it inhabits. Where there is variation corresponding to geographical distribution it is called a geographical variety. A good example of this is Lycæna pseudargiolus, the common small blue butterfly, which ranges from New England to Arizona. The New England,

FIG. 241.—Two flower heads of Gaillardia. The head on the right is the normal type, with ray flowers ligulate. The head on the left is a variation (sport) which frequently occurs. The ray flowers in this are tubular and often quite regular. ×2/3.

Middle, Southern and Southwestern States varieties of this butterfly differ so much that they might well be classed as four distinct species, were it not for the intergrading forms found in the transition regions. Nor is this an isolated example. Extended study of a species almost invariably widens the range of its recognized variability, and sharply defined species are the exception rather than the rule.

782. Opposed to the tendency to vary is a tendency for the species to maintain its character. This is evident in the resemblance of the offspring to the parents. Although the in-

384   GENERAL PRINCIPLES

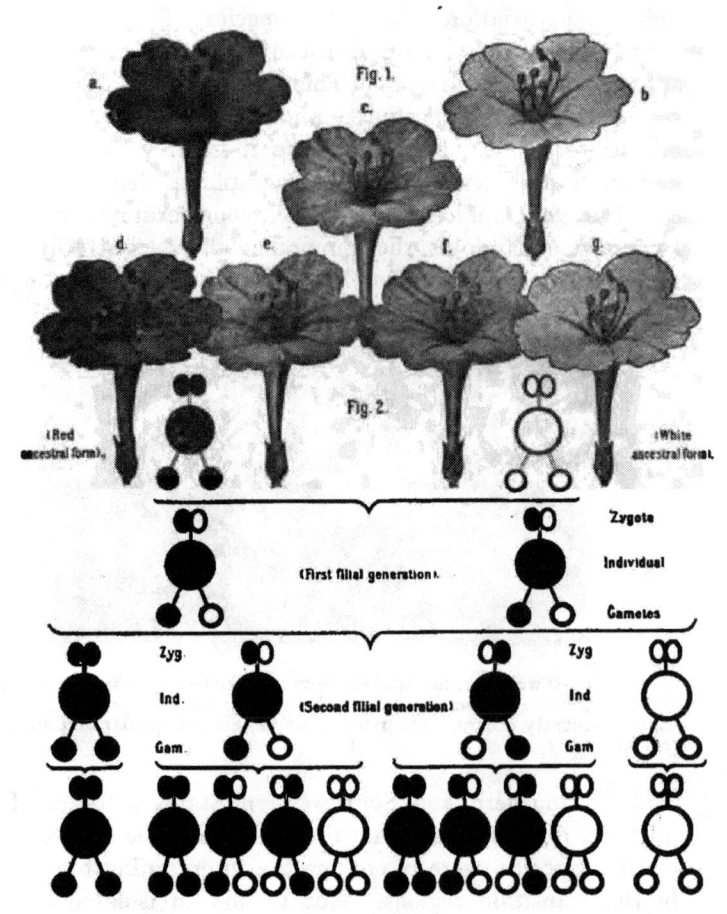

FIG. 242.—Mendelian inheritance in the four-o'clock. If red (*a*) and white (*b*) forms are crossed the offspring are all pink (*c*). These interbred yield 1/4 red (*d*), 2/4 pink (*e* and *f*), and 1/4 white (*g*). The lower part of the figure shows the condition of the zygote and the gametes in the ancestral and first, second, and third filial generations. (From Davenport after Haecker.)

dividuals of the same brood differ among themselves and from their parents they still resemble their parents, and hence each other, more than they do distant relatives or unrelated members of the same species. That is to say, the peculiarities of the parents tend to reappear in the offspring. This, in some cases, has been found to be controlled by very simple laws, known as Mendel's Laws of Heredity. If the two parents differ with regard to a certain character the offspring of the first generation will inherit equally from both parents. In the second generation one-fourth will have the original **paternal** character only, one-fourth will have the original **maternal** character only, and the remaining two-fourths will still be mixed like the first generation. In the third generation the mixed two-fourths of the preceding generation will be divided into a fourth pure paternal, a fourth pure maternal, and two-fourths mixed. In the fourth, fifth, etc., generations this process will continue. In this it must be recognized that a character may be present, though not evident. Such a character is said to be recessive while the opposed character, which is evident, is said to be dominant. To illustrate we may take a simple case. If the red and white varieties of Mirabilis Jalapa (four o'clock) are crossed, the offspring in the first generation are all pink. The second generation (secured by close fertilization of the pink generation), however, consists of three kinds, viz.: One-fourth white, two-fourths pink, and one-fourth red. The white and red forms are said to be pure because they continue to produce only white and red, respectively, in succeeding generations if close fertilized. The other two-fourths of pink flowers in the next generation again break up into white, pink, and red forms in the proportion of 1:2:1, as before, and thus the pink or mixed forms continue in each generation to separate into the three kinds.

783. When the two parental characters are not equally potent, i. e., when one is dominant, the other recessive, the

results are as follows: We will take as an example the pure white and common gray mice. The result of this cross is gray mice like the gray parent, not a lighter gray, as one might expect, following the case of Mirabilis Jalapa. In the second generation there are a fourth white, which are pure, and three-fourths are gray. The gray are in reality of two kinds, though this becomes evident only in the course of succeeding generations, when it develops that one-third of the three-fourths continue to breed only gray, while the other two-thirds yield one-fourth white in the succeeding generation and are thus seen to have been mixed. The second generation of offspring may, therefore, be described as one-fourth white, two-fourths mixed with gray dominant, and one-fourth pure gray. The dominant grays and pure grays can only be distinguished by the character of their offspring.

784. Not every character is controlled in this simple way, for it is readily conceivable that a given character may be due to the combined operation of several factors, each of which may be separately heretible.

785. **Physical Basis of Heredity.**—The phenomena of heredity correspond in a remarkable way with those of maturation, which makes plausible the theory that the chromosomes are the bearers of the hereditary traits of the organism, and that during maturation the readjustment of chromatin determines the ancestral characters which are to be handed on to the next generation. In the process of fertilization the germ cell is provided with equal parts of maternal and paternal chromatin, and this condition is maintained during the subsequent stages of development in all the cells of the body. Let the condition of the chromatin with regard to any hybrid character be represented by (P.M.). Then when the first maturation division occurs in the primary oocyte of the hybrid (F.) the (P.M.) elements divide into $\begin{cases} (P.M.) = \text{1st polar body} \\ (P.M.) = \text{secondary oocyte.} \end{cases}$

But when the reduction division occurs the paternal and maternal elements are separated and the result is..........
........either...................or

$$\text{2d p.b.} = \begin{cases} (P.M.) \\ (P.)(M.) \end{cases} = \text{1st p. b.} = \begin{cases} (P.M.) \\ (P.)(M.) \end{cases} = \text{2d p. b.}$$

If the first polar body divides the result is

$$\begin{cases} (P.) & (M.) \\ (P.) & (M.) \end{cases}$$ in which either one of

the four cells may represent the ripe egg and the other three the three polar bodies. The ova are, therefore, either (P)aternal or (M)aternal in regard to the hybrid character, and the two kinds are probably equally numerous.

786. In the maturation of the sperm the process is similar. The primary spermatocyte (P'.M'.) divides into two secondary spermatocytes,

$$\begin{matrix}(P'.M'.)\\(P'.M'.)\end{matrix}$$ which then divide into

$$\begin{matrix}(P'.)(M'.)\\(P'.)(M'.)\end{matrix}$$ four spermatids. Two of these are (P')aternal and two are (M')aternal, so that the number of (P'.) and (M'.) sperm is also equal, as in the case of the egg.

787. By close fertilizing, the gametes of the F_1 hybrid generation may combine as follows:

(P.P'.), (P.M'.), (P'.M.), (M'.M.). This results in one-fourth pure paternal, two-fourths hybrid and one-fourth pure maternal individuals in the F_2 generation.

788. **Number of Species.**—In spite of the fact that it is often extremely difficult and even impossible to definitely circumscribe a species, yet for convenience of reference animals and plants must be divided into convenient groups, named and classified. And much time has been spent in hunting out and describing species. About 520,000 animal species have thus been listed and over 200,000 plants. Besides these there are many species which have become extinct and are now only

represented by fossil remains. Of these there are about 60,000 known. In addition to these there are many species living which have not been observed by the recording biologist, and hence do not appear in the count, and there have probably been many, many more which became extinct without leaving any trace or the remains of which have not yet been found. It is, therefore, not probable that any one familiar with the facts would regard a million a high estimate for the number of species which have been or are now living on the earth.

789. **Origin of Species.**—The question naturally arises, Whence came they all? It is a question which has always occupied thinking men, and concerning which there has been much difference of opinion. To-day biologists generally, if not all, are of the opinion that species are plastic, as it were, and continually undergoing modification, so that they are not to-day what they were or what they will be, and further that two sections of a species may become modified in different directions and thus come to differ even to the extent of specific distinction. In this way there would arise two species where there had been but one. This is known as the theory of the origin of species by descent with modification. In connection with this theory there are two questions which should be clearly distinguished. The first one is as to fact, the other as to method: (1) What is the evidence that species originate by descent with modification? (2) If a fact, how does it come about? In the following pages we will consider the evidence upon which the theory of descent rests, and in that connection take up a number of important biological phenomena which have not yet been discussed.

790. **The Taxonomic Series.**—Long ago, students of natural history were struck by the fact that animals could be arranged in a series in the order of their various degrees of organization; with the simplest at one end, the most complex at the other, and the interval between more or less completely filled by forms of

intermediate grade. This series is fairly well represented by almost any scheme of classification adopted by systematists to-day. Great similarity in form and structure naturally suggests a blood relationship and a common origin. But the taxonomic series represents a continuous chain of such relations, and hence leads to the conclusion that the entire animal kingdom had a common origin, and that by a process of evolution the higher forms have developed from lower forms as the complex adult develops from the simple egg.

791. The taxonomic series is, however, not adequately represented by a line and it is now more frequently compared to a tree. At its base this genealogical tree divides into two trunks, one representing the vegetable kingdom, the other the animal. The base from which they both spring represents the many unicellular forms which have both vegetable and animal characteristics. Then up along the animal trunk come the less differentiated forms, like some Cœlenterates, Annelids, Peripatus, Branchiostoma, etc. The branches represent the highly differentiated forms and spring from the main stem at various points; the Sponges below, higher, the Echinoderms, Arthropods, Molluscs, etc., while several large branches at the top represent bony Fishes, Reptiles, Birds and Mammals.

792. With the advancement of the study of anatomy much information has been obtained which throws light on this question. In the vertebral column of Vertebrates, for example, we have a structure which indicates clearly a relationship between the five classes of Vertebrates, but when we examine the skull and the appendages we seem at first to have only hopeless diversity. But here also a wonderful uniformity appears on more careful investigation. With regard to the skeletal portions, the wing of a bird, the fore limb of a bat, the flipper of a whale, the fore legs of the horse and dog and the arm of man, are all constructed of the same elements and each one of these appendages may be homologized bone for bone with

the others. It must be kept in mind that bones may fuse, may dwindle by degeneration to the point of disappearance, and even new bones may develop, which have no counterpart in other animals. But such modifications do not detract from the value of homologies. In the same way the skulls of these five classes are also found to belong to the same type, and one can homologize the bones of a frog's skull with those of a dog. The resemblances between Birds and Reptiles are especially numerous in parts of the skeleton, but a detailed knowledge of comparative osteology is necessary to a full appreciation of such points.

793. The plant kingdom, as a whole, does not form as perfect or continuous a series as the animal kingdom, but all the important breaks in the series fall below the Archegoniates. The simple structure of the Algæ and Fungi offers comparatively few features for comparison, and hence makes it difficult to discern relationship. On the other hand, the series from the liverworts to the highest flowering plants is more perfect and more extensive than anything to be found among animals. When we trace the gradual development of the sporophyte and the corresponding reduction of the gametophyte, through the various classes of Bryophyta, Pteridophyta and Spermatophyta we are able to form an almost ideally perfect series. When one studies this series, not only as a whole but in its details, the conviction that it represents a "blood relationship" is irresistible.

794. The anatomist often discovers organs which are clearly without function. It is impossible to account for such organs except on the ground that they are rudiments of organs which were at one time functional. That such is the case is usually evident by comparison with other species in which homologous organs are to be found. When an organ becomes useless for any reason it still persists in a more or less imperfect condition as a vestige of its former state. Some examples of vestigeal organs are of particular interest in the present connection.

795. The whale is a mammal, since it suckles its young, as

RUDIMENTARY ORGANS 391

well as for many other reasons. But it has only two appendages, the flippers, which represent the fore limbs. No evidence of hind limbs is to be found externally, but on dissection a rudimentary pelvic girdle may be found, and in the Greenland whale there are also rudimentary femurs and tibias. The

FIG. 243.—The "Congo Snake," Amphiuma means. This animal is not a reptile but an amphibian. It is found in the southern United States. Note the rudimentary appendages. ×1/3.

Ophidia are classed as an order of Reptilia, but they have no appendages. Yet in the case of the python there is a rudimentary pelvis and also rudimentary appendages which appear at the surface as horny points. Most lizards have two pairs of

392 · GENERAL PRINCIPLES

functional appendages, but in several species the appendages are more or less rudimentary. In one the fore limbs are entirely wanting, while the hind ones are greatly reduced. In still another form there are no limbs at all, but both girdles are present. In all these cases we have animals which are classed with quadrupedal forms, though they do not have four legs. The significance of such rudimentary structures cannot be overlooked.

FIG. 244.—The female luna-moth, Tropaea luna, seen from beneath. The abdomen becomes so heavy before the eggs are deposited that the moth is unable to fly. ×1.

796. The young baleen whale has rudimentary teeth which never develop to a point where they can be of service to the animal. In the middle of the upper surface of the skull of many lizards there is a small opening. Over this place the skin is transparent, and beneath there is an eye which is connected with the fore brain by a long stalk. In the Cyclostomes there

is a similar eye in a functional condition, but in all other Vertebrates it is wanting. In its place there is an organ whose function is not known but which is homologous with the pineal eye of Cyclostomes and lizards, and is probably a functionless rudiment. The rudimentary paired eyes of cave fishes belong in the same category.

797. As an example, from among invertebrates the wings of insects may be mentioned. Most insects have wings, but the order Aptera contains no winged forms. In this group there are no rudimentary wings or other evidence that the insects ever possessed wings. The order Hemiptera contains

FIG. 245.—Hibernia marginaria, a species of moth in which the female has wings much reduced and useless. A, Male; B, female. ×1 1/2.

many wingless forms, but many others are winged and many have rudimentary wings. In this case the wingless forms are regarded as representing a degenerate condition. In other orders there is also evidence of degeneration of wings. The male gipsy moth flies well. The female is also provided with well-developed wings, but she never uses them. Among the species of the geometrid moth genus, Hibernia, the females are, in some cases, wholly without wings, while in others various stages in the reduction of wings may be found. A similar condition exists in the beetle family, Lampyridæ, the common "fire flies." Here the males are always good fliers, and in some species the females are also, but in other species the females have rudimentary wings or the wings are entirely wanting.

798. Among plants the rudimentary leaves and other organs to which frequent reference has been made are further examples of the principle under discussion.

799. In the first series of examples cited in this section we saw how organs adapted for such diverse purposes as swimming, walking, flying and writing may be constructed on a common

Fig. 246.—Hibernia defoliaria. The female is wingless. See preceding figure. A, Male; B, female. ×1 1/2.

plan. No plausible explanation for this remarkable fact has ever been offered except that of a common origin. If these animals had a common pentadactyl ancestor the present diversity as to the condition of their appendages is the result of modification in different directions as a result of different conditions of environment.

800. The vestigeal organs also can only be accounted for on the supposition that the ancestral forms possessed the organs in a functional condition, and that changed conditions, involving a disuse of the organs, resulted in their degeneration. This

means then also that the rudimentary organ is an indication of kinship with forms in which it exists in a functional condition.

801. If this principle is granted the kinship of the entire organic world can be more or less completely established.

802. **The Phylogenetic Series.**—A large part of the rocks of the surface of the earth were formed by the deposits of mud, sand and organic remains under water. Thus originated the shales, sandstones, and limestones. While the rocks were being deposited the bodies of animals and plants were frequently buried and the resistant parts preserved as fossils. Of course, the rocks which were formed first are now beneath those which were deposited later. By the fossils and their relative position in the rocks we have been able to learn something of the character of the former inhabitants of the earth and of the order in which they appeared. The geologist has been able to reconstruct in considerable detail the more recent periods of the earth's history, but the earlier chapters are difficult to decipher.

803. The Cambrian period is the earliest in which we find any evidence of life. It was a period covering a vast extent of time, and at its close most of the invertebrate phyla, if not all, were already represented. The highest Molluscs, the Cephalopods, were present, and also the aquatic Arthropods, the Crustacea. Insects and spiders appeared in the next period, the Silurian, and also the first Vertebrates, Fishes. In the Devonian period Fishes were extremely abundant. The Amphibians and Reptiles appeared in the Carboniferous period. Mammals did not appear until the Jurassic period, and Birds came still later, in the Triassic. So far as this evidence goes it shows that the lower forms appeared first. With regard to Vertebrates, more particularly, the order in which the classes appeared also agrees with what one would expect according to the theory of descent.

804. The fact that Birds appeared after Mammals must not

be misinterpreted. Of two forms, the one which appeared later is not necessarily descended from the other, since both may have arisen independently from still earlier forms. And the one which appeared latest is not necessarily the highest. Birds are as highly specialized as Mammals. But the mammalian type of specialization may be described as a more successful one, and Mammals are, therefore, usually placed above Birds.

805. The geological record is very fragmentary and only occasionally do we get a connected story. The history of the snail, Paludina, has been worked out in detail, and we have an

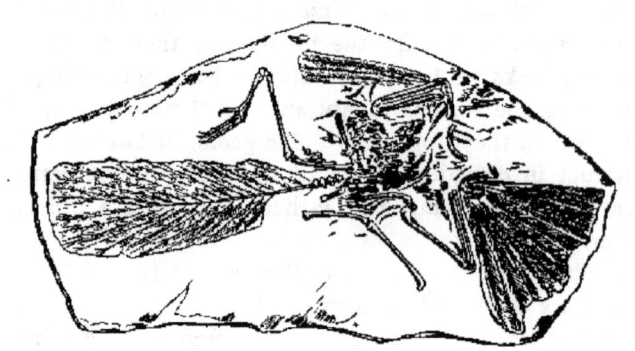

FIG. 247.—Fossil remains of Archæopteryx lithographica. (From Galloway, after Claus.)

account of the changes through which the genus passed during a considerable interval of time. The shell, which was at first very simple, with smooth, rounded contours, became step by step angular and ribbed. So that the later species have little resemblance to the earlier forms.

806. The first bird of which we have any record is the Archæopteryx. This bird had a long tail consisting of a series of vertebræ, fringed on either side with feathers. The wings were provided with three free digits armed with claws. The head was very large and had heavy jaws, both of which were

THE PHYLOGENETIC SERIES 397

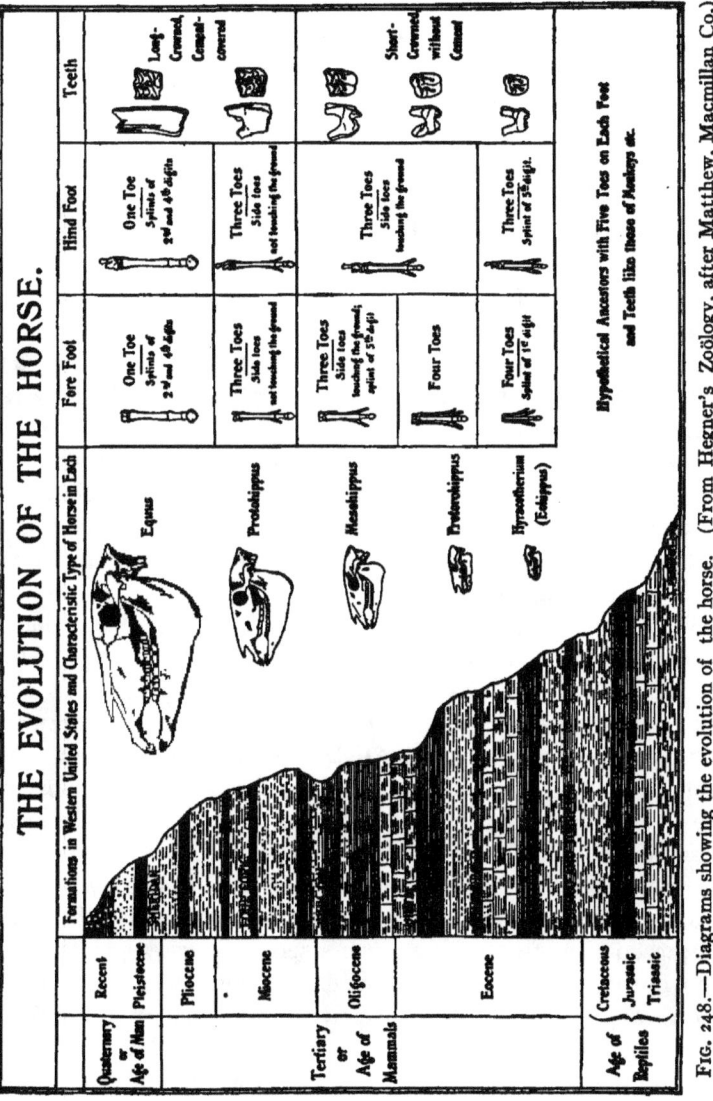

FIG. 248.—Diagrams showing the evolution of the horse. (From Hegner's Zoölogy, after Matthew, Macmillan Co.)

provided with a complete series of teeth. Some of the birds of the Cretaceous period were much more like modern birds, but still had teeth on certain parts of the jaws. The Archæopteryx was almost as much reptile as bird, and even the later types presented many decided reptilian characters.

807. The most complete series of mammalian fossils are those which show the genesis of the modern horse. The earliest mammals were pentadactyl (Phenacodus). The earliest horse-like form had four toes on the fore foot and three on the hind foot. From this we see the number of toes gradually reduced, until in the modern horse there is only one functional digit and small rudiments of the second and fourth. The first digit (I) was the first to disappear and then the fifth (V). These were then followed by the second and fourth.

808. Geological evidence concerning the history of the development of the vegetable kingdom is much like that for animals. The Cryptogams existed in great profusion long before the seed-bearing plants appeared, and the Gymnosperms preceded the Angiosperms.

809. **The Ontogenetic Series.**—The differences between individuals are the greatest when the individuals are mature. The young, the late embryos and the earlier embryonic stages are successively more and more alike, and differences finally vanish in the egg. Hence all metazoa start from the same level. In fact, the differences which exist up to the end of gastrulation are of secondary importance and have no relation to the systematic rank of the developing organism. All metazoa are, therefore, in a real sense alike up to the end of gastrulation.

810. Suppose an observer entirely unacquainted with the characteristics of eggs were given a series of eggs representing, we will say, Coelenterates, Annelids, the lancelet, a fish, a bird and a rabbit. In the eggs themselves the observer would find no means of determining the class to which they belonged. If now these eggs each passed through its appropriate develop-

mental processes the first identification would be possible after gastrulation, because at this point the cœlenterate development ceases. The other embryos continue their development by the formation of the third layer, the mesoderm. The body becomes elongated and the mesoderm assumes the form of a series of mesodermic somites by which the body is divided into a homonomous series of metameric segments. Here the annelid larva has attained the form of the adult worm, and hence the end of its development. The other larvæ develop gill slits, and at this stage the development of the lancelet is virtually completed. The further addition of large cerebral vesicles and paired eyes would indicate vertebrate embryos, the fish, the bird and the mammal. But only the bird and the mammal would develop lungs and pentadactyl appendages. In the bird the aortic arch would lie on the right side of the body, while in the mammal it would be on the left.

811. In this comparison of the development of animals details are, of course, omitted. The purpose of the comparison is to show that the difference in the result of development of the lower and higher forms is due not to a difference in direction of development so much as to its extent. All forms pursue the same course, but the higher forms continue their development farther. Stating the same thing in another way, we may say that the higher forms, in their development, pass through stages which are the permanent adult condition of lower forms. Why? If it is granted that the baleen whale is descended from a terrestrial quadruped with the dentition characteristic of Mammalia, then the rudimentary teeth of the young whale are a relic of the former condition, and in its development the whale passes beyond the tooth-bearing stage to a stage of rudimentary teeth. This argument applies to all rudimentary or vestigeal organs. The same line of reasoning may be applied to another type of development in which an organ, instead of remaining rudimentary, passes beyond the normal type.

For example, the wing of the bat is supported chiefly by the enormously developed phalanges of the II, III, IV, and V digits. In the embryo the bat hand is at first a normal pentadactyl hand, and the great elongation of the four fingers does not take place until very late. The bat being also a Mammal follows the mammalian type of development, and after it has reached the grade of a Mammal it continues its development into the bat stage by transforming the mammalian appendage into the more specialized bat appendage.

812. If the above is a true conception of the origin of vestigeal and highly specialized organs then we are also in a position to understand the parallelism of development described above. It has been stated as a "Fundamental Law of Biogenesis" that "the development of the individual recapitulates the history of the race," which means that in its development each organism passes through stages which represent the adult condition of ancestral forms.

813. The fish has four or five pairs of gill slits and between the slits are the gill arches which bear the gills. Farther back in the mid-ventral line lies the heart, from which a vessel runs forward and divides into as many pairs of vessels as there are pairs of gill arches. These vessels go one to each gill arch, and above as many vessels pass from the arches to the mid-dorsal line, where they unite into a single vessel, the dorsal aorta. By these vessels the blood passes from the heart over the gills for respiration. In the embryo of Amphibia, Reptiles, Birds and Mammals, we also find these gill slits and the same arrangement of blood vessels. In Amphibia this fish-like condition persists in a functional manner until the time of metamorphosis of the tadpole. But in the other three classes respiration by gills never occurs and the gill slits are functionless rudiments. For the arrangement of the several pairs of vessels which pass over these functionless gill arches there is also no explanation to be offered except that they have been inherited from fish-like

MAMMALIAN GILL ARCHES

ancestors. The blood passes through these vessels for a time, but soon an entire rearrangement takes place, and in Birds and Mammals the connection between the heart and dorsal aorta

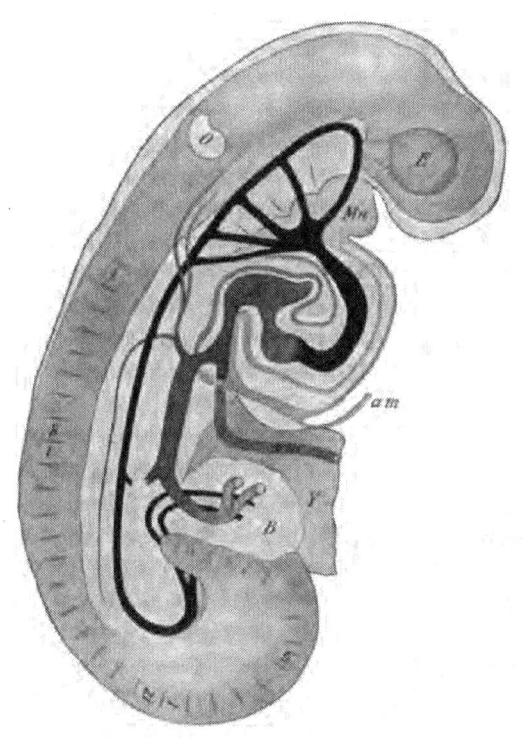

FIG. 249.—Diagram of the human embryo to show the arrangement of the blood-vessels. *E*, Eye; *O*, ear; *Mn*, lower jaw; *H*, heart. From the heart a large vessel leads forward and then divides into five pairs of vessels (only the five of one side are represented). These vessels pass over the gill arches to the dorsal side and there unite to form the dorsal aorta. In the adult, however, only the fourth branch of the left side remains to connect the heart with the dorsal aorta. (From McMurrich after His.)

is maintained only by a single vessel. In Birds this vessel lies on the right side, in Mammals on the left. The other vessels either become connected with other parts of the body or else fail to develop at all. In adult Amphibia and Reptiles a pair of these vessels persists to form the aortic arches.

814. The conclusion seems evident. The gill arches and their blood vessels are a fish character, and their presence in the terrestrial vertebrates can only mean that as vestigeal organs they hark back to fish-like ancestors. But this is only one of many anatomical puzzles which can be explained in this way.

815. The remarkable parallelism which appears between the Taxonomic series, the Phylogenetic series and the Ontogenetic series assuredly warrants the formation of a provisional hypothesis of the origin of species by descent. The value of any hypothesis is gauged by the extent to which it explains phenomena and by the help it gives in the discovery of new facts. We shall proceed to apply this test, but let us first enquire what causes might be supposed to bring about a change in species.

816. **The Struggle for Existence.**—Taking the whole world into account and year after year, there is on the average no great change in the number of individual organisms. Locally and for brief periods there frequently occurs an increase or a decrease in the number of a given species. But extended changes of this kind are comparatively rare even for a single species. This indicates that each pair of adult individuals at the time of death have provided a progeny of the same number to fill the gap. But the rate at which even the slowest breeding animals reproduce is much in excess of this, and for many the rate is many thousand-fold greater. Many plants produce several thousand to several million seeds in a season and, in the case of perennials, this is done for many years. For many animals a single brood of eggs ranges from many thousands to many millions. The conger eel may produce five or six million eggs, while the female Ascaris is credited with a brood of sixty-four million eggs. Yet in these cases only one or two eggs can ultimately have developed into an individual

of reproductive age. The others must in some way be destroyed. Many seeds and eggs are devoured by animals and many are not brought into an environment favorable for development. But one need not observe very closely to discover that the number of young is always much greater than the number of adults. The Nemesis of destruction follows the young throughout the period of development, and indeed throughout life, but the ratio of mortality is greatest during the earlier stages.

817. Now what is it that determines which one of a thousand young should survive? Is it merely a matter of chance or is there a difference between individuals which gives certain ones an advantage? Let us consider an imaginary concrete example. Suppose a litter of young rabbits in a nest at the edge of a forest. These young are more or less like their parents (heredity), but are not all exactly alike (individual variation). One soon shows itself to be puny, is ill-nourished, and perhaps falls a prey to disease or, being less active, is the first to fall a prey to the weasel or other predacious animal. Its more active mates escape the first assault, but one is particularly light in color and is readily seen at night in the open field, where both he and the owl are seeking their food. Perhaps one is too dark and his color fails to blend with the dead grass where he attempts to hide. One may be rather stupid. He fails to sense the enemy until it is too late. But among the rest there is one just the right color, that of his successful parents. He is alert, strong of limb and a nimble dodger. He runs fast, dodges quickly and has the instinct to hide at the right time and place. He is the one most likely to survive to the season when he establishes a family of his own.

818. This is a purely imaginary case, but no unreasonable supposition is made. That rabbits vary in regard to such characters cannot be questioned, nor that deficiency in such matters may be fatal to the individual. The matter may be

summed up in a few words. It is the fittest that survive in the struggle for existence.

819. **Natural Selection.**—In this brood of rabbits we have imagined a process of natural selection to take place by which the unfit are eliminated. Since the parent rabbits succeeded they must have been fit and, therefore, the young ones which resembled the parents closely would be fit also, provided they lived under the same conditions. This process would, therefore, tend to preserve the type of the parents. But conditions change and a locality which at one time is most favorable for a given species may become less so. Moreover, species often migrate. If a locality becomes overcrowded or the food scarce, or enemies too numerous, there is a special impetus given to the migrating tendency. Thus a species may push out into a new and quite different environment where there is a different nature at the work of selecting. Suppose again the rabbits: They have pushed out into colder regions, where the snow lies on the ground for many months. The gray rabbit would be very conspicuous against the snow and a coat of white fur would be decidedly advantageous in winter. Hence individuals with white coats in winter might be selected here, while in other regions the winter gray continues to hold the advantage. The diverse conditions would thus tend to produce two varieties of rabbit or indeed two species, the winter white and the winter gray. So long as the two kinds remain connected by intermediate forms they could be only called varieties, but if the intermediate forms disappear they would be distinct species. This is not intended to be regarded as an explanation of how the two species of rabbits originated. It is simply a hypothetical case which may help one to an understanding of the method by which natural selection, acting through individual variation, may produce new species. The process of natural selection must necessarily be a very slow one, and there are few historical records of such changes.

There is, however, much indirect evidence, which we will now consider.

820. **Animals and Plants Under Domestication.**—All our domestic animals and plants were originally wild species. They have become so changed under domestication that most of them bear little resemblance to their prototypes. The various types of fancy pigeons, the carriers, fantail, tumbler, pouter, etc., have probably all been produced by selective breeding from the wild rock pigeon. The differences in structure of these fancy pigeons is much more than enough to give them specific standing. Such differences found in wild species would be regarded as of generic value. How did they come about? Simply by selection. The breeder selects those which conform to a certain type and thus produces a "breed."

821. Our dogs may be descended from two or three wild dogs or wolves, but the original type has little in common with the hundreds of breeds of dogs, ranging from mastiff to greyhound and from poodle to St. Bernard. In our horses and cattle, cats, poultry, garden vegetables and cereals similar remarkable effects have been produced. In some of these domestic breeds selection has been at work for a long period, but often marked results have been brought about in a short time.

822. The conclusion which we may draw from the facts of varieties under domestication is that species are not immutable, and if man by selection can produce such results it is reasonable to believe that nature by some process may bring about similar results. The natural process is certainly slower, but the time during which it has been at work is vastly longer.

823. **Geographical Distribution.**—If such species had an independent origin (not by descent) then there is no reason why two similar species should be related geographically. They may as well occupy islands on the opposite sides of the globe, provided food, climate, etc., are the same, as live in adjacent countries. If, however, two species had a common origin

(by descent) they must also be related geographically; either they still live in the land where they originated or else there must have been a path along which they could migrate to the place where they are now found.

824. Hence, the present geographical distribution of animals may throw light on the question of the origin of species.

825. Australia is separated from Asia by a barrier which is practically impassable for mammals, and geologists tell us that this has been the case for a long time—since the Cretaceous period. Now if species change in the course of time one would expect to find the Australian mammals unlike those of Asia or elsewhere. This expectation is fulfilled in a remarkable way. All the mammals, except a few which we have reason to believe were carried there, are Monotremes and Marsupials. These are the most primitive mammals and no living forms are found outside of the Australian region except the American opossum. Fossil remains show that Marsupials were at one time widespread, but evidently they were unable to contend with the higher mammals and became extinct. In Australia no higher mammals developed. On the other hand the Marsupials developed in great variety; herbivores, carnivores, gnawers, subterranean mole-like forms and tree-dwelling forms.

826. Africa and South America are also somewhat isolated, and here we also find peculiar faunas. It is not remarkable that a peculiar species of any kind should be confined to a given area, but where several similar species of a remarkable genus are found in the same isolated region, and when, farther, fossils of still other related forms are found in the same region, only the hypothesis of a common origin offers a satisfactory explanation. Numerous examples of this kind occur. Some examples are the following: The kiwi-kiwis of New Zealand, the catarrhine monkeys of the Old World and the platyrhine monkeys of the New World, and the rheas of South America. The Edentates of the Old and New Worlds are also of distinct orders.

827. The fauna of isolated oceanic islands contributes the same kind of evidence. Madagascar has many species found nowhere else, but these species are more like those of the neighboring African coast than those of more remote regions. The Galapagos Islands also have a peculiar fauna, which finds its greatest affinity in the fauna of the nearest part of the South American coast. The fauna of the Azores is related to that of Europe, while that of the Bermudas belongs to America. These resemblances of faunas cannot be attributed to the effect of food and climate or other external causes, for there is often a greater difference in environment between two neighboring localities than between others on opposite sides of the globe.

828. The Hawaiian Islands are very mountainous and the mountains are cut by numerous deep parallel valleys. In these valleys are found numerous species of the snail, Achatinella. The snails cannot cross the mountain barriers and hence there is little migrating of snails from valley to valley. The fact that almost every valley has its own peculiar type of snail, and the way these species are distributed on the island, makes it seem probable that all had a common origin and that each species originated where it is now found. If at any time, in any valley, a new character appears through individual variation that character may in time be transmitted to all the individuals of that valley, and hence become a specific character, but natural barriers will prevent its transmission to other species living in other valleys.

ADAPTATIONS

829. In Part I many examples of modification of the type structures were described and it was shown that these modifications were always associated with peculiarities of life habit or of environment. Such modifications of an organism, in connection with peculiarities of the condition of life, are known

as adaptations. It is a phenomenon not confined to plants. The peculiarities of parasitic animals or of sedentary animals are also adaptations. In fact, the sum total of characteristics of living things is an adaptation to conditions. At various points in this book the idea has been expressed that an organism is what it is because of the conditions under which it lives. For example, one often hears stated that foliage is green because that color is least irritating to the human eye. The same idea is expressed in other forms, but the position or point of view is entirely false. The color of vegetation is part of the environment, and natural selection would result in the development of eyes which were adapted to that color.

830. There are many special types of adaptations which are of interest because they give us an insight into the method of operation of natural selection. We will call attention to a few of these here.

831. The dispersal larvæ so often found among marine animals may be regarded as an adaptation by which the species make use of oceanic currents to secure transportation from place to place. The various devices employed by plants to secure the scattering of their seeds fall in the same category. On the other hand a free-swimming larva would be fatal to many fresh-water animals because the larvæ would be carried to the sea and perish in the salt water. The eggs of very many marine fishes are light and float freely in the water, but the eggs of fresh-water fishes are either attached by means of adhesive secretions or else are so heavy that they lie on the bottom among the pebbles which protect them from the current. Many fresh-water fishes make nests by excavating the bottom and the eggs are often covered by a layer of pebbles. Some marine fishes also attach their eggs or construct nests, but the habit is not general.

832. The eggs of the decapod Crustaceæ are usually attached to the abdomen of the female, but in the marine forms the

young hatch early and are then set free, while the young of the crayfish hatch later and cling to the mother for some time after hatching.

833. The Amphibia generally deposit their eggs in water, but they avoid the streams which have a strong current, preferring quiet pools, ponds or even stagnant puddles. They also often attach the eggs to objects under water by means of the gelatinous envelope which holds the eggs together in masses.

834. The embryo of the marine Lamellibranchs is set free at an early stage as a free-swimming veliger (page 338). At a corresponding stage the young glochidium of the fresh-water mussels, the Unios and Anodontas, become attached to fishes, where they continue their development for perhaps several months longer before they finally become free.

835. Lakes and ponds often swarm with many kinds of minute free-swimming organisms, which are comparatively rare in streams. Only the larger forms, with their stronger swimming powers, can make headway against an ordinary current, and are thereby enabled to maintain themselves in the waters of creeks and rivers.

836. **The insect faunas of oceanic islands** present a similar phenomenon. These insects are either wingless or, if they have wings, are seldom seen to use them. The explanation offered is very simple. Few insects are able to fly against a strong wind, and strong winds are particularly prevalent on oceanic islands. Under such circumstances if an insect were to rise into the air it would most likely be carried to sea and perish. As a result only those insects which cannot, or at least do not, fly have remained.

837. **Adaptations to Water.**—Attention may again be called to the important adaptations which have reference to water. These are particularly well exemplified by comparing Hydrophytes and Xerophytes, or by comparing aquatic and terrestrial animals, especially with regard to the integument.

838. **Adaptations with regard to light** are much more general and important among plants than among animals. As touching plants the matter has already been fully discussed. Animals are much less dependent on light, and adaptation with regard to light affects chiefly the eyes. Animals adapted to absolute darkness, such as the fishes, salamanders and crayfishes of caves have usually little or no pigment in the skin. The most striking peculiarity of these animals is that they are blind and the eyes are usually very rudimentary. The tactile organs, however, are better developed than are those of the normal type. This is especially true of the antennæ of the crayfishes. Blind fishes are found in caves in many parts of the world, and they "belong to many different families, but are always related (similar) to the forms living in nearby streams." This fact is strong evidence that the blind forms have descended from the ancestors of those which now live in the surface streams.

839. **Adaptations to Changes of Temperature.**—All plants and most animals are directly dependent on the temperature of the surrounding medium, so that growth and other vital processes proceed more or less rapidly in accordance with the changes in temperature of the surrounding water or air. The time required for a frog to develop from the egg, for example, may vary from seventy days at a temperature of 60° F. to two hundred and thirty days at 51° F. The temperature of sea water seldom passes the limits within which vital processes are possible. The temperature of the air varies much more widely, and consequently terrestrial organisms present several types of special adaptations with regard to temperature. All the vital activities of all terrestrial plants and animals, except birds and mammals, are suspended when the temperature falls to or below freezing. Insects, Amphibia and Reptiles usually hide in sheltered recesses at such times and remain dormant until

the temperature rises again to a point which will permit the organs to perform their functions.

840. Birds and Mammals present a special adaptation in this regard in the comparatively high and constant temperature maintained by the body. This is done by the expenditure of a considerable amount of energy, specifically for keeping the body warm, and for this reason Birds and Mammals require considerably more food than do other animals of corresponding size. The temperature of the body is kept constant by a control mechanism by which the amount of heat lost is controlled. Much heat is lost by evaporation of moisture from the lungs and respiratory passages and from the mouth cavity also when the animal is panting. Panting greatly increases the amount of vaporization and the accompanying loss of heat. The feathers and hair, when lying close, prevent the loss of heat, but they may be raised on end by the action of special muscles in the skin. This permits free circulation of air and increases the loss of heat by radiation, convection and vaporization. The skin of Mammals is provided with numerous tubular glands which discharge their secretion on the surface. This secretion is chiefly water, which evaporates from the surface as rapidly as it is formed, or may accumulate in small droplets of perspiration. The function of the sweat glands seems to be primarily temperature control.

841. The heat of the body is distributed by the blood. The amount of blood brought to the surface, and there cooled, is regulated by the expansion and contraction of the blood vessels of the skin. The supply of blood to the skin and the activity of the sweat glands are both controlled through nervous stimulation.

842. Some Mammals have in a measure reverted to the primitive condition of variable temperature. Bears and many others pass a considerable portion of the winter in a deep sleep, during which the temperature of the body falls to a low point

and all the vital processes are at a low ebb. This sleep is called hibernation. It permits the animal to tide over the season when food is difficult to find. The small amount of energy required to maintain life in the hibernating condition is furnished by the reserve store in the form of fat which the animal possesses at the beginning of winter.

843. Most Birds have adapted themselves to the changing seasons in another way. At the approach of the winter season they move southward in easy flights of twenty-five to fifty miles a day and thus keep south of the region of ice. In the spring this migration is repeated in the opposite direction. We do not know what impels the birds to begin their migration, for they do not wait until the season has advanced far enough to make conditions uncomfortable. Nor do we know by what means the bird is informed in which direction to fly. We call such actions instinctive, which, however, does not explain them. It may be that they should be classed with such rhythmical physiological processes as the fall of the leaves of deciduous trees, and tropisms like geotropism and heliotropism. But whether the fact is explained or not the real fact remains, and if a bird failed to migrate, that bird would probably not survive the winter and its eccentricities would not be perpetuated.

844. **Adaptations for securing food** are exceedingly manifold. Under this class would fall most of the peculiarities connected with saprophytic and parasitic habits. Insectivorous plants, the teeth and digestive tract of the carnivorous and herbivorous animals, the claws, beak and digestive tract of the birds of prey, and the digestive tract of grammivorous birds may be cited in this connection. The great baleen whale feeds on minute pelagic organisms, which it secures by filling its mouth with the water containing the food and then straining out the food by allowing the water to flow out through the fringe of horny baleen fibres which hangs down from the upper jaw. Many

spiders spin a web which entangles small insects which come in contact with it. Many other animals set traps. Some aquatic insect larvæ construct a trap like a fish net and these open up stream, so that the current may sweep small edible objects into them. The angler fish lies on the bottom, often very much concealed. His most capacious mouth opens upward and above it hangs an attractive-looking bait, which is phosphorescent in some cases. When the prey approaches near enough the great mouth opens suddenly and the rush of water into it carries the prey along. An African snake (Dasy-peltis) feeds largely on eggs, which are swallowed whole. Some of the vertebræ have pointed processes which project into the œsophagus. The shells of the eggs are broken against these points and the empty shell is then disgorged.

845. **Pollination.**—Some of the adaptations of plants, with regard to pollination, have been noted elsewhere, but there are many special cases which are very remarkable. We can only note briefly a few of them.

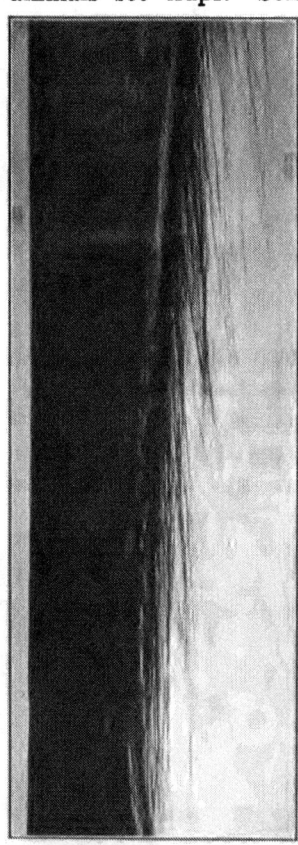

FIG. 250.—Part of one of the horny baleen plates ("whalebone") which hang from the upper jaw of the baleen whale. One edge of the plate is split up into a fringe of hairs which form the filter through which the food is strained out of the water.

846. The papilionaceous blossom of most members of the pea family is familiar to everyone. This flower in its prime

has its axis horizontal. The upper petal (standard) is very broad and stands erect, making the flower very conspicuous. The two lateral petals (wings) form a horizontal platform upon

FIG. 251.—A row of the nets woven by the Caddice fly larvæ, to catch food. In the next figure three of the nets are seen from above.

which an insect (bee) may conveniently rest when visiting the flower for nectar. The two lower petals are slightly curled longitudinally and have their concave faces toward each other (keel), so that they completely enclose the stamens and pistil. The filaments of the ten stamens are all united, except the upper

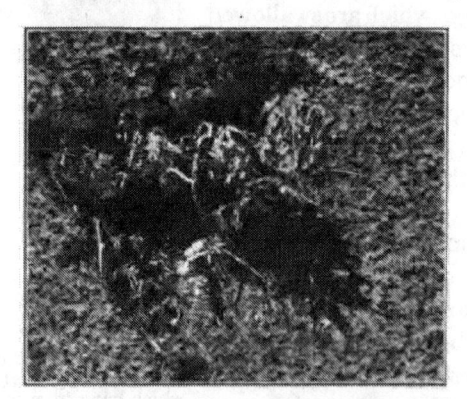

FIG. 252.—Nets of Caddice worm. See Fig. 251.

one, for most of their lengths. The ends only are free and bend upward. The style also bends upward at the end. When an insect like a bee visits the flower its weight presses the

POLLINATION 415

wings and keel down, but the rigid filament tube holds the stamens and style in place. The upper edges of the keel petals separate and the anthers come into view and touch the ventral surface of the abdomen of the insect, leaving upon it a charge of pollen. The insect now visits another flower and takes the same posi-

FIG. 253.—Bumblebee (Brombus) pushing his way under the stigma and stamen of the blue flag (Iris versicolor). See following figure. (From Folsom.)

tion on the wings. The stigma touches the same part of the insect which before came in contact with the stamens and is consequently covered with pollen which came from another flower.

847. In some of the mint family (Salvia) the flowers are somewhat funnel-shaped, with two stamens attached to the

416   GENERAL PRINCIPLES

corolla near the opening of the funnel. Each anther is attached to the upper end of a long lever, which is pivoted in the middle. When an insect enters the flower it brushes against the lower end of this lever, causing it to rise, and the opposite end with the anther comes down on the insect's back, leaving

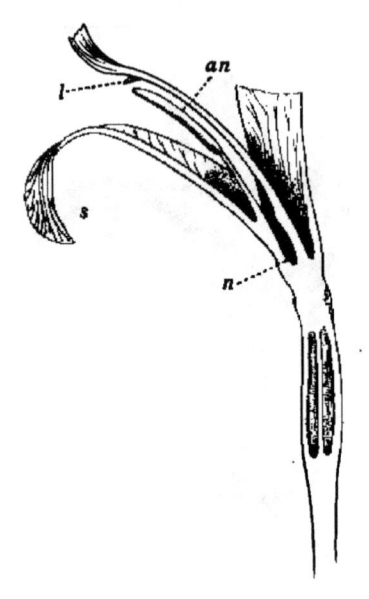

FIG. 254.—Diagram to explain the preceding figure. The bee alights on the spreading lobe of the perianth (*s*) and forces his way under the stigmatic shelf (*l*) and the anther (*an*). In doing so some of the pollen left on his back from a flower previously visited, is scraped off by the stigma and then he is immediately dusted with pollen again by contact with the anther. The nectary is shown at *n*.

a dab of pollen upon it. At this time the stigma is high up under the hood-like edge of the corolla, but later it grows out and down so that it assumes approximately the place where the anther strikes the insect. When now a bee which has previously been dusted with pollen visits this flower the stigma brushes against its body and is pollinated.

848. Some of the orchids present the most remarkable adaptations for pollination through the agency of insects. In Arethusa the pollen is contained in a receptacle which opens by a lid. This lid is torn open by the insect in its efforts to back out of the flower, and the pollen falls upon its back. In backing out of the flower, however, the insect first brushes against the stigma, which would then be pollinated, provided the insect had previously visited another similar flower.

849. The little showy orchid (Galeorchis) has two pollen masses (pollinia) which lie in the throat of the corolla, one on either side of the stigma. Each pollen mass consists of pollen grains bound together by threads and is attached to a sort of stalk which ends in a viscid disc. The pollinium is enclosed in a sack, but the disc is exposed and projects forward toward the entrance to the corolla. When an insect thrusts its head into the throat of the corolla, as it must in order to reach into the deep nectary, the discs of the pollinia adhere to the eyes or some other part of the head and are withdrawn when the insect leaves the flower. The position of the pollinia is now such that when another similar flower is visited by the insect the pollinia are thrust directly upon the broad stigmatic surface.

850. The lady slipper (Cyprepedium) has again another device. The large cup formed by the "lip" of the corolla is readily entered, but exit is difficult because of the way the edges are inrolled. A small opening on either side of the column, which bears the two anthers and the stigma, attracts the attention of the prisoner and he forces his way through one of these. In doing so he must creep under the column and his back brushes against the stigma first and then the anther. If he had previously visited a similar flower some of the pollen on his back would now adhere to the stigma and a new supply of pollen would immediately be obtained as he passes the anther, for the next flower visited.

851. The flower of the common milkweed (Asclepias) is greatly modified. The five stamens are all united around the ovary and they alternate with five funnel-shaped nectaries. Externally nothing can be seen of either anthers or stigmas, but alternating with the five nectaries are five narrow slits which open slightly at the upper end of the pendant flowers. These slits open into the stigmatic cavities. The pollen is not powdery but adheres in masses similar to the pollinia of Galeor-

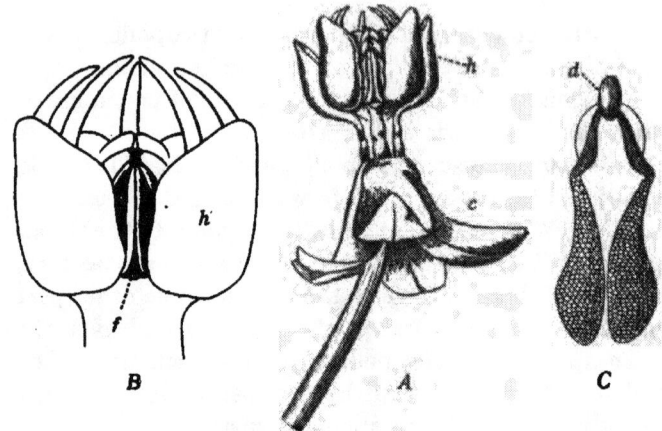

Fig. 255.—Structure of the milkweed flower. (Figures *A* and *B* should be inverted.) *A*, The whole flower; *B*, the upper part of *A* enlarged; *C*, corolla; *f*, slit opening into the stigmatic cavity; *h*, nectary. *C*, a pair of pollen masses connected by a V-shaped appendage and the sticky disc (*d*). (From Folsom.)

chis. There are five pairs of such pollen masses and the pairs are united in the form of a letter V, with a sticky substance at the point of the V. The apex of the V coincides with the lower end of the slit and the pollen masses are embedded in pockets which extend upward on either side of the stigmatic cavity. When the bee is clinging "head down" to the pendant flower his feet readily slip into the slits and are thereby guided to the sticky apex of the V pollen mass. With a strong pull the foot is released, with the pollen masses attached. When later the same foot slips into a similar slit the pollen masses are drawn into the stigmatic cavity, and in part or wholly torn off by the struggle of the insect. Occasionally an insect is not strong enough to free itself from these traps and perishes, suspended by one or several feet. This is the only possible method of pollination in milkweeds.

852. The flowers of the Yucca are pollinated by the Pronuba moth. The moth deliberately collects the pollen with the fore feet, then goes to the pistil **of the same flower,** pierces it with her ovipositor and deposits an egg. She then goes to the fun-

FIG. 256.—A wasp, Sphex ichneumonea, with a number of the milk weed pollen masses attached to its feet.

nel-like stigma and deposits the pollen. This operation is repeated in the same and neighboring flowers until her eggs are all deposited. The carrying of pollen to the stigma is an indirect method of providing food for the young, since it causes the ovules to develop, and these are devoured by the larvæ of the moth after hatching. When ready to pupate the larvæ escape from the ovary by a hole which they bore through its wall. Not all the developing seeds are devoured. The plant sacrifices a part of the seeds as a reward for the services of pollination.

853. It is not only the plants that are affected by the adapta-

tion for pollination. The insects are often as much modified. The worker bee has special organs for carrying pollen, the Moth has a long proboscis for reaching into the extremely deep nectaries of certain flowers and the Pronuba has developed a special instinct for pollinating the Yucca, which is as much a part of the insect as are its legs and wings. In many cases both plant and flower are so modified with respect to each other that one cannot exist without the other.

FIG. 257.　　　　　　　　FIG. 258.

FIG. 257.—Pronuba yuccasella in the flower of the Yucca. (From Folsom after Riley.)

FIG. 258.—Female Pronuba getting pollen from the anther of Yucca. (From Folsom after Riley.)

854. Care of Young.—The food stored up in seeds and in eggs is not the only kind of provision made for the young of the next generation. Birds feed the young until they are able to hunt food for themselves, and the young of Mammals are fed for some time from the secretions of the mammary glands of the female. But many more special adaptations occur. To mention only one from the plants: The mangrove trees grow in shallow water, but the seeds are not allowed to fall and drown or be

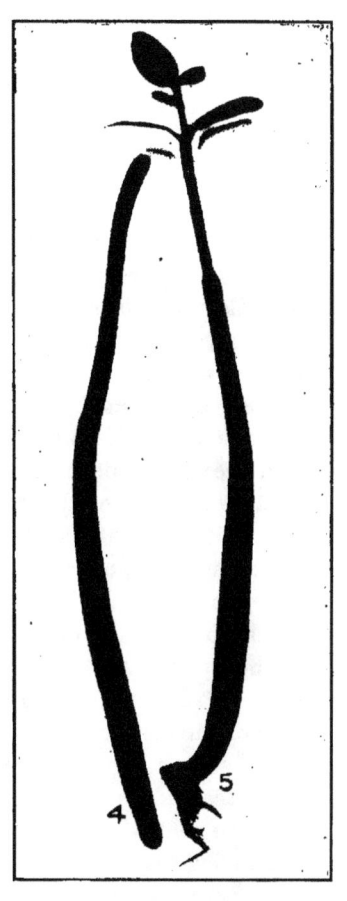

FIG. 259.—The developing seedling of the mangrove. In 1, 2 and 3, the fruit is still hanging on the branch but the hypocotyl grows until it reaches a length of about 12 inches when it drops to the earth and, striking in the mud, remains standing upright, as if planted (4). At a later stage (5) roots have been developed at the lower end and an epicotyl from the upper end.

covered up with the mud or washed away. The seed remains on the tree until it has germinated and developed a heavy hypocotyl about a foot in length. It then falls and strikes deep enough into the mud so that it remains upright as if planted.

855. Among the social Hymenoptera the young are cared for as carefully as they are by the higher vertebrates. In other cases, however, the young are never seen by the mother, and, indeed, in many cases, the mother dies before they are hatched. But even in such cases the mother may make elaborate provision for the young. The Pronuba will illustrate this point, but another more remarkable example is frequently quoted. Many of the solitary wasps (Sphegidæ) excavate channels under ground or build mud nests under the eaves of houses. These nests are then filled with spiders or other insects which the wasp stings in such a fashion that they are paralyzed, but not killed. An egg is then deposited by the wasp and the nest sealed up. The larva soon hatches and feeds upon the spiders. If the spiders had been killed decomposition would soon set in and the result would probably be the death of the wasp larva. If the spiders were not sufficiently stupefied they would probably kill the larva. It is, therefore, of great importance that the spiders should be stung in a very particular manner. But the wasp never returns to the nest and cannot know how it fares with her offspring. If, however, her work was not well done she will have no offspring to inherit her careless ways. Our wonder and admiration of the instinct and skill of the successful wasp are increased when we consider that the proper stinging of the spiders is not a deed that is performed with calm deliberation, for the spiders are also armed and are bold and skillful fighters. The wasp is compelled to place carefully the paralyzing thrust in the midst of a desperate conflict.

856. **Sexual Dimorphism.**—Reference has been made to sexual dimorphism (page 353). This is more general among the higher animals. When there is a notable difference between

the males and females of a species of one of the lower phyla the difference is most frequently a difference of size. The female is usually larger. This is regarded as due to the great demands made upon the female organism in the development of the relatively large mass of egg substance. Among Mammals the male is usually the larger, if there is any marked difference in size. The males of the fur seal and sea lion are about four times as large as the female. In such cases the males fight for the possession of the females, and consequently size and strength are the determining factors in the struggle for existence among the males. Why the size of the male parent should be inherited by the male offspring and not by the female is an interesting problem which still awaits solution.

857. **Sexual Selection.**—In some species of Birds also the males are the larger, and this occurs again in those cases in which the males contend in battle for the possession of the females. Generally, however, the male bird is distinguished from the female by his greater beauty or his superior ability as a vocalist. This introduces us to a particular form of natural selection, called sexual selection. At the time of mating the males vie with each other by displaying their beautiful plumage or singing their best songs. This is done in the presence of the female, and is evidently intended to win her favor. Following this courtship the birds mate in pairs (monogamy), apparently according as the appearance or performance of the male pleases the female. That is to say, in this case the selecting which determines the male parentage of the next generation is done by the female, and the survival

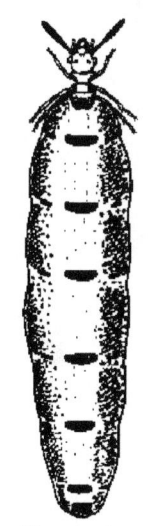

FIG. 260.—Queen of Termes obesus. Natural size. (From Folsom after Hagen). It is said that in some cases the queen attains the size of thirty thousand workers.

424 GENERAL PRINCIPLES

of the male characters in the next generation depends upon the colors, plumage or song, which are fitted to meet with the approval of the female. Sexual selection also occurs in other

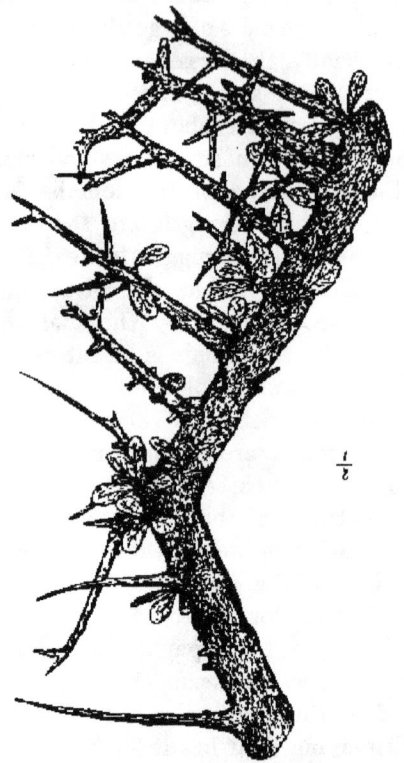

Fig. 261.—Myrrh, a xerophytic plant of the Arabian desert. There are few leaves and the spiny branches offer protection against grazing animals. (From Sayre.)

classes of animals. A particularly interesting case is found among spiders. Here the males are often much smaller than the female, and strive to gain her favor by series of movements which may be called dancing.

ADAPTATIONS

858. Welfare of the Individual and of the Species.—The welfare of a species sometimes makes demands which do not coincide with what is required for the welfare of the individuals of that species. It is sometimes in the interest of the species that certain individuals should perish. It is often better that the weak or inefficient individuals should perish, and in many

FIG. 262.—A sandy beach, the home of a small light-gray grasshopper. The dark patches in the background are green yaupon thickets where two species of green grasshoppers are found. These are remarkably well protected by their coloration when in their proper environment. Coast of North Carolina.

cases the welfare of the species requires the sacrifice of the most efficient individuals. In many instances the female dies immediately after she has properly deposited her brood of eggs. This is not only because her life term has been completed but because of the heavy draught made upon her organism by the development of the ova. Sometimes the body of the female disintegrates normally in order to free the contained embryos.

859. Though such cases are rather numerous they must still be regarded as exceptional. Usually the best interests of the species are served by that which favors the individual. We will, therefore, inquire into that class of adaptation by which the individual profits more directly. Much of the struggle for existence is in reality a struggle between individuals; it may be individuals of the same or of different

FIG. 263.—A Juncus swamp in which is found a large gray and olive-brown striped grasshopper. The color of the grasshopper is protective in such an environment. Coast of North Carolina.

species. Illustrations of this principle are usually taken chiefly from animals, but one from the vegetable kingdom may also be introduced here. The difficult conditions under which desert plants grow makes the number of individual plants which succeed relatively small. Therefore, the life of an individual plant is of more value to the species. It is, therefore, not strange that such plants are wonderfully well protected. The spines of the cacti render them practically immune to the attacks of animals. To a less degree spines

PROTECTIVE COLORATION

are also found on mesophytic vegetation and are also more or less efficient as protection. Many plants are protected by bitter, acrid, poisonous or otherwise disagreeable juices which protect them from the attacks of many, if not all, animals. When we consider how devastating the attacks of insects

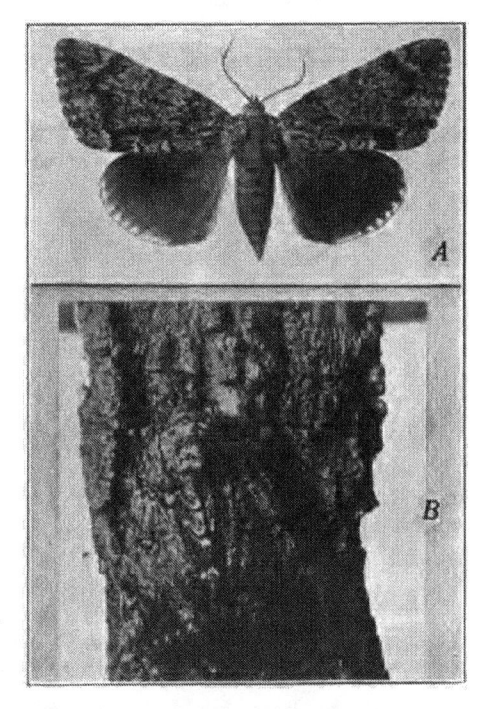

FIG. 264.—Protective resemblance of the moth, Catocala lacrymosa, to the bark on which it rests. *A*, With wings spread, as in flight; *B*, with wings folded and at rest on bark. (From Folsom.)

sometimes become to given species of plants we may realize how useful such protective contrivances may be.

860. Animal Coloration.—If the color of animals has no general significance it does have an extremely far-reaching significance when we consider the life of the individual. The color is often the most remarkable adaptive feature about it. Animals are usually darker above than below. This may be due in part to the direct tendency of light to produce pigment in the skin. But it has also been suggested that the dark upper surface in the bright light and the light under surface

FIG. 265.—Walking-stick insect (Diapheromera). Natural size. An example of protective resemblance. (From Galloway after Folsom.)

in the shadow of the body yield approximately equal light value and tend to render the animal inconspicuous at a distance.

861. Animals generally are colored in harmony with their surroundings. Polar animals are white; animals of the desert and plain are gray, and those of the forest are striped or mottled. Pelagic marine animals are often transparent and those of the bottom are often so much like the bottom that it be-

PROTECTIVE COLORATION

comes difficult to distinguish them from their surroundings, even when one knows precisely their location. Many animals living on or among green foliage are as green as the leaves. These agreements in color between the animal and its environment render the animal difficult to see and, therefore, protect it from its enemies. The same characteristic of the animal enables it to steal upon its prey, but in either case the color is an advantage and may have been developed through natural selection.

862. It has been shown that some color patterns, which at first sight seem to render the wearer conspicuous, have in

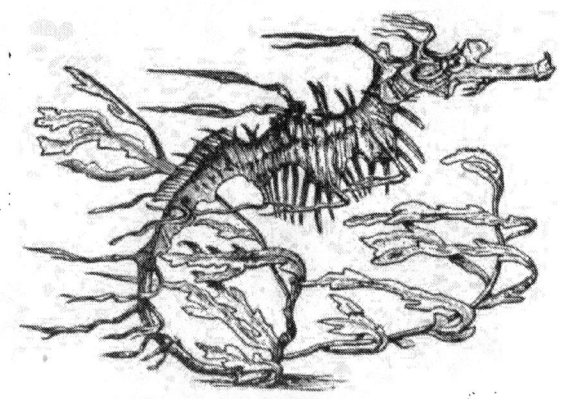

FIG. 266.—Protective resemblance. A sea-horse resembling a sea-weed. (From Galloway after Eckstein.)

reality an obliterating effect when seen at a distance under natural surroundings. Nevertheless, there are many cases in which the color makes the animal conspicuous. This may be illustrated by the many species of birds in which the male is brilliantly colored. An explanation for this coloring has already been given. But the females of these same species are usually very plainly colored and harmonize well with their surroundings. The female usually broods over the eggs, and

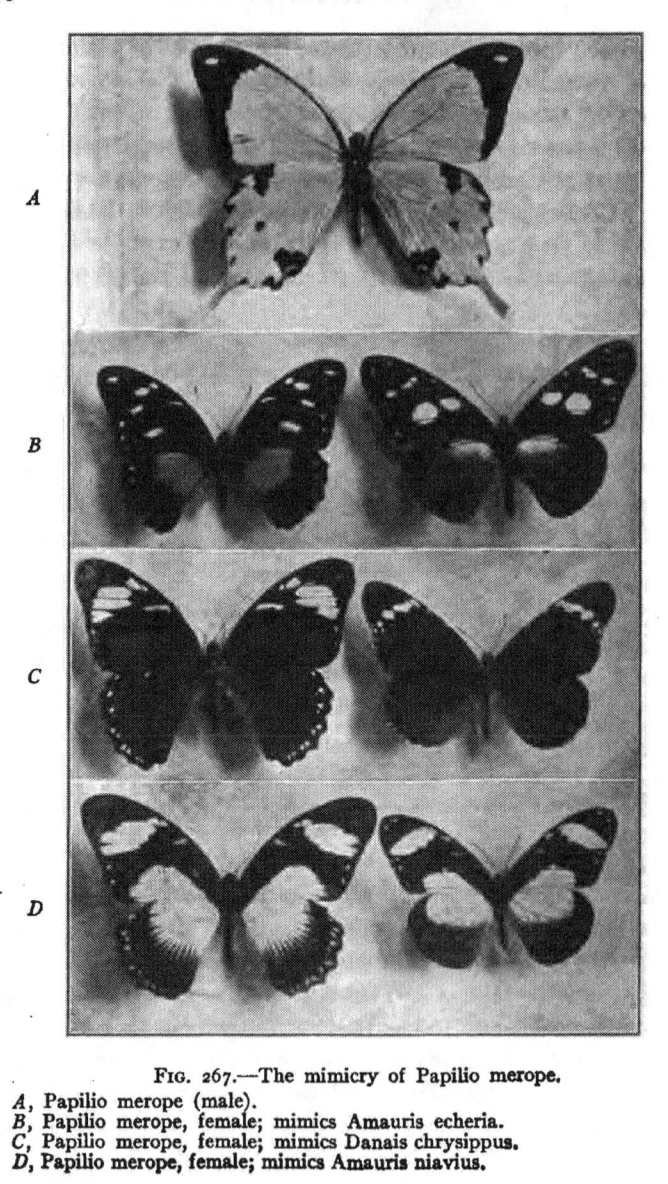

FIG. 267.—The mimicry of Papilio merope.
A, Papilio merope (male).
B, Papilio merope, female; mimics Amauris echeria.
C, Papilio merope, female; mimics Danais chrysippus.
D, Papilio merope, female; mimics Amauris niavius.

when sitting quietly is not readily seen. She is, therefore, probably less frequently molested. The male is free to take to flight when discovered and pursued. The color of the female is explained on the basis of ordinary natural selection, while that of the male is due to the operation of sexual selection.

863. **Protective Resemblance.**—In many cases the animal resembles its environment in form as well as color. This is called protective resemblance. There are insects which resemble dead twigs, rolled and broken dry leaves, dead leaves still on the twig, green leaves, seed pods, patches of lichens, etc. There are fishes which resemble sea weeds and even a mammal, the sloth, resembles a lichen-covered knot on a tree.

864. **Feigning.**—Many animals when threatened by enemies resort to bluff. They assume terrifying attitudes, make a show of great size by swelling themselves or raising hair or feathers on end, or make disconcerting noises like hissing, spitting or growling. Feigning death or "possuming" is another common instinctive method of getting out of a tight place. The opossum is a well-known example and has lent his name to this particular instinct. Beetles often feign death. When attacked they allow themselves to fall to the ground and lie there motionless for some time. They are then difficult to find, whereas if they attempted to run or fly their move-

---

The three types of female Papilios, shown on the left in B, C, and D, belong to the same species, of which the male is represented in A. There is also a type of female which resembles the male, and still another form which is not figured here. There are then five types of females within this species. Three of these, beside the male, have been reared from the same brood of eggs. This species is found in Africa but a similar case of polymorphism is found in India. The origin of the polymorphism in this case is apparently due to mimicry. The species of Amauris and Danais represented on the right in the figure are protected, *i.e.*, they are unpalatable to birds, hence the female Papilios by mimicry also secure immunity from the attacks of birds though they are not otherwise protected. The males are not protected, nor are they mimics, but they are produced in much greater number than the females. In A the predominant color is yellow, in C it is orange, while in B and D it is white, or pale yellow, and dark gray to black. ×1/2.

ments would make them conspicuous and invite a second attack.

865. **Mimicry.**—Many animals are protected in various degree by their stings, poison fangs, malodorous secretions or unpalatable taste. These are naturally avoided by species which would otherwise prey upon them. But this means that the preying species must be able to distinguish between the palatable and unpalatable prey. The unpalatable forms are often conspicuously marked, as if to advertise the fact, and thus prevent an attack which might be disastrous to both pursuer and pursued. Coloring which is regarded as serving such an end is termed warning coloration. It is especially common among insects and protects them from birds.

866. Where species occur which are protected and warningly colored there are also often other species which are not protected by sting or unpalatable, and yet are very like the protected species in form and color. This is called "mimicry," because the one form is supposed to have acquired a resemblance to the other for the purpose of protection. If a bird recognizes a certain form and color pattern as belonging to an undesirable insect another insect resembling the first would be spared an attack if the bird failed to discriminate. Upon this ground mimicry is explained by natural selection. A fact of almost conclusive significance is that the mimic and the model are always found associated in the same regions. Mimicry is very common among butterflies, but many cases are known in which bees, bumbleebees and wasps serve as models and are mimicked by flies, beetles and butterflies. Cases in which poisonous snakes are mimicked by harmless ones are also known.

867. Mimicry also occurs between two species which are both protected. This demands a different explanation from the preceding case. Birds learn that protected species are unpalatable only by experience, and in getting this knowledge, one or more butterflies of the protected species are injured or

destroyed. Therefore, each species profits by the sacrifice the other makes in the education of the bird. In the case of the unprotected mimic, however, the burden of education rests wholly on the protected model.

868. Color Changes.—The color of animals is in the main inherited, but it may often be more or less modified in the individual by the environment. Animals kept in darkness tend to become paler, and if the young flat fishes are illuminated from below there is a tendency for the underside to develop pigment where normally there is none. The color of caterpillars may be determined somewhat by the color of the surrounding objects. If they are surrounded by dark objects they tend to become darker also. Other animals, like many fishes, frogs, tree toads, lizards and cuttlefishes, change color rapidly and repeatedly. The color of a cuttlefish changes in a flash. This is due to the action of contractile pigment cells. When the cells expand the animal takes on the color of the chromatophores, dark brown or orange or a combination of these colors, as the different cells are stimulated. The action is controlled through the nervous system, but it is not clear what service it plays in the animal economy. The chameleon and other lizards, as well as many frogs and fishes, change color more slowly, but by a similar mechanism. In these cases the color assumed is determined by the surroundings. If the animal is blind the changes do not occur, and it is known that the stimulus is received through the eye and transmitted by the nervous system without, however, any voluntary control by the animal. In these cases the colors assumed are protective.

869. Luminescence.—There are two important physiological processes which are practically wanting in all animals above fishes, but are quite common among lower forms. These are the light-producing organs and organs for generating electricity. The production of light or phosphorescence occurs among all classes of animals from the Protozoa to Fishes, and also among fungi. Decaying vegetable and animal matter is often luminous as a result of the action of bacteria. The mycelium of other fungi also yields light at times. In these cases the light is apparently a by-product, which is not to be regarded as having any adaptive function.

870. The light-producing power is especially common among marine invertebrates and Fishes. Phosphorescence occurs among the Protozoa, Cœlenterates, Worms, the smaller Crustaceæ, Bryozoa, Rotifers, free-swimming Ascidians, Fishes and Insects. In some cases the light is produced at certain points within the protoplasm of the cell. In others the slime secreted by glands in the skin is luminous. And again there are special organs which may be simple or complex in structure, but which bear evidence of having been developed from groups of glands, though there is no duct and no external secretion. The more highly developed photogenic organs have a structure resembling that of an eye with a layer of pigment at the back and a lens in front. In the lower animals the light is only emitted when the animal is stimulated, and the purpose of it is unknown. In the higher forms, however, the organ is well supplied with nerve elements and is under voluntary nervous control.

871. Among Fishes the photogenic organs are especially common and well developed in deep sea species. Some "anglers" carry a lantern at the tip of the long anterior dorsal spine. This lantern is suspended directly above the mouth of the animal and is regarded as a bait by which the angler attracts his prey. In other cases the photogenic organs may occur on almost any part of the body.

872. The common "fire fly" is a beetle belonging to the family, "Lampyridæ," which contains many luminescent species. The eggs, larvæ, male and female, may all be luminescent. In some species the female is wingless, but has an

exceptionally brilliant light, which may, therefore, enable the winged male to find her. In many cases the eyes of these nocturnal insects are unusually well developed, as is also the case with the deep sea fishes, a fact that renders probable the view that the luminescent organs are a means by which the sexes find each other. The luminescence of the eggs and larvæ are not understood. Photogenic organs are common in other families of beetles, and also occur among flies.

873. Oxygen is said to be necessary to the action of photogenic organs, but no appreciable heat is generated.

874. **Electrical Organs.**—Organs for generating electricity are developed in a number of Fishes. The electric eel (Gymnotus) of the Amazon and Orinoco rivers, the electric catfish (Malapterurus) of tropical Africa, and the electric rays (Torpedo) of the warmer seas are all capable of producing an electrical discharge sufficient to stun large animals. The electric organ of the Gymnotus is a modified muscle of the ventral side of the long tail. In Torpedo the organ is also of modified muscles, but of the head region. In Malapterurus the glands of the skin have been the starting point from which the electric organ developed. In neither case, of course, does the fully developed electric organ bear any resemblance to muscle or gland. The nerves supplying the electric organs are developed to an extraordinary degree and the electric discharge is under voluntary control. These organs are doubtless organs of offense and defense.

875. **Instinct.**—When the Pronuba moth deposits her egg in the pistil of the Yucca and then stuffs pollen in the stigma she is not aware of the end secured by her acts. She does not know that pollination will cause the ovules to develop. She does not know that there are ovules. She cannot even know that she has deposited an egg. She never sees the eggs; she never sees her offspring. The whole performance is to her without meaning and is enacted in obedience to an internal impulse originat-

ing in physiological processes connected with the organs of reproduction.

876. Practically the same may be said of the actions of the mud dauber when building her mud nest and filling it with embalmed spiders. Another example may be described. There is a family of beetles (Cantharidæ) which are parasitic on other insects during the larval stages. In some cases (Sitaris) the eggs of the beetle are deposited on the ground in the vicinity of a bumblebee's nest. A small active larva hatches from these eggs and this larva reaches the nest of the bumblebee in a very peculiar way. It does not seek the opening of the nest and thus make its way in, but waits until some living object like the bumblebee chances to come within reach, when it attaches itself to the legs or hairs of the body and is thus carried into the nest. The bumblebee builds a large cell of wax. This it fills with honey, and then deposits an egg on the honey and seals up the cell. At the moment when the egg is deposited the beetle larva attaches itself to the egg and is thus sealed up in the cell with the egg and honey. It first devours the egg, which requires almost eight days' time. Then it undergoes a metamorphosis, after which it is adapted for feeding upon honey, which it could not do before. After about forty days' feeding on honey the supply is exhausted and the larva undergoes a second metamorphosis. This is followed by several more metamorphoses, after which the adult beetle (blister beetle) appears. The notable thing about this life history is the means adopted by the minute larvæ for reaching the nest of the bee. They will often attach themselves to other living objects, such as other insects or even a camel's hair brush. When they do this they perish, because they fail to reach the condition necessary for their future development. These larvæ are not taught what they have to do to succeed; they cannot profit by the observation of others, and they cannot learn from experience. They are somehow impelled to attach themselves to other insects. If

they are fortunate enough to attach themselves to the bee they succeed. Otherwise they perish. The female blister beetle is very prolific and deposits many thousands of eggs. Hence it is only necessary that a few of the thousands of larvæ should succeed.

877. Actions like those of the Pronuba, Sphex or blister beetle larva are called instinctive. They are not prompted by a kind of intelligence. Nor are they in any sense akin to intelligence, though among the higher animals it is often difficult to say whether an act is prompted by instinct or intelligence.

878. If a moth habitually rests on surfaces which it resembles it does so instinctively, not because it has an intelligent comprehension that it is thereby protected. When a caterpillar spins a cocoon it does so instinctively and not with the forethought of providing protection. When a young bird builds a nest it is impelled thereto by instinct, and the form and manner of building the nest are also determined by instinct. In the latter case more or less evidence of intelligence may be discernible, but the process as a whole is instinctive.

879. An instinct is a kind of adaptation and subject to the laws of heredity. Instinctive actions may, therefore, be developed under natural selection, just like other adaptive characters of an organism.

880. **Intelligence.**—Intelligence is found only among the most highly organized animals because it is dependent upon **an efficient set of sense organs** which yield accurate information concerning the environment, **a flexible response mechanism** which may react in multitudinous ways to the infinite variation in the conditions of existence, and **an organ of control,** the brain. In practically all Birds and Mammals the first two of these conditions of intelligence are well met, and yet there is a vast difference in intelligence within these classes. This is due to the difference in brain structure. The brain of the lowest Vertebrates is an inconceivably complex organ, and in the higher

forms it is vastly more so. This organ enables the individual animal to profit by experience. A sensation or an experience of any kind to which the organism has once been subjected is in some way registered in the brain (memory) and through it the future responses are modified. The constant stream of highly complex stimuli which pour in upon the organsim from the environment are sifted and analyzed in some way by the brain, and the appropriate responses determined (reason, judgment), and the proper motor stimuli sent out to the organs of response (will). Animals guided by instinct inherit a few sets of more or less complex responses, which are set in motion by corresponding sets of stimuli, and these responses are little if at all modified. Responses prompted by intelligence are more variable as determined by variable external conditions, and the individual exercises an adaptive control. The brain might be called an organ of adaptation, for the degree in which the individual can adapt itself to its environment is a measure of its intelligence.

INDEX—GLOSSARY.

Acarina, 571
Accessory buds. 57
Accipitres, 650
Achatinella, distribution of, 828
Achene, 156
Acicula, a needle-shaped structure, 346
Acrania, (Gk. having no skull), 624
Actinomma, 126
Adaptations, 829
    regarding food, 844
        light 838
        temperature, 839, 840
        water, 837
Adelochorda, 617
Adventitious buds, 57
Æcidiospores, 749
Æpyornithes, 650
African fauna, 826
Agglutinin, 777
Aggregate fruit, 164
Air sacs, 647
Albatross, 650
Albumen, the white of an egg, 677
Aleurone, 19, 95, 672
Alexin, (Gk. to ward off), 776
Alga, pl. algæ (L. a sea weed).
Algæ, 177, 178
    blue-green, 232
Allantois, one of the fœtal membranes of reptiles, birds and mammals, 174, 641, 651
Alligator, 644
Alternation of generations, 525, 741
Altitude and plants, 204
Ambulacral, pertaining to the system of tube feet of an echinoderm.
Ambulacral system, 550
Amiatus, 635
Amnion, one of the fœtal membranes of reptiles, birds and mammals, 641, 651
Amœba, 68, 178, 303
    chemical sense of, 353
    digestion in, 452, 453, 464
    excretion in, 489

Amœba, reproduction in, 495, 496
    respiration in, 476
    response in, 407
    sense of sight, 355
    of touch, 354
    temperature sense, 356
Amœbina, 510
Amphibia, 350, 637
    structure of, 637
Amphineura, 593
Amphioxus, syn. for Branchiostoma (lancelet).
Amphipoda, 561, 563
Amphitrite, 139
Amphiuma, the "congo snake."
Ampulla, 550
Amylolytic, converting starch into sugar, 461
Amylolytic ferments, 463
Amyloplast—a starch forming corpuscle, 93, 672
Amylopsin, 462
Andreaceæ, 277
Andrœcium, 123, 128
Anemophilous, pollinated by the wind, 139, 140
Angiosperms, 171, 298
Angler fish, 844
Animal coloration, 860
Anisopoda, 561
Annelida (L. annellus—a ring) worms with a segmented, ringed body, 542
Annelids, circulatory system of, 469, 470
    locomotion of, 410, 411
    nervous system of, 438
    reproductive system of, 501, 502
    trochophore larva of, 501
Anomostraca, 561
Anomura, 561, 562
Anopheles, 768
Ant bear, 661
Ant eater, spiny, 176
Antedon, 144
Antelope, 666

Numbers refer to paragraphs; Black Face numbers refer to figures.

439

Antenna, one of the first or second pair of jointed appendages, "feelers," on the head of an Arthropod.
Antennæ, of moth, 78
Antennule, one of the first pair of jointed appendages on the head of a Crustacean.
Anterior, 311
Anther, 123
Antheridium, 264
Anthocerotaceæ, 270
Anthozoa, 529
Antibodies, 777
Antimere, 335
Antitoxin, 776, 777
Antlers, 348
Ant lion, 585
Ants, 590
　polymorphism in, 740
Anura, 640
Anvil, 403
Apanteles, 236
Apes, 652, 668
Aphids, 227, 590
Apical cell, 710
Aplanospores, non-motile spores, 247
Apothecium—the concave fruiting surface of a fungus, 258
Appendages, of Arthropods, 412
　of Vertebrates, 170, 413, 792
Apteryges, 650
Apterygogenea, 577
Apteryx, 175, 650
Aquatic plants, 184-191
Aqueous humor, 382
Arachnoidea, 566
Araneida, 569
Archæopteryx, 247, 806
Archegoniates, those cryptogams which bear archegonia, viz., Bryophyta and Pteridophyta, 266
Archegonium, 264
Archenteron, the primitive intestine, 714
Arethusa, 848
Aristotle's lantern, 555
Armadillo, 421, 652, 661
Artemia, 687
Arthostraca, 561, 563
Arthropoda (Gk. jointed foot), 557
Arthropods, appendages of, 412
　chemical sense of, 370
　circulatory system of, 471
　digestion in, 458, 459, 467

Arthropods, eyes of, 378
　exoskeleton of, 417
　glands of, 350
　growth in, 731
　locomotion of, 412
　nervous system of, 443
　segmentation of, 336
　sense organs of, 361
Artiodactyla, 666
Ascaris, 687, 695, 758
Aschelminthes, 538
Ascidians, 621
　structure of, 621
　symmetry of, 321
Asclepias, 851
Ascomycetes, 256
Ascus (Gk. a bag), 256
Ash, 64
Aspidobranchia, 600, 601
Assimilation—the process of transforming food into the living substance, 6, 486
Association fibres, 439-441,
Asteroidea, 552
Asymmetry, 318
Atrium, 621
Attraction sphere—a rounded mass of the cytoplasm which encloses the centrosome, 685
Auditory organ, 396
　meatus, 401
Auricle, 401
Australian fauna, 825
Autobasidiomycetes, 255
Autogamy—self fertilization, 144
Aves, 646
　structure of, 646
Axil, 56
Axillary bud, 56
Axis of locomotion, 310

Babesia, 771
Bacillus, 227
　aceti, 229
　anthracis, 231
　coli communis, 231
　diphtheriæ, 231
　pneumoniæ, 231
　tetani, 231
　tuberculosis, 231
　typhi, 231
　vulgaris, 230
Bacteria, **58-61**, 180, 217, 227-231, 673, 778
　as parasites, 772, 773
　nucleus of, 673

Numbers refer to paragraphs; Black Face numbers refer to figures.

INDEX—GLOSSARY.

Bacterium, 227
Balancers, 587
Balanoglossus, syn. for Dolichoglossus
Baleen whale, 665, 796
    feeding of, 844
Ball and socket joint, 413
Barnacles, 560, 739
    symmetry of, 321
Basidiomycetes, 252
Basidium, 252
Basilar membrane, 398
Basket fish, **147**, 554
Bast, the fibrous portion of the back, 74
Bat, 652
Beak, 347
Bears, 652, 663
Beavers, 652, 660
Bed bugs, 591
Bees, 590
Beggiatoa alba, 229
Berry, 153
Bilateral symmetry, 315
Bile pigments, 483
Bimana, 669
Biology, 1
Birds (see Aves).
Birds and reptiles, 792
Birds, development of, 806
    glands of, 350
    migration of, 843
    reptilian characters of, 649
Blackbirds, 650
Black mold, 250
Blastula, **196, 197**, 712
    of lancelet, 712
Blood, origin of, 721
    -vessels, origin of, 721
Blue crab, ecdysis of, **76**
Blue flag, pollination of, 253, 254
Blue-green algæ, nucleus of, 673
Blue molds, 257
Body cavity, 469
    fluid, 469
Bojanus, organ of, 607
Bone, **95**, 426
Bones, origin of, 721
Bony labyrinth, 399
Book gills, 565
    lungs, 567, 568, 569
Bot fly, 761
Brachiopoda, 549
Brachyura, 561, 562
Bract—the leaf, usually modified, which subtends a floral shoot.
Brain, 444, 580

Brain, of annelids, 438
    of crayfish, **100**
    of shark, **102**
Branchioganoidea, 632
Branchiata, 558
Branchiura, 559
Brand spores, 253
Brittle star, **146**, 554
Bryinæ, 279
Bryophyllum, **34**
Bryophyta—Bryophytes, 176, 264
Bryozoa, 548
Budding, 330, 671
    in hydra, 499
    multiplication by, 169
Buffalo, 666
Bugs, 763
Bulbus arteriosus, a muscular chamber of the heart, in front of the ventricle, 628
Bull-bat, 650
Butterflies, 586
    polymorphism in, 743
Byssus, silky fibres spun from a gland in the foot of certain Lamellibranchs, 610

C—symbol for carbon.
Cactus, **24**
Caddice worm nets, **251, 252**
    shelters, **73, 74**
Cæcum—cœcum—cecum,—a pouch or sac.
Calyptra, part of the archegonium which remains attached to the spore capsule, 277
Calyx, 122, 131
Cambium, 75
Camel, 666
Cameleon, 645
Campodea, **159**
Canaliculi, of bone, 426
Canal system of sponge, 521
Canidæ, 663
Capillary, small blood-vessels having walls composed of a single layer of thin cells.
Capitulum, 119
Caprella, **150**
Capsule, 163
Carapace, a hard case or shell, 643
Carbohydrates—organic compounds of carbon hydrogen and oxygen, with the hydrogen and oxygen in the proportions of H_2O, 94

Numbers refer to paragraphs; Black Face numbers refer to figures.

442 INDEX—GLOSSARY.

Carbohydrates, absorption of, 472
Carbon dioxide, formed in body, 488, 489
    used by plant, 85
Carbon of plant, source of, 89
Carinatæ, 650
Carnivora, 652, 662
Carnivorous — flesh-eating. plants, 218
Carp, 636
Carpels—the leaves modified to form the pistil, **28**, 125
Carpogonium, 248
Carpospores, 248
Cartilage, **49**, 425
    origin of, 721
Caryopsis, 157
Cassia, **42**, **43**
Cassowary, 650
Catarrhina, 668
Catbird, 650
Caterpillar, 723
Catfish, 636
Catkin, 119
Cats, 663
Cattle family, 666
Cave fauna, 838
Cedar apple, 750
Cell, **2**, 16, **179**
    colonies, 704
    division, 683
    masses, 705
    membrane, 672
    regeneration of, 680
    wall, 622
Cellulose, 96, 619
Central nervous system, 325
    of annelids, 438
    origin of, 715
Centrosome, 677, 683, 689
Centipede, 576
Cephalization, 311
Cephalomya, 762
Cephalopoda—Cephalopods, 611, 616
    structure of, 611
Cercaria, 754
Cermatia, 576
Cestoda—Cestodes, 537, 755
Cetacea, 652, 665
Chætopoda, 543
Chætopterus, tube of, **72**
Characeæ, 244
Chela, a pincer-like claw.
Cheliceræ, the first pair of appendages of certain Arthropods, 567

Chemical sense, 353
    of arthropods, 370
    of crayfish, 369
    of earthworm, 368
    of hydra, 367
    of amœba, 353
Chilopoda, 576
Chimpanzee, 668
Chinch bugs, 591, 763
Chiroptera, 652, 659
Chiton, 341, 593
Chlorophyceæ, 238
Chlorophyll, 82
Chloroplasts, 82
    position in cell, 206
$C_6H_{10}O_5$—starch, 87
$C_6H_{12}O_6$—sugar, 90
Chondroganoidea, 633
Choroid layer, 379
Chromatin, 674
Chromatophore—a cell containing pigment or, a protoplasmic granule containing pigment.
Chromoplast—a protoplasmic granule (plastid) containing pigment, 672
Chromosome, 683
Chromosomes, division of, 684, 695
    individuality of, 703
    number of, 687, 695
Cicada, 396, 591, 763
Ciconiæ, 650
Cilium(pl. cilia), minute thread-like, vibratile appendages.
Ciliary body, 381
Ciliata, 514
Circulation, 327, 468–
Circulatory system of annelids, 469, 470
    of arthropods, 471
    of crayfish, **110**
    of man, **114**
    of Nereis, **112**, **113**
    of vertebrates, 472
Circumvallate papillæ, 371
Cirratulus, **140**
Cirripedia, 560
Civet cat, 663
Clam, **166**
Clamatores, 650
Classes of animals, 507–669
    of plants, 170–181, 224–301
Claws, 347
Cleavage, 702–
    types of, 711, 718

Numbers refer to paragraphs; Black Face numbers refer to figures.

Cleistogamic—flowers which do not open and which are self fertilized, 145
Climate and vegetation, 223
Climbing plants, 212
Cloaca, the chamber into which the intestine, ureters, and gonoducts, all open, 556, 637
Closteridium butyricum, 229
Club moss—Lycopodium.
Clypeaster, 65, **148**
Cnidaria, 524
Cnidoblasts, 524
CO_2—symbol for carbon dioxide, 66
Coal, 219, 221
Coccus, 227
Coccygomorphæ, 650
Cochlea, 398
Cockroaches, 582
Cocoon, 586, 590
Cœlenterates, 518
   chemical sense of, 367
   digestion in, 454, 465
   nerve cells of, 435
   sense organs of, 359
Cœlomata, 532
Coleoptera, 589
Collar, of Dolichoglossus, 618
Coloration, protective, 861, 862
Color of animals, 308, 860
Color changes, 868
Columbæ, 650
Columella, 270, 403
Commensalism, 745
Composition of plants, 63–65
Compound eyes, 378, 580
Conchiolin, 605
Conchifera, 594
Condor, 650
Condylarthra, 666
Cones of retina, 380
Coney, 666
Congo snake, **243**
Conidium—spores formed in fungi by budding, 249
Coniferæ, 296
Conjugatæ, 243
Conjugation, **182, 186**, 692–
Conjugation in protozoa, 498, 699
Connective tissue, 96, 325
Connective tissue, origin of, 721
Conus arteriosus, a chamber of the heart lying in front of the ventricle and containing several valves, 628
Copelata, 620

Copepoda, 559
Coral, **75, 135-138**, 349, 529
Cordyceps, 229
Cork, 101
Cork cambium 101
Corm, 111
Cornea, 379
Corolla, 122, 132
Corrodentia, 583, 740
Corydalis, 585
Corymb, 119
Cotyledons, 294
Crabs, 561
Crab, lung of, 563
   terrestrial, 563
Cranes, 650
Cranial nerves, 445
Crayfish, 561, 563
   chemical sense of, 369
   development of, 504, 505
   digestion in, 467
   green gland of, 491
   integument of, 341
   locomotion of, 412
   reproduction in, 503, 504
   respiration in, 477
   statocyst of, 390
Cricket, 396, 582
Crinoids (sea lilies), an order of Pelmatozoa.
Crocodile, 644
Crop, 579
Cross fertilization, 138, 142
Cross-striped muscle fibre, 414
Crows, 650
Crustacea, 558
Cryptogams, 174–181, 220, 292
   reproduction in, 181
Ctenidia, comb-like gills, 593, 595
Ctenobranchia, 600, 601
Ctenoid (of a fish scale)—with a spiny edge, 636
Ctenophora, 531
Cuckoo, 650
Cumacea, 561
Cuscuta (dodder)—a genus of parasitic flowering plants.
Cuticula, of hydroids, 339
   of worm, 340
Cutinized cell walls, 97, 98
Cuttle fish, 611
Cyanophyceæ, 232
Cycadinæ, 294
Cycloganoidea, 635
Cycloid (of a fish scale)—with smooth rounded edge, 635

Numbers refer to paragraphs; Black Face numbers refer to figures.

Cyclosporeæ, 247
Cyclostomata—Cyclostomes, 627
  structure of, 627
Cyme, 118
Cymose inflorescence, 25
Cynips, 764
Cyprepedium, 850
Cypselomorphæ, 650
Cysticercus, 755
Cystoflagellata, 512
Cytoplasm, 672
  division of, 685
  function of, 680, 682

Daddy-long-legs, 570
Damsel flies, 584
Darning needle, 582
Dasypeltis, 844
Day flies, 584
Decapoda, 561, 616
Decay, 670
Deciduous, falling off (especially of leaves).
  plants, 197-198
Deer family, 666
Degeneration, 588
Dehisce (of a fruit)—to open.
Dentine, the bony substance of teeth lying beneath the enamel, 348
Dermis, 70
  of mammal, 343
  origin of, 721
Desmidiaceæ, 235
Development of crayfish, 504, 505
  of insect, 505
  of vertebrate, 506
  progressive, 738
  regressive, 738
  types of, 707
Devil fish, 167
Devil ray, 169
Devil's horse—praying mantis, 582
Diadelphous, 133
Diastatic (of a ferment)—having the power of converting starch into sugar.
Diatomæ, 233
Diatomes, growth of, 727
Dibranchiata, 616
Dichogamy, 31, 142
Dicotyledons, 171, 172, 300
  development of, 709
Difflugia, 1
Differentiation, 323, 725
  of tissues, 22, 96
Digestion, 326, 452—

Digestion by bacteria, 453
  in amœba, 452, 453, 464
  in arthropods, 458, 459, 467
  in cœlenterates, 454, 465
  in crayfish, 467
  in flatworms, 454
  in hydra, 454
  in sponges, 454
  in worms, 455-457, 466
Digestive ferments, 463
  glands of vertebrates, 461
  tract of crayfish, 110
  of grasshopper, 161
  of man, 111
  of Nereis, 104-107, 109
  of vertebrates, 460
Digitigrade (of certain mammals)—
  standing on the toes, 663
Dimorphic—two types of form in the same species, 143
Dimorphism, 225, 226
  seasonal, 742
  sexual, 739, 856
Dinoflagellata, 512
Dinornis, 650
Dinornithes, 650
Diœcious, 128
Dionæa, 50-52
Diphycercal, 631, 632
Diplopoda, 575
Dipnoi, 631
Diprotodontia, 652, 656
Diptera, 587
Discomycetes, 258
Dispersal larvæ, 831
Divers, 650
Division of labor, 725
Dodder, 230, 751
Dodo, 650
Dogs, 652
Dogwood, 33
Dolphin, 652, 665
Dolichoglossus, 618
  gill slits of, 618
  nervous system of, 618
  notochord of, 618
  structure of, 618
Domesticated animals, 820
  plants, 820
Dominant characters (in heredity), 783
Doodle bug, 585
Dorsal, 312
Dove, 650
Dragon flies, 584
Dromedary, 666

Numbers refer to paragraphs; Black Face numbers refer to figures.

INDEX—GLOSSARY.

Drosera, 49
Drupe, 154
Ducks, 650
Duck bill, 177, 652
    mole—duck bill.
Dugong, 652, 667

Eagles, 650
Ear, 84
Ear drum, 401–403
Ear of insects, 397
Ear of vertebrates, 398
Ear sacs, 387
Ear stone, 392
Earthworm, chemical sense of, 368
    locomotion of, 411
    respiration in, 476
Earthworms, 305, 543
Earwigs, 582
Ecdysis, molting, or shedding, the superficial layers of the integument, 214, 731
Echidna, syn. for Tachyglossus, the spiny ant eater.
Echinodermata, 550
Echinoderm larva, 64
Echinoidea, 555
Ecology.—The science of the relation of organisms to each other and to their inanimate environment, 182–223
Ectoderm, 713
    of hydra, 339
Ectoplasm, 672
Edentata nomarthra, 652, 661
    xenarthra, 652, 661
Eels, 636
Effectors, 439–441
Efts, 639
Egg, 671
    apparatus, the egg nucleus and two other nuclei, synergids, which lie together at one end of the embryo sac, 299
    maturation of, 696
    membrane, 702
    of bird, 647
    pronucleus, 698, 699
    size of, 697
    yolk of, 711
Eimeria, 127
Elaters, 267, 287
Electrical organs, 874
Electric eel, 636, 874
    light bug, 591
Elephants, 666

Elytra, 589
Embryo, 43, 44
    human, 249
    of dicotyledon, 189, 709
    of fern, 188, 709
    of hydra, 123
    sac—megaspore, 293
Emeu, 650
Enamel, of scales, 348
Endolymph, 398
Endoskeleton, the internal skeleton, 420, 422–
Endospores, 228
Endosperm, 53
    gametophyte, 299
Endothelium—a thin layer of cells lining a cavity, 379
Energy of animals, source of, 484
    relations of the animal, 446–
Entamœba, 765
    coli, 510
    histolytica, 510
Enteropneusta, 618
Entoderm, 713
Entomophilous—flowers which are pollinated by insects
Emydosauria, 644
Environment, 332
Ephemeroidea, 584
Ephyra, 528
Epidermal hairs, of plants, 21
Epidermis, 20, 70, 101
    of leaf, 27, 80
    of mammal, 343
    of stem, 73
    of worm, 340
    origin of, 715
Epigynous, 134
Epiphysis, the smaller bone formed on the end of a long bone, with which it ultimately unites.
Epiphytes, 213
Epithelium, a layer of cells covering an organ or lining a cavity.
Equilibration, 366
    in vertebrates, 392–395
Equisetinæ, 287
Equisetum, 287
Eustachian tube, 403
Euthyneura, 600, 602
Evolution, 781–
Excretion, 329, 489–
    by liver, 493
    in amœba, 489
    in hydra, 489

Numbers refer to paragraphs; Black Face numbers refer to figures.

Excretory organs of Nereis, **119, 120**
Exoasci, 261
Exogen, a plant whose stem increases in thickness by growth in the region between the bark and the wood.
Exoskeleton, an external skeleton.
    of arthropods, 417
    of molluscs, 418
    of vertebrates, 419
Eye, control of light intensity in, 386
    focusing of, 385
Eyes, **77, 79, 80**
    of arthropods, 378
    of cave fishes, 796
    of insects, 384
    of vertebrates, 379
    of worm, 376, 377
Eyespot, in protozoa, 374
Eyespots, 526, 528

F, F$_1$, F$_2$—first filial, second filial and third filial generations.
Falcon, 650
Fascia, sheets or layers of connective tissue covering organs or forming attachment for muscles, 721
Fasciola—a liver fluke.
Fats, 473
Fauna of Africa, 826
    of Australia, 825
    of caves, 838
    of fresh waters, 831–835
    of oceanic islands, 827
    of South America, 826
Feathers, 347, 646
Feigning, 864
Felidæ, 663
Female, 694
Ferment, a substance which causes a chemical change in other substances without undergoing a permanent change itself.
Fermentation, 230, 453, 670
Fern, development of, 708
    sperms of, 700
Ferns, 281
Ferret, 663
Fertilization, 135, **187**, 694, 698
    in hydra, 500
    stimulus, 700
Filament, 123
Filices, 285
Filicinæ, 281
Finches, 650

Fire-fly, **220**, 872
Fire-flies, rudimentary wings of, 797
Fishes, glands of, 350
    respiration in, 479
    skeleton of, 424
    sense of taste of, 370
Fission—reproduction by division, 671
Fissipedia, 663
Flagellata—Flagellates, 512, 766
Flagellum—a whip-like protoplasmic appendage.
Flame cell, 534
Flamingo, 650
Flat fishes, 322, 636
    worms, digestion in, 454
Flea, **237**, 762
Flies, 587
Flight, adaptation for, 646
Floral structures, **27**
Florideæ, 248
Flounder, **66**
    symmetry of, 322
Flower, function of, 135
    homology of, 115–120
Fly catcher, 650
Fœtal membranes, **173, 174**, 641
    of mammals, 651
Foliate papillæ, 371
Follicle, a minute cavity, sac, or tube, 161
Food of animals, 447–451
Foot, of fern, 282, 708
    of gastropods, 595
    of molluscs, 592
    of mosses, 274
    of rotifers, 539
Form of animals, 308
    of organisms, 7
Four-o'clock, **242**, 782
Fowl, 650
Free nerve terminations, 362
Fresh water fauna, 831–835
Frigate bird, 650
Frog, metamorphosis of, 211
    respiration in, 476
Frogs, 637, 640
Fruit, 149, 151
Fruits, aggregate, 164
    kinds of, 152–165
    function of, 168
    multiple, 165
    simple, 152-163
Fucus, fertilization of, 693
Fulgur, shell of, **213**
Function of the senses, 405
Fungi, 177, 179–180

Numbers refer to paragraphs; Black Face numbers refer to figures.

INDEX—GLOSSARY. 447

Fungiform papillæ, 371
Fur seal, 739

Gaillardia, 241
Galeorchis, 849
Gallinacei, 650
Galls, 764
Gall wasp, 238, 590
Gametangium (of plants)—the organ in which gametes are produced.
Gametes, 694
Gametophyte, 265, 292
Gamopetalous, 132
Gamosepalous, 131
Ganoin, 632
Garpike, 419
Garpikes, 634
Gastric fluid, 641
  glands, 720
  mill, 459
Gastrophilus, 761
Gastropoda, 595
  structure of, 595-
Gastro-vascular cavity, 454
Gastrula, 713
  cavity, 713
  mouth, 713
Gastrulation, 198, 199
Gavial, 644
Geese, 650
Geographical distribution, 823
Geotropism, 49, 50
Germ, 9
Germinal tissue, 724
Germination, 46–50
Germs, 670
Gibbons, 668
Gills, 593, 606
  of crayfish, 477
  of fishes, 479
Gill slits of Dolichoglossus, 618
  of vertebrates, 813, 814
Ginkgo, 295
Ginkgoinæ, 295
Giraffe, 666
Gizzard, 579
Glands, 71, 349–352
  of arthropods, 350
  of birds, 350
  of fishes and amphibia, 350
  of hydra, 349
  of mammals, 351
  of reptiles, 350
Glandular activity, 487
Glossinia, 766
Glowworm, 739

Glucose—a kind of sugar $C_6H_{12}O_6$ (grape sugar).
Glycogen, 472
Gnats, 587
Gnetinæ, 297
Goats, 666
Golden thread — dodder
Gonad—the organ in which the germ cells (gametes) are developed.
Gonads, of hydra, 500
  of insects, 580
  origin of, 721
Gordius, 756
Gorilla, 668
Grallæ, 650
Grasshopper, 396, 582
Gray matter of brain and spinal cord, 444
Grebes, 650
Green gland, of crayfish, 491
Growth, 6, 486
Grub, 587
Grubworm, 589
Guard cell—one of the epidermal cells which bound a stoma, 86
Guinea-pig, 660
Gulls, 650
Gustatory sense — sense of taste.
Gynœcium, 125, 128
Gymnophiona, 638
Gymnospermæ —Gymnosperms, 173–293
Gymnotus, 874

H—symbol for hydrogen.
Hæmocyanin, 483
Hæmoglobin, 483
Hair, 347, 651
  follicle, 70
Hairs, of arthropods, 346
  of plants, 100
Halteres, 587
Hammer, 403
Harvestmen, 570
Harvey, William—English anatomist who discovered the circulation of the blood (1578–1657), 670
Haversian canals, 426
Hawks, 650
Hearing, 366
  and equilibration, 387-
Heart, 471, 472
  origin of, 721
Hedgehog, 652
Heliotropism, 50

Numbers refer to paragraphs; Black Face numbers refer to figures.

INDEX—GLOSSARY.

Heliozoa, 510
Hellgrammite, 585
Hemibasidialis, 252
Hemiptera, 763
  wings of, 797
Hepaticæ, 267
Hepatic, pertaining to the liver.
  cæca, 553
  portal vein, the vein which leads from the intestine to the liver, 472
Herbivorous—feeding on vegetable matter.
Heredity, 782
  Mendel's laws of, 782
  physical basis of, 785
Hermaphrodyte—having the organs of both sexes in one individual, 502
Hermit crab, 562
Heron, 650
Herring, 636
Heterocercal, 633
Heteronymous, 336
Heteropoda, 600, 601
Heterotricha, 515
Hibernia (moth), **245, 246,** 739
  moth, rudimentary wings of, 797
Hibernation, 842
"Higher" and "lower" animals, 332
Hinge joint, 413
  ligament, 605
Hippopotamus, 666
Hirudinea, 546
H₂O — symbol for water.
Holocephali, 630
Holophytic, 744
Holothuria, symmetry of, 320
Holothuroidea, 556
Holotricha, 515
Holozoic, 744
Hominidæ, 669
Homo, 669
Homonymous, 336
Hoofs, 347
Horns, 347
Horse, 666
  evolution of, **248,** 807
  -hair snake, 756
  -shoe crab, 565
Host—an organism that harbors a parasite.
Hosts, of bacteria, 773
  alternation of, 769
Humming birds, 650
Hyænidæ, 663

Hybrid, 147, 781
Hydra, **69,** 304
  budding in, 499
  chemical sense of, 367
  digestion in, 454
  excretion in, 489
  glands of, 349
  gonads of, 500
  integument of, 339
  muscle fibres of, 408
  reproduction in, 499
  response in, 408
  sense organs of, 358
  sensitiveness to light, 375
  sexual reproduction in, 500
  supporting lamella, 415
Hydractinia, **222**
Hydroid, **133, 222**
Hydrophytes, 183–192
Hydropterides, 286
Hydrotropism, 49
Hydrozoa, 525
Hyena, 663
Hymenoptera, 590
  polymorphism in, 740
Hypha—one of the filaments which make up the mycelium of a fungus.
Hypocotyl, 52
Hypoderma, 761
Hypogynous (of stamens, etc.)—attached below the ovary.
Hypotricha, 515
Hyracoidea, 666
Hyrax, 666

Ibis, 650
Ichneumon, 663
  fly, **235,** 590, 762
Imago, 586
Immunity, 775
  acquired, 777, 780
  natural, 776, 780
  active, 778, 780
  passive, 779, 780
Impennes, 650
Incus — anvil.
Indehiscent (of fruits)—not opening.
Indian pipe, 751
Indirect development, 722
Individual, 725
Indusium, the membrane covering or enclosing a sorus, 285
Inferior (of ovary)—below the calyx, 134
Inflorescence, 117–120

Numbers refer to paragraphs; Black Face numbers refer to figures.

Ink gland, 611
Insecta—insects, 578
Insects, development in, 505
    growth in, 732
    integument of, 341
    of oceanic islands, 836
    respiration in, 478
    sense of smell of, 369
      of taste of, 369
    voice of, 396
    wings of, 412
Insectivora, 652, 658
Insertion, of muscle, 429
Inspiration, 481
Instinct, 875
Integument, **70,** 324, 338
    of arthropods, 342
    of insects, 341
    of mammals, 343
    of vertebrates, 733
    special structures of, 346, 347
Intelligence, 880
Internodes—the portion of the stem between two nodes.
Intestinal glands, 720
Invertebrates, eyes of, 379
Invertin, 462
Involucre, 120
Iris, 379
Isoetaceæ, 291
Isoetes, 291
Isopoda, 563

Jaws, 346
Jelly fishes, 528
    nervous system of, 437
Jungermanniaceæ, 271

Kangaroo, 652
Karyokinesis—mitosis, 686
Katydid, 396, 582
Kidneys, 329, 492
    origin of, 721
Kidney tubule, 492
King bird, 650
Kiwi. *See* also Apteryx, 650

Labium, 578
Labyrinth, 392, 393, 398, 399
Lace wing flies, 585
Lacertilia, 645
Lacteals, the lymphatic vessels of the intestine.
Lacteal capillaries, 472
Lactuca, 38, **39**
Lacunæ, 426

Lady slipper, 850
Lamellæ of bone, 426
Lamellibranchiata, 604
    structure of, 604
Lamellirostres, 650
Lancelet, 625
    egg, cleavage of, 712
    notochord of, 422
    structure of, 625
Lantern fly, **163**
Lateral line, 404
Latitude and plants, 204
Lari, 650
Larks, 650
Larvæ, dispersal, 722
Larva, the young of an animal before metamorphosis, when development is indirect.
    of hydra, 500
    of the lancelet, **200, 210**
    of tunicates, 621
    trophic, 723
Law of Biogenesis, 809, 812
Leaves, form of, 23
    storage, 114
    venation of, 26
Leaf, structure of, **14, 16,** 24, 80
Leech, locomotion of, 411
Legume, 162
Lemurs, 668
Lens of eye, 381
Leopards, 663
Leptocardia, 625
Lepidoptera, 586
Leptothrix, 227, 229
Leptostraca, 561
Lice, 583
Lichens, **48,** 216, 263, 745
Life habits, 744
Ligaments, 428
    origin of, 721
Light and plants, 205–208
Light sense in protozoa, 374
Lignified cell-walls, 97
Lilac mildew, 748
Lime, secretion of, 349
Limulus, **151,** 565
Linguatulida, 572
Linin, 675, 690
Lions, 663
Liver, 472, 493, 720
    excretion by, 493
Liver fluke, **231, 232,** 754
Liverworts, 264, 267
Lizards, 645
    rudimentary appendages of, 795

Numbers refer to paragraphs; Black Face numbers refer to figures.

INDEX—GLOSSARY.

Llama, 666
Lobster, 561
Locomotion, 308, 309
    in annelids, 410, 411
    in arthropods, 412
    in vertebrates, 413
Lophophore, 548
Love vine—dodder.
Luminescence, production of light, 869, 873
Luna moth, **244**
Lungs, **118**
    of crab, 563
    of dipnoi, 631
    of snail, 602
    of vertebrates, 480
Lycoperdon, 46
Lycopodiaceæ, 289
Lycopodinæ, 288
Lycopodium, 289
Lymph, 474
    glands, origin of, 721
    origin of, 721
    spaces, 474
    vessels, 474
Lysin, 777

Mackerel, 636
Macrocystis pyrifera, 245
Macrogamete—egg, 694
Macronucleus—meganucleus, 674, 699
Macrospore—megaspore.
Macrura, 561, 562
Maggot, 587, 670
Malacostraca, 561, 563
Malapterurus, 874
Malarial fever, 768
Male, 694
Males, dwarf, 739
Malleus—hammer.
Malpighian tubules, 579
Maltose—a kind of sugar $C_{12}H_{22}O_{11}$.
Mammalia—mammals, 651
Mammals of Australia, 825
    integument of, 343, 344
    of glands of, 351
Mammary glands, 651
Man, 652
Manatee, 652, 667
Mandible, jaw, the lower jaw of vertebrates or one of the first pair of appendages of the mouth in arthropods.
Mandrels, 668
Mangrove seedling, **259**
    tree, 854

Mantle of molluscs, 592
Marchantiaceæ, 269
Marsh plants, 192
Marratiaceæ, 284
Marsupialia, 652, 654, 655
Mastigophora, 511
Maturation, 695
    of ovum, **184, 185,** 785
    of sperm, 786
Maxilla, one of the second or third pair of appendages of the mouth of arthropods, 578, 586
Mechanics of growth, **212-218,** 727
Mechanism of response, 441
Medullary groove, **206, 207,** 715
    plate, **204, 205,** 714, 715
    ray, 62
    tube, **209,** 715
Medusa, 525, 528
Medusæ, light sense organs of, 375
Meganucleus — macronucleus, the larger of the two nuclei of certain protozoa.
Megaspore, 286
Membrane bone, 427
Membrana tectoria, 398
Membraneous labyrinth. See labyrinth.
Mendel's laws of heredity, 782
Meristematic, actively growing.
Mesenchyma, mesodermal tissue which arises as separate cells, not as a continuous layer.
Mesenteries, origin of, 721
Mesocarpaceæ, 237
Mesoderm, 408, 517, 716, 717, 719
Mesodermic somites, **204-210,** 717
Mesoglea, a gelatinous layer between the ectoderm and entoderm of cœlenterates.
Mesophyll, 27, 81
Mesophytes, 183, 195
Mesothorax, 578
Metabolism, 484–
    nuclear control of, 682
Metameres, 334
Metamorphism, 581
Metamorphosis—a marked change of form occurring during development, 320, 506, 637, 723
    in insects, 505
    in tunicates, 621
Metathorax, 578
Metazoa, 517
Mice, 652, 660

Numbers refer to paragraphs; Black Face numbers refer to figures.

INDEX—GLOSSARY. 451

Mice, inheritance of color in, 783
Microgamete—sperm, 694
Micronucleus, the smaller of the two nuclei of certain protozoa, 674, 699
Micropyle, a small hole, 701
Microsome, a small body, 672
Microspore—the smaller spore, when there are two kinds. It gives rise to a male gametophyte, 286
Microspora, growth of, 728
Middle ear, **87**, 403
Migration of birds, 843
Mildew, 257, 748
Milkweed, pollination of, **255, 256**, 851
Mimicry, 865–867
Mink, 663
Mirabilis Jalapa. *See* four o'clock.
Mistletoe, 663, 751
Mites, 571
Mitosis, **180, 181**, 479, 686
Moa, 650
Mocking bird, 650
Modified roots, 103–106
    stems and branches, 107–113
Moles, 652
Mollusca, 592
Mollusc, exoskeleton of, 418
    foot of, 592
    mantle of, 592
    segmentation of, 333
    shell of, 349, 592
    structure of, 592
Molluscoidea, 547
Monotremata, 652, 653
Monkeys, 652, 668
Monocotyledons, 171, 172, 300
    growth of, 729
Monodelphia, 652, 657
Monodelphous, 133
Monœcious, 128
Morchella, 258
Mosquitoes, 587, 768
Mosses, 264, 273
    sperms of, 700
Mother of pearl, 605
Moths, 586
Mougeota, conjugation in, 693
Mouth parts of cockroach, **160**
    of insects, 459
Mucous epithelium, 720
Mud puppies, 639
Mullet, 636
Multiple fruit, 165
Multicellular body, 706

Multipolar nerve cells, 435
Muscle, 325, 429
    fibres, **89–92**, 408, 409
Muscles of annelids, 408–411
    of vertebrates, 414
    origin of, 721
    stimulus, 431
Muscular activity, 488
    contraction, 430
Mushrooms, 255
Mycelium—the mass of threads which constitute the vegetative body of a fungus.
Mycorhiza, 216
Mycetozoa, 225
Mygale, 153
Myxomycetes, 225
Myonemes, **88**, 407
Myriapoda, 574
Myrrh, 261
Myxamœba, 225

N—symbol for nitrogen.
Nails, 347
Narwhal, 665
Natural selection, 819
Nautilus, **168**, 611
Nematoda, 540
Nemertini, 541
Nephridia, 329, 593
Nephridia of worms, 490
Nereis, **67**, 305, 543
    locomotion of, 411
    respiration in, 476
    sense organs of, 360
Nerve cells, **97, 100, 101**
    of cœlenterates, 435
    types of, 435
    -muscle mechanism, 325
Nervous system, 434
    of annelids, 438
    of arthropods, 443
    of dolichoglossus, 618
    of jelly fish, 437
    of nereis, **98**
    of tunicates, 619
    of vertebrates, 444
Nettling cells, 524
Neuroptera, 585
Newts, 637, 639
Nictitating membrane, 648
Nitrate bacteria, 229
Nitrite bacteria, 229
Nitrogen bacteria, 217
    waste, 488, 490
Noctiluca, 512

Numbers refer to paragraphs; Black Face numbers refer to figures.

INDEX—GLOSSARY.

Node—the point on a stem at which the leaves are borne.
Non-ruminants, 666
Notochord, **93, 206,**–210, 422, 423, 716
   of dolichoglossus, 618
   of tunicates, 619
Nuclear membrane, 674, 685
   sap, 676
   spindle, 683
Nucleolus, 674
Nucleoli, 688
Nucleoplasm, 679
Nucleus, 16, 673
   function of, 680–682
   resting, 691
   structure of, 674
Nut, 158

Oak galls, 238
Oceanic islands, fauna of, 827
   insects of, 836
Ocelli, 580
Octopus, 611, 616. (*See* also devil-fish.)
Odonata, 584, 585
Œdogonium, 739
   growth of, 728
Œsophagus of crayfish, 458
Oil, 350, 351, 672
Oils, vegetable, 94
Olfactory sense. (*See* sense of smell.)
Oligochæta, 545
Oligotricha, 515
Ommatidium, **79,** 378, 384
Omnivorous—using all kinds of foods.
Ontogeny, the history of the development of the individual.
Ontogenetic series, 809
Oogonium (in the lower cryptogams)—a cell within which one or more ova are formed.
Oomycetes, 250
Operculum, 279, 632, 633
Ophidia, 645
Ophioglossaceæ, 283
Ophiuroidea, 554
Opilionidea, 570
Opisthobranchia, 600, 602
Opossum, 652, 654
Optic nerve, 380
Opuntia, **24**
Orang-utan, 668
Orchids, 848
Organ of Bojanus, 607
   of Corti, **85, 86,** 398
Organism, 4

Organization of the body, 331
Organs of response, 406–
   of sight, 374–
   of special sense, 366–
Origin of species, 789
Ornithorhynchus. (*See* duck-bill.)
Orthoptera, 582
Oscines, 650
Osmose, diffusion of a solution through a membrane, 69, 71
Osphradium, an olfactory organ found in many molluscs, 597
Ossification of vertebra, **217**
Ostium, an opening, mouth, **471,** 579
Ostracoda, 559
Ostrich, 650
Otters, 664
Ovary, **29,** 125
   of hydra, **121,** 500
Ovules, **29,** 126
Ovum of hydra, **122,** 500
   of nereis, **125**
Owls, 650
Oxidation, 475
Oxygen, 67
   given off by plant, 87
Oxygenation of blood, 482

Palps, a jointed sensory organ attached to the mouth appendages of arthropods, 580
Pain, 364
Palisade cells, 81
Palæostraca, 564
Palisade tissue, 205
Paludina, development of, 805
Pancreas, 462, 720
Panther, 663
Papilio merope, **267**
Papilionaceous blossom, 846
Paramœcium, 128
   conjugation in, **186, 699**
Parasites, 215
Parasitism, 747–
Parrots, 650
Parthenogenesis, development of an egg without fertilization, 581
Parenchyma, 72
Passeres, 650
Pasteur (Louis), 1822–95, French bacteriologist, 670
Pearly nautilus, 611, 616
Pecora, 666
Pedicl, 116
Pedipalpi, 568

Numbers refer to paragraphs; Black Face numbers refer to figures.

INDEX—GLOSSARY.

Peduncle, 116
Pelican, 650
Pellicle, 338
Pelmatozoa, 551
Penguin, 650
Pentadactyl appendages, 637
Pepsin, 461, 463
Peptones—soluble proteid compounds, 459
   absorption of, 472
Perch, 636
Perennial, living on from year to year.
Perianth, 122
Pericardial cavity, 471
Pericardium, origin of, 721
Pericarp—the wall of the ovary when the fruit is mature.
Peridermium, **227, 228**
Perigynous, 134
Perilymph, 399
Peripatus, **157**
Perisarc, 339
Perisperm, 53
Perisporeaceæ, 257
Perissodactyla, 666
Peristome, 247
Periostracum, 605
Perithecium—(of fungi) an urn-shaped fruiting receptacle, 257
Peritoneum, origin of, 721
Peritricha, 515
Petiole, 24, 25
Petals—the parts of the corolla, 132
Phæophyceæ, 245
Phæosporeæ, 246
Phagocytosis, the destruction of bacteria by the white blood corpuscles—phagocytes, 776
Phanerogams, flowering plants, 292
Pharynx, of tunicates, 619
Phascaceæ, 278
Pheasant, 650
Phenacodus, 666, 807
Phloem, the part of the vascular bundle containing the sieve tubes.
Phosphorescence—luminescence.
Phosphorus, 679
Photogenic—producing light.
Photosynthesis—the process by which organic substances, such as starch, are formed by the agency of chlorophyll in sunlight, 87
Phycocyanin, 232
Phycoerythrin, 248

Phycophæin—a brown pigment contained in the brown seaweeds, 245
Phycomycetes, 249
Phyllotaxy—leaf arrangement, 30–33
Phyllopoda, 559
Phylloxera, 763
Phylogey, the history of the development of the race.
Phylogenetic series, 802
Physalia, 134
Physiographic relations of plants, 219–223
Pici, 650
Pigeon, 650
Pigment layer of eye, 379
Pike, 636
Pill bug, 561
Pine, **35**
Pineal eye, 796
Pinnipedia, 664
Pisces, 628
   structure of, 628
Pistil, 29, 125
Pistil—megasporophyll, 298
Pith, 61
Placenta, 126
Plant bugs, 591
Plants, color of, 18–22
Plant hairs, 100
Plantigrade—standing on the whole sole of the foot, 663
Plant lice, 591, 763
Plant series, 793
Planula, 528
Plasmodium—the amœboid stage of the body of a slime mold, 252, 240, 768
Plastron, 643
Platyhelminthes, 534
Platyrhina, 668
Pleura, the membrane covering the lungs and lining the thoracic cavity.
   origin of, 721
Pleurobrachia, 531
Plumule, **55**
Pocket-gopher, 660
Poison gland, 567, 569
Polar body, 696
Pole cat, 663
Pollen, 123
   grain—microspore, 293
   protection of, 137
   selection of, 147
   tube nucleus, 294

Numbers refer to paragraphs; Black Face numbers refer to figures.

INDEX—GLOSSARY.

Pollination, 135–147, 845
  by insects, 140, 143
  by wind, 139
Polychæta, 544
Polygala, **30, 31**
Polymorphism, **221–223**, 527, 458, 581, 583
  in bryozoa, 740
  in hydrozoa, 740
  in plants, 743
Polyps, 525
Polypodium, **40, 41**
Polyprotodontia, 652, 655
Polyzoa, 548
Porifera, 519–
Porpoises, 652
Posterior, 311
Prawns, 561
Praying mantis, 582
Primates, 652, 668
Proboscidia, 666
Proboscis, 586
Procyonidæ, 663
Proglottis, segment of a tapeworm, 537
Pronuba, 852, 853, 875
Prosimiæ, 668
Protective coloration, 861, 862
  in grasshoppers, 262, 263
  resemblance, **264**, 863
Proteolytic—having the property by which proteids are changed into peptones, 461
  ferments, 463
Prothallium, the thalloid gametophyte of certain pteridophytes, 280
Prothorax, 578
Protobasidiomycetes, 254
Protoascales, 240
Protonephridia, 534, 541
Protonema, the green thread-like part of the gametophyte of mosses, 275
Protoplasm, 13
  chemical properties of, 15, 68, 672, 680
  contractility of, 680, 681
  irritability of, 680
  structure of, **178**, 672
Protozoa, 507–
  as parasites, 765
  conjugation in, 498
  sensitiveness to light, 355
Protracheata, 573
Pseudopodium 276
Psittaci, 650
Pteridophyta–Pteriodophytes, 175, 280

Ptyalin, 461
Puff balls, 255
Pulmonata, 600, 602
Pupa, 586, 723
Pupil, 379
Pygopoda, 650
Pyrenomycetes, 259
Python, rudimentary appendages, 795

Quail, 650
Queen conch, shell of, **218**

Rabbits, 652, 660
Raceme, 119
Racemose inflorescence, **26**
Raccoon, 663
Radial symmetry, 316
Rachis, 29
Radiolaria, 510
Radula, 593, 596
Rails, 650
Ratitæ, 650
Rats, 652, 660
Ravens, 650
Receptacle, 122, 130
Receptors, 439, 441
Recessive characters, in heredity, 783
Red blood corpuscles, 483
Redi, Francesco, 1626–98, Italian naturalist, 670
Redii, 754
Reduction division, 695, 696, 698
Regeneration, 726
Regions of growth, 102
Reproduction, 330, 495–
  in amœba, 495, 496
  in annelids, 501, 502
  in crayfish, 503, 504
  in hydra, 499
  in sponge, 523
  in vertebrates, 506
Reptilia—reptiles, 691
Reptiles, glands of, 350
  structure of, 641
Reserve food, 672
Resemblance, protective, 863
Respiration, 308, 327, 475–
  in amœba, 476
  in crayfish, 477
  in earthworm, 476
  in fishes, 479
  in frog, 476
  in insects, 478
  in nereis, 476
  in plants, 91
  in sea anemone, 476

Numbers refer to paragraphs; Black Face numbers refer to figures.

INDEX—GLOSSARY.   455

Respiratory organs of crayfish, 116, 117
    of nereis, 115
    tree, 556
Response, in amœba, 407
    in annelids, 409-411
    in hydra, 408
Retina, 379
Retinal elements, 81, 380
Rhabdom, 384
Rhea, 650
Rhinoceros, 666
Rhizoids, 267
Rhizopoda, 509
Rhodophyceæ, 248
Rhomboganoidea, 634
Rhythmical changes in plants 197, 199 200
Rhynchocephalia, 642
Rhynchota, 585, 591
Ricciaceæ, 268
Rice birds, 650
Rocks, decay of, 222
Rodentia, 652, 660
Rods, of retina, 380
Root, 7
    cap, 102
    hairs, 8, 68-69
    tip. 23
Roots, 37, 39
    aerial, 105
    of epiphytes, 106
    prop, 104
    storage, 103
    structure and function of, 68-71
Rootstock, 111
Rosette habit, 201
Rotatoria, 539
Rotifers, foot of, 539
Round-mouthed eel, 423, 627, 752
Round worms—thread worms, 540
Rudimentary organs, 794-
Ruminants, 666
Runner, 109
Rusts, 254, 749

S—symbol for sulfur.
Saccharomycetes, 262
Sacculina, 560, 739, 760
Sacculus, 393, 394
Salamanders, 637, 639
Salamandra, 171
Salicornia, 37
Salivary glands, 459, 720
    of insects, 579
    of man, 461
    of nereis, 455

Salmon, 636
Salvia, 461, 847
Samara, 159
Sand flea, 561
Saprophytes, 214
Saprozoic—nourished like fungi, i.e., on soluble organic matter.
Sarracenia, 53-55
Scale insects, 591, 763
Scale leaves, 114
Scales, 70
    bony, 348
    of vertebrates, 347
    of worms, 346
Scaly ant eater, 421, 652, 661
Schizocarp, 160
Schizophyceæ, 232
Schizophyta, 226
Schizopoda, 561
Sclera, 379
Sclerenchyma—hard tissue, cells with thick walls.
Scolecida, 533
Scolex, 537, 755
Scorpion, 152
Scorpionidea, 567
Scyphozoa, 528
Sea anemone, 529
    chemical sense organs of, 367
    respiration in, 476
    cow, 667
    cucumber, 556
    horse, 636
    lilies, 551
    squirt, 621
    turtles, 643
    urchins, 555
    weeds, 208
Seal, 652, 661
Seed, the, 148, 151, 292
    distribution, 166-168
Seedling, 51
Seeds, 42-45
Segmentation, of body, 333, 337
    of egg—cleavage, 190-195, 702
Selachii, 629
Selaginella, 290
Selaginellaceæ, 290
Self fertilization, 144
Semicircular canals, 393, 394
Sense of position, 365
    of smell, 366
    of insects, 369
    of man, 373
    of vertebrates, 370
    of taste, 366

Numbers refer to paragraphs; Black Face numbers refer to figures.

456 INDEX—GLOSSARY.

Sense of taste of fishes, 370
    of insects, 369
    of man, 372
    of vertebrates, 370
  of touch, 364
    of amœba, 354
  of weight, 365
  organs, **77**, 325, 353—
    of amœba, 353–357
    of arthropods, 361
    of cœlenterates, 359
    of hydra, 358
    of Nereis, 360
    of vertebrates, 362
    special, 311
Senses of animals, 404
Sensibility, 309
Sensory corpuscles, 362
Sepal—one of the parts of the calyx, 131
Serpent star, 554
Sessile—not raised on a stalk.
Seta, 279, 346
Sex, development of, **182**
Sexual dimorphism, **219, 220**
  reproduction in hydra, 500
  selection, 857
Sharks, skeleton of, 423
Sheep, 666
Shell of animals, growth of, 730
  of gastropods, 595
  of molluscs, 418, 592
  of turtles, 420
Shrew, 652
Shrimp, 149, 561
Sieve tubes, **11**, 74
Sight, 366
Simiæ, 668
Siphon, 605
Siphonales, 243
Siphonaptera, 588
Siphonocladiales, 242
Siphonophore, **221**
Sirenia, 652, 667
Sirenidæ, 639
Sitaris, 876
Size of organisms, limitation of, 8
  and differentiation, 323
Skeletal muscles, 414
Skeleton, 325
  and connective tissue, 415
  cartilaginous, 423, 424
  of sponge, 520
  of vertebrates, growth of, 734, 735
Skull of human embryo, **216**
  of vertebrates, 792
Slaves of ants, 590

Sleeping sickness, 766
Slime mold, **57**
  molds—myxomycetes.
Sloth, 652
Slug, **165**
Slugs, 602
Smell, 366
Smooth muscle fibre, 414
Smut, 253, 259
Snail, **164, 165**
Snails, 595
  fresh water, 602
Snakes, 645
Snapping turtle, 643
Soil and plants, 209–210
  bacteria, 217
Soldier (of Aphids), 583
Solenoconchæ, 603
Sole, symmetry of, 322
Somatic tissue, 724
Sorus, a cluster of sporangia, 284, 285
South American fauna, 826
Sparrows, 650
Species, 781
  number of, 788
  origin of, 789—
Spermatia, 248
Spermatogenesis, **183, 185**
Spermatophyta—spermatophytes, 170, 292
Sperm cells, formation of, 695
  motility of, 697
  nucleus, 698, 699
  of hydra, 500
  nuclei of pollen, 299
Sphagnaceæ, 276
Sphex, 876
Spicules, 522
Spider, 569
  web, 844
Spiders, polymorphism in, 743
Spike, 119
Spinal cord, **103**, 444
  ganglia, 363
  nerves, 444, 445
Spindle fibres, 690
Spiny ant-eater, 652
Spiral valve, 627, 629, 631, 632
Spirillum, 227
Spirobolus, **158**
Spirochæte, 227
Spirogyra, conjugation of, 693
Spirostomum, myonemes of, **88**
Spleen, origin of, 721
Sponge, **129–132**
  structure of, 520

Numbers refer to paragraphs; Black Face numbers refer to figures.

INDEX—GLOSSARY. 457

Sponges, 519–
    canal system of, 521
    digestion in, 454
    reproduction in, 523
Spongilla, 519
Spontaneous generation, 670
Spore, 181, 671
Sporidia, 749
Sporophyll, a leaf bearing spores, 282
Sporophyte, the generation which produces spores asexually, but is produced sexually, 265
Sporozoa, 513, 768, 774
Spring lizards, 639
    tails, 577
Spurs, 347
Squamata, 645
Squash bug, 591
Squid, 611, 616
Squirrels, 652, 660
Stapes — stirrup, 399
Staphylococcus, 231
Starch, **18,** 87, 672
    changed to sugar, 90
Starfish, **141-143, 145,** 552, 553
Statocysts, 83, 387–528, 531
Statolith, 388, 390
Stamen, 123, 124
Steapsin, 462
Steganopodes, 650
Stem, 34, 36
    section of, **10, 12, 13**
"Stemless" plants, 107
Stems of biennials, 107
    of climbers and trailers, 108
    storage, 112
    structure and function of, 72–78
Sterculia, 28
Sterigma—a stalk (of a spore).
Stigma (of plants), 125, 127
Stigmata (of insects), 478, 574
Sting, 590
Stirrup, 403
Stolon, 109
Stoma, pl. stomata, **15, 17,** 80
Stomach of crayfish, 458
    of insect, 579
Stomata of aquatics, 188, 189
    function of, 84
Stomatopoda, 561
Storage stems, 110
Stork, 650
Stormy petrel, 650
Streptococcus, 231
Streptoneura, 600, 601
Striate muscle fibres, 414

Striges, 650
Strobila—a chain of segments or individuals formed by transverse division of the parent organism, **124,** 755
Strobila of microstomum, **124**
Struggle for existence, 816
Struthiomorphæ, 650
Sturgeons, 633
Style, 125
Suberized cell walls, 97
Subterranean stems, 202
Suctoria, 516
Sugar, $C_6H_{12}O_6$, $C_{12}H_{22}O_{11}$, 90
Superior (of the ovary)—attached above the calyx.
Susceptibility, 774
Suspensor, 289, 290, 294, 709
Swallows, 650
Swamp plants, 192
Swarm spore—a ciliated, motile spore.
    conjugation of, 693
Sweat glands, 352
Swine, 666
Symbionts, 216
Symbiosis, 745, 746
Symmetry, 314
    of echinoderm larvæ, 320
    of gastropods, 319
    universal, 317
Synergids, 299
Syphostoma, 528
Syrinx, 647

Tachyglossus. See anteater.
Tadpole of tunicates, 621
Tænia—a tapeworm.
Tapeworm, **233, 234** 755
Tapir, 666
Taste, 366
    buds, **77,** 371
Taxonomy, systematic classification of organisms.
Taxonomic series, 790, 791
Teeth, 348
    of mammals, 651
    origin of, 721
Tegmen, 42
Teleostei, 636
Teleutospores, 749
Temperature and vegetation, 196–203
    control, 840, 841
    sense, 364
    of amœba, 356
Tendons, 429
    origin of, 721

Numbers refer to paragraphs; Black Face numbers refer to figures.

Tendrils, 114
Tentacles, 528
Termes—a genus of termites.
Terminal bud, 55
Termite queen, 260
Termites, 223, 224, 583
　polymorphism in, 740
Terrapin, 643
　diamond back, 215
Testa, 42
Testes of hydra, 121, 500
Testudinata, 643
Tethyodea, 621
Tetrabranchiata, 616
Tetrads (in maturation), 695
Tetraspores—four spores produced asexually in one mother cell, 248
Texas cattle fever, 771
Thaliaceæ, 623
Thallophytes, 177, 224-263
Thoracic duct, 472, 473
Thoracostraca, 561
Thorns, 113, 114
Thousand legs, 574, 575
Thread worms, 540, 756-759
Thrushes, 650
Thymus gland, 720
Thyroid gland, 720
Ticks, 571
Tigers, 663
Tillandsia, 45
Tinamiformes, 650
Tissues, origin of, 719
Titmouse, 650
Toad fish, 636
Toads, 637, 640
Torpedo, 874
Tortoise, 643
　shell, 347, 643
Toxin, 776
Tracheæ, 11, 569, 574, 579
　of insects, 162, 478
Tracheids, 11, 74, 296
Traguloidea, 666
Translocation of food substances, 92, 93
Transpiration, 86
Trap-door spider, 154-156
Tree toads, 640
Trematoda—Trematodes, 536, 753
Trichinella, 757
Trichogyne, 248
Trochophore, 609
　larva of annelids, 501
Tropæa. See luna moth.

Trunk fish, 419, 636
Trypanosome, 239, 766, 767
Trypsin, 462, 463
Tryptic—having the proteolytic action of trypsin.
Tsetse fever, 766
　fly, 766
Tube feet, 550
Tuber, 110
Tuber, 47
Tuberaceæ, 260
Tubinares, 650
Tunic, 619
Tunicata, 619
Turbellaria, 535
Turgid, distended, swollen.
Turkey, 650
Turtles, 643
　shell of, 420
Tylopoda, 666
Tympanum—eardrum, 397, 401

Ulothricales, 241
Umbel, 119
Ungulata, 652, 666
Urea, COH_4N_2, 492
Uredospores, 749
Ureter, 492
Urinary bladder, 492
Ursidæ, 663
Urochorda, 619
Urodela, 172, 639
Uropygal gland, 350
Utriculus, 393, 394

Vacuole, 672
Vascular bundle, 74
Variation, 781
Variety—subdivision of a species, 781
Vegetation and climate, 223
Veliger, a mollusc larva of peculiar form with a ciliated collar, 598
Ventral, 312
　ganglionic chain—ventral nerve cord.
　nerve cord, 438, 580
Vertebral column of vertebrates, 792
Vertebrata—vertebrates, 480, 626
Vertebrate appendage, 413, 799
　eye, 379
Vertebrates, circulation in, 472
　development in, 506
　digestive tract of, 460
　exoskeleton of, 419
　kidneys of, 492

Numbers refer to paragraphs; Black Face numbers refer to figures.

INDEX—GLOSSARY.

Vertebrates, locomotion in, 413
   nervous system of, 444
   reproduction in, 506
   segmentation of, 336
   sense of smell of, 370
     of taste of, 370
     organs of, 362
Vessels (of plants), 74
Vestigeal organs, 794–
Vibrio, 227
Villi, 472
Visceral sac, 595
Vision, 383, 384
Vitreous humor, 382
Viverridæ, 663
Voice, 396
Volvocales, 239
Vultures, 650

Walking stick insect, **265**
Walrus, 664
Warblers, 650
Warm blooded animals, 840
Wasps, 590
   care of young, 855
Water and vegetation, 183–195
   boatmen, 591
   bugs, 591
   striders, 591, 763, 766
   vapor, transpiration of, 84
Weasel, 663
Web of spider, 569
Whales, 652, 665
Whale bone, **250**, 347
   rudimentary limbs of, 795
Wheat rust, 749
"White ants" — termites, 583
White blood-corpuscles — leucocytes, 494, 776

Whip-poor-will, 650
Whorl—three or more leaves, or other parts, set around the same node.
"Witches broom," 261
Wolves, 663
Wood lice, 561, 563
   pecker, 650
Worker (ants or termites), 583
Worms, 349, 542
   connective-tissue of, 416
   digestion in, 455–457, 466
   eyes of, 376
   glands of, 349
   integument of, 340
   nephridia of, 490
   sense organs of. *See* nereis.
   sensitiveness to light, 376

Xerophytes, 183, 193–195
Xiphosura, 565
Xylem, the wood portion of a vascular bundle.

Yeast, 262
Yolk, effect on cleavage, 711
Young, care of, 854
Yucca, 852
   pollination of, **257, 258**

Zooglea, 228
Zygnemaceæ, 236
Zygomycetes, 250
Zygospore, a spore formed by the fusion of two similar gametes. 234
Zygote, a body formed by the fusion of two gametes.

Numbers refer to paragraphs; Black Face numbers refer to figures.

BOOKS FOR STUDENTS OF BIOLOGY.

HAMAKER. Principles of Biology. Including brief outlines for laboratory work. By J. I. HAMAKER, *Professor of Biology, Randolph-Macon Woman's College, College Park, Virginia.* With 267 Illustrations. Octavo X +459 pages. Cloth, $1.50.

MARSHALL. Microbiology. A Text-book of Microörganisms, General and Applied. By various writers. Edited by CHARLES E. MARSHALL, *Professor of Microbiology and Director of Graduate School, Massachusetts Agricultural College.* Discusses Morphology, Culture and Physiology of Microörganisms, including Nutrition and Metabolism, Physical Influences; Bacteriology of Dairy, Soil, Water Supplies, Sewage Disposal, Air, Special Manufactures, Diseases of Man, Animals and Plants. 1 Colored Plate. 128 Other Illustrations. 12mo; xxi+724 pages. Flexible Cloth, $2.50.

MINOT. Embryology. A Laboratory Text-book of Embryology. By CHARLES S. MINOT, S. D., LL. D., *Professor of Comparative Anatomy, Harvard University Medical School.* Second Edition, Revised. With 262 Illustrations. xii+402 Pages. Cloth, $3.50.

VINAL. A Guide for Laboratory and Field Studies in Botany. By WILLIAM GOULD VINAL, A. M. (*Harvard*), *Salem Normal School, Salem, Massachusetts.* Second Edition, Revised. Square Octavo. Paper Covers, $.60.

STEVENS. Plant Anatomy from the Standpoint of the Development and Functions of the Tissues. By WM. C. STEVENS, M. S., *Professor of Botany in the University of Kansas.* Second Edition, Enlarged. 152 Illustrations. 8vo; 394 pages. Cloth, $2.00.

STOHR. Text-book of Histology. Arranged upon an Embryological Basis. By DR. FREDERIC T. LEWIS, *Assistant Professor of Embryology at the Harvard Medical School.* From the Twelfth German Edition by DR. PHILLIP STOHR, *Professor of Anatomy at the University of Wurzburg.* Sixth American Edition, Revised. 450 Illustrations, 45 in Colors. 8vo; 443 pages. Cloth, $3.00.

CRARY. Field Zoology, Insects and Their Near Relatives and Birds. By L. E. CRARY, *Assistant Professor of Biology and Geology, Kansas State Normal College, Emporia.* 117 Illus. 12mo; 376 pages. Cloth, $1.25.

McMURRICH. The Development of the Human Body. A Manual of Human Embryology. By J. PLAYFAIR MCMURRICH, A. M., PH. D., *Professor of Anatomy, University of Toronto; American Editor of Morris' "Text-book of Anatomy."* Fourth Edition, Revised. 285 Illustrations. Octavo; x+495 pages. Cloth, $2.50.

PATTEN. The Evolution of the Vertebrates and Their Kin. By WILLIAM PATTEN, PH. D., *Professor of Zoology, and Head of the Department of Biology, Dartmouth College, Hanover, N. H.* With 307 Figures engraved especially for this book, largely from original sources. Octavo. Cloth, $4.50.

P. BLAKISTON'S SON & CO., PHILADELPHIA.

BOOKS FOR STUDENTS OF BIOLOGY.

KINGSLEY. Comparative Anatomy of Vertebrates. A text-book arranged upon an embryological basis and prepared especially to meet the needs of the under-graduate student. By J. S. Kingsley, *Professor of Biology in Tufts College.* Octavo; 346 Illustrations drawn or redrawn expressly for this book. ix+401 pages.
Cloth, $2.25.

DAVISON. Mammalian Anatomy. With Special Reference to the Anatomy of the Cat. By ALVIN DAVISON, A. M., PH. D., *Professor of Biology, Lafayette College, Easton, Pennsylvania.* Second Edition, Revised. 114 Illustrations.
Cloth, $1.50.

FOLSOM. Entomology with Special Reference to Its Biological and Economical Aspects. By JUSTUS WATSON FOLSOM, SC. D. (Harvard), *Assistant Professor of Entomology at the University of Illinois.* 5 Plates (1 in colors) and 300 other Illustrations. 8vo; 485 pages.
Cloth, $2.00.

GALLOWAY. Zoology. A Text-book for Secondary Schools, Normal Schools and Colleges. By T. W. GALLOWAY, PH. D., *Professor of Biology, James Milliken University, Decatur, Illinois.* Second Edition, Revised. 240 Illustrations. 8vo; 460 pages.
Cloth, $2.00.
Elementary Zoology. A Text-book for Secondary Educational Institutions. 160 Illustrations. xx+418 pages.
Cloth, $1.25.

GREEN. Vegetable Physiology, An Introduction to. By J. REYNOLDS GREEN, SC. D., F. R. S., *Fellow of Downing College, Cambridge.* Third Edition, Revised. 182 Illustrations. Octavo; 482 pages.
Cloth, $3.00.

JOHNSTON. Nervous System of Vertebrates. By JOHN BLACK JOHNSTON, PH. D., *Professor of Comparative Neurology, University of Minnesota.* With 180 Illustrations. Octavo; 390 pages.
Cloth, $3.00.

SCHEFFER. Zoology. Loose Leaf System of Laboratory Notes. Second Edition. Revised and Enlarged. By THEO. H. SCHEFFER, A. M., *formerly Assistant Professor of Zoology, Kansas State Agricultural College.* Square 8vo.
Adjustable Cloth Covers, $.75.

BRUBAKER. Text-book of Physiology. Illustrated. Fourth Edition. A Text-book of Physiology, specially adapted for the use of Students. Including a Section on Physiologic Apparatus. By A. P. BRUBAKER, M. D., *Professor of Physiology and Medical Jurisprudence at Jefferson Medical College.* With an appendix giving a brief account of some essential forms of apparatus suited to those who have not large laboratory opportunities. Fourth Edition. Thoroughly Revised and in Parts Rewritten. 1 Colored Plate and 377 other Illustrations. Octavo; xii+735 pages.
Cloth, $3.00.

BLAKISTON'S SON & CO., PHILADELPHIA.

CPSIA information can be obtained
at www.ICGtesting.com
Printed in the USA
BVHW042312121220
595588BV00032B/611